# The Secret Teachings of the Vedas:

## The Eastern Answers to the Mysteries of Life

### VOLUME ONE

By
Stephen Knapp

## DEDICATED TO

All those who ever gave me any encouragement
on the path to spiritual understanding

---

Cover photo: Sunrise over the Meenakshi temple in Madurai, India.

First edition, August, 1986
Revised edition, 1990
Final revised & re-edited edition, 1993
ISBN 0-9617410-1-5
Library of Congress Catalog Card Number
90-71652

## PUBLISHED BY

PROVIDING KNOWLEDGE
OF
REALITY DISTINGUISHED FROM ILLUSION
FOR THE WELFARE OF ALL

The World Relief Network
P. O. Box 15082
Detroit, Michigan
48215-0082

The many quotes from *Bhagavad-gita As It Is*, *Srimad-Bhagavatam*, *Sri Caitanya-caritamrita*, and *Brahma-samhita*, are used with permission from the Bhaktivedanta Book Trust--International. Copyright (C) 1972.

# Contents

# Foreword

The present work is the first volume of an extensive project of four volumes on *The Eastern Answers to the Mysteries of Life* contemplated by Stephen Knapp in order to provide an exhaustive understanding of the various aspects of human spirituality and spiritual evolution. This volume is titled *The Secret Teachings of the Vedas*. It focuses specifically on the Vedic and post-Vedic philosophical and religious responses to the persistent curiosities and inevitable querries of the human mind in its encounter with the spatio-temporal immensity of the universe, about its whence and whither, and the place and purpose of the human person within it, for whose emergence and existence on the earth, the entire universe is but necessary.

Not only the primordial reality, the *raison d'etre* of the universe, but even the universe itself with its myriad inorganic and organic systems is a *mysterium tremendum et fascicans*, a mystery ever engaging and challenging the human intellect to unravel its not-so-impenetrable visage. It opens up its deepest secrets to the probings of the scientific and religious minds, unless the same human mind through its deviant irrationality decides to precipitate a general catastrophe that spells destruction of all its erstwhile achievements.

The author authentically and ably presents the ancient Indian thoughts and insights in dealing with numerous questions regarding life and its origins, the whys of life and the material world surrounding it, the soul and its passage through various life-forms and through various human planes to its ultimate destiny, the nature of God, our spiritual identity, the law of *karma* and reincarnation, the modes of *Prakriti* and the consequent character of actions, *karmic* disposition and free will that determine the quality of future existence, the nature of good and bad *karmas*, vegetarianism, the structure of the universe, including heaven and hell, and the description of Vaikuntha or the spiritual world. The discussion of the brain-mind-consciousness question (pp 39-45) is of special interest. The author has also appended an informative and interesting chapter on the historical sites and temples of South India to demonstrate the striking spiritual dimension of India's culture.

The book is a labor of love and an act of devotional service. It is a genuine expression of what Stephen Knapp has thought through in his spiritual journey and the conviction he has found in the course of his personal life-experiences. That is the reason why the book is written with such simplicity, lucidity, and accuracy. It is enlivened by examples from practical life to bring home spiritual ideas. The main basis of exposition of these ideas is the *Bhagavat Purana* which the author copiously cites.

The book is not only a discussion of the issues concerning the mystery of existence and of human life in terms of Indian teachings of the Vedic literature, but also a conscious effort to relate those insights to the contemporary age and its ethos.

In conclusion, Stephen Knapp advocates that the Vedic teachings offer us guidance through the maze of modern maladies brought about by the complex industrial and technological civilization, and make human life worthwhile.

The book is a welcome introduction to the teachings of the Vedic and Puranic literature on the various topics of metaphysical and spiritual interest.

Prof. Mahesh Mehta
Department of Religious Studies
University of Windsor
Windsor, Ontario, Canada

# Preface

There are many books being written these days on spiritual or occult subjects by authors who present their ideas and teachings as if they were facts, but do not provide any traditional references or scriptural evidence to justify what they write. This book, *The Secret Teachings of the Vedas: The Eastern Answers to the Mysteries of Life*, is written to establish an alternative to the highly speculatory, inconclusive, and often times problematic theories about the universe, the soul, life after death, where we have come from, where we are going, and the various ideas about the Absolute that are presently being spread and accepted today.

The truths that are contained in the ancient texts often hold the clearest understanding of life that can be found anywhere. This will become more apparent as we present various parts of the Vedic teachings to clarify many theories that an increasing number of people are starting to seriously consider. These include such concepts as the eternality of the soul, reincarnation, *karma*, destiny, who we are, the meaning of life, and all the questions that often go unanswered for lack of knowledge.

We have seen, for example, that many times children will ask their parents questions concerning matters about life and death that the parents hardly understand themselves. The elders may take questions to their own spiritual leaders, such as the local minister or priest, who often leave their congregational members with little more understanding than what they already had. In this way, many difficult questions about life go unanswered and are dismissed because precise information does not seem to exist.

Sometimes it is taught that, "It's not meant for us to know," or "God will tell us when we are fit to receive it." Or we may even be told that we will not know the answers until after we die, so just keep the faith. But this book is an attempt to show that this is hardly the case. There are many answers awaiting us, especially in the area of Eastern philosophy. And any person is fit to receive this knowledge when they care enough to search for it. However, to receive full understanding you must approach that source of complete knowledge in the proper way, which is in a mood of respect and humility. A challenging attitude will not do. After all, we are born in ignorance and, regardless of whatever technological skills we may acquire, we can easily die in spiritual ignorance unless we qualify ourselves with spiritual knowledge. When this knowledge and the laws of the universe become known, then the mysterious reasons and causes for the present day problems of the world become obvious. Then the reasons why we are in this world and why we go through the things we do are also understood.

For those, however, who feel hesitant to consider alternative viewpoints due to a feeling of allegiance to a certain religion or philosophy, I hope you will read this book with an open mind. If, for example, you are a Christian, you should have the attitude of following in the footsteps of Jesus Christ while reading this, since there are many recorded references of his traveling through the East and studying the Vedic writings. However, some people may say that they have their own religion, so what more do they need? Why should they study the philosophy of the East or the science of yoga? The point is that the word *religion* comes from the Latin word *religio*, which means to bring back or to bind, while the Sanskrit word *yoga* means to connect with or to unite. To bind or unite with what? The Supreme, of course. Thus, there is no difference between the purpose of religion and the goal of yoga: they are the same. Yet it has been shown that the knowledge of the *Vedas* is much more expansive and deeper than that found in most conventional religious philosophies. It is like the difference between an abridged dictionary and one that is unabridged. They are essentially the same; yet, one is more complete. Therefore, one can get a much better understanding of whatever spiritual philosophy he or she follows by studying the Eastern texts.

In fact, for many hundreds of years, the East, especially India, has been the focal point when it comes to spiritual knowledge. As we will see in Chapter Two, many great writers, poets, theologians, etc., have increased their understanding of themselves and their own viewpoints of life simply by investigating the wisdom of the East. So now let us begin the grand adventure of examining the essential, universal, spiritual truths as presented in this discourse on Eastern philosophy.

THE AUTHOR

# Introduction

This book takes information that is widely scattered throughout many volumes of Vedic literature and condenses it into the present work for an in-depth introduction to the Vedic teachings. For the average person, it would take many years of study to acquire or assimilate what is presented here. Thus, the purpose of this book is to supply the reader with clear and concise knowledge and references of spiritual topics that normally would be difficult to find, or would be reached only after many years of research. I recognize that in this age not everyone has time to do everything he or she would like, and our priorities may require so much of our day that there is no time left to do anything but work for our essential needs. In light of this, I have tried to compile this book so that with a limited amount of time and expense one could still have access to some of the most elevated knowledge and spiritual realizations ever recorded or known to man.

This book, however, is not meant to be read and digested in a few days like an adventure novel. Of course, one may try to do that if they wish and will still get much insight from it. But I suggest that readers go through it and absorb it at their own pace, reading certain portions of it each day and meditating on various parts of it that they may find especially enlightening.

In supplying this information, I have tried not to write too extensively, but only enough to make things clear for the reader without being vague. I have also used direct quotations from the Vedic literature whenever possible to allow the *Vedas* to speak for themselves, and to let the reader get a better understanding of the kind of knowledge and wisdom the *Vedas* contain. The reader may want to study some of these chapters more than once, since it is well-known that Vedic knowledge remains ever-fresh and reveals newer and newer insights as one advances in spiritual understanding. Of course, if you are only looking for specific information, the chapters are divided into segments by sub-titles making it easier for you to find those references in which you may be particularly interested.

Each chapter is complete in itself and will convey a thorough understanding of the topic with the most essential information in the beginning portions of the chapter. As one continues through the chapter, deeper knowledge is revealed. For the beginner in Eastern philosophy, the most important chapters in this book are Chapters One and Four, which give clear insights into who and what your real identity is and how the *Vedas* offer guidance that help us understand the real purpose of life. The information in these chapters also provides a better understanding of other spiritual philosophies. Chapters Two and Three explain how the Vedic literature has influenced many of the great men of our times, and give information on the background of the *Vedas* and how they were compiled. Chapter Five gives a thorough view of what the law of *karma* and reincarnation is and how it affects us. Chapter Six may seem a little detailed but the information is an integral part of understanding how we incarnate into different types of bodies in different lives. Chapter Seven describes a little about the structure of the universe and the heavenly and hellish planets, and shows how there are many levels of existence and consciousness throughout this universe. Chapter Eight puts it altogether and discusses the theory of evolution and describes the Vedic concept of spiritual evolution and how the living being goes up and down through the higher and lower planets and species of life according to his or her consciousness, and how to get out of this cycle of repeated birth and death. Chapter Nine explains why we have to go through all of this and why we exist at all. Chapters Ten and Eleven explain how God is not only an impersonal force that pervades everything, but is also the Supreme Person whose influence can be recognized in all areas of our everyday life. Chapter Twelve, which is all about the spiritual world, provides information that is found no where else in such detail except in the Vedic literature.

For some readers, the information in this book may seem so different that it may border the fantastic and be quite controversial. For others, it may make a lot of sense and provide an understanding of life for which they have long been looking. For others, it may kindle a reawakening of what, deep in their hearts, they already know but could not quite remember. Nonetheless, if there are specific questions the readers have, whether about something in the book or a topic that is not covered in this volume, they may correspond with me at the following address and I will be glad to give further assistance:

The World Relief Network
P. O. Box 15082
Detroit, Michigan
48215-0082

Spiritual knowledge is meant as much for women as it is for men, so if it seems like I use the words "he" or "him" a lot in this book when referring to the individual, the aspirant, or yoga practitioner, it actually means anyone, he or she. I use the word "he" mostly for ease of writing, not to show some bias.

Further information on the knowledge of the East will be supplied in Volume Two of *The Eastern Answers to the Mysteries of Life*, which is titled *The Universal Path to Enlightenment*. This book will explain the real purpose of yoga and the religious systems, how they work, the development and analysis of the major world religions and their effectiveness, and how to follow the path for spiritual self-realization that is meant for this age. It also contains a comparative study of the philosophical systems of the East, an explanation of mystic abilities, the qualifications of a true spiritual leader, the Vedic teachings found in Christianity, and much more. There is also a chapter presenting the origins of modern religion based on the linguistic and archeological evidence that shows how the major religions of the world are all related to each other, and how they expanded from one ancient but common source: which is the Vedic Aryan culture. It is a volume that provides important information and much enlightenment for those on the path, or those seeking a path to the Absolute.

Presently, we are also considering Volume Three. This will be another important book based on the ancient Eastern texts which will explain such things as the Vedic predictions of the near and distant future, how the worlds are finally annihilated, how we fit into this cosmic plan, and the reason for it. After this, there are also plans for a possible fourth volume in this series which will explain the process of universal creation, how society can be structured to avoid the common social problems we find today, and how we can find individual fulfillment according to the process as described in the Vedic literature.

To help make these books more authentic and complete, I have included a section on seeing the spiritual side of India. In this volume there are over 75 photographs of many aspects of life in India. The hardest part about doing this section was choosing the photographs from the thousands of slides I have. In this volume we will journey through South India and go on an important pilgrimage to many of the holy places that few others are able to visit in one trip, if at all. We will visit many of the important temples in this region and hear about the ancient legends that make these places sacred. Many of the temples are like none you will see anywhere else in the world, and are held in high esteem by followers of the Vedic philosophy. In the following volumes of *The Eastern Answers to the Mysteries of Life* we will continue our travels through other sections of India to see some of the holiest cities in the world.

## A NOTE TO SCHOLARS

As most scholars on Vedic philosophy know, when you say *Vedas* you refer to the original four *Vedas*: the *Rig, Yajur, Sama*, and *Atharva Vedas*. When you say *Veda* (without the *s*) you not only refer to the four *Vedas*, but also to the *Upanishads, Vedanta-sutras, Brahmanas*, and *Aranyakas*: all the texts which are considered to be *Shruti*. *Shruti* is considered to be the original revealed knowledge. The remaining parts of Vedic literature consists of the *Mahabharata* and *Bhagavad-gita*, the *Ramayana*, and the *Puranas*. These are the *Itihasas* or histories and supplemental portions of the Vedic literature, which is called *Smriti*, or that which is remembered. When you say Vedic literature, you refer to both *Shruti* and *Smriti* in a general way. But some scholars think that the *Shruti* is more important than the *Smriti*. So some may object to the way I alternately use the words "*Vedas*" and "Vedic literature" to refer to the same thing, which is all of the Vedic texts, both *Shruti* and *Smriti*.

The reason I do this is because I present Vedic evidence from any portion of the Vedic literature, and I often use quotes from the *Puranas*. Furthermore, some of the greatest of spiritual authorities, like Shankaracarya, Ramanujacarya, Madhvacarya, and others, have presented *Smriti* as valid evidence of spiritual truths and wrote commentaries on *Bhagavad-gita*. In fact, Madhvacarya, in his commentary on the *Vedanta-sutras* (2.1.6), quotes the *Bhavishya Purana*, which states: "The *Rig-veda, Yajur-veda, Sama-veda, Atharva-veda, Mahabharata, Pancaratra*, and the original *Ramayana* are all considered Vedic literature. The Vaishnava supplements, the *Puranas*, are also Vedic literature." Even the *Chandogya Upanishad* (7.1.4) mentions the *Puranas* as being the fifth *Veda*. And the *Srimad-Bhagavatam* (1.4.20) clearly states: "The four divisions of the original sources of knowledge (the *Vedas*) were made separately. But the historical facts and authentic stories mentioned in the *Puranas* are called the fifth *Veda*." So I point this out simply for those scholars who feel that there should be some distinction between *Shruti* and *Smriti* and may object to the way I use the terms "*Vedas*" and "Vedic literature" to mean the same thing, although I am sure the general reader will not be very concerned about it.

# CHAPTER ONE

# *Why Study The Vedas*
# *In Our Search*
# *For Happiness*

While living in this material world there are two things that everyone is working for: to increase our happiness and pleasure, and to decrease our suffering and problems. This means that being happy is our natural constitutional position which we are always endeavoring to attain, and that different types of misery and problems are a constant factor in this world with which we are always forced to deal.

Let's face it--being happy is probably the most important factor on everyone's list. But how do you stay happy? First you have to find what makes you happy; then you can worry about how to maintain it. In the attempt to find happiness, people choose one of two ways to accomplish this. As we can see, the most common way people try to become happy is by adjusting their material situation to increase their comforts and pleasure. The other way is by progressing spiritually. These are the only ways to become happy. But the happiness found in one way is genuine; whereas the other is illusory, as we shall see.

Naturally, everyone would like to be eternally happy and free from problems. Many people also strive to be rich, beautiful, famous, knowledgeable, and strong. These are the major attributes that everyone is struggling to achieve to some degree. Of course, it is rare to see someone with all of these qualities. These attributes are often difficult to get. So, in most cases, we have to work for only one or two of these qualities at a time, of which riches and beauty seem to be the most sought after.

For becoming rich or famous, everyone has a different plan. This plan-making usually involves a lot of competition between others who may also want the same position. Therefore, whether between athletes, movie stars, authors, politicians, musical groups, or those within businesses and corporations, there can be a lot of envy and jealousy in the fight for promotion and

1

recognition. There may also be other problems such as discrimination against minorities and women, or even sexual harrassment that one may be forced to tolerate in the hopes of climbing the ladder of material success.

In such an environment, many people are not as satisfied as they would like to be, or are actually frustrated with no idea of what else to do but "make the best of it." The point is that we end up working more and enjoying it less, while the primary goal of simply being happy often evades us. Unfortunately, we usually have to find this out for ourselves, but we can learn this from such ancient Vedic texts as the *Srimad-Bhagavatam*, where says: "Although the performer of fruitive activities desires perpetual happiness, it is clearly observed that materialistic workers are often unhappy and only occasionally satisfied, thus proving they are not independent or in control of their destiny. When a person is always under the superior control of another, how can he expect any valuable results from his own fruitive actions." (*Bhag*.11.10.17)

This would seem to indicate that whether we are working under the control or direction of a local boss, foreman, or manager, or even under the power of a Supreme Controller, it can not be guaranteed that we will be successful simply by working hard for money and position. Thus, it becomes obvious that very few people who are absorbed in trying to attain materialistic happiness are really satisfied with their position in life.

Of course, as we can observe, there are ways people endeavor to become happy other than simply working hard for fame and fortune. In fact, no matter what else we accomplish in life, it may seem rather empty or shallow without someone with whom to share it. Therefore, most people agree that the highest happiness one can attain is that found in a loving relationship. Even if we do become successful, how much happiness can it bring without our having someone with whom to share it?

There are many levels and types of love that can exist between people. For example, due to a love for humanity, we may work hard in trying to relieve the problems of the world by organizing food distribution for the hungry or shelter for the homeless. Out of a love for our friends, we may like to associate with them and offer our help if they may need it. Out of a love for one's wife or husband and family, one may spend many hours a day working to provide them with all the necessities of life. Thus, a person may feel very satisfied to work hard due to his or her love for someone.

Even if people do not have a family or someone special to love, it is often seen that some of them will get pets which become the objects of their affection. Then they feel some satisfaction that they have someone to love and someone who needs them. There is evidently a need in all of us to express our love, and being able to express that love is a cause for our happiness. In this way, everyone is looking for a lover, or at least a very close friend with whom we can depend on, talk with, and reveal our hearts to, and share experiences.

There may be ordinary friends or acquaintances, and there may be best friends or close lovers. But if we could, everyone would want to find that supreme lover with all the qualities for which we are hankering: someone to be our everything. And out of all the pleasures in this world that we may share with someone, it is generally accepted that the most intense pleasure is that of sexual affection. Therefore, it is seen that intimate love between two people and sexual expression are often times closely related. But how often are we actually able to find true love in this world? How often does something that at first seemed so deep, later turn out to be so superficial?

The problems that can take place in relationships are innumerable. This is shown by the fact that almost 50% of all marriages end in divorce. This indicates that a lot of people do not know exactly what they are looking for. When there is good sex between two people, the infatuation and attraction they feel for each other, which can be mistaken for love, greatly increases. However, when the emphasis for expressing love is centered around sexual affection, if a problem develops with sexual performance, the relationship falls apart. The partners then start to become frustrated with each other and may begin to look for someone else with whom to share their sexual love.

So there is pressure on people to make sure they know how to perform sex perfectly. If there is some difficulty, there are psychiatrists, sex therapy classes, etc., waiting to take your money to help you work out your problems. It would almost seem to indicate that finding the perfect sex partner is more important than finding a true loving relationship.

Sex often promises, but not necessarily brings, great physical and mental pleasure, relief, satisfaction, happiness, and sometimes adventure. Thus, for most people the pursuit of it is an essential part of life. Of course, how long these good feelings may last has been shown to be extremely unpredictable. But the anticipation for it usually outweighs any thoughts of the aftereffects. The fact of the matter is that during sex one becomes vulnerable to certain risks and dangers which can affect one for years after the momentary pleasure has gone. These may include your partner not being satisfied by your endeavors to satisfy him or her, the acquiring of incurable diseases like herpes or AIDS, problems from the types of birth control used, or a pregnancy which may or may not be wanted. If the child is not wanted, there may be the decision to have an abortion, which is also a risk to one's health and has many times left deep psychological scars of guilt lasting for years with the would-be mother.

Therefore, the question could be asked, how can sex be the central activity for expressing love if there are so many potential risks or dangers involved? Or an even more basic question would be, if we are just trying to find happiness, why does there seem to be such a variety of things that can go wrong or problems that get in the way?

First of all, let us look at what these problems are. In the first paragraph of this chapter, I mentioned that one of the things we are always working toward is to decrease our suffering and problems. What these problems consist of and what they are caused by is explained in the *Vedas*.

The *Vedas* describe three basic types of suffering which affect us all. There are the sufferings caused by natural events, such as earthquakes, tornadoes, hurricanes, severely hot summers and dreadfully cold winters, as well as floods, draughts, and so on. These natural disasters can influence or change the lives of thousands, even millions of people at a time. Many people may die or be left homeless and never again be the same after being involved in such an occurence. When such things take place, it becomes obvious how utterly powerless we are against the forces of nature.

The second type of suffering, which we are constantly having to deal with, is the kind caused by other living beings. These may be problems caused by people we work with, neighbors we do not get along with, trouble with our wife or husband, bad drivers on the highway, dogs barking at night and disturbing our sleep, insects trying to bite us, or termites eating our house, etc. There may be other disturbances, such as the decisions of politicians to raise our taxes, a doctor's mistake on our operation, or living in a war-torn country where our family is killed, supplies of food and water are cut off, etc. These are definitely types of difficulties caused by others which are always taking place somewhere at some time that disturb or destroy our happiness.

The third type of suffering is caused by our own material body. These problems can be anything from common illnesses that we all get from time to time, such as colds, the flu, headaches, toothaches, or things like constipation, sore muscles, ulcers, broken bones, or poor hearing and eyesight. There can also be the more serious illnesses which affect us in old age like heart trouble, arthritis, cancer, and so on. There can be the mental problems as well, such as retardation, confusion, depression, anxiety, senility, or paranoia and schizophrenia.

Basically, just having a material body guarantees us so many problems with which we must deal. This means that for most people life can be a long struggle of trying to solve all these problems as well as working to attain the simple things they need or want for being alive and happy. Therefore, it should easily be understood that happiness in this world mostly amounts to nothing more than temporarily feeling a lack of distress, or forgetting our problems for a little while. This, obviously, is not real happiness at all.

A sensible person, therefore, may begin to question: where is real happiness? What are we supposed to do in this world? Are we just pushed into this creation without a choice of whether we want to be here or not? Are we nothing more than lost soldiers in a wilderness, struggling to survive without knowing why? Who can make sense of it all and answer my questions? How do I fit into all this? And what do I do if I am more desparate and want a definite way out of here? Or is life nothing more than a series of events, trying to do the best we can, with nothing more than death waiting for us in the end? And what happens after death? Do we just take another birth to go through the whole cycle all over again? And if we do, for what? What are we progressing towards? And if there is nothing after death, then what is the use of this life anyway? What is the meaning of it all?

## FINDING THE ANSWERS

Fortunately for us, all these questions have detailed answers found in the *Vedas*, the ancient knowledge of the East. This is real knowledge. Real knowledge means truth, or that which does not change. It means to know who and what you are, how you got here, where you are going, how this universe works, who or what God is, what your relationship is with all this, and how to work according to that relationship for the ultimate benefit and happiness.

The highest truth is the divine knowledge of the soul because that is the real identity of the individual. When one approaches the highest truth, all other mysteries and questions are automatically solved and answered. However, there are many people who have questions about life and the beyond, yet have not been able to find an authorized source from which they can get detailed answers. Even with all our modern conveniences, this is a problem which is reflected by the confusion, the high level of crime, and the general lack of moral stability in society today. However, when one can approach genuine spiritual knowledge for actual guidance, this problem can easily be rectified.

The sages and mystics who were well versed in the knowledge of the *Vedas* knew the fruitlessness of activities that are not based on spiritual information. They also knew that, although we are looking for love in our attempt to find happiness, we are looking for love in a world that is primarily filled with lust.

Lust means the desire to satisfy your own mind and senses. People may say they love someone, but the reasons for that love may be, "Because he takes care of me," or, "He gives me what I need," or, "She's the prettiest girl I've ever seen and makes me feel like nobody else can." This is nothing more than being in love with your own desires and feeling some appreciation toward someone who satisfies those desires for you. And, of course, you may feel obliged to do something in return to satisfy their desires. (You scratch my back and I'll scratch yours.) But in almost all cases, if that person did not satisfy you or did something to disappoint you, your feelings of love would immediately change into anger or regret.

This kind of "loving" exchange has nothing to do with real love. It is nothing more than a business relationship because your feelings for a particular person depend on what he or she does for you. Actually, in materialistic society, all relationships are based on this kind of "mutual behavior," or the medium of sense gratification. When people like to enjoy doing something, they may do that activity with others who become their friends. But once one of them starts to change interests or behavior, the relationship generally fades away.

The sages and Vedic scholars also knew where to find real happiness and which kind of activities would lead to disappointment. For example, if it were possible, most people would like to have a thrill at every moment: a lifelong vacation with new things to do, new adventures in which to engage, and no concerns about which to worry. People like to cater to the various sensual delights of the body by enjoying the ears with nice things to hear, the eyes with lovely objects at which to look, the nose with fragrant aromas to smell, the tongue with delicious foods to taste, and the skin with nice things to feel and touch. This is the standard for material pleasure that most people would like. And it is generally considered that the more people can surround themselves with such comforts, the happier they will be. In this way, as long as we have something to stimulate the senses and mind, we feel some pleasure and happiness.

This kind of happiness is called "soda pop pleasure." As long as we have soda pop to tingle the tongue, there may be some enjoyment. But in due course, the soda pop is finished and so is the delightful sensation that went with it. So, then you have to get another soda. To support this habit of buying soda to supply tingle to the tongue, one must work to get money. And when there are a variety of such sensual habits to support, it can become quite expensive and require more and more money. The problem with this kind of pleasure is that, in spite of all our well-made plans, it always comes to an end or is interrupted by the previously mentioned threefold miseries. Then we hanker for what we want and work in hopes of acquiring it, or we lament for what we have lost.

This hankering and lamenting is the continual activity of the mind which always looks for something new to attain and laments if we must lose or give up something. However, we can see that too much of any one kind of pleasure makes us disgusted with it, like hearing the same song on the radio over and over. We need a variety of things to keep us happy. And this simply motivates us to seek out newer thrills, which, being based on the mood of the mind, either satisfies us until we get disgusted with it or until we are forced to deal with another unexpected problem of life. This is the temporary nature of material happiness.

This is why the sages and mystics did not engage in pursuing such flickering pleasure. By their study of the *Vedas*, and from their own spiritual vision, they knew that to work hard for that which is temporary is like working hard for nothing at all. You may have something for a short time, but then it is gone. As pointed out in the *Bhagavad-gita*: "An intelligent person does not take part in the sources of misery, which are due to contact with the material senses. O son of Kunti, such pleasures have a beginning and an end, and so the wise man does not delight in them." (*Bg*.5.22)

What happens when one works for material sense gratification is explained as follows: "While contemplating the objects of the senses, a person develops attachment to them, and from such attachment lust develops, and from lust anger arises. From anger, delusion arises, and from delusion bewilderment of memory. When memory is bewildered, intelligence is lost, and when intelligence is lost, one falls down again into the material pool." (Bg.2.63)

This is the typical pattern of thoughts for one who hankers to enjoy some material object and then develops attachment to it, which turns into lust. Lust turns the attachment a person feels for something into a blind endeavor to acquire it no matter what the consequences are, which then turns into anger and frustration if he cannot have it. After this, he loses his intelligence and becomes bewildered, thus failing to see that his lust for acquiring a certain object or type of pleasure is actually the cause of his own suffering. Failing to see this, he is hopelessly controlled by the idea that he can achieve happiness by adjusting his material situation. This only increases the desires he endeavors to satisfy, which simply implicates him further in the cycle of continued ups and downs in material life.

To begin rectifying this situation, it is explained: "The nonpermanent appearance of happiness and distress, and their disappearance in due course, are like the appearance and disappearance of winter and summer seasons. They arise from sense perception, O scion of Bharata, and one must learn to tolerate them without being disturbed." (Bg.2.14)

Happiness or distress, which is essentially a state of mind, manifests according to our perspective of what seems pleasant and unpleasant through our senses. The senses deliver information to the mind, the center of the senses, which then accepts or rejects it as either agreeable or disagreeable. Such happiness and distress follow each other like winter and summer.

No matter who or where we are, the ups and downs will follow. This is the ordinary course of events. Whatever our situation, there will be particular conveniences as well as inconveniences that we will have to tolerate. However, just knowing this will help us to be less affected by such changes as they go on around us. After all, change is the only constant in this world, and change means not knowing what the future will bring. In this way, it is evident that we cannot find security in a world that offers only insecurity through constant change. And how can we be happy or peaceful if we feel insecure?

Anxiety, which is brought on by insecurety, is from hoping for particular results and being afraid that something else will happen. This is another aspect of being attached to our desires. But as long as we have this body, we will naturally have various desires. We cannot really stop them. However, the body will one day be finished and all things related to the body will also be finished. Ultimately, when the body dies, it is buried and deteriorates into earth, or is burned and becomes ashes, or it is eaten by others, such as animals and insects, and becomes stool. For earth, stool, or ashes we are taking so much care, and for that we are in so much anxiety. For what reason? Because we are attached to this body and our desires. Therefore, it is stated: "A person who is not disturbed by the incessant flow of desires--that enter like rivers into the ocean which is ever being filled but is always still--can alone achieve peace, and not the man who strives to satisfy such desires." (*Bg*.2.70)

The point is that this body is a tool which can be used to accomplish many kinds of goals in life. But it is just that, a tool, a machine or vehicle within which we are presently situated. The more we think that these bodies are what we really are, the more we limit ourselves and the more we become fearful of things that may limit our hopes for material happiness. But the more we realize that our real identity is actually above and beyond this body, the more our potential becomes unlimited and the more we will see that all problems are simply temporary illusions, challenges for our growth. But if our real identity and potential is beyond the bodily platform, then the real happiness we are looking for must also exist on that same spiritual level. So, which way do we turn if we are looking for real happiness since bodily enjoyment and pleasure will always come and go?

As we mentioned on the first page of this chapter, there are two ways to find happiness: one is by working for material arrangements, and the other is by progressing spiritually. The reason for progressing spiritually is pointed out in the *Srimad-Bhagavatam*: "My dear sons, there is no reason to labor very hard for sense pleasure while in this human form of life; such pleasures are available even to the hogs. Rather, you should undergo penance in this life by which your existence will be purified, and, as a result, you will be able to enjoy unlimited transcendental bliss." (*Bhag*.5.5.1.)

Since material pleasures can never promise complete fulfillment and cause further entanglement in material life, the wise engage in activities which spiritualize their consciousness. According to the above verse, such activity makes one eligible for experiencing unlimited bliss, as confirmed in the *Padma Purana*: "The mystics derive unlimited transcendental pleasures from the Absolute Truth, and therefore the Supreme Absolute Truth, the Personality of Godhead, is also known as Rama."

That unlimited happiness is further described in *Bhagavad-gita*: "The stage of perfection is called trance, or *samadhi*, when one's mind is completely restrained from material mental activities by the practice of yoga. This is characterized by one's ability to see the self by the pure mind and to relish and rejoice in the self. In that joyous state, one is situated in boundless transcendental happiness and enjoys himself through transcendental senses. Established thus, one never departs from the truth, and upon gaining this he thinks there is no greater gain. Being situated in such a position, one is never shaken, even in the midst of greatest difficulty. This indeed is actual freedom from all miseries arising from material contact." (*Bg*.6.20-23)

This means that with patience, enthusiasm, and determination, one should practice the process of yoga (which we discuss more thoroughly in *The Universal Path to Enlightenment*) through which attaining the ultimate stage of enlightenment will be guaranteed. This is confirmed by the following verses:

"Those who are free from anger and all material desires, who are self-realized, self-disciplined and constantly endeavoring for perfection, are assured of liberation in the Supreme in the very near future. (*Bg*.6.28). . . In this world there is nothing so sublime and pure as transcendental knowledge. Such knowledge is the mature fruit of all mysticism. And one who has achieved this enjoys the self within themselves in due course of time." (*Bg*.4.38)

By developing transcendental or spiritual senses, which exist in a completely different dimension than our dull and limited material senses, one becomes fully joyful in contact with the spiritual atmosphere. Being established in such a position, one is not concerned with petty difficulties in the same way a millionnaire is no longer concerned with ten dollar problems. This is actual freedom, as further explained in *Bhagavad-gita*: "Steady in the Self, being freed from all material contamination, the yogi achieves the highest perfectional stage of happiness in touch with the Supreme Consciousness." (*Bg*.6.28)

As we read this, we may feel that this is too much to think possible for us. How are we to reach such a state of being?

Needless to say, reaching a state of enlightenment is no overnight process. And in an age when people want everything yesterday, it might seem almost troublesome to attempt a spiritual path when we may not get any immediate results from it. But, regardless of what our position is, the *Vedas* offer many levels of assistance.

## GUIDANCE FROM THE VEDAS

The above information is just the beginning of the guidance the *Vedas* can offer us in regard to the many questions we may have about life and beyond. The Vedic literature has many verses filled with much wisdom and information along with innumerable stories that help us understand spiritual knowledge.

One such story that helps elaborate on the topics we have been discussing is from the Eleventh Canto of the *Srimad-Bhagavatam*, about Pingala, a woman who, like many of us, wanted to find happiness through sex pleasure and the accumulation of money.

In the city of Videha there dwelled a prostitute named Pingala. She had become very anxious to get money. Being a prostitute, she dressed herself in a way to attract men who would pay her for the pleasure of having sex with her. Desiring to bring a lover into her house, she stood outside her front door at night and displayed her beautiful form.

As she stood there on the street at night, she studied all the men who were passing by, thinking, "Oh, this one surely has money. I know he can pay the price for my company and enjoy me very much." In this way, she thought about all the men on the street. But many men walked by her house and she, in anxiety, thought, "Maybe this one who is coming now is very rich... But he is not stopping. But I'm sure someone else will come. Surely here is a man who is coming now who will pay me for my love. He will give lots of money." Thus, with vain hope, she remained leaning against her doorway, unable to finish her business and go to sleep.

Out of anxiety, she would sometimes walk back into her house and then out towards the street. Gradually the midnight hour arrived. As the night wore on, the prostitute, intensely desiring money, became very morose. Being filled with anxiety and most disappointed, she began to feel a great detachment from her situation and, thereby, happiness arose in her mind. She felt disgusted with her material situation and thus became indifferent to it. Indeed, detachment acts like a sword, cutting to pieces the binding network of material hopes and desires for which one continues working in so many ways. Just as a human being who is bereft of spiritual knowledge never desires to give up his false sense of proprietorship over many material things, similarly, a person who has not developed detachment never desires to give up the bondage of the material body.

Pingala said, "Just see how greatly I am illusioned. Because I cannot control my mind, just like a fool I desire lusty pleasure from the most insignificant man. I am such a fool that I have given up the service of that person who, being eternally situated within my heart, is actually most dear to me. That most dear one is the Lord of the universe, who is the bestower of real love and happiness and the source of all prosperity. Although He is in my own heart, I have completely neglected Him. Instead I have ignorantly served insignificant men who can never satisfy my real desires and who have simply brought me unhappiness, fear, anxiety, lamentation, and illusion.

"I have uselessly tortured my own soul! I have sold my body to lusty, greedy men who are themselves objects of pity. Practicing the abominable profession of a prostitute, I hoped to get money and sex pleasure."

"This material body is like a house in which I, the soul, am living. The bones forming the spine, ribs, arms, and legs are like the beams, crossbeams, and pillars of the house, and the whole structure, which is full of urine and stool, is covered by skin, hair, and nails. The nine doors (the two eyes, two nostrils, two ears, mouth, anus, and genitals) leading into this body are constantly excreting foul substances. Besides me, what woman could be so foolish as to devote herself to this material body, thinking that she might find pleasure and love in this contraption?

"Certainly in this city of Videha I alone am completely foolish. I neglected that Supreme Person who awards us everything, even our original spiritual form, and instead I desired to enjoy sense gratification with many men. The Supreme Personality of Godhead is absolutely the most dear one for all living beings because He is everyone's well-wisher and Lord. He is the Supreme Soul situated in everyone's heart. Therefore, I will now pay the price of complete surrender, and thus purchasing the Lord I will enjoy with Him just like Lakshmidevi, the goddess of fortune.

"Men provide sense gratification for women, but all these men, and even the demigods in heaven, have a beginning and end. They are all temporary creations who will be dragged away by time. Therefore, how much actual pleasure or happiness could any of them ever give to their wives? Although I most stubbornly hoped to enjoy the material world, somehow or other detachment has arisen in my heart, and it is making me very happy. Therefore, the Supreme Lord Vishnu must be pleased with me. Without even knowing it, I must have performed some activity satisfying to Him.

"A person who has developed detachment can give up the bondage of material society, friendship, and love, and a person who undergoes great suffering gradually becomes, out of hopelessness, detached and indifferent to the material world. Thus, due to my great suffering, which was actually a blessing in disguise, such detachment awoke in my heart. Therefore, I am in fact fortunate by the mercy of the Lord. I am now completely satisfied, and I have full faith in God's mercy. Thus, I will maintain myself with whatever comes of its own accord. I shall enjoy life with only the Lord, because He is the real source of love and happiness.

"The intelligence of the living entity is stolen away by activities dedicated to the pleasure of the senses, and thus he falls into the dark well of material existence. Within that well he is then seized by the deadly serpent of time [in the form of old age, disease, and death]. Who else but that Supreme Person could save the poor living entity from such a hopeless condition? When the living entity sees that the entire universe has been seized by the serpent of time, he becomes sober and sane and at that time detaches himself from all material sense gratification. In that condition the living entity is qualified to be his own protector."

Material desire is undoubtedly the cause of the greatest unhappiness, and freedom from such desire is the cause leading to the greatest happiness. Thus, her mind completely made up, Pingala cut off all her sinful desires to enjoy sex pleasure with many lovers and became situated in perfect peace. She then sat down on her bed and happily went to sleep.

* * *

The realizations Pingala had in this narration are beneficial for everyone to understand. There are several things to note in this story. First of all, Pingala was consumed by desires for money and sexual pleasure. These are certainly desires that affect everyone. But where do such desires come from?

Practically speaking, the whole world turns on the basis of attraction to sex life. The *Vedas*, however, point out that this material world is a perverted reflection of the spiritual world. Therefore, sex life is not unreal, but the reality of sex is originally experienced in the spiritual world. Material life is only a perverted reflection of reality. So, those without information of spiritual sex, which originates in the Absolute Truth, think that material sex is the highest pleasure.

When the living entities are in the state of pure consciousness, they exhibit desires of pure spiritual love and affection. Therefore, desires are there both in the spiritual as well as material worlds. The difference is that when the spirit soul is embodied in material elements, those spiritual urges are expressed through the material body and are thus pervertedly reflected in the selfish desire to satisfy the body and mind. The example can be cited that a flashlight may send out a beam of pure light, but when it is covered by a piece of red tinted paper, it then sends out a red light. In this way, you could say that the red light is perverted since it is no longer the original pure light. Similarly, when the pure spirit soul is covered by the body, the needs and urges of the living entity manifest themselves in the form of lust rather than pure love. This is further explained in the *Bhagavad-gita*:

"As fire is covered by smoke, as a mirror is covered by dust, or as the embryo is covered by the womb, similarly, the living entity is covered by different degrees of this lust. Thus, a person's pure consciousness is covered by his eternal enemy in the form of lust, which is never satisfied and which burns like fire. The senses, the mind, and the intelligence are the sitting places of this lust, which veils the real knowledge of the living entity and bewilders him. Therefore, O Arjuna, best of the Bharatas, in the very beginning curb this great symbol of sin (lust) by regulating the senses, and slay this destroyer of knowledge and self-realization." (*Bg*.3.38-41)

In this way, by the practice of yoga we can remove the influence of the contamination of lusty desires which exist in the body and mind, and can once again reach the transcendental platform which is completely spiritual, beyond the realm of material imperfections. Upon reaching this spiritual platform, or even getting a glimpse of it, a person feels a happiness which far outweighs any material pleasure. This is pointed out in *Bhagavad-gita*: "Such a liberated person is not attracted to material sense pleasure or external objects but is always in trance, enjoying the pleasure within. In this way, the self-realized person enjoys unlimited happiness, for he concentrates on the Supreme." (*Bg*.5.21)

From this we can realize that a person who is dedicated only to satisfying the body shows his lack of knowledge of satisfying the spiritual needs of the soul. As long as the needs of the soul are neglected, the body and mind, being whipped by the relentless masters of lust, greed, anger, and lamentation, are always hungry for newer thrills and excitement. This keeps one bound to the bodily conception of life and the struggle to acquire and maintain impermanent material happiness.

Pingala also mentioned her disgust for the material body. At first she had wanted to indulge in satisfying her bodily desires, but later realized that actually the body is a structure filled with urine and stool, covered with skin, hair, and nails, and continually excretes foul substances. Of course, this does not mean that the body is not a most useful tool for accomplishing many things, material as well as spiritual. But the point is that one should not think that the material body is one's real identity, nor be so attached to the body that serving and trying to satisfy all of the body and mind's sensual desires becomes the goal of life.

While reading about Pingala's attitude toward the material body, I thought of the time when I had visited the Museum of Science and Industry in Chicago. There was an exhibit in which a local professor had put on display thin, horizontal and vertical slices of the bodies of a man and a woman. Each slice was set up between two pieces of glass so everything could be seen clearly. There were slices of the skull which showed the mouth, throat, eyes, nasal passages, and brain matter. There were slices of the arm and knee joints showing the muscles, tendons, bones, and blood vessels. There were slices of the torso cut from the shoulder or throat area down to the groin region that showed the outside skin, backbone or ribs, and all the internal organs, such as the heart, lungs, liver, kidneys, and intestines. It was not a pretty sight.

At first, when I saw it, I was not sure what it was. Then suddenly it dawned on me, and I felt a little shocked. But then I started looking at it and thinking, "Just see the reality of this body. Where is the pleasure in such a thing?"

As I stood there looking at this exhibit, I was also listening to comments from other people as they walked by looking at it. Some men would walk up to it, give a low gasp or say nothing at all and continue looking. Then, in a few instances, their wives would walk by and say something like, "What's this? Oh, God. Come on, Fred, we don't want to look at this" and then would grab the man's arm and pull him away. A few said something like, "Oh, jeez, is this real? Are these real bodies? I'm not hanging around here." Even children would sometimes walk up and say, "Yech. Gross. Let's go find something else."

It was quite amusing. It definately made you realize that we are more than just these material bodies. But if you think this body is your real identity, to see it displayed like that can be a little embarrassing. It is like being afraid to be seen in a bathing suit because someone might notice your crooked toes, your knobby knees, the warts on your back, or whatever other faults the body has. But as long as we keep this body covered with fancy clothes, glamorous hair styles, fine perfumes and facial make-up, it does not seem so bad. In fact, we may start thinking it looks pretty good. That is the illusion.

However, there are powerful businesses based on this illusion. Therefore, the spreading of this spiritual knowledge, which can tear down the veil of this illusion, is often felt as a threat by those who think they may have something to lose from it. So, it is not surprising to see those with the power to do so attempt to suppress the channels which spread this knowledge in order to maintain the profits they get which may be based on the general ignorance of society.

It can also be seen throughout history at various times in which groups of people or governments sanctioned the withholding of knowledge, or the manipulation of information, or proceeded with mass burnings of books. Since it is known that knowledge is strength and ignorance is weakness, the idea is that your ignorance is my strength. Of course, that is when the science of propaganda and the manipulation of the news media comes into play in order to control the opinion of the general populace. This book is not really intended to discuss such matters. But we feel it is important to mention that any philosopher, humanitarian, politician, visionary, etc., who wishes to do anything truly beneficial for themselves, their friends, or humanity at large, must be able to see beyond this illusion. Otherwise, one is just another cog in the wheel, falling into the same rut and playing the same materialistic game as everyone else.

Another important point Pingala mentions is that everything in this universe is affected by the time factor. Everything composed of material elements goes through the six changes of birth, growth, maintenance, production of by-products, dwindling, and death. Therefore, even though we may be enjoying life like anything, the machine of the body begins to break down and finally dies. At that time we are forced to leave our body as well as everything connected with it, such as wife or husband, relatives, friends, home, bank account, and everything else. The *Vedas* describe these as fallible soldiers who cannot help us at the time of death. And once we die, where we go, we do not know.

It is described that death is that journey from which no one returns, and many people are afraid of death. This fear can be seen constantly. One may have fear of heights, fear of the dark, fear of swimming in deep water, fear of the future or the unknown, and so on. All this is simply the reflection of the fear of death, the ultimate unknown. So we work very hard at trying to relieve our anxiety over our inevitable death, or at least in trying to forget about it.

In the Vedic classic *Mahabharata*, there is a story of how Lord Yamaraja, the lord of death, asks King Yudhisthira what is the most wonderful thing in the world. The King answered that the most wonderful thing is that day after day countless people die all around us, but those who live believe that death will not yet happen to them, and they carry on as if it does not matter. What could be more wonderful than this?

*Srimad-Bhagavatam* points out that even though we are busily engaged in our family, business, or recreational affairs and may forget about the problem of death, death does not forget about us.

"Insurmountable, eternal time imperceptibly overcomes those who are too much attached to family affairs and are always engrossed in their thought." (*Bhag.* 1.13.17)

"This frightful situation cannot be remedied by any person in this material world. It is the Supreme Personality of Godhead as eternal time that has approached us all. Whoever is under the influence of eternal time must surrender his most dear life, and what to speak of others such as children, wealth, honor, land, and home." (*Bhag.* 1.13.19-20)

"Despite your unwillingness to die and your desire to live even at the cost of honor and prestige, your miserly body will certainly dwindle and deteriorate like an old garment." (*Bhag.*1.13.25)

"Even if people know how to achieve happiness and avoid unhappiness, they still do not know the process by which death will not be able to exert its power over them. Death is not at all pleasing, and since everyone is exactly like a condemned man being led to the place of execution, what possible happiness can people derive from material objects or the gratification they provide?" (*Bhag.*11.10.19-20)

"For one who is in the grips of death, what is the use of wealth or those who offer it, sense gratification or those who offer it, or, for that matter, any type of fruitive activity, which simply causes one to again take birth in the material world?" (*Bhag.*11.23.27)

In these verses it is made very clear that anything material which we may have accumulated in life, such as wealth, fame, honor, our possessions, or even scientific knowledge, cannot help us when death is approaching. But when is death not approaching? One may say he is twenty-five years old, or thirty-five years old, or sixty-five years young, but whatever the case, he is actually that many years already dead. And he cannot be sure when the exact moment death will strike. It may be years from now, or it may be in a few moments. Therefore, it is stated that a wise man always lives as if each day may be his last. This means always remembering the real purpose of life and that life is nothing but a moment on our great path toward spiritual self-realization. Life holds many lessons to be learned and how long it takes to learn those lessons will determine how many lifetimes we must go through before we graduate to a higher level of existence. The highest of all levels of existence is where we regain our constitutional spiritual position.

In our attempt to regain our natural spiritual state, we should remember that in the material world, in order to be successful, all activities must be completed within this lifetime. However, it is still temporary, as it is said, "You can't take it with you when you go." But spiritual activities and their profits stay with the soul lifetime after lifetime, even if not fully completed. In other words, if we make only 25% of the needed spiritual progress in this life, we can attain the remaining 75% in a later life, or continue working towards it over many lifetimes until we finally reach the goal. Thus, Sri Krishna says in *Bhagavad-gita*: "In this endeavor there is no loss or diminution, and a little advancement on this path can protect one from the most dangerous type of fear." (*Bg.*2.40)

The most dangerous type of fear is that of not knowing where death will take you. It is difficult to say for certain whether our next life will be better or worse. It may turn out heavenly or hellish or a little of both. Why take the risk? We must prepare for it. Death is a problem which must be reckoned with. But once we have solved this problem of death and understand what it is, there is no longer anything of which to be afraid. This is real fearlessness. Fearlessness does not mean just looking into the far reaches of the unknown, or even into the face of death itself with a hardened, steady gaze. But it means attaining those realizations and that knowledge by which the unknown becomes knowable. After all, how much fear can be generated by those things which we understand?

Naturally, we may rationalize in our overexaggerated opinions of ourselves that we must surely be heading towards the "promised land," or a better future after death. But what makes us think so? What have we really done to deserve such a fate? Therefore, it is recommended that we use the Vedic instructions for guiding ourselves along the path that will assure us of developing virtuous spiritual assets. These assets will guarantee our further advancement in this life and in the hereafter until we can return to the original spiritual atmosphere. This is how one actually conquers death. The importance of this is mentioned in the following verses:

"The Blessed Lord said: Son of Pritha, a transcendentalist engaged in auspicious activities does not meet with destruction either in this world or in the spiritual world; one who does good, My friend, is never overcome by evil." (Bg.6.40)

"That is the way of the spiritual and godly life, after attaining which a person is not bewildered. Being so situated, even at the hour of death, one can enter into the kingdom of God." (Bg.2.72)

"Because of his spiritual assets, the doubts of duality were completely cut off. Thus, he was freed from the three modes of material nature and placed in transcendence. There was no longer any chance of his becoming entangled in birth and death, for he was freed from the material form." (Bhag.1.15.31)

This is the importance of acquiring the necessary spiritual qualifications for the benefit of our future existence.

One more important point mentioned by Pingala is that, after giving up the desire to enjoy with many lovers, she would enjoy with the Lord. She had attained perfect peace and was now intent on directing her affection towards God. But how is this possible? How can one have a loving relationship with the Absolute Truth, which the Vedas describe as full of all potencies, all power, all consciousness, all knowledge, all beauty, all love, beyond our ability to comprehend, and the source from which everything else emanates?

The answer is described in the Vedic literature. That Supreme Person is said to be not only a powerful force or energy that pervades everything in and outside this universe, but also the Supersoul within our hearts, as well as the Supreme Person who can reveal Himself in a way we can understand according to our sincerety. It is impossible for us to know God by our own endeavor, but it is no great matter for Him to reveal Himself to us. Most people in society may not be so interested to know God. In fact, only a handful of the population may ever make a serious attempt to understand the Absolute Truth. However, God is very interested in allowing us to know Him and, therefore, He supplies so much information in the Vedic literature on how to do so.

The fact of the matter is that in all of the creation there are ultimately only three things which are eternal: (1) God, (2) the living entities, and (3) the relationship between them, which is love. The love in this case is that which is pure, unselfish, and spiritual, above and beyond the need for physical or sexual expression. It is much higher than that. Due to this spiritual love, the Lord maintains the spiritual world where we can engage in eternal loving activities that are full of bliss and knowledge. However, when we wish to forget the loving relationship we have with the Supreme and be independent, we enter into the material worlds where we search for small, temporary energies of God towards which we may become attracted for a while. These may include various friends, lovers, or we may have a love for sports cars, beautiful paintings, sunsets at the Grand Canyon, etc. But these are all small energies of the Supreme and cannot nearly give all the pleasure for which we are hankering. That is the problem with trying to be happy with material pleasure.

We can stay in this material world lifetime after lifetime for as long as we want to remain forgetful of our relationship with the Supreme. But once we start becoming frustrated with our temporary material relationships and long to find the ultimate object of our love and affection, then a way is supplied by which we can accomplish this and again spiritualize our consciousness. When the student is ready, a teacher appears in order to give one the process for reaching perfection. Do not think that God would establish the fantastic arrangement of the material creation and then be so neglectful as to leave us here without providing a process for getting out. By this process, we can attain the real happiness for which we are always desiring. We can again remember who we actually are and what God is and what our relationship is with God. This is the ultimate goal of life, which the *Vedas* fully describe. This knowledge is continually being offered throughout history for the well-being of everyone in the form of Vedic knowledge, which we will continue to explain in the following chapters.

# CHAPTER TWO

# *What Are The Vedas*

The word *veda* means knowledge. Any knowledge may be *veda*, but it is understood that the Vedic literature contains the original knowledge. This includes knowledge both within and from beyond our sensory perception. We acquire most of our knowledge by the way we see, touch, taste, smell, or hear things that go on around us. By the use of our mind, the center of the senses, we adjust our view of life and the world according to the type of knowledge we acquire through experience. If we cannot experience everything for ourselves but want to know about a particular topic, we then must hear from others who have experienced or know what we wish to learn. People go to school or college to acquire knowledge of what is beyond their present experience. Everyone can see, therefore, that no one is born with all knowledge. They must learn and be taught by one who knows. This means that we must accept the idea of approaching higher authority. And the ultimate higher authority, in terms of spiritual subject matter, is considered to be the *Vedas*, the ancient knowledge of the East.

The *Vedas* are regarded as a system of higher understanding which can explain how best to utilize one's present situation, just as when you buy an appliance or a car, you also get an owner's manual to help explain how to use and take care of it. In the same way, the *Vedas* were given to people of the world so that they may know who they are, how they got here, how this world works, and how to utilize this life for the best advantage and avoid unseen dangers. This is confirmed in the *Yajur-veda* (31.7) where it states that God created the *Vedas* and reveals all things through them (40.8). This is also stated in the *Atharva-veda* (11.7.24 and 19.6.13).

Ultimately, the main purpose of the Vedic literature is to establish knowledge of self-realization and provide the way to attain freedom from suffering. This means becoming liberated from material entanglement by using this human form of life for reaching (or returning to) the spiritual platform of

18

existence. But no matter what level of desires you may have, there is a particular portion of the *Vedas* you can use for continuing your progress.

The *Vedas* first teach how to regulate ordinary work and channel that activity into actions which reward the performer with future benefits. As a person's life becomes channeled or organized accordingly, he naturally grows toward a superior stage of philosophical understanding. As one gains deeper enlightenment by practical experience, one also perceives through the *Vedas* the real purpose of life. This is explained in the *Srimad-Bhagavatam*: "Your word in the form of the *Veda* is the one excellent eye possessed by the ancestors, gods and human beings, enabling them to obtain insight into the unseen purpose of life, such as final liberation, heavenly bliss, as well as the goal to be attained in this very life and the means of attaining it, O Lord." (*Bhag*.11.20.4)

The *Bhagavad-gita* also states: "This knowledge is the king of education, the most secret of all secrets. It is the purest knowledge, and because it gives direct perception of the self by realization, it is the perfection of religion. It is everlasting and it is joyfully performed." (*Bg*.9.2)

However, one must also be careful. "Because a person who has been covered over by ignorance since time immemorial is not capable of effecting his own self-realization, there must be some other personality who is in factual knowledge of the Absolute Truth and can impart this knowledge to them." (*Bhag*.11.22.10) Therefore, we must be cautious about who to approach to understand the Vedic teachings. This means not only which teacher you hear from, but which translation of the *Vedas* you read.

Some scholars, for example, have complained that the *Vedas* are too vague and unclear. Therefore, due to their own lack of understanding, they dismiss the Vedic teachings as not being very significant. There is a reason for this. It has been said that knowledge in the hands of an envious person can be very dangerous. Thus, the *Vedas* may deal in esoteric terms so the inimical will not understand. As Lord Krishna says in *Srimad-Bhagavatam*: "The *Vedas*, divided into three divisions, ultimately reveal the living entity as pure spirit soul. The Vedic seers and *mantras*, however, deal in esoteric terms, and I am also pleased by such confidential descriptions. The transcendental sound of the *Vedas* is very difficult to comprehend and manifests on different levels within the *prana* (life energy), senses, and mind. This Vedic sound is unlimited, very deep, and unfathomable, just like an ocean." (*Bhag*.11.21.35-36)

To explain further, to understand the highest levels of Vedic philosophy properly, one must practice or participate in it. One can study it simply to attain a much higher understanding of one's real identity, but this type of erudition is limited in its perspective and typical of the Western approach to researching philosophy. A full view of Vedic philosophy will increase as one studies as well as practices the teachings found in the Vedic writings. These practices help one develop the inner realizations for more fully understanding and directly perceiving the spiritual information within the *Vedas*. We will present some of these practices and explain the different types of yoga in *The Universal Path to Enlightenment*. But for now you should realize that whomever you learn from must be fully developed and experienced in both the study of the philosophy as well as the practices prescribed in the Vedic literature. The reason is that, naturally, the student cannot advance further than the teacher. Therefore, the teacher or author of any book you read on this subject must be qualified.

For example, the statements that are made by some so-called scholars who write books on Eastern philosophy, and who are supposed to be expert enough to teach others, are sometimes so misguiding that they clearly impede the progress of any sincere seeker of truth. Their interpretations, which often show every sign of being limited by their own atheistic tendencies, reveal that such teachers and writers will never be able to grasp the expansiveness or fathom the depths of the truths that are revealed through the process of submissive hearing of the *Vedas*. This is because they refuse to approach a spiritual authority or an experienced master from whom to learn. They think they can understand Vedic philosophy on their own simply by reading a Vedic text. But the Vedic system does not work like that. *Bhagavad-gita* points out: "Those who are thus bewildered are attracted by demonic and atheistic views. In that deluded condition, their hopes for liberation, their fruitive activities, and their culture of knowledge are all defeated." (*Bg.*9.12.)

One of the funniest examples of how misinformed some of these professors can be is in a popular book in which the word *gosvami* is interpreted to mean "cow-lord." As anyone who is even slightly informed on the subject of yoga knows, the Sanskrit word *go* also means the senses, and the word *svami* means master or controller. Therefore, *gosvami* refers to one who is master of his senses. By mastering the senses and controlling the mind, one makes the connection with the self within. By being a lord or master of a cow, this is hardly achievable. If such were the case, every cowboy and rancher in the world may wake up one day to suddenly find themselves as fully enlightened mystics.

So, a person must be very careful in this regard if he or she is serious about gaining authentic spiritual knowledge and not to be the victim of trying to understand what is actually inaccurate information. Many years ago, this problem did not exist because not just anyone was allowed to study the *Vedas*. They were generally kept in the possession of the priestly *brahmana* class. Only qualified students who would spend the proper time studying under the guidance of a spiritual authority were allowed to delve into the Vedic mysteries. This way, the *Vedas* would always maintain their purity, and unqualified or envious people would not be able to abuse or misuse them.

The point is also mentioned that since the *Vedas* are spiritual energy in the form of sound vibration, they are difficult to comprehend, except by the pure-hearted who alone can grasp the real meaning. Therefore, the general populace must take care not to be misguided by incompetent teachers. But if one is persistent and finds a pure-hearted soul who can explain the *Vedas* properly, then he has every chance of being successful. As stated in the *Vedanta-sutras* (4.4.23): "One who properly hears Vedic knowledge does not have to return to the cycle of birth and death." In other words, one is sure to reach the perfectional platform of spiritual existence and happiness, free from the physical and material limitations, simply by understanding the real teachings of the Vedic literature, which we are trying to present in this volume.

## THE INFLUENCE THE VEDAS HAVE HAD ON THE WEST

The *Vedas* are not new to the Western world. There have been seekers, writers, poets, philosophers, and people of all levels who have appreciated the depth, inspiration, and insight of Vedic thought for many years. For centuries, interest in India, where the Vedic literature originated, was usually for reasons of trade. Goods like spices, jewels, and fine cloth were always in demand. Even Marco Polo wrote of seeing the great wealth of India and described it as one of the richest countries in the world. Christopher Columbus read Marco Polo's descriptions and devised a plan to find a new route to India. (He discovered America instead.)

This interest in India continued, but in the early 1800's the traders of Indian goods also began bringing with them books in Sanskrit. Sanskrit literature started to become popular. Up to the end of the civil war in America, the influence of Vedic thought continued to spread. This was especially noticeable in places such as Concord, Massachusetts where personalities like Henry David Thoreau, Ralph Waldo Emerson, Amos Bronson Alcott, Minister James Freeman Clark and others began to express in their writing the philosophical insight which was inspired directly by the Vedic literature. Emerson in particular was known to have read such Vedic books as the *Bhagavad-gita, Vishnu Purana, Laws of Manu, Bhagavat Purana,* and even the *Kathopanishad.* One quote of his is: "I owed a magnificent day to the *Bhagavad-gita.* It was the first of books; it was as if an empire spake to us, nothing small or unworthy, but large, serene, consistent, the voice of an old intelligence which in another age and climate had pondered and thus disposed of the same questions that exercise us."

Henry David Thoreau is also well known for his philosophical leanings in his writings. He was an avid reader of Vedic literature and openly expressed his admiration for Vedic thought. During his stay at Walden Pond, he would regularly read *Bhagavad-gita.* Thoreau once remarked, "What extracts from the *Vedas* I have read fall on me like the light of a higher and purer luminary, which describes a loftier course through a purer stratum." Also, "In the morning I bathe my intellect in the stupendous and cosmogonal philosophy of the *Bhagavad-gita,* since whose composition years of the gods have elapsed and in comparison with which our modern world and its literature seems puny and trivial." (*Walden,* Chapter XVI)

Thoreau was so impressed with the *Bhagavad-gita* that he went on to say: "The reader is nowhere raised into and sustained in a bigger, purer or rarer region of thought than in the *Bhagavad-gita*. The *Gita's* sanity and sublimity have impressed the minds of even soldiers and merchants." He also admitted that, "The religion and philosophy of the Hebrews are those of a wilder and ruder tribe, wanting the civility and intellectual refinements and subtlety of Vedic culture." Thoreau's reading of literature on India and the *Vedas* was extensive: he took it seriously. Even Mahatma Gandhi respected him and accepted him as his teacher.

Other recognized writers that were influenced by Vedic philosophy were T.S. Eliot, Paul Elmer More, and Irving Babbitt, all of whom had studied at Harvard under the great Sanskrit teacher Charles Rochwell Lanman, who taught for over forty years and also published works on Sanskrit and Hindu philosophy. As Harvard had a succession of outstanding teachers of Sanskrit, so did Yale, but even earlier. In fact, Elihu Yale had a deep respect for Vedic philosophy.

Part of the reason for introducing the study of Sanskrit and Eastern philosophy in universities was due to the influence of such organizations as the American Oriental Society, which was founded in 1842. Through the years, there have been many great Sanskritists and American Indologists who have helped point out how unique the Vedic philosophy is. Such people include Edward Elbridge Salisbury (1814-1901), who went to India and continued his studies there; Fitzedward Hall (1825-1901); William Dwight Whitney (1827-1901); Edward Washburn Hopkins (1857-1932); James Bradstreet Greenough (1833-1900); and many others. Not only in America but in other Western countries the ideas from India were received among interested intellectuals, some of whom were Max Mueller and Aldous Huxley of England, Romain Rolland of France, Tolstoy of Russia, and Schlegel, Deussen and Schopenhauer of Germany. In fact, Schopenhauer went so far as to predict that the *Vedas* would one day be accepted as the religion of the world.

As there were great thinkers in America and other countries years ago who were attempting to increase their understanding of the Vedic philosophy from India, there were also those in India who were eager to send such literature to the West. In 1896, Bhaktivinode Thakur (1838-1914) sent several copies of his book, *The Life and Precepts of Chaitanya Mahaprabhu*, to the West. A few of them found their way into the library of McGill University in Canada and the library of the Royal Asiatic Society of London. Though a small work, the book was indeed admired by Western scholars.

This concept of exchanging ideas and culture can no doubt more easily be seen in recent times as many sages and *svamis* from India have come to America to teach students, and Western students have gone to India in search of teachers. Surely, this is no accident: for while America is rich in modern technological know-how but seems to lack spiritual vision, India, on the other hand, is poor materially but rich in spiritual heritage.

This is similar to the example of a blind man and a lame man working to help each other. The blind man may be able to walk or even run, but without eyes he may run many miles in the wrong direction. And a lame man may be able to see where to go but move only with great difficulty. By working together, the lame man can advise the blind man of the route he can take, and the blind man can help the lame man to get around. In this way, they help each other accomplish their goals. So it is natural, as in this example, for the East (the lame man) and the West (the blind man) to assist each other until a proper combination is found. It has been understood by great thinkers that this combination of East and West can be accomplished through the study and utilization of the Vedic philosophy.

In this way, numerous writers and poets of the West, which we have admired for years, have gotten much of their inspiration from Eastern philosophy. Thus, the *Vedas* have already made a definite contribution to the spiritual and intellectual development of Western society.

## REDISCOVERING VEDIC SCIENCE

Not only do the *Vedas* contain a high level of philosophical and spiritual knowledge, but they also hold information on material science. The Vedic literature includes such works as the *Ayur-veda*, the original science of wholistic medicine as taught by Lord Dhanvantari; *Dhanur-veda*, the military science as taught by Bhrigu; *Gandharva-veda*, which is on the arts of music, dance, drama, etc., by Bharata Muni; *Artha-sastram*, the science of government; *Sthapatya-veda*, the science of architecture; and the *Manu-samhita*, the Vedic lawbook.

There is also the *Shulba Sutras*, which contains the Vedic system of mathematics. These *sutras* are a supplement of the *Kalpasutras*, which shows the earliest forms of algebra. The Vedic form of mathematics is much more advanced than that found in early Greek, Babylonian, Egyptian, or Chinese civilizations. In fact, the geometrical formula known as the Pythagorean theorem can be traced to the *Baudhayana*, the earliest form of the *Shulba Sutras* prior to the 8th century B.C. It was this Indian system that originated the decimal system of tens, hundreds, etc., and the procedure of carrying the remainder of one column over to the next. It also provided a means of dividing fractions and the use of equations and letters to signify unknown factors. These Indian numbers were used in Arabia after 700 A.D. and then spread to Europe where they were called Arabic numerals. It is only because Europe changed from Roman numerals to these Arabic numerals that originated in India that many of the developments in Europe in the fields of science and math were able to take place.

The *Puranas* contain a variety of information on the creation of the universe, its maintenance, and destruction. Other subjects include astrology, geography, use of military weapons, organization of society, duties of different classes of men, characteristics and behavior of social leaders, predictions of the future, analysis of the material elements, symptoms of consciousness, how the illusory energy works, the practice of yoga, meditation, spiritual experiences, realizations of the Absolute, and much more.

The *Vedas*, written many hundreds of years ago, also completely disprove the theory of modern scholars who think that all ancient civilizations thought the earth was the center of the universe and the stars and sun revolved around it. In the Vedic description of the cosmological arrangement, it is explained that all planets, as well as the sun, have their particular orbits of travel through the universe. Furthermore, in the earliest of Vedic writings, such as the *Yajur-veda*, we find other sciences mentioned as well. Take, for example, the following verse:

"O disciple, a student in the science of government, sail in oceans in streamers, fly in the air in airplanes, know God the Creator through the Vedas, control thy breath through yoga, through astronomy know the functions of day and night, know all the *Vedas, Rig, Yajur, Sama,* and *Atharva,* by means of their constituent parts.

"Through astronomy, geography and geology, go thou to all the different countries of the world under the sun. Mayest thou attain through good preaching to statesmanship and artisanship, through medical science obtain knowledge of all medicinal plants, through hydrostatics learn the different uses of water, through electricity understand the working of ever-lustrous lightening. Carry out my intructions willingly. . ." (*Yajur-veda*, 6.21)

Among all the different sciences mentioned in the above verse, it may be surprising to find a reference to airplanes. But, actually, the mention of airplanes is found many times throughout Vedic literature, including the following verse from the *Yajur-veda* describing the movement of such machines:

"O royal skilled engineer, construct sea-boats, propelled on water by our experts, and airplanes, moving and flying upward, after the clouds that reside in the mid-region, that fly as the boats move on the sea, that fly high over and below the watery clouds. Be thou, thereby, properous in this world created by the Omnipresent God, and flier in both air and lightening." (*Yajur*, 10.19)

Other discoveries of modern technology is that of atomic energy and its by-products. Most people agree that no civilization before us had knowledge of such things. But time and again we find in the Vedic literature discriptions of weapons that had a similar amount of energy as the atomic bombs we use today. And to what else would these next few verses from the *Atharva-veda* be referring if they are not a description of the basic principles of atomic energy?

"The Atomic Energy fissions the ninety-nine elements, covering its path by the bombardments of neutrons without let or hindrance. Desirous of stalking the head, i.e., the chief part of the swift power, hidden in the mass of molecular adjustments of the elements, this atomic energy approaches it in the very act of fissioning it by the above-noted bombarments. Herein verily the scientist know the similar hidden striking force of the rays of the sun working in the orbit of the moon." (*Atharva-veda*, 20.41.1-3)

Another point illustrating the advanced nature of the Vedic Aryan civilization is their conception of the universal time scale. The time factor is calculated as affecting various levels of the universe differently. For example, a day for 'he demigods is equal to six months for humans on planet earth. And a year is calculated as 360 human years, while 12,000 years of the gods is said to be but one blink of the eye of MahaVishnu. For Lord Brahma, the highest of all the demigods, his day equals one thousand cycles of the combined four ages of Satya, Treta, Dvapara, and Kali-yugas. This amounts to 4.3 billion years, at the end of which is his night when there is a partial annihilation of the universe, which includes the earth. After an equal number of years, Brahma's day begins again, and that which is destroyed is again created or revived. Interestingly, modern science has also estimated that the age of the earth is about 4 billion years. Scholars feel it is uncanny that the Vedic Aryans could have conceived of such a vast span of time over 3,500 years ago that would be similar to the same figure estimated by science today.

The reason this is possible is not because of speculatory thoughts about life by the sages thousands of years ago, but because the Vedic knowledge is, as we have previously stated, established by the Supreme so that the living entities can understand their position in this world. Thus, this knowledge has been descending down through time, ready to be taken advantage of by anyone qualified to do so. Through the above examples, we can see that many of the sciences and inventions that we feel proud of today, thinking they are but recent achievements, were known many years ago. Therefore, we should be careful not to feel that no civilization before us has ever been so advanced. It is quite possible, and from the Vedic literature very evident, that we have failed to see that what has been known for many years we are now, at great expense and with much research, only rediscovering.

# CHAPTER THREE

# *The History And Traditional Source Of The Vedas*

How were the *Vedas* established? What were their origins? What is their history? How were they divided, and why does it seem that there are different paths from which to choose within the *Vedas*?

First of all, there are two ways to answer these questions: one is to consider the theories presented by some of the contemporary scholars and historians in regard to when the *Vedas* appeared, and the second way is to consider the traditional account as presented in the Vedic literature itself.

Many historians have held the idea that it was the Aryans who invaded India in the second millennium B.C. and were the founders of the Indian culture and Vedic traditions. They said that the Aryans came from somewhere near the southern part of Russia and brought their Vedic rituals and customs with them.

This theory, however, does not hold as much weight as it used to amongst modern historians for various reasons. For example, the culture of the Indus valley, where the Aryans are said to have invaded, flourished between 3500 and 2500 B.C. The two main cities were Harappa and Mohenjo-daro. Many finds have come from the archeological excavations from Harappa, which give evidence to suggest that many aspects of later Hinduism were already a part of the early Indus valley culture. Such things have been found as images of yogis sitting in meditation, as well as many figures of a god similar to Lord Shiva. Evidence has also been found to suggest that temple worship played a major role in daily life, which is what the *Vedas* prescribe as the process for attaining the greatest amount of spiritual advancement for people of that time. Evidence also shows that fire worship played an important role, and fire was a representation of Vishnu. And traditionally constructed fire altars have been found that were made according to the descriptions in the ancient *Brahmana* texts.

Another point is that the Indus valley enveloped a vast area and the cultural traits of that society continued to survive for a long time, so how could the

26

pre-Aryan language of the Indus valley people, which is not known today, die out without leaving any trace of its existence? Maybe there actually was not any pre-Aryan language. And if not, if this is where the Aryan invaders were supposed to have appeared when they brought their Vedic culture with them, it is to be concluded that there really was not any Aryan invasion, not at least the way some scholars seem to think. It is more likely that the Vedic Aryans were already there.

Furthermore, most scholars agree that the earliest Vedic hymns seem to belong to a pre-1500 B.C. date. Some researchers, however, feel that parts of the *Rig-veda* date back to several thousand years earlier than 1500 B.C. This means it was not necessarily invaders who had brought Vedic culture with them, since at least the oldest Vedic books, if not most of them, had already been in existence by the time any invaders arrived.

Let us consider another point, using nothing more than our common sense. It is generally accepted that Lord Buddha appeared about 2,500 years ago, and we know that Lord Buddha preached against the *Vedas*. So, the *Vedas* had to have been existing at that time, otherwise how could he have preached against them? In fact, the reason why he no longer accepted the *Vedas* was because many of the leading Vedic followers were no longer truly following them but were abusing them. And any student of history knows that abuse of something takes place after there is a flourishing. So, if the deterioration reached such an extreme 2,500 years ago that people embraced Buddha's teachings, then clearly such gradual degeneration had been going on for many hundreds of years. Since the *Vedas* were a highly developed form of philosophy, it would indicate that they must have been in existence and quite widespread several thousand years before that. Therefore, we can easily understand how old the *Vedas* must be. (I give this kind of research much deeper consideration in Chapter Seven of *The Universal Path to Enlightenment*.)

Furthermore, let us not forget that it was the British Sanskritists and educators in India, during the 1700 and 1800's, who first portrayed Vedic literature and culture as something barbaric, inferior, and recent. They formed estimated dates on when the different Vedic books were written according to such things as the contents of the books and style of writing. But it should be pointed out that even the Vedic tradition describes that after the Vedic knowledge was divided and the different volumes were written, they were handed down to sages who became expert in the content of that portion of Vedic knowledge who then continued to hand it down to others who formed subbranches of it. Thus, it may look like the *Vedas* gradually evolved as if they had been influenced and changed by many authors over a long period of time, but, actually, that is not necessarily the case.

We also have to remember that for many years the Vedic literature was written on palm leaves and would have to be copied when they wore out or when other copies were wanted. Down through the years, as other copies were repeatedly made, certain conventional modifications of the script would have taken place, making some scholars think their origin was more recent. But in the case of the *Bhagavat Purana*, the Sanskrit text still contains the archaic form of writing, verifying its antiquity. Nonetheless, the English scholars said the author of the *Purana* must have purposely used the archaic script to make people think it was older than it was. The fact that the English proposed this sort of theory in an attempt to disqualify its ancient origins simply shows how biased they were against the Vedic literature.

This cultural prejudice was the result of deliberate undermining with the disguised intention of asserting the superiority of their own Christian-based values and outlook, as well as the perpetuation of colonial rule. This intention actually played a prominent role in the reason why they wanted the Sanskrit texts translated into English and to have their Christian scripture translated into Sanskrit. And many of the notable professors at the time had the audacity to consider themselves to be better authorities on their questionable translations of the *Vedas* than the Indian scholars.

In any case, the attempt to belittle the Vedic literature made only a minor impact. In fact, by translating such texts, many of the notable writers and poets in the West, as mentioned in the previous chapter, were allowed to see what lofty views of the world the Vedic literature held and were indeed very impressed and influenced by them.

So, where did the *Vedas* come from? Though modern historians may offer their many changing theories about how the *Vedas* were compiled and where they originated, we can see that this is their attempt to find an oversimplified key to understanding Vedic thought, or to even discredit the value of the *Vedas*. But they must admit that they are still unsure of their theories and lack detailed evidence for many of their opinions. In fact, most historians today feel that any accurately recorded history only goes back to around 600 B.C., and prior to this period all events and stories related in the scriptures are simply imaginary myths and legends. This reflects an extremely narrow-minded way of looking at things. Many Vedic authorities and self-realized sages in the past have accepted the stories, as found in the *Mahabharata* and *Puranas*, to be factual, and have also attained lofty states of consciousness by following the Vedic instructions for spiritual perfection. Therefore, the best way to understand the history of how the *Vedas* were formed is to simply let the Vedic literature speak for itself.

According to Vedic tradition, when the Supreme Lord created this material world, His transcendental energy pervaded every corner of it. This spiritual energy was the pure vibration, *shabda-brahma*, in which the Supreme Himself can be found. This pure sound vibration is manifested as the *om mantra*, comprised of the letters "A," "U," and "M". The spiritually elevated Gosvamis of Vrindavana have explained that the letter "A" refers to the Supreme Person, Bhagavan Krishna, who is the master of all living entities of the material and spiritual planets and is the source from which everything emanates. The letter "U" indicates the energy of the Supreme, and "M" indicates the innumerable living entities. Therefore, *omkara* (*om* or AUM) is the resting place of everything, or, in other words, all potencies are invested within this holy vibration. As further explained in the *Caitanya-caritamrta*:

"The Vedic sound vibration *omkara*, the principal word in the Vedic literature, is the basis of all Vedic vibrations. Therefore one should accept *omkara* as the sound representation of the Supreme Personality of Godhead and the reservoir of the cosmic manifestation." (*Cc.Adi-lila*, 7.128)

Krishna also explains: "I am the father of this universe, the mother, the support and the grandsire. I am the object of knowledge, the purifier and the syllable *om*. I am also the *Rig-veda, Sama-veda* and the *Yajur-veda*." (*Bg*.9.17)

Further confirmation is found in the *Yajur-veda*, (Chapter 31, verse 7): "From that Absolute God unto Whom people make every kind of sacrifice, were created the *Rig-veda*, the *Sama-veda*. From Him were created the *Atharva-veda* and also the *Yajur-veda*."

These verses indicate that the pure Absolute Truth and the pure spiritual sound vibration are nondifferent and that the *Vedas* are the expansions of that Absolute Truth. By understanding Vedic knowledge, one can understand the Absolute. Therefore, the end result of all spiritual realizations, based on the authority of the *Vedas*, is to understand that Supreme Personality.

It is said that originally the *pranava* or *om mantra* expanded into the sacred *gayatri mantra* (*om bhur bhuvah svah tat savitur varenyam bhargo devasya dimahi dhiyo yo nah pracodayat*). The *gayatri* was then expanded into the following four central verses of the *Srimad-Bhagavatam*, called *Catuh-sloki*:

"Prior to this cosmic creation, only I exist, and nothing else, either gross, subtle, or primordial. After creation, only I exist in everything, and after annihilation, only I remain eternally.

"What appears to be truth without Me is certainly My illusory energy, for nothing can exist without Me. It is like a reflection of real light in the shadows, for in the light there are neither shadows nor reflections.

"As the material elements enter the bodies of all living beings and yet remain outside them all, I exist within all material creations and yet am not within them.

"A person interested in transcendental knowledge must therefore always directly and indirectly inquire about it to know the all-pervading truth." (*Bhag*.2.9.33-36)

These *Catuh-sloki* verses were taught by the Supreme Lord Vishnu to Brahma at the time of creation, and all other Vedic literature was expanded from them. The *Bhagavatam* (*Bhagavat Purana*) is considered to be the complete expansion of these four verses.

From this we can now begin to see how incorrect the assumption is of some scholars who think the *Vedas* were written by ordinary men over a length of time which displays the gradual evolutionary changes in man's religious thinking. The fact of the matter is that the Vedic knowledge was given by the Supreme in order for us to understand this world, who we are, and our relationship with the Absolute Reality and how to work according to that relationship. Sri Krishna says in the *Bhagavatam*: "As the unlimited, unchanging and omnipotent Personality of Godhead dwelling within all living beings, I personally establish the Vedic sound vibration in the form of *omkara* within all living entities. It is thus perceived subtly, just like a single strand of fiber on a lotus stalk." (*Bhag*.11.21.37)

What this means is that since we are all spiritual in nature, our constitutional position is to be full of eternal knowledge and bliss. The purpose of the Vedic literature is to reawaken that knowledge within us. Our spiritual position is of a very subtle nature and we cannot force our entry into the understanding of this knowledge simply by the deliberate manipulation of intelligence or logic. As pointed out earlier, one must practice the Vedic system to get the full results. By this process, one develops the power to perceive that which exists on the spiritual platform. Otherwise, how can one become qualified for understanding the higher principles of spiritual self-realization?

The next few verses clearly indicate that the *shabda-brahma* exists in the Absolute Truth before creation, during the creation, and after the annihilation of this material world. Therefore, the source for all kinds of knowledge stems back from the *Vedas*.

"Just as a spider brings forth from its heart its web and emits it through its mouth, the Supreme Personality of Godhead manifests Himself as the reverberating primeval vital air, comprising all sacred Vedic meters and full of transcendental pleasure. Thus, the Lord, from the ethereal sky of His heart, creates the great and limitless Vedic sound by the agency of His mind, which conceives of variegated sounds such as the *sparsas* (Sanskrit consonants). The Vedic sound branches out in thousands of directions, adorned with the different letters expanded from the syllable *om*: the consonants, vowels, sibilants, and semivowels. The *Veda* is elaborated by many verbal varieties, expressed in different meters, each having four more syllables than the previous one. Ultimately, the Lord again withdraws His manifestation of Vedic sound within Himself." (*Bhag*.11.21.38-40)

Since the *Vedas* are a manifestation of the Absolute Truth and exist eternally, the *Manu-samhita* (the first law book for human civilization) explains that all other doctrines or philosophies not based on Vedic knowledge are impermanent. They exist for short times in history while they undergo constant transformations because of mankind's ever-changing attitudes of likes and dislikes. We can especially see this happening today in many religions where people want changes to be made in the basic precepts. Eventually, all that is left as the years go by is simply a watered down hodgepodge with no potency. Therefore, the *Manu-samhita* says: "All those traditions (*Smriti*) and all those despicable systems of philosophy, which are not based on the *Veda*, produce no reward after death; for they are declared to be founded on darkness. All those doctrines differing from the *Veda*, which spring up and (soon) perish, are worthless and false, because they are of modern date." (*The Laws of Manu*, Chapter 12, verses 95-96)

"Of modern date" means that it is recent, emerging within the last several hundred years, or arising from someone's imagination who gives something completely new or makes up a doctrine that combines a number of different traditions. Thus, it is a philosophy of questionable benefit for the people in general. It is what is called a cheating process, though it may be in the name of religion. It may have some flowery language and basic wisdom in its scripture, but it is nothing that will give people tangible results on the spiritual level. At best, all you will have is a group of people, whether a small community or several nations, who are temporarily united in their blind faith and who work together for a cause which produces no truely beneficial outcome.

## THE COMPILING OF THE VEDAS

If the *Vedas* are eternal and were manifest from the Supreme, then how were they first compiled into written form?

This is how it is explained. After the creation of the universal elements, Brahma was born from Lord Vishnu, the incarnation of God who directly manifests the material ingredients. Brahma is the first living entity in the universe and helps engineer the part of the creation which includes all the different forms of humans, vegetation, insects, aquatics, planetary systems, etc.

When Brahma was first generated, he was not sure what this material world was or who he was. There was no one else to enlighten him; so, he thought about it for a long time and tried to search out the cause of his existence but came to no conclusion. This is the same result that people will come to if they try to understand this universe and who they are simply by observing things through their senses. By analyzing the world with the mind and senses, they are bound to make many mistakes in their perception of things. Even with instruments like telescopes or microscopes, mistakes will be there because such machines are simply extensions of the same faulty senses. Therefore, retiring from his searching and mental speculation, Brahma engaged in deep meditation by controlling the mind and concentrating on the Supreme Cause.

By Brahma's meditation and practice of penance for many years, the Supreme Lord Vishnu became satisfied with him and from within Brahma's heart there awakened all transcendental knowledge and creative power. From his spiritual realizations, Brahma manifested the *gayatri mantra*. He also manifested the four primary *Vedas*. This is confirmed in the *Vishnu Purana* as well as the *Vayu, Linga, Kurma, Padma, Markandaya,* and *Bhagavat Puranas.*

Lord Vishnu taught this Vedic knowledge to Brahma and Brahma in turn taught this knowledge to other great sages who became manifest, including Narada Muni, who also taught it to others. This is where the oral tradition began, and how the Vedic knowledge was spoken from one person to another for thousands of years before it was written and compiled into the original *samhitas.* The *Vedas* were taught to the great saints and mystics who had such mental capabilities that they could memorize anything by hearing it once. This should not be considered too unusual because even today there are those who have memorized large amounts of scripture. For thousands of years the *Vedas* were carefully handed down in this way. This is further elaborated in the *Bhagavatam.*

"Out of the aforesaid (AUM or *om mantra*) the almighty Brahma (the creator born from Lord Vishnu) evolved the alphabet, comprising *Antahsthas* (semi-vowels), *Usmas* (aspirants), *Swaras* (vowels), *Sparsas* (sibilants) and the short, long, and prolated measures of sound. With this alphabet Brahma gave expression through his mouth to the four *Vedas* along with the *om* and *Vyahritis* (mystical names of the three planetary systems, Bhuh, Bhuvah and Svaha) with the intention of pointing out the duties of the four priests (officiating at a sacrifice, namely *Adhwaryu, Udgata, Hota,* and *Brahmana*). He then taught them to his (mind born) sons (Marichi and others) who were *brahmana* sages and expert in reciting the *Vedas.* The latter in their turn proved to be the promulgators of righteousness and taught the *Vedas* to their sons (Kasyapa and others). Received from generation to generation in the course of the four *yugas* by the pupils of the various sages--pupils who observed the vow of (lifelong) celibacy [in order to retain the *Vedas* in their memory]--the *Vedas* were later divided by great seers at the end of the Dvapara age. Perceiving the men to be shortlived, deficient in energy and dull-witted due to the action of time (in the form of unrighteousness prevailing in it) the *brahmana* seers rearranged the *Vedas* as directed by the immortal Lord residing in their heart.

"Descended from the sage Parasara through (his wife) Satyavati in the form of Vedavyasa (Vyasadeva) as prayed to by Brahma, Lord Shiva, and other guardians of the spheres for the vindication of righteousness, the almighty Lord, the life-giver of the universe, divided the *Veda* into four parts. Picking out and classifying in four (distinct) groups the multitudes of *mantras* belonging to the categories of *Rig, Atharva, Yajus,* and *Sama,* as various kinds of gems are assorted into so many groups, the sage Vyasadeva compiled four *samhitas* or collections of those *mantras.*" (*Bhag.* 12.6.42-50)

This is the basic story of how the *Vedas* appeared and were then divided. However, *Srimad-Bhagavatam* also explains: "In Saty-yuga, the first millennium, all the Vedic *mantras* were included in one *mantra--pranava* (*om*), the root of all Vedic *mantras.* In other words, the *Atharva-veda* [some say the *Yajur-veda*] alone was the source of all Vedic knowledge. The Supreme Personality of Godhead Narayana (an expansion of Krishna) was the only worshipable Deity; there was no recommendation for worship of the demigods. Fire was one only, and the only order of life in human society was known as *hamsa* [the swanlike sages who were all spiritually self-realized]." (*Bhag*.9.14.48)

This indicates that originally there was no need for expanding the Vedic literature because everyone was self-realized. In Satya-yuga, the age of purity and peace, everyone knew the ultimate goal of life and they were not confused about this as people are today. There was only one *Veda* (which was unwritten until Vyasadeva compiled the Vedic literature at the end of the Dvapara-yuga), one *mantra*, one process of spiritual self-realization, and one form of worship. But as time passed and unrighteousness began to spread, things changed and there was a need for further elaboration of Vedic knowledge. Other processes of self-realization were also presented to accommodate the various levels of consciousness of the people. Thus, the primary purpose of the *Vedas*, which was the worship of the Supreme Lord for material liberation, changed and began focusing on the worship of demigods for the attainment of various material rewards through the performance of detailed rituals, as can especially be seen from the verses in the *Rig* and *Sama Vedas*.

To explain further, in Satya-yuga, which lasts 1,728,000 years, people live a very long time and the process for self-realization is meditating on Narayana. In the next age, Treta-yuga, which lasts 1,296,000 years, the spiritual tendency of the people declined by twenty-five percent, and the process for self-realization was the performance of ritualistic sacrifice, which the early *Vedas* fully describe. In the next age, Dvapara-yuga, which lasts 864,000 years, people engaged in opulent temple worship as the prescribed process for spiritual self-realization, but the religious inclination of people again declined by another twenty-five percent. In the present age of Kali-yuga, which lasts 432,000 years and started 5,000 years ago, people are all short-lived and exhibit almost no interest in self-realization or spiritual topics. For this reason, the *Vedas* were expanded and put into written form so that less intelligent people could more easily understand them. This is confirmed in the *Bhagavatam* in its description of the different incarnations of God who appear in this world:

"Thereafter, in the seventeenth incarnation of Godhead, Sri Vyasadeva appeared in the womb of Satyavati through Parasara Muni, and he divided the one *Veda* into several branches and subbranches, seeing that the people in general were less intelligent." (*Bhag*.1.3.21)

Here we also find that Vyasadeva was in fact an incarnation of the Supreme who appeared with the purpose of establishing the *Vedas* in writing. The *Vedas* had previously been passed down through an oral tradition, but now there was a need for them to be written. How exactly Vyasadeva divided the *Vedas* is nicely told in *Srimad-Bhagavatam* in the following story:

"Once upon a time he (Vyasadeva), as the sun rose, took his morning ablution in the waters of the Sarasvati and sat alone to concentrate. The great sage saw anomalies in the duties of the millennium. This happens on the earth in different ages, due to the unseen forces in the course of time. The great sage, who was fully equipped with knowledge, could see, through his transcendental vision, the deterioration of everything material, due to the influence of the age [of Kali]. He could see also that the faithless people in general would be reduced in duration of life and would be impatient due to lack of goodness. Thus he contemplated for the welfare of men in all statuses of life." (*Bhag*.1.4.15-18)

Srila Vyasadeva could see that in the future men would be very short-lived, quarrelsome, impatient, easily angered, and their memory would be very inefficient. So, there was now the need to put the Vedic sound vibration into writing. Otherwise, people would never be able to remember it as they had in the past, what to speak of studying and understanding it.

"He (Vyasadeva) saw that the sacrifices mentioned in the *Vedas* were means by which people's occupations could be purified. And to simplify the process he divided the one *Veda* into four, in order to expand them among men. The four divisions of the original sources of knowledge (the *Vedas*) were made separately. But the historical facts and authentic stories mentioned in the *Puranas* are called the fifth *Veda*." (*Bhag*.1.4.19-20)

How the one *Veda* was divided into four is explained more fully in the following quote from the *Vishnu Purana*: "There was but one *Yajur-veda*; but dividing this into four parts, Vyasa instituted the sacrificial rites that are administered by four kinds of priests: in which it was the duty of the *Adhvaryu* (priest) to recite the prayers (*Yajus*) (or direct the ceremony); of the *Hotri* (priest) to chant other hymns (*Sama*); and of the *Brahmana* (priest) to pronounce the formula called *Atharva*. Then the Muni, having collected together the hymns called *Richas*, compiled the *Rig-veda*; with the prayers and directions termed *Yajushas* he formed the *Yajur-veda*; with those called *Sama, Sama-veda*; and with the *Atharvas* he composed the rules of all ceremonies suited to kings, and the function of the *Brahmana* agreeably to practice." (*Vishnu Purana*, Book Three, Chapter Four)

What follows in the *Vishnu Purana* is a detailed description of how these four *Vedas* were handed down from spiritual master to disciple through many generations and how many different branches of Vedic knowledge were formed. To keep the length of this chapter from getting unnecessarily long, we will use the considerably shorter account as given in the *Bhagavat Purana*:

"After the *Vedas* were divided into four divisions, Paila Rishi became the professor of the *Rig-veda*, Jaimini the professor of the *Sama-veda*, and Vaisampayana alone became giorified by the *Yajur-veda*. The Sumantu Muni Angira, who was very devotedly engaged, was entrusted with *Atharva-veda*. And my (Suta Gosvami's) father, Romaharsana, was entrusted with historical records [the *Puranas*]. All these learned scholars, in their turn, rendered their entrusted *Vedas* unto their many disciples, grand-disciples, and great grand-disciples, and thus the respective branches of the followers of the *Vedas* came into being. Thus, the great sage Vyasadeva, who is very kind to the ignorant masses, edited the *Vedas* so they might be assimilated by less intellectual men.

"Out of compassion, the great sage thought it was wise that this would enable men to achieve the ultimate goal of life. Thus, he compiled the great historical narration called the *Mahabharata* for women, laborers, and friends of the twice-born (unqualified *brahmanas*). O twice-born *brahmana*, still his mind was not satisfied, although he engaged himself in working for the total welfare of all people. Thus, the sage, being dissatisfied at heart, at once began to reflect, because he knew the essence of religion, and he said within himself: 'I have, under strict disciplinary vows, unpretentiously worshipped the *Vedas*, the spiritual master, and the altar of sacrifice. I have also abided by the rulings and have shown the import of disciplic succession through the explanation of the *Mahabharata*, by which even women, laymen, and others can see the path of religion. I am feeling incomplete, though I myself am fully equipped with everything required by the *Vedas*. This may be because I did not specifically point out the devotional service of the Lord, which is dear both to perfect beings and to the infallible Lord.'" (*Bhag.*11.4.21-31)

Even though Vyasadeva had worked for the welfare of all by writing the Vedic literature, still he felt dissatisfied. This is a great lesson. Naturally, we all desire freedom from the problems that material life causes us, but only by engaging in direct spiritual activities does the spiritual living entity, the soul within these temporary material bodies, begin to feel any real relief or happiness. How to do this by engaging in service or *bhakti-yoga* to the Supreme Being is what the *Vedas* are meant to establish, and because this had not yet been prominently presented in the literature Vyasadeva had written, such as the four *Vedas*, the *Upanishads*, and *Vedanta-sutras*, he was still feeling dissatisfied. Now he was trying to understand the cause of his dissatisfaction.

In all the literature compiled by Vyasadeva, there were many descriptions of the temporary universe, prayers to the demigods, the process for attaining material necessities, information about the soul, the Brahman, the Supersoul, and the process of yoga for attaining spiritual realizations. There was also information about the Supreme Lord Bhagavan, Krishna. But the detailed descriptions of God, His form, His incarnations, His names, activities, potencies, and energies, and how He is the source of everything, including the ever-increasing spiritual bliss which we are always seeking, had not yet been fully described.

While questioning his unexpected dissatisfaction, Vyasadeva was at that very moment greeted by the sage Narada Muni, who had just arrived at Vyasadeva's cottage. Acting as Vyasadeva's spiritual master, as described in *Srimad-Bhagavatam* (Canto One, Chapters Five and Six), Narada Muni instructed him in the cause of his problem. He said that Vyasa had not actually broadcast the sublime and spotless glories of the Supreme Personality. Therefore, Narada Muni encouraged Vyasadeva to write and describe the eternal spiritual truths in a more direct manner:

"O Vyasadeva, your vision is completely perfect. Your good fame is spotless. You are firm in vow and satisfied in truthfulness. And thus you can think of the pastimes of the Lord in trance for the liberation of the people in general from all material bondage. The Supreme Lord is unlimited. Only a very expert personality retired from the activities of material happiness, deserves to understand this knowledge of spiritual values. Therefore, those who are not so well situated, due to material attachment, should be shown the way of transcendental realization, by Your Goodness, through descriptions of the transcendental activities of the Supreme Lord. Persons who are actually intelligent and philosophically inclined should endeavor only for that purposeful end which is [spiritual and] not obtainable even by wandering from the topmost planet down to the lowest.

"The Supreme Lord is Himself this cosmos, and still He is aloof from it. From Him only has this cosmic manifestation emanated, in Him it rests, and unto Him it enters after annihilation. Your good self knows all about this. You yourself can know the Supersoul Personality of Godhead because you are present as the plenary portion of the Lord. Although you are birthless, you have appeared on this earth for the well-being of all people. Please, therefore, describe the transcendental pastimes of the Supreme Personality of Godhead, Sri Krishna, more vividly."

After Narada Muni took leave of Vyasadeva, Vyasa, in his own *ashrama*, on the bank of the River Sarasvati, sat down to meditate. He fixed his mind, perfectly engaging it by linking it in devotional service (*bhakti-yoga*) without any tinge of materialism, and thus he saw the Absolute Personality of Godhead along with His external energy, which was under full control. Then the learned Vyasadeva compiled the topmost fruit of the tree of Vedic knowledge, the *Srimad-Bhagavatam* [*Bhagavat Purana*], which is in relation to the Supreme Truth, as well as being Vyasadeva's own commentary on all the other Vedic writings.

In this way, the different levels of Vedic literature came into being. This includes the four primary *Vedas*, namely the *Rig, Yajur, Sama,* and *Atharva-vedas*, the *Upanishads*, the *Vedanta-sutras*, the *Mahabharata*, the *Puranas*, and finally, as related in the above story, the *Bhagavat Purana*. Within these literatures and their many supplementary books on health, architecture, music, etc., are contained the essential teachings of spirit, the material sciences, and the processes for attaining transcendental realizations, which will be explained further in Volume Two of *The Eastern Answers to the Mysteries of Life*, which is titled *The Universal Path to Enlightenment*.

# CHAPTER FOUR

## *Our Real Identity: The Science of the Soul*

This chapter has some of the most valuable information one can ever read in regard to spiritual knowledge. Within the next few pages we will establish, by Vedic evidence, the real identity and nature of the living being. Only by understanding who we are will we be able to know what to do with ourselves, where we fit in this world, and so on. We will also be able to see through the bodily differences between us, and, if everyone could understand this knowledge, we could establish peace in the world. But without comprehending this information, there is little hope that true peace will ever be found. Furthermore, regardless of what philosophy or religion towards which you are inclined, without understanding the detailed information about the soul, whatever spiritual progress you think you have made is, practically speaking, only superficial and hardly scratches the surface of spiritual reality. Therefore, we encourage everyone to follow the course of this chapter to enter into another level of spiritual realization.

### FINDING OURSELVES

People in every part of the world are very much the same in the respect that everyone is trying to find themselves. The only difference is how they do it. In this regard, everyone is a philosopher to some degree because everyone is trying to figure out how to arrange life in order to find happiness, peace of mind, and so on. But what most people assume you are talking about when you mention the idea of finding yourself is choosing the one thing you would most like to do in life. Actually, this is merely analyzing the mind and trying to discern your likes and dislikes.

Someone might want to become a businessman and work in an office in a skyscraper from nine to five everyday. Someone else may want to become a famous movie star. Another may want to become a politician, or a priest, or just learn a trade and raise a family in the countryside somewhere. There are so many things a person could do, depending on his or her ideals.

In identifying with these ideals, there may be certain clubs we join, or particular people with whom we associate, or activities we do with others. For example, when fans of a certain sports club, like in football or baseball, go to watch their favorite team play, they might wear the same colors as the team's uniforms. Or they may wear something like a hat or shirt with an emblem on it which signifies their loyalty to the team. They cheer for the team, maybe even fight for the team, and if the team wins they feel happy and proud and will celebrate with other fans.

Younger people especially may put a lot of energy into identifying with particular ideals and in expressing them in personal ways. They may wear certain clothes and hairstyles, listen to a special kind of music, and meet similarly interested friends at clubs that cater to their likes. They may even engage in propagandizing their ideals to others. This is all part of the endeavor of trying to find our material identity.

If, however, we cannot find our own identity, then we may stylize ourselves in the fashion of a particular celebrity we admire. We may dress like they do, talk like they do, walk like they do, etc. But as we grow older, we may change the way we do things. We may not dress as outlandishly as we used to, or keep our hair as long, or stay out as late. Our identity and ideals seem to change as we mature through life. So who are we? Which of these identities is the real us?

As ideals are changeable, so are our names. We may call ourselves by certain names, either out of necessity, such as a family name, or for individuality, like names some entertainers use. We may call ourselves Robert or Roberta, Stephen or Stephanie, Henry or Henrietta. Or we might use names like Sparky, Rocky, Paul Punk, Happy Hippie, Sally Sweetheart, Ralph Redneck, Workingman Williams, Peter Politician, etc. We can call ourselves by any kind of name we want and change it accordingly. Names, therefore, are not that important in regard to our real identity. So who are we?

Not only can we change our names, but we can also change our religion or philosophical viewpoint. We may be Catholic, Protestant, Baptist, Mormon, Amish, Jewish, Muslim, Hindu, Buddhist, or whatever. We may feel very strong towards our particular faith, but we have seen many times when people, for some reason, give up their faith or may change it. We may be a Buddhist one day and a Hindu the next. Or maybe we will become an atheist and give up religion altogether.

So, what is the difference between one religion and another? It is simply the way we see things and how we want to worship or relate to God. But of what religion is the soul? To what religion does God belong? We may say we are Catholic or Protestant, but does that change the nature of the soul? Does that really change our eternal, spiritual relationship with the Supreme? Therefore, on a personal basis, religions, ideals, clothes, names, and even careers, can all be changed as easily as one changes his mind. Yet how does all this affect our real identity? How do we really find ourselves and know who we are? What is it that does not change? Even our bodies slowly change from a young body to a middle-aged body, and finally to an old body. So who are we?

First of all, let us look at ourselves. Do we really know who or what we are? Maybe not. But take a look at who you think you are. See your hands? Point to them. Now point to your leg. Now your head. Now your stomach. Now point to your heart. Now point to your self. What are you? Are you the body, mind, or something else?

## REVIEW OF WESTERN PHILOSOPHIES

This is a big question that people have been debating for many centuries: is the self separate from the body, or is it a part of the body?

One of the first Western philosophers to consider this was Socrates (469-399 B.C.) who believed that the soul was different from the body. He concluded that the soul was released from the body at the time of death, and after death the soul, being immortal and immaterial, would again live in another realm.

Plato (427-347 B.C.) also believed that the soul is immortal and unchangeable and exists before the birth and after the demise of the impermanent physical body. But he considered that there are three parts to the soul: one part holds truth and wisdom, another part holds the emotional ambitions or expressions, and the third part consists of the bodily appetites and desires. When all three parts work harmoniously, the individual feels balanced and happy. If one part, say the bodily appetites, are unbalanced or out of control, then life will be frustrating and unsatisfying. Thus, death, wherein the soul attains freedom from the body, becomes a welcome release, rather than something to be feared.

Aristotle (384-322 B.C.) at first accepted Plato's ideas of the soul but later changed his views. He compared the body to a ship and the soul to its captain. The soul is that which animates the living body. That which has a soul is alive, and that which has no soul is dead. Thus, even animals and plants have souls, although they are not as developed as humans. However, Aristotle did not believe the soul is eternal or exists beyond death. Death is the end of both body and soul. Aristotle's ideas became the basis for thinking that the body and soul are but one mechanism (monism), rather than two separate substances working together (dualism).

Later on Descartes (1596-1650), a French philosopher, mathematician, and scientist, propounded the idea of dualism in which he stated that the self and body are completely separate. He claimed that there are two kinds of substances;

spiritual or mental, and physical. The mind, which is immaterial, immeasurable and invisible, proves its existence by its attribute of thinking: "I think, therefore I am." The physical substance does not think and has no conscious or spiritual attributes.

Descartes proposed that the body and soul work so closely that together they make a whole being, and that one can affect the other as when injury to the body creates pain or alarm in the mind. Later in his life, he claimed that the soul must be seated in the pineal gland in the brain because this had to be the link where interaction between the soul and body takes place. However, he could not answer the questions of his contemporaries in regard to how the self, if separate from the body, interacts with the body, or what the mechanism is by which it interacts. He also could not fully explain how conditions of the body affect the mind.

It is obvious that different states of physical condition have an effect on our mind, and because of that it appears that the mind is dependent on the body. When you alter conditions of the brain, the mind is affected, which makes it seem like it is a product of the brain and not independent of it. Since Descartes could not explain this, his ideas were defeated by other philosophers. So, after Descartes, dualism was not so popular.

Philosophy and science both disputed Descates' notions, and even the Church viewed him as a threat to its authority. In fact, in 1663, the Church condemned his books, but by then it was too late. Descartes' reasoning helped bring in the Age of Enlightenment in the seventeenth and eighteenth centuries throughout Europe and North America. During this time, the intellectual renaissance challenged the Church's interpretation of social order and opened wide the door to newer philosophies.

Malebranche (1638-1715), another French philosopher, presented the philosophy of Occasionalism, in which God came in between the mind and body and enabled the two to interact. A person, or the soul which was separate from the body, would decide to do something, and then God would give the necessary force or mobility. This is very similar to the Vedic concept which we will discuss later. Through Occasionalism, the uniting force between the will to act and performing the act was God. But how God was situated in the body and what our relationship was with this localized form of God was not fully explained. So this philosophy was also not conclusive.

Another philosophy introduced was called Interactionism. Interactionists try to conceive of the mind as somewhat separate yet somewhat dependent on the body. They try to figure out the cause of the interaction between the mind and brain to explain how the mind was a little bit separate. This is actually the biggest problem in Western philosophy: how the mind and body work together but seem to be separate at the same time. In fact, all Western philosophers, including Pythagoras, Plato, Aristotle, and others like David Hume, Immanuel Kant, Georg Hegel, and so on, have all, at some time or other, pondered over this mind/body problem. However, as with Interactionism, they were not able to explain exactly how the mind was separate from the brain.

There were also other philosophers, like Spinoza, who had a big influence on Einstein, and who stated that there was only one substance in all existence. Call it God or matter, it makes no difference, but everything is one and has within it the natural characteristics of consciousness. In other words, according to this idea, atoms, molecules, chemicals, etc., are all conscious, and depending on how they were organized would make the difference between lesser or greater consciousness. When they are organized into neurons of the brain, then you would have greater consciousness. Of course, this is absurd because if each cell was conscious of itself, then that consciousness would extend only to an awareness of the other cells around it. So how do all the brain cells develop one collective, integrated consciousness of what exists outside the body? In other words, why am I conscious of others or of experiences and memories rather than just neurons beeping around me? So this philosophy is another which does not answer the question of how consciousness becomes integrated.

The point is that as modern science discarded all these philosophies, they were left with nothing but pure mechanism. This meant that every single idea related to consciousness, such as our perceptions, our feelings, experiences, and so on, must all be explained in a mechanistic way. In other words, they feel that just by understanding the neurons in the brain, everything can be explained. This ultimately means that everything is reduced to chemistry: chemicals are the essence of life, and life comes from chemicals. By chemical manipulation, consciousness and everything related to it can be controlled.

It is the same idea in physics, evolution, and the basis of all neurological research and microbiology: that by proper chemical arrangement, as soon as the scientists find out what that is, they will create life. Obviously, with this view in mind, if chemical arrangement must be all there is to consciousness, then through our technology we can recreate consciousness and bring our computers to a stage where they are as good or better than humans.

Very often scientists have a desire to do something that determines or proves the philosophy they use. Rather than simply basing their philosophy on the facts alone, they may tend to base their viewpoints or interpret their experiments on what they desire. In this way, they may use the idea that life comes from chemicals because if it is true, there are then so many things science can do. With science we could build a better human machine, a better brain, or create immortality. But if it is not true, then science cannot recreate life, or build machines as good as humans, or overcome death. Therefore, science does not want to face that. Instead they may choose to take an idea and follow it as far as it will go by using many taxpayers' hard-earned dollars to investigate many useless and unnecessary things.

One very famous physicist stated that if there is such a thing as the conscious self, a nonmaterial particle that possesses consciousness which does not come about from chemicals, then scientists might as well retire and become truck drivers. This is an example of the bias in science and the motivation behind rejecting any nonmechanistic idea, and in clinging stubbornly to mechanistic and physical explanations of life. Only in this way can they become like God, with their hopes of creating life and doing so many wonderful things, and denying any need to recognize a Supreme Being.

Today, scientists hardly talk about the mind. They just talk about the brain. There are over a billion neurons in the brain and each of these little brain cells discharge electrical impulses which send out particular kinds of signals. So the scientists are conceiving of mapping which parts of the brain control cognitive functions, like thinking, memory, motor responses, sensory impressions, etc. Then they hope to stimulate artificially the activity of specific neuron cells with chemicals or electrical shock to negate those neurons that affect one's feelings of anxiety or depression, or similar unwanted feelings. In this way, one could simply take a chemical in order to feel a particular feeling. This is based on the Western concept that the mind is the self and is not separate from the brain, but is a part of it.

The basis of this kind of modern research of the mind was set by the British biologist T. H. Huxley more than a century ago. He said that all states of consciousness are caused by molecular changes of the brain. In other words, this is all that causes our changes of mood or the way we feel when experiencing good or bad events in our life. On the basis of this theory, the mind is merely a by-product of a properly functioning brain, and the mind can be controlled simply by adjusting the brain in various ways.

There are, however, a few who do not agree with this. The Australian neurophysiologist and Nobel laurate, Sir John Eccles, thinks that mind or consciousness is separate from the brain. While performing experiments on the cerebral cortex, which controls movements in our bodies by sending appropriate signals to various muscles, he has noted that before any voluntary act is performed, the 50 million or so neurons of the supplementary motor area (SMA) within the cortex begin to act. Thus, the SMA acts before the cerebral cortex sends the necessary signals to the muscles needed to perform the desired activity. Eccles concludes that conscious will, separate from the brain, must first be there before the chain of neurological events begin. Therefore, the mind controls matter rather than matter (the brain) controling the mind. In this way, we can begin to understand that, as Sir Karl Popper, a philosopher of science, describes, the mind and brain exist in two separate realities. The brain is a functioning material organ of the body, and the mind or consciousness is the immaterial symptom of the living entity or soul which motivates the body. Thus, as explained in the *Vedas*, the two work together like a driver seated in a car.

# PROBLEMS WITH SCIENTIFIC THEORIES OF CONSCIOUSNESS

The current idea that the mind is part of the brain is held not only by many biologists, neurologists, etc., but by others in all branches of science, including physics, computer science, and psychology. We might, however, point out a number of problems with this current thinking. Let us suggest that it is just as reasonable to consider an alternative view, and that the Vedic concept is actually more consistent and does not have as many problems as their concept has.

For example, does a person have the same experience in seeing a sunset as a machine programed to say "I see a red light," when it registers a sunset taking place? In other words, is merely recognizing light waves all there is to consciousness? If the mind works simply in a mechanistic way, as science tends to propound, then simply registering that we see a sunset would be all there is to consciousness. It would be exactly like a mechanical reflex to a particular stimuli. The point is that we could say a tape recorder hears music, but does it actually hear or enjoy it? Does it get goosebumps or inspiration from listening to it?

The experiences of enjoying something cannot be measured or broken down into a simple mathematical equasion. Therefore, in an eliminative or reductionary philosophy, which science uses, it is believed that if something cannot be broken down into a measurable and simple equasion, then it is not real and leaves no room for discussion. With this viewpoint, reductionary scientists can begin throwing out a word like "consciousness" because it does not have any meaning or reality. It does not fit into an equasion. You can break the movement of braincells down to a mathematical formula, but not consciousness. And since the word "mind" also does not fit into an equasion, we can throw that out as well. And, of course, the concept of a soul has been given up long ago. After all, everything is seen as an extension of the mechanical workings of the brain. So the idea is that we should only use vocabulary which is related to physical, identifiable, and quantifiable formulas.

By understanding these examples of a machine responding to a red sunset, or a tape recorder hearing music, we can know that there is something in consciousness far beyond the ability of any machine giving simple reactions to external stimuli. Machine reactions are similar to our senses sending electrical messages to the brain. But, obviously, we experience more than a simple sensual or physical stimulus. A machine cannot describe the experience of hearing a Beethoven symphony and cannot recognize one piece of music from another. A machine has no emotions, so how can it describe the experience? Therefore, scientists who just try to show that our own responses are a mechanical reaction to sensory stimuli are simply trying to negate the idea of consciousness or the existence of the soul. But, if there is a conscious particle, then they cannot make something else conscious, or create life, or be a Dr. Frankenstein without first creating that conscious particle or soul, which they cannot do.

From the Vedic literature, we learn that there is a conscious self that is separate from the machine or body. Obviously, we are conscious of every single impulse that the senses of our body/machine deals with. There is perfect interaction. So science will question how the self can interact so well with the machine if it is not part of the machine. And why is consciousness affected when changes are made to the brain? If the self is separate, then consciousness should not be affected. These are the arguments of science, and the Vedic literature offers some very interesting answers. If these arguments are answered, then why not consider an alternative viewpoint, as described in the Vedic literature?

The idea that consciousness is changed by changes of the body or machine can be understood more clearly if we use the example of a person driving a car. Obviously, the driver is separate from the car, but if the driver gets in his car and is hit by another car, he will immediately say, "You hit me." It is not that the driver was hit, it was the car that was hit, but the driver identifies with the car, as if he were a part of it. So the driver is affected by changes in the machine. Similarly, when the self depends on the body and strongly identifies with it, he will think he is the body and will be disturbed if there is some problem with it, although he is actually separate from it.

Another example is that there have been carefully controlled and documented experiments done with epileptic patients. In these experiments, the patients have been treated with electric shock to certain parts of the brain in order to respond in a particular way. The findings of these experiments have shown, however, that in almost every case the patient would respond to a certain stimuli stating that he was not doing it, but that the doctor, by controlling the electrical impulses, was making the patient's body respond in a certain way. Thus, the mind's inclination was different or separate from the response of the body. So simply by applying electric shock to parts of the brain for certain responses does not give any adequate explanations of what is the mind.

In considering the mind, we also have to consider the will. If all that the patients did was respond to stimuli, then, according to the mechanistic theory, that is all that would be expected of being conscious. But the patients were protesting that it was not they who were voluntarily reacting. It was against their will. So if there was no such thing as a separate self with an individual will, there would have been no protest, like a robot programmed to act in a certain way. So these experiments that showed that the mind had an identity and will separate from the brain were startling in neurological circles. The reason was because it brought up the old argument that there is something separate between the mind and the brain--it is not all one.

Another example of this is in the field of near-death experience. There have been top scientists at such places as the University of Virginia using the strictest standards for documenting and researching particular phenomena. They have been able to demonstrate conclusive findings in over hundreds of test cases with patients who were, according to all known laws of physics, technically in a state of unconsciousness, or in a coma due to a heart attack or accident. The patients, after being brought back to consciousness, explained in detail what procedures had been performed to revive them. They described themselves as floating out of their body, up into the room, looking down and watching the medical procedures the doctors were performing on them. There was no possibility that they could have dreamed this as subsequent tests have shown. This shows that there is a difference between the brain and the mind, and that the mind or consciousness can continue working even though the brain is impaired and hardly functioning at all, as in a comatose state.

## VEDIC RECOGNITION OF THE SOUL'S PRESENCE

In the near-death experience we have the description of what happened to the individuals when they were revived, but what if they had not re-entered their body? What if the patients could not be revived? If they had died, where would they have gone? Or is death simply the end of everything? When someone dies, the relatives may cry and exclaim, "Oh, he is gone, he has left us." But what is gone? He is lying there, or at least the body is. So if he is gone, then it is that part you have not seen that is gone. So what is it?

As we have shown in the last several pages, philosophers and scientists have all questioned this and have arrived at no final conclusion. But the Vedic literature gives detailed descriptions of the self. The *Chandogya Upanishad* (6.10.3) begins explaining that the subtle essence in all that exists is the self. It is the true and thou art it.

In the Twelfth and Thirteenth Khandas of the *Chandogya Upanishad*, it gives further examples in which it states that a tall tree has its essence, the self, originally in the small seed from which it grew. Yet to break a seed open will reveal no such potency for it to grow into such a huge plant. But the power is there. Likewise, to take salt and mix it with water renders the salt invisible; yet, by tasting the water, we can know the salt is there. Similarly, in the material body, the self exists, though we do not directly perceive it. However, *Bhagavad-gita* (13.34) explains: "O son of Bharata, as the sun alone illuminates all this universe, so does the living entity, one within the body, illuminate the entire body by consciousness." Therefore, just as we cannot perceive the salt mixed in the water except by taste, we also cannot see the soul in the body except by recognizing the symptom, which is consciousness.

Consciousness can be recognized easily by performing a small experiment. Pinch part of your body and you will feel pain. This is a sign of consciousness, not only in humans but also in cats, dogs, or other animals. In any type of species of life, there are two types of bodies; the body which is alive, and the body which is dead and deteriorating. The live body is pervaded and illuminated by the consciousness of the self. The *Mundaka Upanishad* (3.1.9) says: "The soul is atomic in size and can be perceived by perfect intelligence. This atomic soul is floating in the five kinds of air (*prana, apana, vyana, samana,* and *udana*), is situated within the heart, and spreads its influence all over the body of the embodied living entities. When the soul is purified from the contamination of the five kinds of material air, its spiritual influence is exhibited."

Thus, the self is the motivating factor within the body and when it leaves, the body breaks down and slowly disintegrates. Therefore, the *Brihadaranyaka Upanishad* (2.4.3-5) points out that whomever is dear to us, whether it be our wives, husbands, sons, daughters, teachers, guardians, etc., they are dear to us only due to the presence of the self within the body, who in reality is what is dear to us. Once the self leaves the body, the body becomes unattractive to us because it rapidly gets cold, stiff, and begins to decompose. Therefore, the body is not our real identity, but we are the self within.

## THE SOUL IS ETERNAL

The *Chandogya Upanishad* (6.11.3) also states that although the body withers and dies when the self leaves it, the living self does not die. The Bible also explains: "While we look not at the things which are seen, but at the things which are not seen; for the things which are seen are temporal; but the things which are not seen are eternal." (*II Corinthians* 4:18)

Further enlightenment is given in the *Srimad-Bhagavatam* (7.2.22): "The spirit soul, the living entity, has no death, for he is eternal and inexhaustible. Being free from material contamination, he can go anywhere in the material or spiritual worlds. He is fully aware and completely different from the material body, but because of being misled by misuse of his slight independence, he is obliged to accept subtle and gross bodies created by the material energy and thus be subjected to so-called material happiness and distress. Therefore, no one should lament for the passing of the spirit soul from the body."

The eternal nature of the self is also explained in *Bhagavad-gita* by Sri Krishna: "Never was there a time when I did not exist, nor you, nor all these kings; nor in the future shall any of us cease to be. As the embodied soul continually passes, in this body, from boyhood to youth to old age, the soul similarly passes into another body at death. The self-realized soul is not bewildered by such a change." (*Bg.*2.12-13)

"Know that which pervades the entire body is indestructible. No one is able to destroy the imperishable soul. Only the material body of the indestructible, immeasurable, and eternal living entity is subject to destruction. (*Bg.*2.17-18). . . For the soul there is never birth nor death. Nor, having once been, does he ever cease to be. He is unborn, eternal, ever-existing, undying and primeval. He is not slain when the body is slain. (*Bg.*2.20). . . As a person puts on new garments, giving up old ones, similarly, the soul accepts new material bodies, giving up the old and useless ones." (*Bg.* 2.23)

Certainly this knowledge can relieve anyone from the anxiety that comes from thinking our existence is finished at death. Spiritually, we do not die; yet, the body is used until it is no longer fit to continue. At that time, it may appear that we die, but that is not the case. The soul continues on its journey to another body according to its destiny. And if one has sincerely practiced and perfected a genuine spiritual path, then their next body will not be material, but can be completely spiritual.

Further descriptions of the indestructability of the soul is explained in a way that reveals how it is beyond the influence of all material elements.

"The soul can never be cut into pieces by any weapon, nor can he be burned by fire, nor moistened by water, nor withered by the wind. This individual soul is unbreakable and insoluble, and can be neither burned nor dried. He is everlasting, all-pervading, unchangeable, immovable and eternally the same. It is said the soul is invisible, inconceivable, immutable, and unchangeable. Knowing this, you should not grieve for the body." (*Bg.*2.23-25)

"Some look on the soul as amazing, some describe him as amazing, and some hear of him as amazing, while others, even after hearing about him, cannot understand him at all. O descendant of Bharata, he who dwells in the body is eternal and can never be slain. Therefore you need not grieve for any creature." (*Bg.*2.29-30)

Let us point out that when it says one should not grieve for any creature, it does not mean that if we see a creature or a person who is suffering that we remain indifferent or callous to the situation. When we see someone who is suffering, we should feel compassion. Compassion is a quality that will make one feel soft-hearted and concerned for the well-being of others. Such a quality is necessary for one who is trying to become fit to receive knowledge of the self. Therefore, we should feel compassion and help resolve the problems of others if we can. But feeling compassion does not mean simply giving hungry people something to eat. Of course, that should be done if we are capable of doing it, but real compassion means helping them understand their real situation and spiritual identity.

For example, as we have explained, the body dwindles and dies but the soul does not die: it simply changes bodies. Therefore, the body is like a shirt or coat which we wear for some time, and when it is worn out, we change it for a new one. So if we should see someone who is suffering and struggling with material nature, such as a drowning man, what is the use of going out to him and saving only his shirt or coat? We will swim back to shore thinking, "I've saved him," and find that all we have brought back is his shirt, while the real person is still suffering in the ocean of material energy. We must also take care of the person or soul within the shirt or material body. As long as one has a material body, whether in this life or any number of lifetimes after this, there will be so many unavoidable problems, such as birth, disease, old age, and death. Therefore, the

Vedic literature, such as the *Chandogya Upanishad* (8.1.1), mentions that knowledge of the self within is what should be sought and understood by all. Realizing one's spiritual identity solves all the problems of life, as we shall further clarify in this chapter.

The more we realize our spiritual identity, the more we will see that we are beyond these temporary material bodies, and that our identity is not simply being a white body, or black, or yellow, or fat, skinny, intelligent, dumb, old, young, strong, weak, blind, etc. Real blindness means not being able to see through the temporary and superficial bodily conditions and into the person within. Seeing reality means to recognize the spiritual nature of everyone.

## THE VEDIC DESCRIPTION OF THE SOUL

The *Srimad-Bhagavatam* (11.28.35) explains that the self is self-luminous, beyond birth and death, and unlimited by time or space and, therefore, beyond all change. The *Bhagavatam* (11.22.50) also points out that as one witnesses the birth and death of a tree and is separate from it, similarly the witness of the birth, death, and various activities of the body are separate from it. The *Bhagavad-gita* also states: "One who can see that all activities are performed by the body, which is created of material nature, and sees that the self does nothing, actually sees. When a sensible man ceases to see different identities, which are due to different material bodies, he attains to the Brahman conception. Thus, he sees that beings are expanded everywhere. Those with the vision of eternity can see that the soul is transcendental, eternal, and beyond the modes of nature. Despite contact with the material body, O Arjuna, the soul neither does anything nor is entangled. The sky, due to its subtle nature, does not mix with anything, although it is all-pervading. Similarly, the soul, situated in Brahman vision, does not mix with the body, though situated in that body." (*Bg.*13.30-33)

Although the soul is situated in the body, it is very small and is seated in the heart, according to the *Chandogya Upanishad* (6.3.3). We can see this since all energy within the body is expanded from the heart. If the heart stops functioning, the whole body collapses. But the heart is simply a seat, which means the seat can be changed, as we can observe from heart transplant operations, or even from the use of a mechanical heart. But even with such scientific advancement, if the soul leaves the body, not even a mechanical heart will keep the body functioning for long.

The size of the soul is described in the *Svetasvatara Upanishad* (5.9): "When the upper point of a hair is divided into one hundred parts and again each of such parts is further divided into one hundred parts, each such part is the measurement of the dimension of the spirit soul."

The *Bhagavatam* also states: "There are innumerable particles of spiritual atoms, which are measured as one ten-thousandth of the upper portion of the hair." So, obviously, if you take the pinpoint tip of a hair, which usually measures three thousandths of an inch in diameter, and cut it into ten thousand pieces, one such piece will be practically invisible, atomic in size. Therefore, if it takes special equipment to detect the atoms of material substances, it is no wonder that scientific equipment cannot detect atomic particles which are spiritual. Even though scientists want documented proof that there is such a thing as a soul, by studying the Vedic literature, we learn that the soul cannot be observed by ordinary scientific equipment. Of course, as we have established, there are other ways to perceive the soul, especially through the science of yoga and through the study of the Vedic science. We suggest that these scientists study the *Vedas* to learn about what is beyond their limited sense perception.

The fact is most people have not seen atoms such as protons and neutrons, etc., that scientists talk about. They can only take the word of scientists that such things exist. Similarly, many people have not directly seen the soul. They can only accept the word of those who are supposed to know. But, as previously explained, anyone can recognize the consciousness that pervades the body. This is not difficult. If you pinch or cause some pain to any living entity, whether a person, cat, dog, etc., or approach some wild animal like a bird or squirrel, it will try to get away. This is not some instinctive reflex, but it is due to consciousness. And this is, according to Vedic science, the direct evidence for the existence of the soul, from which consciousness expands through the body.

According to the *Vedas*, the body is compared to a chariot in which the self is riding. "Transcendentalists who are advanced in knowledge compare the body, which is made by the order of the Supreme Personality of Godhead, to a chariot. The senses are like the horses; the mind, the master of the senses, is like the reins; the objects of the senses are the destinations; intelligence is the chariot driver; and consciousness, which spreads throughout the body, is the cause of bondage in this material world." (*Bhag*.7.15.41)

In this example, the senses are like horses always pulling the mind towards the objects to which they are attracted. The mind is always restless, turbulent, obstinate, and very strong. Only through practice of yoga can the mind be controlled. Otherwise, the mind is always trying to convince the intelligence to make plans to satisfy the senses. In this way, the intelligence, referred to as the chariot driver, will take the body here and there in hopes of arriving at the destination of sense objects, such as nice things to see, taste, feel, hear, and smell. Meanwhile, the self within the body is riding and observing all these bodily activities.

In the *Katha Upanishad* (1.3.3-12), which gives the same example, there is further elaboration where it states that he who has no understanding and whose mind (the reins) is never firmly held, his senses (horses) are unmanageable, like vicious horses of a charioteer. But he who has understanding and whose mind is firmly held has senses that are under control like good horses of a charioteer. He who has no understanding enters into the rounds of rebirth; whereas, he who has understanding, who is mindful and pure, reaches that place from whence he is not born again. He reaches the end of his journey, which is the highest abode of Sri Vishnu in the spiritual atmosphere.

The *Katha Upanishad* also explains that within the body, higher than the senses and the sense objects, exists the mind. More subtle than the mind is the intelligence, and higher and more subtle than the intellect is the self. That self is hidden in all beings and does not shine forth, but is seen by subtle seers through their sharp intellect.

From this we can understand that within the gross body, composed of various material elements, such as earth, air, water, etc., there is also the subtle body composed of the finer subtle elements of mind, intelligence, and ego. The psychic activities take place within the subtle body, and when the unbridled senses and mind are the controllers of a person's goals and desires, much time may be spent in catering to the demands of the mind, or in psychoanalysis with the hopes of calming the mind and figuring out the problems that exist within it. In this way, many people feel that achieving satisfaction of the mind is the goal of life and, therefore, participate in various and sometimes costly programs that promise to accomplish this.

Having the mind pacified may be a relief for anyone who has such mental problems and is looking for a way to relax or sleep better, or lead a happier and healthier life. This is becoming more important to people these days, especially in Western civilization where they may use psychiatric treatments, or take special courses in mind control or hypnosis, or use special subliminal-message tapes to try to get more control over their mind or change their attitude and their life. But this is also one of the purposes of yoga, which has been very effectively practiced for thousands of years. Therefore, *Bhagavad-gita* stresses that one must control the lower self by the higher self. The mind will always want to engage in activities of sense gratification and, therefore, must be guided by the intelligence after having cultivated knowledge of the goal of life. The mind absorbed in sense objects is the cause of bondage to material activities, and the mind detached from sense objects is the cause of liberation.

"A person must elevate themselves by their own mind, not degrade themselves. The mind is the friend of the conditioned soul, and enemy as well. For one who has conquered the mind, the mind is the best of friends; but for one who has failed to do so, their very mind can be the greatest enemy." (*Bg*.6.5-6).

In *Bhagavad-gita*, Sri Krishna also advises: "As a lamp in a windless place does not waver, so the transcendentalist, whose mind is controlled, remains always steady in his meditation on the transcendent Self. From whatever and wherever the mind wanders due to its flickering and unsteady nature, one must certainly withdraw it and bring it back under the control of the Self. For one whose mind is unbridled, self-realization is difficult work. But he whose mind is controlled and who strives by right means is assured of success. That is my opinion." (*Bg*.6.19,26,36)

In these modern times, however, we see that it is generally recommended that whatever you want to do, if it does not hurt anyone, it is alright. If it feels good, do it. But in the Vedic texts we see that this modern philosophy of allowing the mind to be as free as it can be simply adds fuel to the fire of confusion in society today. By taking advice from *Bhagavad-gita*, we can certainly learn how to solve mental problems. These disturbances of the mind are still on a very superficial level because the real self is higher than the mind and the intelligence which can control the mind. Therefore, we have to rise above the subtle elements of mind and intelligence to perceive the self:

"Beyond this gross conception of form [the body] is another, subtle conception of form [the subtle body or mind, intelligence, and false ego] which is without formal shape and is unseen, unheard, and unmanifest. The living being has his form beyond this subtlety, otherwise he could not have repeated births. Whenever a person experiences, by self-realization, that both the gross and subtle bodies have nothing to do with the pure self, at that time he sees himself as well as the Lord." (*Bhag.*1.3.32-33)

Since we are separate from the gross and subtle bodies, why do we so strongly identify with the material body? This is explained as follows: "Although the material body is different from the self, because of the ignorance of material association one falsely identifies oneself with the superior and inferior bodily conditions. Sometimes a fortunate person is able to give up such mental concoction." (*Bhag.*11.22.48)

"The false ego gives shape to illusory material existence and thus experiences material happiness and distress. The spirit soul, however, is transcendental to material nature; he can never actually be affected by material happiness and distress in any place, under any circumstance or by the agency of any person. A person who understands this has nothing whatsoever to fear from the material creation." (*Bhag.*11.23.56)

"No other force besides one's own mental confusion makes the soul experience happiness and distress. His perception of friends, neutral parties and enemies and the whole material life one builds around this perception are simply created out of ignorance." (*Bhag.*11.23.59)

In these verses it is clearly explained that only due to the false ego do we think we are the material body, and from such a conception we immediately experience various material desires which cause happiness or distress. There is, however, the sense of real ego, such as, "I am," or, "I am existing," or, "I am spirit." But when one identifies with the body and then thinks, "I am this body," "I am black," "I am white," or thinks they are fat, skinny, short, tall, American, European, Hindu, Muslim, Catholic, Protestant, etc., this is all false ego. It is superficial to our real identity, but this ignorance is the cause of the barriers, quarrels, and misunderstandings between people, communities, neighbors, or nations around the world. However, when the false ego, a product of *maya* or illusion, which veils the true nature of the self, is cut asunder by the dagger of inquiry into the wisdom of the self, the all-perfect soul then stands revealed. This condition is called the lasting dissolution. Only in this condition will the people of the world ever really experience peace, either individually or on a worldwide basis.

One story that helps elaborate on how the self is separate from the body is found in *Srimad-Bhagavatam* (Fifth Canto, Chapter Ten), in which a self-realized devotee named Jada Bharata is forced to help carry the palanquin of King Rahugana, who is traveling nearby. The King needs an extra carrier and when the King's men find Jada Bharata, they force him to help.

The palanquin is not being carried very smoothly and the King, discovering the cause to be Jada Bharata, chastises him very severely. Being very angry, the King says, "You rascal, what are you doing? Are you dead despite the life within your body? Do you not know that I am your master? You are disregarding me and not carrying out my order. For this disobediance I shall now punish you and give you proper treatment so that you will come to your senses and do the correct thing."

Thinking himself a king, King Rahugana is in the bodily conception and is influenced by material nature's mode of passion and ignorance. Due to madness, he chastises Jada Bharata with uncalled for and contradictory words. Jada Bharata is a topmost devotee. Although considering himself very learned, the King does not know about the position of an advanced devotee situated in *bhakti-yoga*, nor does he know his characteristics. Jada Bharata is the residence of the Supreme Lord; he always carries the form of the Lord within his heart. He is the dear friend of all living beings, and does not entertain any bodily conception. He therefore smiles and speaks the following words:

"My dear King and hero, whatever you have spoken sarcastically is certainly true. Actually these are not simply words of chastisement, for the body is the carrier. The load carried by the body does not belong to me, for I am the spirit soul. There is no contradiction in your statements because I am different from the body. I am not the carrier of the palanquin; the body is the carrier. Certainly, as you have hinted, I have not labored carrying the palanquin, for I am detached from the body. You have said I am not stout and strong, and these words are befitting a person who does not know the distinction between the body and soul. The body may be fat or thin, but no learned man would say such things of the spirit soul. As far as the spirit soul is concerned, I am neither fat nor skinny; therefore, you are correct when you say that I am not very stout. Also, if the object of this journey and the path leading there were mine, there would be many troubles for me, but because they relate not to me but to my body, there is no trouble at all.

"Fatness, thinness, bodily and mental distress, thirst, hunger, fear, disagreement, desires for material happiness, old age, sleep, attachment for material possessions, anger, lamentation, illusion and identification of the body with the self are all transformations of the material covering of the spirit soul.

A person absorbed in the material bodily conception is affected by these things, but I am free from all bodily conceptions. Consequently I am neither fat nor skinny nor anything else you have mentioned.

"My dear King, you have unnecessarily accused me of being dead though alive. In this regard, I can only say that this is the case everywhere because everything material has its beginning and end. As far as your thinking that you are a king and master and are thus trying to order me, this is also incorrect because these positions are temporary. Today you are a king and I am your servant, but tomorrow the position may be changed, and you may be my servant and I your master. These are temporary circumstances created by providence. Everyone is being forced into these positions by the laws of material nature; therefore, actually no one is master and no one is servant."

Jada Bharata continues teaching the king in this way. He has tolerated the harsh words of the king and remained peaceful and replied properly. Jada Bharata is not affected by the anger and ignorance of the king and has agreed to carry the palanquin out of humility with the idea that he is simply undergoing the results of his past misdeeds. This is certainly how we must tolerate those around us who act on the bodily platform of life. If we are quick to return their criticism of us, this will accomplish nothing but disturb our own peace of mind and arouse our own false ego, which causes us to identify with the bodily platform as well.

On the bodily platform we engage in defending our honor and reputation. But what are these? Whatever honor, distinction, fame, power, riches, or strength we have clings to the body only, and we lose it all at the time of death since the soul is above such things. All material situations are temporary and have nothing to do with the spiritual self. Therefore, we should understand that we are all here only for a short time, like travelers on a bus or plane. We have been given a seat or position which we have for a little while, and then will be forced to give it up at the end of the journey. Why, therefore, should we be so attached or ready to fight over a temporary seat?

Just as in the case of King Rahugana, we see today that there are many rulers along with their followers who are proud and ready to fight for their honor and possessions, such as land or country. But in the *Vishnu Purana* (Book Four, Chapter Twenty-four) the Earth laughs at all those who think they can possess her. Many kings with perishable bodies have stood upon this planet, who, blinded with deceptive notions, have indulged the feeling that suggests, "This earth is mine, it will be my son's, it will belong to my dynasty." But they have all passed away. So many who reigned before them, many who succeeded them, and many who are yet to come, have ceased or will soon cease to be.

The Earth (whom the *Vedas* accept as an individual living being) therefore thinks, "How great is the folly of leaders, who are endowed with the faculty of reason, to cherish the confidence of ambition, when they are nothing but foam upon the waves. They seek to reduce their ministers, their servants and subjects under their authority, and then endeavor to overcome their foes. 'Thus,' they say, 'we will conquer the ocean-circled earth,' and intent upon their project, do not see death standing not far away. It is through infatuation that kings desire to possess me, whom their predecessors have been forced to leave, and whom their fathers have not retained. Beguiled with such selfishness, fathers fight with sons, and brothers with brothers, for my possession.

"Foolishness has been the character of every king who has boasted, 'All this earth is mine, everything is mine, it will be in my house forever,' for he is dead. How is it possible that such vain desires should survive in the hearts of his descendents, who have seen their progenitor forced to relinquish me and tread the path of dissolution, though he was absorbed by the thirst to dominate everything? When I hear a king sending word to another by his ambassador, 'This earth is mine, immediately resign your pretensions to it,' I am moved to violent laughter at first, but it soon subsides into pity for the infatuated fool."

## THE NATURE OF THE SOUL

In the last few segments of this chapter, we have established that the soul is eternal, separate from the gross and subtle body, is situated in the heart, and is atomic in size. But what is the nature of the soul?

The *Chandogya Upanishad* (8.1.5-6) explains that the self is free from sin and old age, death and grief, hunger and thirst, lamentation and sadness, and desires only what it ought to desire, and imagines nothing but what it ought to imagine. Those who depart from this life without having discovered the self and those true desires have no freedom in all the worlds. But those who depart from here after discovering the self and those true desires have freedom in all the worlds.

The soul's nature, in essence, is to love and be loved and to serve it's lovable object. This is quite obvious even in our day-to-day experience. The instinct to love is within everyone and, due to that love, we engage in serving and working to satisfy those we love. We become happy by making those we love happy. Thus, there is the saying, "Better to give than to receive." Therefore, it is recognized that our natural constitutional position is to serve the object of our love.

From this love, on the material platform, we may work hard to get money to satisfy our wife or husband and children. We may do something to please our friends or take care of our parents. We may wish to reach a high political office by promising to be a good servant of the people. Even in the animal kingdom, the parents will take care of and serve their young by securing food, protecting them, and then training them to take care of themselves.

Even if we are working simply to satisfy our own minds and senses, it still must be admitted that it requires work to do so. When our senses want something, we must work to acquire it. We then become the servant of our senses. Or we must work to pay our monthly rent to the landlord or be evicted. Or we must pay the government the taxes we owe on our property. Then we are servants of the government. If we do not wish to be servants of the government and refuse to pay our taxes, then we might be caught and thrown into jail where we will be forced to do work for the government, such as making license plates. Then we are servants of the government by force.

In so many ways, we are working as servants. We cannot avoid it. Every creature is engaged in serving someone else. The constitutional position of the soul is to serve, but in the material world of *maya*, illusion, the entity engages in serving what is illusory and temporary, and receives very little benefit or appreciation in return. Of course, in the material atmosphere, no one wants to be a servant. Everyone wants to become the master or controller of the things around them. But this is an illusory mentality because even if one thinks he is so powerful, he still remains a servant of the material energy.

For example, when death comes to take you, you cannot escape. You may be so proud and think you are so beautiful, rich, powerful, and independent, but that does not matter. When death approaches you, your position is finished. You cannot stand and defiantly say, "No, I will not go." You will be forced to bow and surrender to the power death has over you. Then you are a servant of death. And where you will go after death is not up to you, but up to higher authorities. So then you are a servant of those higher authorities.

Rather than being a forced servant, the Vedic literature, therefore, encourages all living beings to begin directing their love toward the Supreme. The Supreme Absolute Truth is the source of everything, including the ultimate loving relationship. Since the living being is a spiritual part and parcel of the Supreme, the loving relationship is natural. In other words, there is never any question whether God loves us or not. Being a spiritual entity also means that we are naturally part of the spiritual atmosphere, where complete knowledge and bliss exist eternally. However, while in this material world, a person easily forgets his spiritual, constitutional position and then tries to be happy independently. In this endeavor, he works to adjust his material situation for personal gain and sense gratification. This is all due to illusion under the spell of false ego. In such an unsteady situation within the material energy, the living being experiences such things as anger, hatred, envy, lamentation, anxiety, and undergoes the threefold miseries brought about by the body, other living beings, and natural events. But in reality, such feelings are completely absent in the pure spirit soul.

It is stated that for the living being to remain within the material conditions of life, he must forget his real identity. Otherwise, it is not possible for one to be content with material activities and undergo the constant ups and downs of life, and ignore one's natural spiritually blissful condition. How else could the living beings direct their service and loving propensity toward temporary objects within the illusory energy? How else could one be satisfied in the pursuit of acquiring such flickering material pleasures? If people could actually see their real identity, they would immediately realize their mistake of accepting the material body to be who they are. They would also realize what their relationship is with the Supreme. It is for this reason that the Vedic texts urge the materially conditioned souls to rectify their position and engage in *bhakti-yoga*, by which our loving propensity can become spiritualized and fulfilled. Such fulfillment is reached when the living beings understand that the Supreme is the topmost lovable object and regain their loving relationship with the Supreme. This loving relationship is ultimately all that can completely satisfy the self, as stated in *Srimad-Bhagavatam*: "That occupation (*dharma*) for all humanity is best which causes its followers to become ecstatic in loving devotional service to the transcendent Lord which is unmotivated and uninterrupted, for that only can completely satisfy the self." (*Bhag*.1.2.6)

## SUPERSOUL: THE UNIFYING FACTOR

The whole process of spiritual self-realization involves not only understanding who we are, but also what our relationship is with the Supreme, beginning with the Supersoul. Yoga is the system by which we regain our forgotten relationship with the Supersoul, the localized expansion of the Supreme Being within our hearts.

As we had pointed out earlier in this chapter, one of the big questions among philosophers and scientists was how there could be such interaction between consciousness (the self) and the body. By what mechanism does consciousness interact so wonderfully with the body/machine and yet not be a part of the machine?

Before answering this we should point out that modern scientists have a fundamental problem they should answer in order to prove their theory that there is no separate self and that the body is nothing but a machine. For example, the embryo begins as a one-celled organism and then starts dividing. Over a period of nine months, billions and billions of cells come into existence. Almost all of the brain cells come into existence while we are in the womb. So this happens very quickly. So by what mechanism do these brain cells know with what to connect? How is it that one billion or more neurons, tiny little brain cells, manage to combine together in exactly the right sequence and connect with the right neuron in a perfect pattern, which if formed otherwise would leave the brain useless?

More importantly, what is it that makes all these individual brain cells create an integrated awareness? What creates the consciousness of "I am," or "I am thinking," or "I am desiring"? What brings it all together in one consciousness? If this body is only a machine, how could it have an ego? These are the questions to the problems which scientists must try to answer. Otherwise, they should set aside their unproven theories and research the Vedic version. At least then they would have a foundation upon which to base their experiments instead of relying on their continually changing speculations.

Science is always looking for something that unifies everything--the grand unified theory. They think that that will be the origin from which everything else separates, including electromagnetism, gravity, and so on. Actually, a few scientists, quantum mathematicians especially, are beginning to realize that consciousness is not a mechanistic element. And if it is not mechanistic, it would mean that it is not material and, therefore, not subject to being created or destroyed as are other material elements. Thus, consciousness would also not be subject to evolutionary change and development as some philosophers, such as Darwin, have theorized. If such is the case, it would also indicate that consciousness exists both before and after the creation and annihilation of the material cosmic manifestation, what to speak of both before and after the birth and death of the material body.

The next question would be, "Where is the ultimate source and cause of consciousness?" If there is a powerful source, or a Supreme Consciousness, how do we find out about it since it would be unlimited compared to our own tiny power of consciousness? And if our own consciousness has desires and feelings and personality, then why would it be surprising if the Supreme Consciousness and source of everything, the Absolute, is also a person with a personality in the form of the Supreme Being and Supersoul? This Supreme Person, with super consciousness, would therefore be the source of everything else. The fact is the Vedic literature provides descriptions of this Supreme Being.

The Vedic texts establish that the substance in which everything is unified is called the Paramatma, Super or Universal Consciousness. Just as our individual consciousness unifies all our tasting, hearing, seeing, feeling, and willing into one collective experience, so the universal consciousness unifies and is aware of everything within the universe. It is this universal consciousness that exists within each of us which integrates the individual soul with the body.

To begin establishing what the integrating mechanism is, the Vedic literature explains that in addition to the conscious self that is existing within the body, there is also a higher principle of consciousness--Superconsciousness or Supersoul. So on one side you have the gross material body, including the brain and senses, along with the subtle body of mind, intelligence and false ego. On the other side you have the conscious self or spirit soul. Then what integrates the self and makes it so attuned to the gross and subtle body is that which is between them, known as the Supersoul.

So this Superconsciousness or Supersoul is able to unify the machinery of the body and the conscious self. Without the presence of the Supersoul, it is not possible. In other words, the conscious self is dependent on the Superself for it to have the power to use its body, brain, and intelligence. Otherwise, the soul is simply existing within the body without any means of interacting or expressing itself through the vehicle of the body. In this way, the Supersoul gives us the power to move our body or think with our brain or have a collective consciousness that extends throughout the body.

Another example is what is called inspiration. Many great achievements, either in science or the arts, come from what is called inspiration. Mozart once described how he created his music. He explained that sometimes he would walk along and suddenly from outside himself music would start coming into his ears and forming musical arrangements to which he would just listen. Also, in the sciences, a scientist may labor and struggle with his equasions and formulas, but just cannot get it right. Then he goes off somewhere, and then out of the blue the answer comes.

Many great men who have given the world its greatest gifts in music, art, and science say that many of their achievements have come to them from some outside source--through inspiration. The Vedic literature explains that this is an example of the Supersoul, the principle of a higher universal consciousness which integrates and connects the conscious self to intelligence, the brain, and senses. Without the presence of the Supersoul, there would be no integration at all. This is the Vedic philosophy. And whether one accepts or rejects it, no one else, not even modern science, has any better explanation of these things.

The Vedic philosophy also establishes that consciousness is something nonmechanistic and irreducible, meaning that it does not come from chemicals, nor can it be broken down into subparts. The conscious self is an irreducible particle of spirit within the body. So if we accept that there is something in nature which is conscious, a particle of consciousness, and another particle which is superconsciousness, which are both irreducible, we have a complete system for explaining consciousness. We have a system which explains the interaction between the self and the brain. We have an explanation for how the brain cells and bodily organs are actually organized together during the embryo's devplment under the direction of the higher consciousness, being designed rather than happening randomly. And we have an explanation for all the things science is trying to explain.

Once these Vedic explanations are understood, and once people become aware of the self by direct perception, which they can experience and verify for themselves through the higher Vedic science and yoga, people will ultimately come to the knowledge that the self has a very special relationship with the Superself or Universal Consciousness. This is what is integrating everything within the body as well as the universe. This level of awareness has been achieved by many mystics and yogis for thousands of years. It is certainly nothing new. So through this Vedic process, we can actually begin to understand and then reach the stage of perfect realization of who we are and what our real relationship is with this world and the Absolute.

## DESCRIPTION OF THE SUPERSOUL

According to the Vedic texts, the Supersoul is the plenary expansion of God, who is situated within the body. How we begin to understand and perceive the Supersoul is described in *Bhagavad-gita* by Sri Krishna: "I shall now explain the knowable, knowing which you will taste the eternal. This is beginningless, and it is subordinate to Me. It is called Brahman, the spirit, and it lies beyond the cause and effect of this material world. Everywhere are His hands and legs, His eyes and faces, and He hears everything. In this way the Supersoul exists. The Supersoul is the original source of all senses, yet He is without [material] senses. He is unattached, although He is the maintainer of all living beings. He transcends the modes of nature, and at the same time He is the master of all modes of material nature. The Supreme Truth exists both internally and externally, in the moving and nonmoving. He is beyond the power of the material senses to see or to know. Although far, far away, He is also near to all. Although the Supersoul appears to be divided, He is never divided. He is situated as one. Although He is the maintainer of every living entity, it is to be understood that He devours all and develops all. He is the source of light in all luminous objects. He is beyond the darkness of matter and is unmanifested. He is knowledge, He is the object of knowledge, and He is the goal of knowledge. He is situated in everyone's heart." (*Bg*.13.13-18)

"In this body there is another, a transcendental enjoyer who is the Lord, the supreme proprietor, who exists as the overseer and permitter, and who is known as the Supersoul. That Supersoul is perceived by some through meditation, by some through the cultivation of knowledge, and by others through working without fruitive desire. Again there are those who, although not conversant in spiritual knowledge, begin to worship the Supreme Person upon hearing about Him from others. Because of their tendency to hear from authorities, they also transcend the path of birth and death. One who sees the Supersoul accompanying the individual soul in all bodies and who understands that neither the soul nor the Supersoul is ever destroyed actually sees. One who sees the Supersoul in every living being and equal everywhere does not degrade himself by his mind. Thus he approaches the transcendental destination." (*Bg*.13.23,25-26,28-29)

The Supersoul is here explained to be eternal, completely spiritual, the source of everything, and expanded everywhere, yet dwelling within the hearts of everyone. He is the source of all light and knowledge and the goal of all knowledge. Although the Supersoul appears to be divided by expanding into the Paramatma form situated within the hearts of every living being, He is still existing as the one Absolute Truth. This is confirmed in the following verses:

"Physical nature is known to be endlessly mutable. The universe is the cosmic form of the Supreme Lord, and I [Sri Krishna] am that Lord represented as the Supersoul, dwelling in the heart of every embodied being." (*Bg*.8.4)

"The one Supreme Lord is situated within all material bodies and within everyone's soul. Just as the moon is reflected in innumerable reservoirs of water, the Supreme Lord, although one, is present within everyone. Thus every material body is ultimately composed of the energy of the one Supreme Lord." (*Bhag.*11.18.32)

"The Supreme Personality of Godhead has created many residential places like the bodies of human beings, animals, birds, saints, and demigods. In all these innumerable bodily forms, the Lord resides with the living beings as Paramatma. Thus He is known as the *purushavatara*." (*Bhag.*7.14.37)

"As the one sun appears reflected in countless jewels, so Govinda manifests Himself [as Paramatma] in the hearts of all living beings." (*Caitanya-caritamrita, Adi.*2.19)

The material bodies of the living entity, although seeming to appear in different sizes and shapes, are nonetheless all made of the same basic ingredients, namely earth, air, water, etc. By understanding that within the body exists the spirit soul along with the Supersoul, there is no reason to disrespect anyone. Every living entity is spiritually part and parcel of the Supreme, and the Supreme is situated within the heart next to each of His spiritual parts and parcels. The difference is that the individual soul is situated within only one body and cannot understand what is going on in the bodies and minds of others. The Supersoul, however, is present in everyone's body and knows quite well what is happening in the minds and bodies of everyone.

How to perceive the Supersoul is through one of three ways: by perfection in meditation, by cultivation of knowledge, or by engaging in the process of yoga. Others can understand the Supersoul by hearing from spiritual authorities. In any case, if one attains such spiritual vision he will actually see things as they are and the transcendental destination then becomes achievable.

Further ways of recognizing how the Supersoul integrates the body and soul are described in the *Taittiriya Upanishad* (3.10.2). It is pointed out that one can perceive the Supersoul by the action of speech, as action in the hands, and walking in the feet and other bodily activities. This is further substantiated in *Srimad-Bhagavatam* (2.2.35) where it states: "The Personality of Godhead Lord Sri Krishna is in every living being along with the individual soul. And this fact is perceived and hypothesized in our acts of seeing and taking help from intelligence." Therefore, through the Vedic literature we can understand that the unifying factor between the desires of the self and the response of the brain and body to our desires can be recognized as the power of the Supersoul within.

The size, shape, and dress of the Supersoul, who is realized and seen by those sages who have reached the goal of knowledge through yoga, is also described in *Srimad-Bhagavatam* as follows: "Others conceive of the Personality of Godhead residing within the [human] body in the region of the heart and measuring only eight inches, with four hands carrying a lotus, a *chakra*, a conchshell and a club respectively. His mouth expresses His happiness. His eyes spread like the petals of a lotus, and His garments, yellowish like the saffron of the *kadamba* flower, are bedecked with valuable jewels. His ornaments are all made of gold, set with jewels, and He wears a glowing head-dress and earrings. His lotus feet are placed over the whorls of the lotuslike hearts of great mystics. On His chest is the Kaustubha jewel, engraved with a beautiful calf, and there are other jewels on His shoulders. His complete torso is garlanded with fresh flowers. He is well decorated with an ornamental wreath about His waist and rings studded with valuable jewels on His fingers. His leglets, His bangles, His oiled hair, curling with a bluish tint, and His beautiful smiling face are all very pleasing. The Lord's magnanimous pastimes and the glowing glancing of His smiling face are all indications of His extensive benedictions. One must therefore concentrate on this transcendental form of the Lord, as long as the mind can be fixed on Him by meditation." (*Bhag.*2.2.8- 12)

## RELATIONSHIP BETWEEN THE SOUL AND SUPERSOUL

The relationship between the soul and the Supersoul is a very special one, although the materially conditioned beings within the cosmic manifestation are unaware of it. In the Vedic literature one can find descriptions which give detailed information as to what is that relationship. For example, the *Srimad-Bhagavatam* (11.11.6-7) states: "By chance, two birds have made a nest together in the same tree [of the material body]. The two birds are friends and are of similar nature. One of them, however, is eating the fruits of the tree, whereas the other, who does not eat the fruits, is in a superior position, due to His potency. The bird who does not eat the fruits of the tree is the Supreme Personality of Godhead, who by His omniscience perfectly understands His own position and that of the conditioned living entity, represented by the eating bird. That living entity, on the other hand, does not understand himself or the Lord. He is covered by ignorance and is thus called eternally conditioned, whereas the Personality of Godhead, being full of perfect knowledge, is eternally liberated."

The Supersoul knows exactly what His position is as well as that of the living entity. But the living entity is not aware of the glories of his spiritual nature and, therefore, tries to attain happiness by tasting the sweet and bitter fruits of bodily pleasures. These sweet and bitter fruits cause the living entity to feel happiness as well as sorrow. But this anxiety can be put to an end if the soul looks toward the Supersoul, as explained in the *Svetasvatara Upanishad* (4.6-7): "Although the two birds are in the same tree, the eating bird is fully engrossed with anxiety and moroseness as the enjoyer of the fruits of the tree. But if in some way or other he turns his face to his friend who is the Lord and knows His glories--at once the suffering bird becomes free from all anxieties."

Similar descriptions are found in the *Mundaka Upanishad* (3.1.1-3) and *Katha Upanishad* (1.2.20). These descriptions point out that the living entity can get relief from all temporary pleasures and problems by looking toward his friend next to him, the Supersoul. The living entity is desiring different kinds of situations and is completely dependent on the Supersoul to empower him with the ability to perform actions with the body in hopes of achieving various desires. Therefore, the *Bhagavad-gita* states: "The Supreme Lord is situated in everyone's heart, O Arjuna, and is directing the wanderings of all living entities, who are seated as on a machine, made of the material energy." (*Bg.*18.61)

The Supersoul guides the individual souls, although He does not personally take part in fulfilling their desires. He arranges the fulfillment of such desires by the workings of material nature. The living entities are independent in the respect that they are free to desire whatever they want. Only the Supreme allows them to fulfill their desires, but the Supreme is never responsible for the actions and reactions of the situations which may be desired by the living entities. In other words, as the living beings pursue their various desires by the power the Supersoul has given them, they must realize that this universe is governed by certain laws which the Supreme has established. If we perform activities that break those laws, particular reactions will automatically follow. The Lord is neutral to everyone and does not interfere with the desires of the living beings. We, therefore, cannot blame God for those reactions that we will have to endure which were caused by our own unlawful desires. And, as they say, ignorance of the law is no excuse.

Because of their various good or bad activities, the living entities get what they deserve and are carried by the material energy to either happiness or misery. A person may not remember all of his or her good or evil deeds, but the Supersoul can remember everything we have done either in this life or any other previous life. The Supreme, through previously established universal laws, thus causes material nature automatically to award or punish the living beings accordingly. Therefore, one Vedic hymn states: "The Lord engages the living entity in pious activities so he may be elevated. The Lord engages one in impious activities so he may go to hell. The living entity is completely dependent in one's distress and happiness. By the will of the Supreme one can go to heaven or hell as a cloud is driven by the air." A similar statement is also found in the *Kaushitaki Upanishad* (3.8). In this way, the Supreme guides the living beings according to their desires and witnesses all the activities that they perform.

Through all this enjoyment or suffering, the Supersoul is the individual soul's constant companion. As previously stated, if the living beings, after becoming exhausted from the continuous ups and downs of happiness and distress, look toward their friend the Supersoul, they can be relieved from all suffering. At that time, the Supersoul helps the conditioned soul by giving real intelligence for understanding one's ever-blissful, spiritual position. However, the ability for one to perceive the Supersoul depends on one's sincerety to advance spiritually:

"O King Yudhisthira, the Supersoul in every body gives intelligence to the individual soul according to his capacity for understanding. Therefore, the

Supersoul is the chief within the body. The Supersoul is manifested to the individual soul according to the individual's comparative development of knowledge, austerity, penance, and so on." (*Bhag*.7.14.38)

It has been said that for every step we take toward the Supreme, He takes ten steps toward us. We could actually experience His concern for us if we, by putting our sincerity into action, develop knowledge of our spiritual position by studying the Vedic literature and by purifying our consciousness through the practice of yoga. By such practices, we can understand the message the Supersoul is giving us when we feel discontent with our present situation. Every so often, we feel our conscience asking us, "Do you think you should be doing this? Have you really found what you're looking for? Are you satisfied yet?" This is simply the Supersoul within whom, if we were more aware, would give us a more direct message, such as the following:

"Sometimes you think yourself a man, sometimes a chaste woman or sometimes a neutral eunuch. This is all because of the body, which is created by the illusory energy. This illusory energy is My potency, and actually both of us--you and I--are pure spiritual identities. Now just try to understand this. I am trying to explain our factual position. My dear friend, I, the Supersoul, and you, the individual soul, are not different in quality, for we are both spiritual. In fact, My dear friend, you are qualitatively not different from Me in your constitutional position. Just try to consider this subject. Those who are actually advanced scholars, who are in knowledge, do not find any qualitative difference between you and Me." (*Bhag*.4.28.61-62)

Here we find that the Supersoul is always encouraging us to look toward Him for guidance, and to understand our real identity as a spiritual being, beyond the temporary body and its trials and tribulations. The living being is qualitatively the same as the Supreme, but in quantity the Lord is infinite and the living entity is very small. Thus, the finite entity can be overcome and bewildered by the material energy and needs help from the omnipotent Supersoul in every situation.

"In this way, both swans live together in the heart. When the one swan is instructed by the other, he is situated in his constitutional position. This means he regains his original Krishna consciousness, which was lost because of his material attraction." (*Bhag*.4.28.64)

## BEING IGNORANT OF THE SELF

To be ignorant of the self means not to know who you are. For example, if some adult started thinking that he was actually a rabbit and wanted nothing more than to hop around the yard and nibble on the weeds, flowers, and grass, it would soon become very embarrassing for the other members of the family. If the person could not be convinced that he was not a rabbit, he would have to be taken away to the funny farm. In such a condition a person is called insane or a madman.

At the funny farm the human rabbit can mix with others who are also acting out their fantasies and who do not know who they really are. In this way, they are not a nuisance to society because they have been removed to where they can be cared for while they are engrossed in their own little world that exists in their minds. Of course, sometimes the fantasies or desires of one may clash with the fantasies of another, causing fights or quarrels. Likewise, if one is a criminal and cannot abide by the laws of the state or is harmful to others, he is put into prison where he is stripped of his liberties and forced to confine his activities to a limited space where he cannot be a danger to the rest of society.

In a similar way, this material cosmic creation is manifested to give facility to those who do not really know who they are, or who may want to act according to their own materialistic and whimsical ideas and speculations. In society, this creates a civilization consisting of millions of people who are all going in different directions. They all have different ideas on what should be done, how the world should be run, and what the purpose of life should be. And none of them are really sure of where the world is heading or where they will end up.

When no one knows what his or her real identity is, no one knows exactly what to do. But people everywhere are concocting so many plans to make life more enjoyable according to their own opinions, and, therefore, they are madly engaged in material activities in the hopes of finding pleasure and happiness.

"In this way, the conditioned soul living within the body forgets his self-interest because he identifies himself with the body. Because the body is material, his natural tendency is to be attracted by the varieties of the material world. Thus the living entity suffers the miseries of material existence. Just as a deer, because of ignorance, cannot see the water within a well covered by grass, but runs after water elsewhere, the living entity covered by the material body does not see the happiness within himself, but runs after happiness in the material world." (Bhag.7.13.28-29)

As further explained in *Srimad-Bhagavatam* (4.20.31), all living beings in this material world have forgotten their real constitutional position, and out of ignorance they are always desirous of material happiness by trying to surround themselves with society, friendship, and love. In this way, a common man tries to be happy in the illusory energy. A person devoid of knowledge of the self does not inquire into the problems of life, such as birth, disease, old age, and death. Such a person is more attached to the body and bodily relations, such as wife, husband, children, relatives, house and home, country, wealth, etc. Although we are sufficiently experienced to know that all such objects are ultimately destroyed, we overlook this point and think we can make a permanent settlement here in this world. But this has never been done by anyone. After sixty, seventy, or at most one-hundred years, our body deteriorates and dies.

Then we lose everything. To ignore this fact is the foolishness of materialistic society. Such ignorance keeps one bound to the illusion that we are these temporary bodies and the pleasure of the body is the goal of life. Such a mentality is actually the cause of our suffering.

## THE CAUSE OF SUFFERING

Through our bodily conception of life, we are always hankering after material enjoyment and, therefore, try to hold on to so many things in hopes of maintaining that enjoyment. The thought of losing our so-called valuables and what we cherish gives us great anxiety. But this material happiness and anxiety are two sides of the same coin, and they are superficial to the soul since they exist only within the mind. The spirit soul is actually above such miseries and temporary pleasures:

"O my Lord, the material miseries are without factual existence for the soul. Yet as long as the conditioned soul sees the body as meant for sense enjoyment, he cannot get out of the entanglement of material miseries, being influenced by Your external energy." (*Bhag*.3.9.9)

As indicated here, the miseries of life are caused only by the influence of the illusory energy which the living beings are subjected to as long as they refuse to understand their real identity. This is confirmed in *Srimad-Bhagavatam*: "O my Lord, the people of the world are embarrassed by all material anxieties-- they are always afraid. They always try to protect wealth, body, and friends, they are filled with lamentation and unlawful desires and paraphernalia, and they avariciously base their undertakings on the perishable conceptions of 'I' and 'mine.' As long as they do not take shelter of You, they are full of such anxieties." (*Bhag*.3.9.6)

"Sri Kavi said: I consider that one whose intelligence is constantly disturbed by his falsely identifying himself with the temporary material world can achieve real freedom from fear only by worshipping the lotus feet of the infallible Supreme Lord. In such devotional service [*bhakti-yoga*], all fear ceases entirely." (*Bhag*.11.2.33)

From this Vedic evidence it is clear that by whatever material arrangements we make, or by whatever mechanical yoga process we may practice for peace of mind, ultimately the only way to attain freedom from fear is to realize our true spiritual identity and the connection we have with the Supreme Spirit. We cannot control the topsy-turvy nature of this material world. Nature is controlled by the Supreme. But by taking shelter of the Supreme, we begin to understand the difference between the material and spiritual energies, and no longer undergo the temporary ups and downs as we did before. This, however, cannot be achieved if we cling to the material energy in the shape of the temporary body and its relations. This is also pointed out in the Bible (*John* 2.15-17): "Do not set your hearts on the godless world or anything in it. Anyone who loves the world is a stranger to the Father's love. Everything the world affords, all that panders to the appetites or entices the eyes, all the glamour of its life, springs not from the Father but from the godless world. And that world is passing away with all its allurements, but he who does God's will stands forevermore."

Those, however, who remain attached to sensual pleasures and temporary material accomplishments will never be able to see with spiritual vision or attain freedom from fear and anxiety. In fact, all spiritual realizations appear to such people as crazy talk for they are unable to understand it. As the Bible explains: "The sensual man perceiveth not the things that are of the Spirit of God, for it is foolishness to him, and he cannot understand it. A man who is unspiritual refuses what belongs to the Spirit of God; it is folly to him; he cannot grasp it, because it needs to be judged in the light of the Spirit." (*I Corinthians*.2.14)

Furthermore, the *Katha Upanishad* (2.6.4) states that those persons who cannot understand such knowledge before they die will be forced to take birth in another body in the worlds of creation to continue struggling to fulfill their material desires. This is further elaborated in the *Bhagavatam* (starting at 11.28.12) where Lord Sri Krishna explains that as long as the living being identifies with the pleasure and pain of the body, though it has no reality in the self, the entity will continue through cycles of birth and death and the suffering therein the same way the calamities of a dream occur to a person as long as the dream is not broken. But those who have awoken from the dream will not be infatuated by that which continues to affect the dreaming person. Therefore, what brings sorrow to the ignorant does not affect the wise. Grief, delight, fear, anger, greed, infatuation, craving, and other moods, as well as birth and death, are seen in relation to the ego (the body) and not to the soul. But with the sword of wisdom, whetted by devotion to the Supreme, the tree of ego can be cut down.

The *Brihadaranyaka Upanishad* (4.4.12,14-15) also says that those who know their real identity as the self and see the Superself as God are no more afraid of anything in this material creation and they become immortal. With such understanding, what more could they desire for the body? This, of course, comes from realizing that one is above and beyond material pleasure and pain and that spiritual happiness is never affected or decreased by external circumstances. In fact, as related in *Srimad-Bhagavatam* (11.23.49-56), we can blame no one and nothing else for our trials and tribulations. We may say that certain people are the cause of our happiness or distress, but this is just the interactions of material bodies and does not pertain to the soul. Therefore, how can we be angry with others over our troubles? Even if there are natural disasters in our lives, or if our destiny seems to bring us misfortune as if dictated by the way the stars are astrologically arranged, how does this relate to the soul? The effect of planets applies only to things that have taken birth. We can say that the situation around us affects our mood, but do such changes of mood apply to the soul? Changes of mood apply only to the mind. Therefore, the soul, being completely transcendental to material nature, can never actually be affected by material happiness and distress in any place, under any circumstance, or by the agency of any person. One who realizes this and reaches this platform is no longer affected by any fear or anxiety and is free from all suffering.


## ACHIEVING PEACE
## FOR THE INDIVIDUAL AND THE WORLD

To begin seeing how things really are, we have to start adjusting our consciousness, which takes place by being trained in spiritual knowledge and by the practice of yoga which purifies the mind. When the mind becomes purified and the false ego no longer influences our vision, we become a sensible person. As the *Bhagavad-gita* (13.31-32) says: "When a sensible man ceases to see different identities, which are due to different material bodies, he attains to the Brahman conception. Thus he sees that beings are expanded everywhere. Those with the vision of eternity can see that the soul is transcendental, eternal, and beyond the modes of nature. Despite contact with the material body, O Arjuna, the soul neither does anything nor is entangled."

Naturally, until our consciousness is cleansed, we recognize various beings according to their body. We may see a person that appears to be a man, or a woman, a child, a baby, or a black person, a white person, and so on. Or we may recognize those who appear to be cats, dogs, cows, horses, insects, birds, aquatics, or plants. However, once we can see beyond these material bodies, we will see that all these entities are the same in that they are all spirit souls.

The *Svetasvatara Upanishad* (5.10-11) states that the self is not man, woman, nor neuter, but appears in different types of bodies only due to previous activities and desires of the living entity. This is how the entity chooses whatever status in which one presently appears. But one in divine consciousness can perceive that he or she is beyond all designations and activities.

"The humble sage, by virtue of true knowledge, sees with equal vision a learned and gentle *brahmana*, a cow, an elephant, a dog, and a dog-eater (outcaste). (*Bg*.5.18) . . . A person in divine consciousness, although engaged in seeing, hearing, touching, smelling, eating, moving about, sleeping, and breathing, always knows within himself that he actually does nothing at all. Because while speaking, evacuating, receiving, opening or closing his eyes, he always knows that only the material senses are engaged with their objects and that he is aloof from them." (*Bg*.5.8-9)

Herein we can understand that the body is like a dress we are temporarily wearing. Someone may wear a white shirt and someone else a black or red shirt. If we see only the dress, then we think we are different. If we think we are different and that we oppose each other, then there may be fights or even wars because one side is wearing a white shirt and the other a red shirt. There may be soldiers or communities divided into different sides fighting against each other, but without their uniforms, the dead killed in the night all look the same in the morning sunlight.

If we can simply look beyond the dress, the temporary uniform of this material body, we would see that we are all the same. We are all trying to find love and happiness in this world. We are all residents of the same planet. After all: "All of us on the surface of the globe are living entities in different forms. Some of us are moving and some not moving. All of us come into existence, remain for some time and are annihilated when the body is again mingled with the earth. We are all simply different transformations of the earth. Different bodies and capacities are simply transformations of the earth that exist in name only, for everything grows out of the earth and when everything is annihilated it again mingles with the earth. In other words, we are but dust, and we shall but be dust. Everyone can consider this point." (*Bhag.*5.12.8)

In this way, we can understand that either spiritually or materially we are all composed of the same elements. By understanding these points one can begin to realize that, "No other force besides one's own mental confusion makes the soul experience happiness and distress. His perception of friends, neutral parties and enemies, and the whole material life he builds around this perception are simply created out of ignorance." (*Bhag.*11.23.59)

As one gets free from this ignorance and becomes spiritually enlightened, it also becomes obvious that whatever material differences exist between us are all superficial and illusory--they are not real. As stated in *Sri Isopanishad* (*Mantras* 6-7): "He who sees everything in relation to the Supreme Lord, who sees all entities as His parts and parcels and who sees the Supreme Lord within everything, never hates anything nor any being. One who always sees all living entities as spiritual sparks, in quality one with the Lord, becomes a true knower of things. What, then, can be illusion or anxiety for him?"

Thus, as one attains spiritual vision, he becomes completely free from illusion, anxiety, anger, and hatred. This freedom is felt in a natural joy that comes from realizing one's eternal spiritual identity. But this freedom is attained to its fullest extent when one is released from all material limitations and is independent to express one's love and happiness in the unbounded loving relationship between the finite living being and the infinite Supreme Lord. It is this experience and the knowledge of such which is the ultimate uniting factor between all living entities. In this way, we are certainly all brothers and sisters, being sons and daughters of the same Supreme Father. Without this vision we simply remain like uncivilized, quarrelling animals. Therefore, it is obvious that to see the difference between the body and soul, and to recognize the qualitative spiritual oneness amongst us all, are absolutely necessary if we expect to establish real peace in the world.

## ATTAINING THE HIGHEST HAPPINESS

By understanding our spiritual identity, we also become free from the day to day turmoil and hassles that many people take so seriously. Some people let such problems control their lives. Life is too short for that. Allowing such circumstantial difficulties to increase our stress and anxiety only decreases our duration of life.

Life is meant for being happy. But real happiness, which exists on the spiritual platform, is always steady and, in fact, is continually increasing according to one's spiritual advancement. Such persons who understand their spiritual identity and are self-satisfied and content within themselves find happiness everywhere.

The *Chandogya Upanishad* (starting at 7.25.2) explains that he who perceives and understands this, loves the self, revels, rejoices, and delights in the self. Such a person is lord and master of the worlds because he has already attained all that he needs. He knows that he may be in this material world but is not of it. He is actually of the spiritual world and has regained his connection with it. Therefore, he looks at this world as if he were simply a tourist. He sees all the busy activities of people and society, the confusion, but he walks through it all unaffected. But those who think differently live in perishable worlds and have other mortal beings as their rulers. They are limited and controlled by their own material designations. But he who sees the soul of everyone, the spiritual identity beyond the body, does not see death, nor illness, nor pain; he who sees this sees everything and obtains everything everywhere. This certainly is the quality of those who have attained their own internal, self-sufficient happiness.

A similar verse is found in the *Katha Upanishad* (2.5.12-13) where it says that those who have realized their self and also see the Supreme Being residing within their heart and in all beings as the Superself, to them belongs eternal happiness and eternal peace, but not to others.

The original spiritual form of the living being is *sac-cid-ananda*: eternal, full of knowledge, and full of bliss. The living being's spiritual form is never limited by the body or one's situation. The only limiting factor is the living being's consciousness or lack of spiritual awareness. When the living entity, after many births, finally regains his original spiritual consciousness, realizing he is not the body, he naturally feels very happy and jolly, being freed from the limited and temporary perspective one has while being controlled by the illusory, material energy. He also understands that this material world is not his real home, and it has nothing substantial to offer him since real pleasure and happiness actually come from within on the spiritual level. As stated in *Bhagavad-gita* by Lord Sri Krishna: "One who is thus transcendentally situated at once realizes the Supreme Brahman and becomes fully joyful. He never laments nor desires to have anything; he is equally disposed to every living entity. In that state he attains pure devotional service to Me." (*Bg.*18.54)

In this state of spiritual consciousness, there is no limit to the joy and ecstasy one may attain. One may become so absorbed in this state of being that he may be like one in trance. Let us point out, however, that a trance does not necessarily mean that a person is immovably sitting in the lotus position with closed eyes and incapable of doing anything else. A trance may also be like a lover thinking of his beloved. No matter what kind of activities he may do throughout the day, his thoughts are always of his beloved. Similarly, a mystic or yogi, especially one following the path of *bhakti* or devotional service, may also be engaged in many different kinds of activities, but he is always concentrating on the Supreme and relating to the world on the basis of his real spiritual identity. His body simply goes through the necessary motions to accomplish the needful, while his thoughts and consciousness are on a much higher level of existence. Such a person may then feel, as the *Svetasvatara Upanishad* (1.12) states, that that which rests eternally in the self should be known, and beyond this nothing else has to be known.

In this way, "The yogi whose mind is fixed on Me [Lord Sri Krishna] verily attains the highest happiness. By virtue of his identity with Brahman [the absolute spiritual nature], he is liberated; his mind is peaceful, his passions are quieted, and he is freed from sin. Steady in the Self, being freed from all material contamination, the yogi achieves the highest perfectional stage of happiness in touch with the Supreme Consciousness." (*Bg*.6.27-28)

"Such a liberated soul is not attracted to material sense pleasure or external objects but is always in trance, enjoying the pleasure within. In this way the self-realized person enjoys unlimited happiness, for he concentrates on the Supreme." (*Bg*.5.21)

This, therefore, is the highest level of happiness which is attained when one understands his or her true spiritual identity and becomes spiritually self-realized.

# CHAPTER FIVE

# Reincarnation
# And
# The Law of Karma

Reincarnation is called *samsara* in the *Vedas* and means being bound to the cycle of repeated birth and death. The materially conditioned soul transmigrates through different bodies according to his desires and past activities. It is stated that as a man sows, so shall he reap. Similarly, as people live their present life, they cultivate a particular type of consciousness by their thoughts and activities, which may be good or bad. This brings about the kind of life after death that they will enjoy or suffer. The living beings get a certain kind of body that is suitable for the type of consciousness they have developed. Therefore, according to the *Padma Purana*, there are 8,400,000 species of life, each offering a particular kind of body for whatever kind of desires and consciousness one may have in this world. In this way, the living entity is the son of the past and the father of his future. Thus, he is presently affected by his previous life's activities and creates his future existence by the actions he performs in this life.

Nonetheless, one is not condemned to stay in this cycle of repeated birth and death forever. There is a way out. In the human form one can attain the knowledge of spiritual realization and attain release from *samsara*. This is considered to be the most important achievement one can accomplish in life. This is why every religious process in the world encourages people not to hanker for sensual enjoyments which bind them to this world but to look towards what is spiritual and gives eternal freedom from *samsara*. In fact, the only religion which does not acknowledge this science of reincarnation is modern day Christianity.

71

## REINCARNATION IN CHRISTIANITY

Only in contemporary Christianity is it taught that, in essence, the soul has a beginning with this present life and then lives eternally hereafter, either in heaven or hell, but never existed in a previous life. After death, the body lives again with the resurrection of the dead. In this way, they teach that there is but one chance in one life to make it or break it in this one and only universe.

The philosophy of the early Gnostic Christians, however, was similar to the Oriental teachings regarding rebirth and *karma*. But somehow, due to unknown circumstances, the Second Council of Constantinople in 553 A.D. decreed that, "Whosoever shall support the mythical doctrine of the pre-existence of the soul and the consequent wonderful opinion of its return, let him be anathema." Therefore, all such teachings regarding reincarnation stopped and all inner, esoteric teachings of the Bible were thrown out or lost. There are, however, still some powerful references in the Bible which hold the idea of reincarnation intact.

For example, in *Matthew* (16:13-14) it says: "When Jesus came into the coasts of Caesarea Philippi, he asked his disciples, saying, Who do men say that I am? And they replied, Some say that thou art John the Baptist; some, Elias; and others, Jeremias, or one of the other prophets."

This shows that the idea of reincarnation was certainly not a strange or foreign idea to Jesus or his disciples. On the contrary, they accepted it and actually expected the prophets to return again to continue teaching the people. This is exactly in line with the traditional Vedic and Buddhist teachings that propound the idea that the masters may decide to return in another incarnation to continue their teachings.

Further proof of this is found in *Matthew* (17:9-13): "And as they came down from the mountain, Jesus charged them saying, Tell the vision to no man, until the Son of Man be risen again from the dead. And his disciples asked him, saying, Why then say the scribes that Elias must first come? And Jesus answered them, Elias truly shall first come, and restore all things. But I say unto you, that Elias has come already, and they knew him not, but have done unto him whatsoever they listed. Likewise shall the Son of Man suffer from them. Then the disciples understood that he spake unto them of John the Baptist."

This means that the scribes predicted that the prophet Elias would return by taking another birth and that John the Baptist was Elias but was never recognized as such, for Herod had already beheaded him.

"Jesus began to say unto the multitudes concerning John. . . this is he, of whom it is written, Behold, I send my messenger before thy face, which shall prepare thy way before thee. . . and if ye will receive it: this is Elias, which was for to come. He that hath ears to hear, let him hear." (*Matthew* 11:7,10-11,14-15)

A similar reference is in *Luke* (4:7-9): "Now Herod the tetrarch heard of all that was done by Jesus, and he was perplexed, because that it was said of some, that John was risen from the dead; and of some, that Elias had appeared; and of others, that one of the old prophets was risen again. And Herod said, John have I beheaded; but who is this of whom I hear such things?" In *Mark* (6:14-16), the same incident is described.

There are more references which we could point out in the Bible which relate to the idea of reincarnation. However, the goal of this chapter is not to engage in such controversy but to establish what is the science of reincarnation by Vedic evidence. After all, it is a science just as much as the mathematical formula of two plus two equals four. You may believe it or not--it does not matter--but if you do not understand the simple formula of two plus two, there is no chance of understanding any higher mathematical principles. Similarly, if you cannot understand the science of reincarnation, you will hardly understand anything higher in regard to spiritual science.

## OTHER REFERENCES AND BELIEVERS IN REINCARNATION

Quotations can be found in texts from all over the world regarding reincarnation. For example, the *Koran* (2.28) states: "How can you deny Allah? Did he not give you life when you were dead, and will He not cause you to die and then restore you to life? Will you not return to Him at last?"

The *Zohar* also mentions that for the living beings to return to the Absolute, they must develop all the perfections, which if not done in one life must be accomplished in a second, third, or however many lifetimes is necessary to attain reunion with God. The *Cabala* (or *Kabbala*), which is a very important book amongst Hebraic scholars, also has information about past and future lives.

The Buddhist and Taoist scriptures also contain much information about rebirth. In fact, all over the world you can find the idea of reincarnation mentioned in many ancient customs and texts. It was also found in the philosophy of the Gallic Druids, African Zulus, Eskimos of Greenland, North American Indians such as the Hopi tribe, Dayaks of Borneo, Karens of Burma, and even the natives of New Guinea.

It would take a large book to list all who have accepted the idea of reincarnation and explain what their views were on it. A partial list includes the Greek philosophers such as Socrates, Pythagoras, and Plato, Italy's philosopher and poet of the Renaissance Giordano Bruno (who was later burned at the stake by the Inquisition because of his beliefs), as well as the great philosopher Voltaire. Some of America's founding fathers, such as Benjamin Franklin, as well as former Presidents John Adams and Thomas Jefferson, also believed in reincarnation. Napoleon made mention of his accepting reincarnation as did the German poet Wolfgang von Goethe. In Russia, Count Leo Tolstoy believed in reincarnation as did such early American philosophers and poets as Ralph Waldo

Emerson, Walt Whitman, Henry David Thoreau, and Charles Dickens, who mention their beliefs in many of their writings.

We can also include U. S. Auto magnate Henry Ford, U. S. General George S. Patton, Nobel Laureates Herman Hesse and Isaac Bashevis Singer, Psychologist Carl Jung, British biologist Thomas Huxley, American Psychoanalyst Erik Erikson, and Mahatma Gandhi.

No matter how many people believed in reincarnation or how much they knew about it, the basis of all knowledge concerning reincarnation is found in the ancient Vedic teachings. This is especially obvious when one studies Greek philosophy because there are many reports of how the Greeks had been influenced by the religions of India (some of which I detail in *The Universal Path to Enlightenment*). This is the same with Buddhism, being an outgrowth of the Vedic school of thought. Such being the case, let us take a closer look at what the *Vedas* can teach us.


## APPROACHING DEATH

One thing for sure, before you can be reborn you have to die. And as long as the hands on the clock keep turning and the sun keeps rising and setting, the gap between our present situation and our ever approaching death is continually getting smaller. When we will die is not certain. It might be years from now or it may be at any moment. And what our consciousness is like when we die will determine what our next life will be.

This is explained in the *Bhagavad-gita* (8.6): "Whatever state of being one remembers when he quits his body, that state he will attain without fail." This means that all of our thoughts and actions throughout our life will influence the state of being we are in at the time of death. This state of being carries over from this life into the next: "The living entity in the material world carries his different conceptions of life from one body to another as the air carries aromas." (*Bg.*15.8)

One's state of being or conception of life exists in the subtle body of mind, intelligence, and false ego. We shape this consciousness according to our desires, thoughts, words, and deeds. The soul is covered by this subtle body, which exists within the gross material body, as we explained in Chapter Four. When the gross material body can no longer function, the subtle body and soul are forced out of the gross body and are then placed in another physical form which properly accommodates the state of mind of the living entity. Therefore, that subject which attracts the dying man determines how he begins his next life. If the dying man is absorbed in thoughts of material gain or sensual pleasures of wife, family, relatives, home, etc., then he must get another material body to continue pursuing his material interests. After all, how can one satisfy his material desires without a material body? In this way, all who are absorbed in material consciousness at the time of death will continue in the cycle of repeated birth and death: "According to the *Vedas*, there are two ways of passing from this world--one in light and one in darkness. When one passes in light, he does not come back; but when one passes in darkness, he returns." (*Bg*.8.26)

We can begin to understand that dying in the right consciousness in order to become free from the cycle of birth and death is an art that takes practice. We have to prepare for the moment of death so that we are not caught offguard or in an unsuitable state of mind. This is the purpose of yoga. This is explained in the *Katha Upanishad* (1.3.6-8) where it states that one who has understanding and whose mind is always firmly held, his senses are under control like good horses of a charioteer. But one who has no understanding, who is unmindful and always impure, enters the rounds of rebirth. One, however, who has understanding, who is mindful and pure, reaches that place from which he is not born again.

How the soul leaves the body is explained in the *Brihadaranyka Upanishad* (4.4.1-4): as a person dies and slips, as it were, into unconsciousness, the life energy descends into the heart and the living being ceases to recognize those around him. The point where the veins and *nadis* (channels through which energy flows through the subtle body) go out of the heart becomes lit up within and by that light the Self departs. According to the qualifications of the living entity, the soul and subtle body may leave the material body through the eye, nose, mouth, or through the top of the skull. Or it may leave through other openings of the body such as the anus if he is to take a lower birth. When he departs, the chief *prana* (life force) departs after him and all the other *pranas* follow. Then both his consciousness and work (*karma*) take hold of him along with his familiarity with former things or past desires. Then he takes to his new form of existence.

The above verses mention that certain energy channels become filled with light showing the path for the soul to take while departing from the body. This occurrence indicates that the soul, in leaving the body, is beginning to enter the subtle level of existence. The subtle level of existence is that in which the unembodied living beings exist, such as ghosts and wandering spirits on the lower level of the subtle realm, and angels and guardian spirits on the higher level of the subtle realm. Actually, there is such a wide variety of beings on the subtle platform of existence that they cannot all be named here.

In many near death experiences there is often a description of the person leaving the body through a tunnel that has a light at the end of it, as mentioned above. In many cases, the light is described as very peaceful, kind, gentle, etc. Some feel that it is God or the entrance into heaven. Sometimes the people also describe meeting old loved ones who have passed away.

But let us remember that this is near death, when one still has a connection with his present body. In such a state, people may float above the body, as during a medical operation or after a serious accident, and view what is happening to their body, or see astral beings; yet, advanced yogis can also do that at will. It is nothing special, unless, of course, you have never experienced it before. If that is the case, then reaching a stage beyond the limits of your body may seem quite blissful. But that is like the weightlessness felt when you are between two planets. You are not completely on one or the other; you are in between. But once you are completely disconnected with your present body, as in the case of total death, then the effects of your consciousness and past activities, or *karma*, swiftly deliver you to your next form of existence. Some of this *karma* may be experienced on the subtle platform, such as when one takes the form of a ghost. But there are also different levels of subtle existence. In any case, various forms of life are expanded on many levels, throughout the universe and beyond, for accommodating those who are destined to exist on such levels.

As a caterpillar reaches the end of a blade of grass and then reaches for another, similarly the soul gives up one body and approaches another. Such a form of body may be like the Fathers, Gandharvas (angels), Devas (demigods), or other beings. But as a man acts or behaves, so will he be. A man of good acts will take a good birth. A man of bad deeds takes a bad birth. Therefore, as a person desires, so is his will; as his will, so is his deed; and as whatever is his deed, so he will reap.

If people have not practiced yoga in order to purify their consciousness so they can face death in the right frame of mind, then they will not be able to utilize death to their advantage. Instead, they will simply go through the experience of death and another round of rebirth as described in *Srimad-Bhagavatam*: "Lord Krishna said: The material mind of men is shaped by the reactions of fruitive work. Along with the five senses, it travels from one material body to another. The spirit soul, although different from this mind, follows it. The mind, bound to the reactions of fruitive work, always meditates on the objects of the senses, both those that are seen in this world and those that are heard about from Vedic authority. Consequently, the mind appears to come into being and to suffer annihilation along with its objects of perception, and thus its ability to distinguish past and future is lost. When the living entity passes from the present body to the next body created by his own *karma*, he becomes absorbed in the pleasurable and painful sensations of the new body and completely forgets the experience of the previous body. This total forgetfulness for one reason or another of one's previous material identity is called death." (*Bhag.*11.22.37-39)

## REBIRTH

What happens after death is explained in the *Katha Upanishad* (2.5.7,9,10). Some enter a womb in order to have a body as organic beings, and others go into inorganic matter according to their work and knowledge. Thus, the soul, although one in spiritual quality with all beings, appears differently according to whatever kind of body it enters.

This is further elaborated in the *Yajur-veda* (12.36-39): "O learned and tolerant soul, after roaming in waters and plants, thou enterest the womb and art born again and again. O soul, thou art born in [the body of] plants, thou art born in trees, thou art born in all created animate objects, and thou art born in waters. O soul, blazing like the sun, after cremation, having reached the fire and the earth for rebirth, and residing in the belly of thy mother, thou art born again. O soul, having reached the womb, again and again, thou auspiciously liest in thy mother, as a child sleeps in her mother's lap."

"O most charitable Uddhava, what is called birth is simply a person's total identification with a new body. One accepts the new body just as one completely accepts the experience of a dream or a fantasy as reality. Just as a person experiencing a dream or daydream does not remember his previous dreams or daydreams, a person situated in his present body, although having existed previously to it, thinks that he has only recently come into being." (*Bhag*.11.22.40-41)

Thus, the living being, placed into a new material body, immediately begins to identify with his pleasurable and painful sensations and also begins to think of the same kind of desires he had while in his previous body. This is when the living entity forgets his past life and feels that this present body is his first existence. This is the illusion.

What all this means is that as we engage in different types of activities and thoughts, our mind is affected by the kind of desires we have. When we work, we are pursuing some goal. Such activities produce good or bad reactions that affect our consciousness. This consciousness, consisting of thinking, feeling, and willing, is held within the subtle body, which is made up of the material elements of mind, intelligence, and false ego. The shape of the subtle body is said to change according to the type of consciousness we develop. This subtle body travels with the soul from one material body to another as we go through the rounds of repeated birth and death. It is the mind that, being attached to achieving various goals and desires through material activities, always meditates on the pleasures of the senses, and this causes one to be born in another material body after death. The mind is not an object which we can perceive with our eyes, so it will seem as though the mind is created at birth and annihilated at death. But, actually, according to the above information, this is not the case.

From this Vedic knowledge, written many hundreds of years ago, we can understand that after death the soul continues to exist by entering the womb of its new mother in whatever particular species of life for which one is qualified. Regardless of the present day arguments of whether the fetus in the womb is alive or not, by understanding this knowledge of the soul and the science of reincarnation, we learn that the soul enters the womb at the time of conception. Therefore, the embryo is definitely alive and will continue to grow as long as the soul remains within. Otherwise, there is no conception during sexual intercourse. If society could understand this science, the whole controversy about abortion between pro-choice and pro-life could easily be resolved.

Another point here is that the soul is born in other species of life. This is a controversial topic among many occultists or sentimental believers in reincarnation who think that the soul will always go upwards to a better or higher birth after this life. But there is no evidence in Vedic literature that this is the case. In fact, we find that as easily as one may go upward in his next birth, he may also go downward. The reason is that the type of consciousness you develop in this life determines what kind of body you will get in the next. The *Bhagavad-gita* explains: "The living entity, thus taking another gross body, obtains a certain type of ear, tongue, nose, and sense of touch, which are grouped about the mind. He thus enjoys a particular set of sense objects. (*Bg*.15.9). . . The living entity in material nature thus follows the ways of life, enjoying the three modes of nature. This is due to his association with that material nature. Thus he meets with good and evil amongst various species." (*Bg*.13.22)

From this, we can understand that according to one's lifestyle and activities, a person's consciousness becomes infected with high or low qualities. If we are simply interested in the pursuit of animalistic endeavors, such as eating, sleeping, mating, and defending like the cats and dogs, then in our next life we will get a certain type of body to provide the kind of senses we need to enjoy such animalistic pleasures. For example, if we simply want to eat anything and have sex, pigs can eat anything without difficulty and have sex very indiscriminately with other pigs. If we simply like to sleep, then bears sleep for several months at a time. If we like the taste of blood, then tigers eat meat and taste blood quite naturally. But human life is one of particular responsibilities which should not be ignored. If we misuse this human life, then it means we are more fit for one of the other 8,000,000 species of life, and our consciousness at the time of death will determine what kind of body we will get in the future. The point is that an entity within the body of a dog must act like a dog. He cannot act differently. An entity put into the body of a bird must act in that way. But as a human being, one has choice and can act in different ways, thus creating a type of consciousness that will begin taking the shape of the kind of body he will get after death. In some cases, you can almost see what people will be in their next life when they begin to look similar to dogs or cats or even pigs. They are beginning to change into what they will become.

Without being trained in this spiritual science, it is very difficult to understand how the living being leaves his body or what kind of body he will get in the future, or why there are various species of life which accommodate all the living entities' innumerable levels of consciousness. As stated in *Bhagavad-gita*: "The foolish cannot understand how a living entity can quit his body, nor can they understand what sort of body he enjoys under the spell of the modes of

nature. But one whose eyes are trained in knowledge can see all this."
(*Bg*.15.10)

Exactly how it is determined what our next life will be and what reactions
through which we may be forced to experience because of our present activities
can be understood by learning about the law of *karma* and destiny.

## THE LAW OF KARMA AND DESTINY

The law of *karma*, according to Vedic literature, is the law of cause and
effect. For every action there is a cause as well as a reaction. *Karma* is produced
by performing fruitive activities for bodily development. One may perform pious
activities that will produce good reactions or good *karma* for future enjoyment.
Or one may perform sinful activities which produce bad *karma* and future
suffering.

All kinds of good or bad *karma* forces one to continue in the wheel of
transmigration to suffer and enjoy according to his past activities. Therefore, the
living entity creates his own *karma* which he experiences in his future. You
might say that he writes his own script which he acts out in the movie of his life.
Thus, the living being creates his own destiny of good or bad situations.
Therefore, the *Srimad-Bhagavatam* explains: "The living entity, who has
received his present body because of his past fruitive activity, may end the
results of his actions in this life, but this does not mean that he is liberated from
bondage to material bodies. The living entity receives one type of body, and by
performing actions with that body he creates another. Thus he transmigrates
from one body to another, through repeated birth and death, because of his gross
ignorance." (*Bhag*.7.7.47)

The *Chandogya Upanishad* (5.10.7) says that those whose conduct has been
good, will quickly attain some good birth, such as in the family of *brahmanas*
(the spiritually enlightened), or a *kshatriya* (a ruler or administrator), or a
*vaishya* (a prosperous businessman, banker, or farmer). But those whose conduct
has been evil will quickly attain an evil birth, such as a dog, or hog, or a sinful
*chandala* (dog eater or outcaste).

In this way, according to our past deeds which we may have forgotten, we
are born in a particular type of body which may be rich, beautiful, intelligent,
healthy, or a member of an aristocratic family if we have good *karma*. If we
have bad *karma* from performing sinful activities, we may be born ugly, poor,
sickly, with little facility for education, or in a low and degraded family. By the
reactions of our work, we are forced to wander up and down and appear in
various types of bodies within different kinds of families. But these situations are
all temporary and we should not be unduly attached to them whether they are
good or bad, as explained in *Srimad-Bhagavatam* in the following verses:

"My dear mother, in a restaurant or place for drinking cold water, many travelers are brought together, and after drinking water they continue to their respective destinations. Similarly, living entities join together in a family, and later, as a result of their own actions, they are led apart to their destinations." (*Bhag*.7.2.21)

"The association of children, wife, relatives and friends is just like the brief meeting of travelers. With each change of body one is separated from all such associates, just as one loses the objects one possesses in a dream when the dream is over." (*Bhag*.11.17.53)

The above points are very interesting in light of the fact that these days there are many people who are preoccupied with the idea of finding their "soulmates." We admit that the people with whom we may have strong relationships and close ties are a part of our destiny, but any wise follower of the *Vedas* knows that this is due to our *karma* and is temporary because with each change of body our situation is completely different. Even if we do come in contact again with those we knew in previous lives, we will hardly be able to recognize them if we have changed bodies. But since everyone must follow his or her own destiny, it cannot be expected that we will continue to meet people from our past lives very many times. Only if there is a very special reason for it could it possibly happen.

Sometimes, however, we can remember the people, places, or activities of our past lives because the memory still exists in our minds, which is part of our subtle body, as previously explained. Because the subtle body also travels with the soul to another material body, such memories may be awakened. This may happen in dreams or in other ways, as explained in the *Srimad-Bhagavatam*: "Sometimes we suddenly experience something that was never experienced in the present body by sight or hearing. Sometimes we see such things suddenly in dreams. Therefore, my dear King, the living entity, who has a subtle mental covering, develops all kinds of thoughts and images because of his previous body. Take this from me as certain. There is no possibility of concocting anything mentally without having perceived it in a previous body. Sometimes in a dream we see something never experienced or heard of in this life, but all these incidents have been experienced at different times, in different places and in different conditions." (*Bhag*.4.29.64-65,67)

Anyway, whether our life is good or bad depends on our *karma*. In fact, as explained in *Srimad-Bhagavatam* (12.6.25-26), the life and death of a living being is determined by our own doing. Nothing else can bring happiness or misery. When a living being, for example, meets death through the medium of a snake, thief, fire, lightning, or through starvation, thirst, disease, etc., it is only the fruit of one's *karma* that is being experienced.

If we can understand this, we will be able to see that universal justice will follow us wherever we go. We may break man's laws and avoid punishment for our crime, but if we break the universal laws, there is no way we will be able to avoid the reaction. According to our specific *karma* accumulated by the particular activities of our past, we will have certain fortunes and misfortunes happen to us throughout life, up to and including the way we are meant to die. In this way, we can understand that nothing we do goes unaccounted for. All our acts and desires follow us and will affect our next life.

We can relate a very graphic example of how this happens. There was once a woman who had therapy to help solve the many problems that she had. As a child she was raised by an aunt who had a husband who constantly molested her. Even though she told her aunt what he was doing, the aunt did nothing to stop the uncle from forcing the girl to sleep with him. At the age of sixteen, the girl was able to escape the situation by getting married. Over the years she had twelve children by her husband who then left her when she was twenty-seven. Left to take care of the children herself, she worked and later remarried. After some years she came to learn that her second husband had been molesting every one of her children. Needless to say, she was very upset and got a divorce.

Trying to reduce her mental anguish that was caused by all the problems she had experienced through life, she entered therapy with some doctors who were also hypnotists. In an attempt to help her find some answers, the doctors hypnotized her and regressed her to her previous life. While under hypnosis, she saw that in her last life she was not only a child molester herself, but she was a ring leader that included twelve other people who also molested children. She was the one who would make all the arrangements for this to go on. So, now in this life, she was simply experiencing the reactions of her previous life and had helplessly been molested as she had done to others. Furthermore, while under hypnosis she realized that the twelve people who had been a part of her little club in her previous life had now taken birth as her twelve children. It is not known for sure, but I would not be surprised if the uncle who had molested her while she was young was previously one of the children that she had molested in her past life who had come back to give her the same treatment that she had forced on him.

In any case, this is how the law of *karma* can affect us. It may have looked like the woman was merely an unfortunate victim of circumstance and was being abused for no apparent reason. But, of course, things are not always as they seem. Whatever happens in our life is not without some cause and it is important for us to understand this.

As previously mentioned, our past desires and familiarity with former things also follows us. Therefore, as children we may experience a spontaneous interest in particular objects or activities that we unknowingly had done in former lives. For example, a young child may seem especially gifted in playing the piano or some instrument. He may be able to play quite well with almost no training. This may be due to the abilities that he had developed in a previous life rather than a random interest in something at which he seems to be good. This is verified in the Vedic literature: "The mind of the living entity continues to exist in various gross bodies, and according to one's desires for sense gratification, the mind records different thoughts. In the mind these appear together in different combinations; therefore these images sometimes appear as things never seen or never heard before." (*Bhag*.4.29.68)

How we receive the appropriate bodies to carry out our just *karma* and desires is due to higher authorities. When we are newly born, the Paramatma or Supersoul reminds us of our past desires and interests. We then begin to search out those interests. It is also due to the universal laws of God and the agents of God that we are placed into various kinds of families, or in a certain species, or under particular astrological influences. An expert astrologer can ascertain the general fate of a person by drawing up one's horoscope. Such astrological influences are not absolute but tend to affect our life in subtle ways according to the position of the planets at the time of our birth. This also shows that the pattern of our life is not simply a creation of man's will but is affected by superior arrangement of the Supreme. Therefore, we should understand that all the ups and downs, prosperity or loss, are arranged by God according to our *karma* and not simply by our own endeavor, as explained: "From Him only, all our kingly opulence, good wives, lives, progeny, control over our subjects, victory over our enemies, and future accommodations in higher planets have become possible. All this is due to His causeless mercy upon us." (*Bhag*.1.14.9)

This is essentially how *karma* works and how the living being is affected by his past activities and acquires his destiny according to the arrangement of the Supreme. With this knowledge, we should try to be satisfied with whatever happiness is given by destiny, knowing that it is only our own activities which have put us into our present situation, whether it be good or bad. Therefore, the *Bhagavatam* says: "One should be satisfied with whatever he achieves by his previous destiny, for discontent can never bring happiness. A person who is not self-controlled will not be happy even with possessing the three worlds. Material existence causes discontent in regard to fulfilling one's lusty desires and achieving more and more money. This is the cause for the continuation of material life, which is full of repeated birth and death. But one who is satisfied by that which is obtained by destiny is fit for liberation from this material existence." (*Bhag*.8.19.24-25)

If we are too discontent with our present situation, ignoring any respect for the law of *karma*, we will be influenced by our unlawful desires to engage in any number of activities in the effort to satisfy our lusty mind and senses. This will only implicate us further in transmigrating through lifetimes filled with various good and bad reactions. To act in such a way may be due to the influence of our *karma*, but we also have free will to choose how we wish to live and carry on with our lives. This is our minute independence of which we can take advantage in order to progress upward, or to misuse and go downward.

## FREE WILL AND CHOICE

If every move we made was completely controlled by fate, destiny, or astrological influences, how could there be such a thing as sinful acts, and why feel regret toward something we did? If we are controlled by something stronger than ourselves, call it what you will, then how can we be held responsible for what we do? If there is going to be right and wrong activities, morality, judgement, or punishment, there must be some free will and choice.

What must be understood is the difference between the spiritual and material energies. The body is material and is therefore influenced by material forces, such as *karma* or astrological powers. The living entity within the body is spiritual and is transcendental to all such material energies and influences. The more the living entity realizes his spiritual position and acts on the spiritual platform, the more he can become free from the material energies which are actually limitations to one's spiritual freedom. The more a person identifies with the material body, the more he is influenced and controlled by the material forces, such as *karma*, destiny, the modes of nature, sensual desires, etc.

The freedom we have is in the way we desire. As we explained earlier in Chapter Four of this volume, we may desire in particular ways to achieve or experience something, but it is up to the Supersoul to enable us to act out our desires and to arrange the material energy to fulfill our longings. If we desire in a virtuous, pious, or spiritual way, we then act in a particular mode of nature. If we desire in a materialistic, passionate, lusty, or immoral way, we then act in a different mode of nature which produces completely different results. So how does all this fit together?

In this life we are destined to experience certain circumstances from the results of our past *karma*. When these circumstances take place, we have a limited amount of freedom to decide how we are going to react. Once we decide what we wish to do, we come under the influence of a certain combination of energies which produce a series of events. These events, brought on by our decisions, thus lead to good or bad consequences.

For example, we may be destined to have a member of our family die of cancer. When such a thing happens, we may feel sad and then simply lament with other family members over how cruel life can be and how bad is cancer. We then become locked into feeling melancholy about so many things around us. This melancholy mood may be a pattern in our lives due to our *karma* that affects us when the slightest thing goes wrong. But we could change our outlook and decide to do something productive like start a foundation for cancer research, or give a donation or something for helping other cancer patients.

Another example may be that we are destined to lose our job at a particular point in life. When it happens, we may feel that things are really tough, but we decide to make the best of it and go look for another job. This may actually be a *karmic* arrangement for us to find a new and better job. All reversals in life are a chance to grow and overcome the so-called obstacles by learning or experiencing things that we need to know or understand in order to progress in life. Nothing really happens without a reason, and often times it is seen that a person makes the most progress toward his goals right after he has overcome various challenging problems or adversities. We have to remember that life is not merely a matter of working to acquire whatever goals we set for ourselves. Life is a continual evolutionary process that molds us and causes us to learn as much about ourselves and life as we can. How much success or failure there is in this process is not always something that immediately can be determined. The universe has a plan behind it, and we are certainly a part of that plan, although there may be times when we cannot understand what or why things are happening the way they are. Nonetheless, things usually become clear sooner or later, depending on our level of understanding and perceptiveness.

A person who has little maturity and understanding might also lose a job. Say, for example, that someone thought he was goofing off, so he gets fired. The person who got fired from his job then might get very angry and even seek revenge. When the anger takes control, he might lose all rationality and go home, get his guns, go back to his job, and start shooting. When it is over, he has to face the consequences of his decision to get revenge. When we allow ourselves to become predictably angry in any adverse situation, this may be a tendency due to our *karma*, but it is also a matter of choice. Such being the case, we may feel regret over the foolish things we do when we are angry, or even face moral and legal judgements for any crimes we have committed due to our anger and foolish activities.

This is the independence and freedom of choice we have in how we view things around us, or how we react to the experiences that take place in our life. How we accept things and what is our attitude is our responsibility. A positive attitude can help make even the worst situations better. But a negative attitude can cause even a person who has everything to become sickly, unhappy, and decrease his duration of life. This is why it is mentioned in *Bhagavad-gita* (2.15) that one must become undisturbed both in happiness or distress, and (3.43) that one must know that he is above the material senses, mind, and intelligence, and, by spiritual strength, control the lower self by the higher self and conquer the insatiable enemy of lust. And where there is lust, there is also is anger, greed, envy, intolerance, etc.

The key, therefore, is how to tolerate the *karma* we have coming to us from our previous life, and how to get free from accumulating any more *karma*.

## GETTING FREE OF KARMA

If you now think that it is our *karma* that binds us to this material world and the cycle of continuous birth and death, and that it is something very difficult of which to be free, you are absolutely right. But there is a process which allows us to get free from accumulating any more *karma*.

Understanding exactly how to be free of *karma* is not so easy. Many times I have heard pseudo-spiritualists say that they are just working out some bad *karma* when they are going through some difficulty. Although they may understand the cause of some adverse condition in their life and peacefully accept it, they often do not know how to keep from developing more bad *karma*. As it is stated: "The intricacies of action are very hard to understand. Therefore one should know properly what action is, what forbidden action is, and what inaction is." (*Bg.*4.17)

So we have to understand that not only is there *karma*, but there is also *akarma* and *vikarma*. *Karma* pertains to those actions that are performed for one's social, economic, or bodily development, or which direct one to a higher birth in terms of prescribed duties as described in the *Vedas*. *Akarma* are those actions which are performed for one's spiritual growth and are absent of *karma* or reactions, which thereby free one from the cycle of birth and death. Whimsical actions performed on the basis of selfish desires, which direct one towards a lower birth, are called *vikarma*. Knowing that both good and bad activities equally bind one to the material world and all its miseries, an intelligent man will naturally wish to learn how to perform those acts which free one from the bondage of *karma*. To do this, we must study the instructions as explained in the Vedic literature, particularly *Bhagavad-gita* and *Srimad-Bhagavatam*, which can regulate our activities in such a way that we can transcend the modes of material nature and perform actions which can free us from further reactions and bondage to birth and death.

First of all, we must understand that action cannot be avoided. No matter what our situation is, we are forced to work; so, we must know what actions to perform. "Not by merely abstaining from work can one achieve freedom from reaction, nor by renunciation alone can one attain perfection. All men are forced to act helplessly according to the impulses born of the modes of material nature; therefore no one can refrain from doing something, not even for a moment. (*Bg.*3.4-5). . . Perform your prescribed duty, for action is better than inaction. A man cannot even maintain his physical body without work. (*Bg.*3.8). . . One should understand what is duty and what is not duty by the regulations of the scriptures. Knowing such rules and regulations, one should act so that he may gradually be elevated. (*Bg.*16.24). . . Regulated activities are prescribed in the *Vedas*, and the *Vedas* are directly manifested from the Supreme Personality of Godhead. Consequently the all-pervading Transcendence is eternally situated in acts of sacrifice." (*Bg.*3.15)

This means that by engaging in regulated acts of sacrifice we can enter into the spiritual strata, as confirmed as follows: "Therefore, without being attached to the fruits of activities, one should act as a matter of duty; for by working without attachment, one attains the Supreme." (*Bg.*3.19)

What these prescribed duties are is also explained: "Acts of sacrifice, charity and penance are not to be given up but should be performed. Indeed, sacrifice, charity and penance purify even the great souls. All these activities should be performed without any expectation of result. They should be performed as a matter of duty, O son of Pritha. That is My final opinion. Prescribed duties should never be renounced. If by illusion, one gives up his prescribed duties, such renunciation is said to be in the mode of ignorance. Anyone who gives up prescribed duties as troublesome, or out of fear is said to be in the mode of passion. Such action never leads to the elevation of renunciation. But he who performs his prescribed duty only because it ought to be done, and renounces attachment to the fruit--his renunciation is of the nature of goodness, O Arjuna." (Bg.18.5-9)

Sacrifice, charity, and penance all refer to activities related to developing spiritual merit. Charity is a matter of giving your money, time, intelligence, etc., for such things as worship of the Supreme or for the benefit of others who are less fortunate. Sacrifice and penance refer to activities such as fasting on holy days, spending time chanting, meditating, or reading sacred texts for acquiring spiritual knowledge, abstaining from causing any injury to other living beings, or making the endeavor to go on pilgrimages to holy places, and so on. These may seem troublesome, but they are done for developing spiritual advancement, without expecting material rewards. Such activities ensure happiness in this life and the next.

The above-mentioned prescribed duties are of different kinds. There are those that are described in the Vedic literature for realizing and acting on the level of our true spiritual identity, and those that describe our duties in regard to our status of life. For example, if we are married, it may be our duty to raise our family very carefully. Thus, we may have to work and make money to accomplish the many things necessary to do this. It may certainly seem like a burden, but we have to do it out of duty. If we consider that it would be better to leave our family and go off simply to work for ourselves, or be free of unwanted responsibilities, then such renunciation is said to be in the mode of darkness. This brings unwanted reactions both socially and individually. Therefore, once having accepted certain obligations in life, we must perform our duties in a dependable manner, without personal attachment, to continue our spiritual growth.

How these acts should be performed are described as follows: "One is understood to be in full knowledge whose every act is devoid of desire for sense gratification. He is said by sages to be a worker whose fruitive action is burned up by the fire of perfect knowledge. Abandoning all attachment to the results of his activities, ever satisfied and independent, he performs no fruitive action, although engaged in all kinds of undertakings. Such a man of understanding acts with mind and intelligence perfectly controlled, gives up all sense of proprietorship over his possessions and acts only for the bare necessities of life.

Thus working, he is not affected by sinful reactions. He who is satisfied with gain which comes of its own accord, who is free from duality and does not envy, who is steady both in success and failure, is never entangled, although performing actions." (Bg.4.19-22)

"O Dhananjaya, rid yourself of all fruitive activities by devotional service, and surrender fully to that consciousness. Those who want to enjoy the fruits of their work are misers. A man engaged in devotional service rids himself of both good and bad actions even in this life. Therefore strive for yoga, O Arjuna, which is the art of all work." (Bg.2.49-50)

These verses describe how one remains free from being entangled in the karmic reactions of one's work, although engaged in many kinds of activities. But as it is stated, one should not endeavor to enjoy the fruits of one's actions in a greedy or lusty way. To do so simply reveals our attachment to temporary material desires which bind us to this material world. So, if we cannot avoid performing activities but are not meant to enjoy selfishly the results ourselves, then for whom do we perform these acts of sacrifice and charity, and what is the necessity of such activities?

This is explained in Bhagavad-gita: "Work done as a sacrifice for Vishnu has to be performed otherwise work binds one to this material world. Therefore, O son of Kunti, perform your prescribed duties for His satisfaction, and in that way you will always remain unattached and free from bondage. (Bg.3.9). . . One who performs his duty without attachment, surrendering the results unto the Supreme God, is not affected by sinful action, as the lotus leaf is untouched by water. (Bg.5.10). . . Therefore, O Arjuna, surrendering all your works unto Me [Sri Krishna], with mind intent on Me and without desire for gain and free from egoism and lethargy, fight. One who executes his duties according to My injunctions and who follows this teaching faithfully, without envy, becomes free from the bondage of fruitive activities." (Bg.3.30-31)

This is the essence of how to be engaged in activities which will free us from all adverse reactions and from the cycle of birth and death. Through this system, one can remain free from accumulating any more good or bad karma, thereby allowing us to rise above the influence of the material energies. This is the process of bhakti-yoga, or devotional service to the Supreme.

The science of bhakti-yoga, which is especially useful in this age, does not necessitate one to give up all his present activities or change his occupation. Through bhakti-yoga a person can learn how to dovetail his or her present activities in a way which enables one to make spiritual advancement. By understanding bhakti-yoga along with the law of karma, one can easily make rapid spiritual progress in his present situation and reach both material as well as spiritual success. Learning how to use what you presently know and have in spiritual activities is what devotional service is all about. (We will further explain the process of bhakti-yoga in later chapters and in Volume Two of this series: The Universal Path to Enlightenment.)

There are, of course, certain people in society who have no faith in this knowledge and who feel that the verses we have presented here are simply myths from a bygone era that are not relevant to this day and age. But in *Bhagavad-gita*, we find the foolishness of such an attitude clearly explained:

"But those who, out of envy, disregard these teachings and do not practice them regularly, are to be considered bereft of all knowledge, befooled, and doomed to ignorance and bondage. (*Bg*.3.32). . . My dear Arjuna, a man who does not follow this prescribed Vedic system of sacrifice certainly leads a life of sin, for a person delighting only in the senses lives in vain." (*Bg*.3.16)

This last verse gives an indication that sinful activity is centered around living only to satisfy the senses. When the living being is ignorant of his real identity as spirit soul, he is under the impression that he is the temporary body and that satisfaction of the mind and senses is the goal of life. But this conception is the very cause of our repeated birth and death. "The Supreme Personality of Godhead said: Those who give up these methods of achieving Me, which consist of devotional service, analytic philosophy and regulated execution of prescribed duties, and instead, being moved by the material senses, cultivate insignificant sense gratification, certainly undergo the continual cycle of material existence. (*Bhag*.11.21.1). . . If an ignorant person who has not conquered the material senses does not adhere to the Vedic injunction, certainly he will engage in sinful and irreligious activities. Thus his reward will be repeated birth and death." (*Bhag*.11.3.45)

This points out that the purpose of the Vedic literature is to give the necessary instructions for those interested in attaining the best situation possible for their future. Everyone is struggling to do this anyway by making plans to improve their financial income, career opportunities, living conditions, love life, or so many other areas of their existence. In fact, almost everyone lives in the hope that things are going to get better. But we see that they do not always know exactly how to make things better or what should be done. The Vedic literature is there to provide this information. But as *Bhagavad-gita* further explains: "He who discards scriptural injunctions and acts according to his own whims attains neither perfection, nor happiness, nor the supreme destination." (*Bg*. 16.23)

If one, therefore, performs activities which cater only to the whims of the senses and mind, he will certainly become more and more absorbed in irreligious and degrading behavior. This secures more bad *karma* that one will be forced to endure in another round of birth and death, which can take them further into the lower forms of existence. This is what any intelligent person should try to avoid. "The material body certainly moves under the control of supreme destiny and therefore must continue to live along with the senses and vital air as long as one's *karma* is in effect. A self-realized soul, however, who is awakened to the absolute reality and who is thus highly situated in the perfect stage of yoga, will never again surrender to the material body and its manifold manifestations, knowing it to be just like a body visualized in a dream." (*Bhag*.11.13.37)

"One who is in knowledge of the Absolute Truth, O mighty-armed, does not engage himself in the senses and sense gratification, knowing well the differences between work in devotion and work for fruitive results." (*Bg.*3.28)

"By refraining from a particular sinful or materialistic activity, one becomes freed from its bondage. Such renunciation is the basis of religious and auspicious life for human beings and drives away all suffering, illusion and fear." (*Bhag.* 11.21.18)

From this we can understand that we may have reactions from past activities to experience, but if we are patient and let such conditions caused by our previous fruitive work exhaust themselves while not engaging any further in *karmic* activities, we will become free from this material existence. Then we will be able to reestablish ourselves in our natural spiritual identity. "Thus the knot in the heart is pierced, and all misgivings are cut to pieces. The chain of fruitive actions is terminated when one sees the self as master." (*Bhag.*1.2.21)

This is the sign of one who is free from *karma* and the influence of the various material modes: all misgivings and misidentifications with the body cease to disturb him or her. In such a condition the living entity can see things as they are. "Whenever a person experiences, by self-realization, that both the gross and subtle bodies have nothing to do with the pure self, at that time he sees himself as well as the Lord. If the illusory energy subsides and the living entity becomes fully enriched with knowledge by the grace of the Lord, then he becomes at once enlightened with self-realization and thus becomes situated in his own glory." (*Bhag.*1.3.33-34)

"O great sage, as soon as I [Narada Muni] got a taste of the Personality of Godhead, my attention to hear of the Lord was unflinching. And as my taste developed, I could realize that it was only in my ignorance that I had accepted gross and subtle coverings, for both the Lord and I are transcendental." (*Bhag.*1.5.27)

As one progresses in the practice of yoga and increasingly feels less affected by the material influences, one's fate and destiny also begin to change. *Karmic* reactions that are yet to happen actually become less severe as one engages in the prescribed activities on the path of yoga. By seriously engaging in spiritual practices, our *karma* may become so reduced that we suffer only a fraction of what we had coming to us. For example, it may be our destiny that at some point in time we will suffer a serious leg injury. But because of our spiritual progress our *karma* is minimized so that we suffer only the stubbing of our toe on a chair rather than a broken leg in a car crash. This is confirmed in the *Brahma-samhita* (5.54) where it states: "I adore the Primeval Lord Govinda, Who burns up to their roots all fruitive activities of those who are imbued with devotion and impartially ordains for each the due enjoyment of the fruits of one's activities, of all those who walk in the path of work, in accordance with the chain of their previously performed works. . ."

This is further explained by Lord Krishna: "My dear Uddhava, just as a blazing fire turns firewood into ashes, similarly, devotion unto Me completely burns to ashes sins committed by My devotees." (Bhag.11.14.19)

This is how one's karma can change by the performance of devotional service. Therefore, a bhakti-yogi is under the special protection of the Supreme and is not limited by the material energies which influence and control the life of a karmi (one who, by performing selfish and fruitive activities, accumulates more karma). Thus, by practicing bhakti-yoga, one has every chance of not only becoming free of past karmic reactions without accumulating more karma but also to enter back into direct spiritual existence, which is the actual goal of becoming free from karma as confirmed in the Bhagavatam and Bhagavad-gita.

"Just as gold, when smelted in fire, gives up its impurities and returns to its pure brilliant state, similarly, the spirit soul, absorbed in the fire of bhakti-yoga, is purified of all contamination caused by previous fruitive activities and returns to its original position of serving Me [the Supreme] in the spiritual world." (Bhag.11.14.25)

"Persons who have acted piously in previous lives and in this life, whose sinful actions are completely eradicated and who are freed from the duality of delusion, engage themselves in My service with determination." (Bg.7.28)

"My dear Uddhava, the unalloyed devotional service rendered to Me by My devotees brings Me under their control. I cannot be thus controlled by those engaged in mystic yoga, Sankhya philosophy, pious work, Vedic study, austerity or renunciation. Only by practicing unalloyed devotional service with full faith in Me can one obtain Me, the Supreme Personality of Godhead. I am naturally dear to My devotees, who take Me as the only goal of their loving service. By engaging in such pure devotional service, even the dog-eaters can purify themselves from the contamination of their low birth." (Bhag.11.14.20-21)

"That is the way of the spiritual and godly life, after attaining which a man is not bewildered. Being so situated, even at the hour of death, one can enter into the kingdom of God." (Bg.2.72)

Free from karma and the effects of the material modes of nature, we can easily see our natural spiritual position and the relationship we have with the Supreme. But under the influence of karma, materialists always think of their plans and activities for attaining sensual pleasure. Thus, when they die they are meditating on their bodily desires which force them to take birth in another material body. So an intelligent person meditates on the Supreme at the time of death which is the means for returning back to the spiritual atmosphere. This, therefore, as described in the ancient Vedic texts, is the science of karma and destiny, and the ultimate way to get free from all karma and stop the cycle of reincarnation.

# CHAPTER FIVE (PART B)

## Avoiding Activities
## That Cause Bad Karma

To start making the most of our spiritual progress, we must learn which activities do the most harm to our *karma* and create the heaviest reactions. We have already mentioned that pious or religious activities, as well as actions performed to help others, confer good future results to the performer. These results may be experienced as birth in a rich, aristocratic family, or being beautiful, intelligent, talented, healthy, in a comfortable situation, and so on. From sinful activities one may suffer miserable reactions, such as being sickly, ugly, uneducated, born in a poor family or in a war-torn country, not having enough food to eat, etc. Even on this planet we can see that certain areas are like hell and other areas are like heaven. People may suffer hellish miseries or enjoy heavenly pleasures. Where we get placed depends on our *karma*.

Throughout the Vedic literature, one can find prescriptions for virtuous deeds and warnings against sinful acts. Sinful activities are of different kinds, such as physical, mental, and verbal. The *Manu-samhita* explains: "Coveting the property of others, thinking in one's heart of what is undesirable, and adherence to false (doctrines), are the three kinds of (sinful) mental action. Abusing (others, speaking) untruth, detracting from the merits of all men, and talking idly, shall be the four kinds of (evil) verbal action. Taking what has not been given, injuring (creatures) without the sanction of the law, and holding criminal intercourse with another man's wife, are declared to be the three kinds of (wicked) bodily action. (A man) obtains (the result of) a good or evil mental (act) in his mind, (that of) a verbal (act) in his speech, (that of) a bodily (act) in his body. In consequence of (many) sinful acts committed with his body, a man becomes (in the next birth) something inanimate, in consequence (of sins) committed by speech, a bird or a beast, and in consequence of mental (sins, he is re-born in) a low caste." (*Manu*.12.5-9)

The above information shows the results that can be expected from different impious activities. Thus, if we see someone suffering due to deformity, blindness or any other bodily or mental disorder, it is not just a twist of fate, but there is a cause for it. "Some wicked men suffer a change of their (natural) appearance in consequence of crimes committed in this life, and some in consequence of those committed in a former (existence). Thus in consequence of a remnant of (the guilt of former) crimes are born idiots, dumb, blind, deaf, and deformed men." (*Manu*.11.48-53) In this way, we can see that unwanted conditions in this life are the reactions from the degrading activities in our past lives.

Different parts of the Vedic literature further describe the results which are produced from particular activities. To know this is encouraged by the *Vedas*, because then one understands the seriousness of the law of *karma* from which there is no escape.

"In consequence of attachment to (the objects of) the senses, and in consequence of the non-performance of their duties, fools, the lowest of men, reach the vilest births. What wombs this individual soul enters in this world and in consequence of what actions, learn the particulars of that at large and in due order." (*Manu*.12.52-53)

After this verse in the *Manu-samhita*, there is a long list of the different births one gets due to the performance of certain actions. We will include only the following samples.

"Those who committed mortal sins, having passed during large numbers of years through dreadful hells, obtain, after the expiration of (that term of punishment), the following births. The slayer of a *brahmana* enters the womb of a dog, a pig, an ass, a camel, a cow, a goat, a sheep, a deer, a bird, a *chandala*, and a *pukhasa*." (*Manu*.12.54-55)

"Men who delight in doing hurt (become) carnivorous (animals); those who eat forbidden food, worms; thieves, creatures consuming their own kind; those who have intercourse with women of the lowest caste, *pretas* (ghosts)." (*Manu*.12.59)

Herein, we can see how implicating certain actions can be. What we do in this life can affect us for many lifetimes in the future, not just one or two. How this works is explained: "With whatever disposition of mind (a man) performs any act, he reaps its result in a (future) body endowed with the same quality." (*Manu*.12.81) This means that if we want to enjoy a certain feeling or activity that is not conducive to human behavior, then we may not be fit for human life. Therefore, at the time of death, we could be forced to enter back into a lower species where we may enjoy the activities that are suitable for that particular species of life.

For example, if we are cruel or like to eat meat, then we may take birth as a tiger which enjoys blood by hunting other animals. The tiger may not always be able to catch its prey and may go hungry for days. But when it does catch the creature, the tiger serves as a necessary element in the ecological balance of nature to help prevent overpopulation of various kinds of animals. Nature functions neutrally, and every species of animal has a certain purpose. This is how the different varieties of entities act as suitable servants of nature. Therefore, if we are human beings who act sinfully or without proper human responsibility, then the laws of nature will place us in a lower birth where we will not be such a disturbance to the rest of society. Instead, we will remain as menial servants by acting according to the instincts that are natural to the particular species in which we appear. This is not only a kind of punishment, but also mercy, because if we work out our animalistic propensities while in the subhuman forms, then upon entering the human species we will be able to use it properly. The danger is that, by once entering the lower forms of life, it may be many lifetimes before one sees another human birth. If, however, our activities in this human life are too atrocious and abominable, we will not only take a lower birth but also enter into the hellish planets. Just as we have somehow taken birth on this planet, we can just as easily be born in the hellish planetary systems. It all depends on our *karma*, or what we desire and deserve.

The hellish planets are described in *Srimad-Bhagavatam* (5.26.5) as being located in the intermediate space between the major planetary systems and the Garbhodaka Ocean on the southern side or lower portion of the universe. How one is forced to enter into the hellish planets is described as follows: "The King of the *pitas* [forefathers] is Yamaraja, the very powerful son of the sun-god. He resides in [the planet of] Pitriloka with his personal assistants and, while abiding by the rules and regulations set down by the Supreme Lord, has his agents, the Yamadutas, bring all the sinful men to him immediately upon their death. After bringing them within his jurisdiction, he properly judges them according to their specific sinful activities and sends them to one of the many hellish planets for suitable punishments." (*Bhag.*5.26.6)

With this Vedic evidence of heaven and hell, it is clear that they both exist within this universe. Therefore, existence in either region is temporary. "My dear King Pariksit, in the province of Yamaraja there are hundreds and thousands of hellish planets. The impious people I have mentioned--and also those I have not mentioned--must all enter these various planets according to the degree of their impiety. Those who are pious, however, enter other planetary systems, namely the [heavenly] planets of the demigods. Nevertheless, both the pious and impious are again brought to earth after the results of their pious or impious acts are exhausted." (*Bhag.*5.26.37)

This means that from good *karma* one may go to heaven and from bad *karma* one may go to hell, but when such good or bad *karma* is used up, one again returns to this middle planetary system to start over again. To assure us that we will not be forced to enter a lower birth and to purify ourselves of whatever sinful acts we knowingly or unknowingly commit, "Penances, therefore, must always be performed for the sake of purification, because those whose sins have not been expiated, are born (again) with disgraceful marks." (*Manu.*11.54)

Such penance for purification is based on maintaining control over our senses, body, and mind. This is encouraged in every age and in every religious philosophy and is a goal that everyone, sooner or later, must assert himself toward accomplishing. "That man is called a (true) *tridandin* in whose mind these three, the control over his speech (*vagdanda*), the control over his thoughts (*manodanda*), and the control over his body (*kayadanda*), are firmly fixed. That man who keeps this threefold control (over himself) with respect to all created beings and wholly subdues desires and wrath, thereby assuredly gains complete success." (*Manu*.12.10-11)

"Studying the *Veda*, (practicing) austerities, (the acquisition of true) knowledge, the subjugation of the organs, abstention from doing injury, and serving the Guru are the best means for attaining supreme bliss. (If you ask) whether among all these virtuous actions (there be) one which has been declared more efficacious (than the rest) for securing supreme happiness to man, (the answer is that) the knowledge of the Soul is stated to be the most excellent among all of them; for that is the first of all sciences, because immortality is gained through that. Among those six (kinds of) actions (enumerated above, the performance of) the acts taught in the *Veda* must ever be held to be most efficacious for ensuring happiness in this world and the next." (*Manu*.12.83-86)

This is a partial description of the important process of how people can purify themselves from whatever bad *karma* they have accumulated and attain happiness in their next life. But in this age of Kali, there are four principles especially recommended that must be followed for purification. These are truthfulness, austerity, cleanliness, and mercy. These may seem simple enough, and they certainly are when compared to the rules that yogis and ascetics had to follow years ago. But just to follow these four principles is considered quite an accomplishment for the average person in this age. The reason why is that these relate to the four kinds of activities to which people of this age are most addicted. Therefore, if one can follow these principles, he will make a great amount of spiritual progress, as well as avoid some of the heaviest *karmic* reactions that implicate one in many future rounds of birth and death.


## BEING TRUTHFUL

The first principle is that of truthfulness. Truthfulness means to be honest, open, and straightforward with no lieing, cheating, or stealing. Therefore, the one most important rule to follow to maintain truthfulness is not to gamble. This means not engaging in unnecessary chances with hopes of gaining something cheaply. Gambling includes betting on games or races, being involved in illegal or immoral acts, or even engaging in questionable business ventures. If you win or make a profit, it can feel very nice. But when you start losing your money, you begin to feel intense anxiety. Soon one's mind is totally absorbed in nothing else but scheming to get money by whatever means necessary. In such a situation, you become mentally and emotionally unbalanced, unable to make good judgements, and when you are desparate for money no one can fully trust you. And if you lose all your money or your business goes under, you may also lose your friends. Some people become so distraught when they lose their money or business that they feel suicidal. These situations should be avoided by not gambling or taking unnecessary risks.

By keeping the mind peaceful and being content with what you have earned by an honest means, truthfulness becomes easy to maintain. When you have nothing to hide, you can be truly honest and trustworthy, and then the mind is peaceful, and ready for cultivating spiritual knowledge. If the mind is too agitated with thoughts of questionable ventures, there is no chance that one can feel content or happy, what to speak of developing spiritual consciousness. And engaging in lieing, stealing, or cheating produces detrimental *karmic* reactions that become definite obstacles in one's material or spiritual development.

Truthfulness also means knowing the truth, and the *Vedanta-sutras* explain that the Absolute Truth is the source from which everything else emanates. Therefore, to be truthful, one should know the Ultimate Truth as explained in the *Vedas* and explain this truth to others, allowing everyone to benefit from it.

## PRACTICING AUSTERITY

Austerity means several things. It means, of course, being austere and not always giving in to the dictation of the senses. This is similar to being on a diet when one must not cater to the hankerings of the tongue, but must intelligently distinguish between what is good and what is not good to eat in order to reach the goal, whether it be losing weight or staying healthy. To do this, a person must have some realization that he or she is more than just the body, that he is the consciousness within and can control the senses and tolerate various bodily urges and difficulties without being disturbed. The austerity we speak of also means to be grave, sober, mentally equipoised, and determined to make progress, especially spiritual progress. Association with like-minded people can help one significantly in this regard. The best rule to follow to remain austere is to stay free from intoxicants.

Intoxicants mean anything that disturbs one's normal physical condition and mental stability. These things include drugs, such as cocaine, heroin, L.S.D., marijuana, alcoholic beverages, cigarettes, coffee, etc. The caffein in coffee stimulates the nervous system and can make one feel jittery and on edge and easily agitated. And we all know what damage tobacco does to the body.

Intoxicants definitely cause people to lose their sense of austerity. When a person becomes intoxicated, even to a slight degree, he begins to think more in terms of bodily comforts and adopts the attitude that if it feels good, do it. If a person gets too intoxicated, he may begin to do many reckless things that he normally would not do. Or he may see himself as being better than he really is. The next morning, after a night of getting wasted, he may not even remember what he did the night before. He may be more concerned about simply finding some aspirin to ease his headache.

The use of intoxicants not only gives one bad *karma* for deliberately misusing one's body and mind, but also paves the way for one to do many more foolish acts that will create even worse *karma*. We could discuss many problems people have had due to drug abuse or alcoholism and drunk driving, but we have all heard it before. Generally, people resort to drugs and liquor as a crutch or escape because they cannot handle life as it is. They may want an alternative, but such cheap thrills and kicks simply make things worse as they become more dependent on such a low means of attaining happiness, or attempting to avoid misery. Getting intoxicated causes many reactions which one has to endure, either in this life or in the next.

Some people say that they need certain drugs to help their spiritual awareness, but such spiritual visions that people think they get while on L.S.D. or other psychedelics are not spiritual at all. These drugs may show that different levels of consciousness exist but they cannot actually take you there. It is like looking into the window of a house but not being able to enter. Psyche means mind, and using psychedelics is still a long way from entering into the spiritual strata. Such drug-related experiences take place within the mind or on the subtle level, but do not touch the soul. Therefore, drugs can be a great hindrance for one who wants to progress spiritually because they keep one attracted to remaining on the mental and physical level of consciousness. They can also form a drug dependency, which is dangerous for many reasons. Even though the feeling one gets while intoxicated on certain drugs may fool one into thinking it is a spiritual experience, this is simply an illusion for those who want to be cheated.

Anyone who is trying to progress in this life on a spiritual basis is recommended to undergo the penance and austerity of avoiding all kinds of intoxicants. Of course, if one is not very spiritually advanced, this may seem like a difficult task. But the more progressed people become in their spiritual realizations, the more all forms of intoxication become distasteful. Intoxication of any kind will pose no temptation whatsoever for one who advances in spiritual and inner strength. After all, the word intoxication literally means to poison the body or mind with toxins. What kind of person will remain attracted to that if offered a higher form of pleasure and happiness? Such spiritual happiness is attained by keeping the mind and senses under control, not by catering to their every whim or allowing them to go crazy through intoxication. The more austere one becomes, the more determined he will be, and the obstacles that once used to be major problems will cease to pose any threat. This is the beginning of qualifying oneself to perceive the natural happiness within.

There may be those who take drugs, mushrooms, or peyote buttons in religious rituals, like Shamans. This is much different than ordinary drug abuse. But, nonetheless, it is often used to see what is actually nothing more than another level of material reality. These visions are not spiritual. At best, they are the result of a chemically induced way to make contact with the subtle platform of existence. Yoga is the natural way of spiritualizing oneself, and the more spiritual one becomes the more he will be able to perceive the higher realms of life. But through such Shamanic drug use, a person may come in contact with what is said to be healing spirits, plant spirits, or helpful and harmful beings that one works with for different reasons. This is not a path for everyone and can be quite dangerous if one tries it and does not know what he is doing. Some of the visions can be horrific, and some of the drugs can be so powerful that it may take days to pull out of its effects, what to speak of remembering what actually happened while you were under the drug's influence. Therefore, such drug use cannot be a positive or sure way of understanding the higher aspect of things.

## INNER AND OUTER CLEANLINESS

As the saying goes, cleanliness is next to godliness, and in this regard it does not simply mean keeping your home neat and clean and taking a daily bath. It also means keeping the mind clean and free from useless and dirty thoughts. One cannot remain on a spiritual path, attempting to become free from *karma* while the mind is always devising plans to gratify the senses. And the most intense kind of sense gratification is sex life. For many, the thought of sex is a very big motivating factor. So many songs are written describing the glories of sex. Many activities are based on the prospects of finding someone with whom to enjoy sex. In fact, modern society evolves around this longing for sex.

The problem with this kind of sex meditation is that the more one thinks about it, the more they long to engage in it. Thus, the more firmly one embraces the bodily concept of life. For those who are serious about a spiritual path, such meditation must be brought to a minimum, if not completely avoided. Thinking of sex is not the way to maintain a clean mind or heart. Therefore, a person must control the mind by proper spiritual meditation and by avoiding illicit sex. It is not that one should not engage in any sex at all, but if one must have it, then it is best to get married and raise a decent family in spiritual consciousness. Otherwise, one simply remains like an animal looking to eat, sleep, mate, and defend. Human life begins when one asks himself who he is and starts the search to find out. But if one remains interested only in the animalistic propensities, such as sex, then even though he may be in a human form, he misuses it and is nothing more than a polished, two-legged animal.

In *Bhagavad-gita*, Sri Krishna says: "I am sex life which is not contrary to religious principles." (*Bg*.7.11) Therefore, sex can be utilized in a spiritual way if it is according to religious principles. However, illicit sex, which is outside of marriage, with another man's wife, or for useless purposes such as simply experiencing the tingling sensation of the genitals, carries extremely heavy *karma*, not to mention the many diseases one takes the risk of getting from such frivolous conduct with others. Such diseases are nature's way of warning us to be careful, but many do not listen and various diseases spread throughout society because of this.

Also, when there is illicit sex, there easily can be unwanted children. Unwanted and unloved children grow up in a harsh environment and often develop an equally harsh and cruel mentality. We can easily see this in society today; yet, we also find the cause of it mentioned in *Bhagavad-gita*: "When irreligion is prominent in the family, O Krishna, the women of the family become corrupt, and from degradation of womanhood, O descendent of Vrishni, comes unwanted progeny. When there is increase of unwanted population, a hellish situation is created both for the family and for those who destroy the family tradition." (*Bg*.1.40-41)

"Destroyers of family tradition" refers to those who advocate giving up religious and moral standards for the so-called freedom of engaging in illicit sex and other frivolous activities. Therefore, irresponsible men and leaders who promote sexual promiscuity in society, or try to take advantage of independent women, must also share the consequences of the breakdown in social moral values. "Due to the evil deeds of the destroyers of family tradition, all kinds of community projects and family welfare activities are devastated." (*Bg*.1.42) Therefore, the practice of mental and physical cleanliness will prevent people from becoming implicated in these kinds of problems.

Let us, however, point out that the Vedic teachings never recommended merely repressing sexual desires. This is not very effective because people will always have such desires unless they experience a higher spiritual awakening. Such a higher taste comes from an elevated stage of one's spiritual practice in yoga and in the Vedic process of spiritual self-realization. When one attains this level of consciousness, sensual desires gradually fall away like dead leaves from a tree until the idea of sex pleasure becomes insignificant. Then one easily rises above such base desires. Also, on this platform of spiritual experience, one can enter levels of realization that are beyond the reach of those who remain absorbed in sexuality. Thus, one feels an inner bliss, as described in Chapter Four, that far outweighs what a person may feel from sensual pleasure.

## THE ISSUE OF ABORTION

These days, to help rid themselves of unwanted population or unwanted pregnancies, many use abortion. The *karmic* reaction of having or performing an abortion is an extremely heavy one. In the law of *karma*, whatever pain we cause for others will return to us later on. Even unnecessarily stepping on an ant is noted. If we purposely do harm to a more important and significant creature, such as a growing human embryo, the reaction is very severe.

The law of *karma* does not consider that an abortion was performed because the situation was not right for raising a child, or that the woman was going to college and wanted to finish school and could not afford a baby, or that the marriage was not stable enough, or the mother was only fifteen, or so many other reasons. The law of *karma* only recognizes that a man and woman engaged in sex and at that time must accept the responsibility for whatever consequences might occur. Even if one "responsibly" used birth control which failed and therefore allowed a pregnancy to develop, the couple who engaged in sex is still accountable.

Today, women say that abortion is strictly a women's issue, and that they want to have the right to choose what to do with their body and their future, or whether to be rid of a pregnancy if it is not right for them. Women have been making these kinds of personal decisions for centuries, but perhaps with more freedom now than before. Not much will really change that. If they decide to have an abortion, someone somewhere will be willing to do it. But the point is that the law of *karma* recognizes that before conception takes place, there must be a sexual act or insemination. That is where the choice is made and when the responsibility begins.

Sex is primarily a procreative function. Anyone who does not understand this is incredibly naive or desperately needs some education in this matter. Through intercourse, the couple is inviting a child to come; therefore, the choice to have or not have a child should be made before conception. Thus, no two people should participate in sex unless they are willing to share the responsibility if a child results. Once a child is conceived, the choice is considered to have already been made. If one has no desire for children and does not want or cannot take the obligation of raising and taking care of them, then one should simply control the sex urge. So much trouble is then avoided. And if a person feels too sexually agitated to avoid sex, then practicing yoga and adjusting to a diet with fewer sweets and rich foods are a couple of things that can help solve that problem. Otherwise, using abortion to be free from an unwanted pregnancy that resulted from irresponsible sex is the epitome of selfishness.

Another part of the abortion issue is whether the embryo is actually alive before birth and whether or not it can feel anything. If it is not alive, then there is nothing wrong with having an abortion, or so the logic goes. But science has already proven that the child in the womb is alive. After only a few weeks the embryo has its own heartbeat and brainwaves, which are separate from the mother's. So women may want the right to decide what to do with their bodies, but the child in the womb is also a developing individual with its own body.

A graphic example of this took place in Karstad, Sweden, when Doctor Mats Waktel aborted a fetus no bigger than a large peanut from the womb of 22 year old Else Kallstrom. When the fetus is still so small, it is generally referred to as merely being a piece of human tissue. But in this case, once the fetus was removed from the womb, Doctor Waktel, Else, and several nurses saw the fetus tremble and heard it scream before it was dropped into a bucket of formaldehyde. Else claimed to have been psychologically devastated by the experience, and Doctor Waktel, who had been a strong advocate of abortion and had made a living through the trade for years, vowed never to perform another abortion for the rest of his life. Some people still ignored this proof of life within the womb, such as Eva Hanson of 'Mothers for Mothers, Not Children,' who callously said, "I don't care if that thing did scream, they shouldn't have said a word about it."

Though people may still argue over whether the embryo is alive or not, this is something that has been known for hundreds of years in the East, as described in such early writings as the *Yajur-veda* (12.38-39) which states: "O soul, blazing like the sun, after cremation, having reached the fire and the earth for rebirth, and residing in the belly of thy mother, thou art born again. O soul, having reached the womb, again and again, thou auspiciously liest in thy mother, as a child sleeps in her mother's lap." This shows that the soul is within the womb from the very moment of conception. We can understand, therefore, that if there is no conception, then no soul entered the womb.

The *Bhagavatam* (11.22.47) also explains: "Impregnation, gestation, birth, infancy, childhood, youth, middle age, old age, and death are the nine ages of the body." This means that the body is alive and developing in the womb, as it will continue to develop outside the womb if allowed to be born, because the soul is there.

We also find in the *Yajur-veda* (19.87) that it is the duty of the husband and wife to take care of the child, even if it is still in the womb. "It is incumbent upon both (husband and wife) to give food to their parents and protect the embryo in the womb." Protection of the child in the womb is an obligation, in the Vedic point of view, that must be taken up by both parents.

Furthermore, we should understand that the child can actually feel pain while in the womb. Therefore, the Vedic literature advises that a pregnant woman should care for her child by not eating foods which are too spicy and thereby cause the child to suffer. "Owing to the mother's eating bitter, pungent foodstuffs, or food which is too salty or too sour, the body of the child incessantly suffers pains which are almost intolerable." (*Bhag*.3.31.7)

If the child suffers intolerable pain from spicy food, we can only imagine how it suffers from something like an abortion. This is why the act of having or performing an abortion on a defenseless child in the womb carries such a heavy *karmic* reaction. This act of abortion makes the womb a dangerous place to be found during these modern times because it drastically reduces the chances for a person to get to take birth. The *Mahanirvana Tantra* (Chapter 11, verses 69-70) states: "The woman who causes a miscarriage before the completion of the fifth month, as well as the person who helps her thereto, should be heavily punished. The woman who after the fifth month destroys the child in her womb, and the person who helps her thereto, are guilty of killing a human being." Thus, even in the ancient Eastern texts we see that abortion is considered to be a serious offense to human life, and that after the fifth month, killing the child in the womb is equal to killing a grown person. Of course, materialistic people will employ whatever means they choose to make their life easier and use any argument to justify it. But if the above quote from the Eastern texts is in accord with the universal laws, then all who are trying to follow a moralistic life or a spiritual path will avoid the use of abortion, knowing full well that the *karmic* reaction will follow them into their future existence.

What the actual *karma* is for those who have an abortion is that after death they will be placed in the womb of a mother who will suffer a miscarriage or also have an abortion. Thus, they will experience for themselves what it is like to be tightly packed up in a womb and then miscarried. But they do not go through it just once. After they are miscarried from one womb, the soul will be forced to enter another womb again. For many months they will go on like this and not be allowed to see the light of day. Only after the bad *karma* is exhausted will they be able to enter a womb where they will be allowed to take birth. If they should make the same mistake and have an abortion again, the same bad *karma* is acquired. And if a woman or doctor engages in several or more abortions, their future after death becomes extremely dark. If thousands or even millions of women in a single country have abortions, this infects the whole country with horrible *karma*. We cannot even guess what the reactions will be in a country like Russia, where the average woman has about eight abortions during her life. The least effect is that the country will become a very miserable place to live.

Some people claim that in the case of rape or incest an abortion to end a pregnancy is justified. But how can one wrong justify another? We should know that the cases of pregnancy from rape or incest are extremely few. But if it should happen, we should realize why there is ever a conception in any womb. It is not up to us, but a living being is placed in a womb due to his or her destiny, as confirmed in *Srimad-Bhagavatam* (3.31.1): "The Personality of Godhead said: Under the supervision of the Supreme Lord and according to the result of his work, the living entity, the soul, is made to enter into the womb of a woman through the particle of male semen to assume a particular type of body."

From this we can realize that whenever there is a conception in the womb, it is because a living entity was meant to be born by that mother and fulfill its destiny in a certain body. The pregnancy then is no "accident." It was meant to be. But if we assume the position of God and decide to terminate the pregnancy, then we also make it difficult for that living being to live out its own particular fate and evolutionary growth and development. If we cannot take care of the child, then we can still remain merciful enough to allow it to be born and then give it up for adoption. In that case, the baby can still grow and develop and fulfill its destiny according to its *karma*. The child may be adopted by a loving family, and the real mother can see the child's growth and not be so severely implicated in the heavy *karma* that she would otherwise obtain if she had had an abortion.

In this way, people should understand the risks and the *karma* involved if they insist on engaging in illicit sex or having abortions. By understanding the law of *karma* and the science of the soul, such issues can more easily be resolved.

## SEX OR NO SEX

From the more spiritual point of view, especially for those who are practicing a spiritual path, it is advised that they should avoid sex as much as possible. To engage in sex, a person must lower his or her consciousness down to the bodily concept of life. In other words, you have to see yourselves as this body, which you are trying to satisfy, in order to have sex at all. Otherwise, how will you be aroused? But if you see the reality of the situation, that this body is but a smelly skin bag of blood, guts, and bones, with a soul inside which is transcendental to the body and is the real identity of the individual, then you will lose interest in trying to have sex. In this way, one who is making some spiritual progress will see that sex is, basically, a distraction from the goal.

It is especially advised for men who are practicing yoga or who are serious about spiritual enlightenment to avoid sex and not pass semen any more than necessary. In fact, if one can stay celibate, that is best. If the semen is retained in the body, one can develop great strength, strong will, determination, and good memory. Unfortunately, in modern civilization, it is generally considered that the more ways you can pass semen, the more successful and happier you will be. But we have seen that from frequent sex, men often can become weak-minded, apathetic, and lose their moral character, energy, as well as their physical endurance and health.

Semen or *shukra* is also known as *virya*, or vital essence. This vital essence is not only in the reproductive organs but pervades the entire body and radiates what is known as the bodily lustre or aura. When retained, this *virya* gives strength, courage, and determination, and the loss of it brings the opposite qualities, such as weakness, cowardice, and scattered intelligence. Therefore, the *Ayur-veda* stresses that a man should retain his semen, as does also the *Atharva-veda* (19.26.1-2): "The life-prolonging semen, which is produced by *jathragni* bodily temperature, is maintained in the mortal bodies through and through. He who knows the importance of it, does deserve it and who keeps it intact, attains to long, long old age before he dies. O soul, the semen produces the radiance and splendour, (due to well-protected semen) having the beauty and glow like the Sun, which the men, who have gone before you, were able to attain. That very semen will produce in you the pleasant glory. He who bears it, attains to long life."

In the *Yajur-veda* (11.84) we also find the warning that excessive discharge of semen causes harm to the body, whereas retaining the semen increases one's duration of life. In fact, many yogis in the East have lived up to three hundred or even seven hundred years simply by voluntarily retaining the semen. The more one is addicted to sexual enjoyment, the more he decreases his longevity. Therefore, retaining the semen is always recommended for those situated on the spiritual path, as confirmed in the *Atharva-veda* (2.35.1): "The yogis, who live for the purity of the soul, full of noble thoughts, preserve the precious semen for the body, that it may last for a hundred years, so I, thy preceptor, O pupil, advise thee to preserve it for longevity, glory, strength, and a long life of a hundred autumns."

Further elaboration on this is found in the *Ayur-veda*, which states that the body is built and sustained by the elements of the body which are formed from the food we eat. With the help of the heat energies in the body, the *sapta-agnis*, each element converts itself into the next element. For instance, the usable portion of food, when digested, forms lymph, which then also forms blood. These combine and form muscle. This process continues in the following order: first there is lymph, then blood, muscle, fat, marrow, bone, and finally semen or ovum. Semen contains a combination of all the other elements. Therefore, when excessive semen is lost through unrestricted sex, all the other bodily elements are also depleted.

For example, if from 100 c.c. or 1 lb. of food we get 10 c.c. of lymph, 5 c.c. of blood, 3 c.c. of muscle, 2 c.c. of fat, 1 c.c. of marrow, .5 c.c. of bone, and .25 c.c. of semen, then it will take 60 lbs. of food and 4 lbs. of blood to replenish the loss if through ejaculation we lose 20 c.c. of semen. This takes time. Therefore, by continuing to pass semen, we are constantly taxing the body of its other elements. This causes various parts of the body to deteriorate faster than necessary.

We can use another example. Say we own a nice big house. If, however, we take a sledge hammer and begin knocking down some of the inside walls, the supports, braces, and foundation, even though it looks good on the outside, it will not take long before it begins to fall apart. This is what happens to the inside of the body from excessive loss of semen. So, from an excessive loss of semen a man may become more easily susceptible to disease and rapid aging.

Even though we quote many verses from the *Vedas*, the Bible also has some very good advice, as found in the following verses:

"It is my [Paul's] opinion,then, that in a time of stress like the present this is the best way for a man to live--it is best for a man to be as he is (celibate)... If, however, you do marry, there is nothing wrong in it; and if a virgin marries, she has done no wrong. But those who marry will have pain and grief in this bodily life, and my aim is to spare you... I want you to be free from anxious care. The unmarried man cares for the Lord's business; his aim is to please the Lord. But the married man cares for worldly things; his aim is to please his wife; and he has a divided mind. The unmarried or celibate woman cares for the Lord's business; her aim is to be dedicated to Him in body as in spirit; but the married woman cares for worldly things; her aim is to please her husband. In saying this I have no wish to keep you on a tight rein. I am thinking simply of your own good, of what is seemly, and of your freedom to wait upon the Lord without distraction." (*I Corinthians* 7.25-26,28,32-35)

"...The disciples said to him, 'If that is the position with husband and wife, it is better not to marry.' To this he replied, 'That is something which not everyone can accept, but only those for whom God has appointed it. For while some are incapable of marriage because they were born so, or were made so by men, there are others who have themselves renounced marriage for the sake of the kingdom of Heaven. Let those accept it who can.'" (*Matthew* 19.10-12)

"Fornication and indecency of any kind, or ruthless greed, must not be so much as mentioned among you, as befits the people of God... no one given to fornication or indecency, or the greed which makes an idol of gain, has any share in the kingdom of Christ and of God." (*Ephesians* 5.3)

"Agree together, my friends, to follow my [Paul's] example. You have us for a model; watch those whose way of life conforms to it. For as I have often told you, and now tell you with tears in my eyes, there are many whose way of life makes them enemies of the cross of Christ. They are heading for destruction, appetite is their god, and they glory in their shame. Their minds are set on earthly things." (*Philippians*.3.17-19)

"I [Jesus] say unto you, that whosoever looketh on a woman to lust after her hath committed adultery with her already in his heart." (*Matthew* 5.32)

"For this is the will of God, even your sanctification, that ye should abstain from fornication: that everyone of you should know how to possess his vessel [body] in sanctification and honor." (*I Thessalonians* 4.3-4))

## SHOWING MERCY AND BEING VEGETARIAN

The fourth principle that one must follow in the endeavor to be free from acquiring bad *karma* and for spiritual advancement is being merciful. Mercy means more than just being nice. Mercy means being kind to all living entities, not just to humans, but also to animals, birds, insects, etc. This is because the living entity, depending on its consciousness, can take a material body in any one of the 8,400,000 species of life. Therefore, to develop and maintain the quality of mercy, one must follow the principle of no meat-eating. This includes no eating of meat, fish, eggs, or insects. This way, those who are serious about a spiritual path remain free from so many unnecessary *karmic* reactions.

It is stated that meat-eating is actually the grossest form of ignorance. To kill other living entities for the pleasure of the tongue is a cruel and selfish activity which requires one to be almost completely blind to the spiritual reality of the living being. It also causes one to remain hard-hearted and less sensitive to the concern for the well-being and feelings of others.

As previously explained, according to the law of *karma*, whatever pain we cause for others we will have to suffer in the future. Therefore, a wise man does not even want to harm an insect, what to speak of slaughtering an animal in order to taste blood. The sinful reaction for animal slaughter is received by six kinds of participants, which include, (1) the killer of the animal, (2) one who advocates or advertises meat-eating, (3) one who transports the meat, (4) one who handles or packages the meat, (5) one who prepares or cooks the meat, and (6) one who eats it.

The sinful reaction shared by these six participants in animal slaughter is very severe. In fact, the Bible compares the killing of cows to murdering a man: "He that killeth an ox is as if he slew a man." (*Isaiah* 66.3) It is also explained in the *Sri Caitanya-caritamrta*,(*Adi-lila*, Chapter 17, verse 166): "Cow killers are condemned to rot in hellish life for as many thousands of years as there are hairs on the body of the cow." An intelligent person will try to avoid this fate.

The cow and bull are very important to human civilization. Until the recent invention of the tractor, the bull was used for helping to cultivate fields for producing food, and the cow has always supplied milk for human consumption. Milk is important and a moderate supply of it in our diet provides the proper nutrients for developing a good brain for understanding spiritual topics. From milk one can make many other foods that are used in thousands of recipes that we all appreciate, such as cheese or curd, yogurt, kefir, butter, ghee, ice cream, and so on. This means that, according to the *Vedas*, the cow is one of our mothers and the bull is like a father for the benefit they have done for society. To do outright harm to such creatures is considered extremely serious.

I have heard many people criticize India for not slaughtering its cows. Uncultured tourists talk about how there would be no more starving children if they would just eat the cows. For one thing, I have traveled all over India and have seen no more hungry people there than here in America. For another thing, cows are one of India's greatest resources. They produce food, fuel, and power. Bullocks do as much as two-thirds of the work on the average farm. They help plow the fields, hall produce, and turn the presses. For India to convert to machinery to do these tasks would cost as much as 20 to 30 billion dollars. For a country like India, that is out of the question and a waste of time and money.

The cows also supply up to 800 tons of munure each year for fuel. Cow dung gives a slow even heat, good for cooking. Using coal for cooking would cost 1.5 billion dollars a year. And besides, believe it or not, cow dung kills bacteria and is antiseptic. And keeping cows is cheap since they eat things like wheat stuble, husks, and rice straw, which people cannot use.

So why raise cattle for meat consumption when it takes seven times more acreage for a pound of beef than a pound of milk? Only four to sixteen pounds of flesh food is produced for every hundred pounds of food eaten by cattle. Ten to twenty tons of nutritive vegetable food can be produced from the same amount of land that can produce only one ton of beef. In one year, you can get much more protein from a cow in the form of milk, cheese, etc., than in the several years it takes for a cow to mature enough to produce meat. To produce one pound of wheat takes 25 gallons of water, whereas one pound of beef requires 2500 gallons. And water is not always a plentiful resource in countries like India. Obviously, using agricultural resources for meat production is nothing but wasteful.

Furthermore, if we are so concerned about the starving people in the world and the environment we live in, then let us consider the fact that 60 million more people in the world could be fed if Americans reduced their meat consumption by only 10%. Plus, an estimated 216,000 acres of rainforest is lost every day in various countries, and it is said that 50% of that is directly linked to raising cattle for meat production. And though 76% of Americans consider themselves concerned about the environment, only 2.8% are vegetarians. Many Americans may say they love animals, but they still eat them on a regular basis. Obviously, they need to raise their consciousness about this. In any case, there are many books on the market that present this type of environmental information much more thoroughly.

Some readers may say, however, that the sacrifices in the early Vedic literature prescribed animal slaughter. But this is refuted by Sri Caitanya Mahaprabhu in the *Caitanya-caritamrita*, (*Adi-lila*, Chapter 17, verses 159-165):

"The *Vedas* clearly enjoin that cows should not be killed. Therefore any Hindu, whoever he may be, does not indulge in cow killing. In the *Vedas* and *Puranas* there are injunctions declaring that if one can revive a living being, he can kill it for experimental purposes. Therefore the great sages sometimes killed old animals, and by chanting Vedic hymns they again brought them to life for protection. The killing and rejuvenation of such old and invalid animals was not truly killing but an act of great benefit. Formerly there were great powerful *brahmanas* who could make such experiments using Vedic hymns, but now, because of Kali-yuga, *brahmanas* are not so powerful. Therefore the killing of cows and bulls for rejuvenation is forbidden. 'In this age of Kali, five acts are forbidden: the offering of a horse in sacrifice, the offering of a cow in sacrifice, the acceptance of the [renounced] order of *sannyasa*, the offering of oblations of flesh to the forefathers, and a man's begetting children in his brother's wife.' Since you Mohammedans [and others] cannot bring killed animals back to life, you are responsible for killing them. Therefore you are going to hell; there is no way for your deliverance."

This quotation makes it perfectly clear how anyone who paticipates in killing other living beings is responsible for such acts which cause one to attain a hellish future. We mentioned the *karmic* reactions for killing the cow, but the *karmic* results one acquires from killing other entities is to suffer a similar pain or die in a similar way. Whatever you do unto others will later return to you, either in this life or in a future life. For every action there is an equal and opposite reaction. That is the law of *karma*.

We can now begin to understand how dark the future is for someone who owns or manages something like a hamburger or fried chicken stand. Not only is he responsible for the animals that are killed, cooked, and then sold by his business, but he is also responsible for those he hires to help with it.

For example, let us say there is a Sergeant Fowler who starts a country fried chicken outlet, and he calls it Sergeant Fowler's Country Fried Chicken. He hires people to help operate it and finds where he can get good deals on dead chickens which he fries and sells to customers. His business picks up, and he starts establishing a chain of stores. He hires more people, does national advertising, and sells franchises. All the people involved, from the hired help to the people doing the advertising, are implicated and responsible in the activity of creating a big business of selling dead chickens to people who eat them. The people who are eating them, however, might have been satisfied eating something else. But due to the convenience or the advertising, they have become convinced that Sergeant Fowler's Country Fried Chicken is the way to go.

Of course, no one cares about the chickens. But they are often times grown in quarters so cramped that they cannot move properly, and they peck at each other and suffer diseases. One such disease is airsacculitis, a pneumonia-like disease in which pus-laded mucus collects in the lungs. The lungs are cleaned with air suction guns which cause the lungs to burst, allowing the pus to seep into the meat. The government allows such chickens to be sold.

When the chickens are taken for slaughter, they are hung upside down and their throat is sliced to drain the blood. While sometimes only half-dead, they are scalded in boiling water and then defeathered and prepared for butchering and shipment. The low standards of the slaughter houses, which often overlook federal regulations, result in the shipment of carcasses that may have been laying on the floor for some time and contaminated with rodent feces, cockroaches, dirt, and rust. The chickens Sergeant Fowler buys for his stores are only a small percentage of the more than 3 BILLION birds slaughtered every year in America, along with 134 million other mammals.

There are, of course, people who say one has to eat meat to get enough protein. Animal flesh may be a source of protein but a poor source of vitamins, minerals, and carbohydrates. They overlook the fact that plenty of protein is found in such foods as beans, nuts, rice, corn, whole wheat, and diary products, like milk and cheese. Also, one palmful of raw almonds (which is approximately ten) can give one as much protein as found in a half-pound of meat and is much more easily assimilated by the body. The meat that is eaten is not always fully digested since humans, who are considered herbivores, produce stomach acid less than one-twentieth as strong as that found in carnivores. Carnivores also have an intestinal tract only three times their body length to allow rapidly decaying meat to pass out quickly. Humans have an intestinal tract 12 times their body length. Therefore, a part of a corpse will take longer to pass through and quickly becomes putrid, creating many poisonous wastes within the body. Such toxins will put an added strain on kidneys and increase the chances of cancer and high blood pressure. This is why for cancer of the colon or high blood pressure, most doctors recommend no intake of red meat.

Meat-eating also increases saturated fats in the body that cause an accumulation of fatty deposits in the walls of the arteries. This raises the potential for problems such as heart attacks, hardening of the arteries, and strokes. This does not include all the chemicals used with meat that greatly increase the chances of disease in the body, especially when combined with such things as alcohol, beer, wine, or tabacco.

Unfortunately, not too many people think about these things and Sergeant Fowler's business keeps right on prospering. But as time goes on, this successful entrepreneur grows old, diseased, and finally dies. He has arranged his dead-chicken-selling empire very nicely and it will continue for many years after he is long gone. By this time, Sergeant Fowler's Country Fried Chicken outlets all advertise that several million chickens are slaughtered and sold every year, all due to the hard work of Sergeant Fowler. But now he is no longer around to enjoy the profits and has gone to meet his fate.

It is too bad that Sergeant Fowler did not know about the law of *karma*, because he will bear most of the responsibility for all the chickens that have been killed, as well as the millions of chickens that will continue to be killed in the future because of the business he started. According to the law of *karma*, to suffer for the pain he has caused to be inflicted on others, he will be born and be similarly slaughtered innumerable times. In such a case, it is impossible to know when he will ever see another human birth. His fate and the fate of others like him is extremely dark.

The only time when the eating of meat may be considered is when it is an emergency and there is absolutely nothing else to eat in order to stay alive. Otherwise, there is no reason to eat meat when so many other kinds of food are readily available. This is why the *Manu-samhita* recommends that, "Meat can never be obtained without injury to living creatures, and injury to sentient beings is detrimental to the attainment of heavenly bliss; let him therefore shun the use of meat. Having well considered the disgusting origin of flesh and the cruelty of fettering and slaying corporeal beings, let him entirely abstain from eating flesh." (*Manu*.5.48-49)

"He who permits the slaughter of an animal, he who cuts it up, he who kills it, he who buys or sells meat, he who cooks it, he who serves it up, and he who eats it, must all be considered as the slayers of the animal. There is no greater sinner than that man who though not worshipping the gods or the ancestors, seeks to increase the bulk of his own flesh by the flesh of other beings. (*Manu*.5.51-52). . . As many hairs as the slain beast has, so often indeed will he who killed it without a (lawful) reason suffer a violent death in future births. (*Manu*.5.38). . . By subsisting on pure fruit and roots, and by eating food fit for ascetics in the forest, one does not gain so great a reward as by entirely avoiding the use of flesh. Me he [*mam sah*] will devour in the next world, whose flesh I eat in this life; the wise declare this to be the real meaning of the word 'flesh' [*mam sah*]. (*Manu*.5.54-55). . . He who injures harmless creatures from a wish to give himself pleasure, never finds happiness in this life or the next." (*Manu*.5.45)

"He who desires to augment his own flesh by eating the flesh of other creatures, lives in misery in whatever species he may take his birth. (*Mahabharata, Anu*.47.116). . . The purchaser of flesh performs violence by his wealth; he who eats flesh does so by enjoying its taste; the killer does violence by actually tying and killing the animal. Thus, there are three forms of killing. He who brings flesh or sends for it, he who cuts off the limbs of an animal, and he who purchases, sells, or cooks flesh and eats it--all these are to be considered meat-eaters. (*Mahabharata, Anu*.115.40). . . The sins generated by violence curtail the life of the perpetrator. Therefore, even those who are anxious for their own welfare should abstain from meat-eating." (*Mahabharata, Anu*.115.33)

## BIBLICAL QUOTATIONS ABOUT MEAT-EATING

The Bible also has many quotations against meat-eating as can be seen from the following: "But flesh with the life thereof, which is the blood thereof, shall ye not eat. And surely your blood of your lives will I require; at the hand of every beast will I require it." (*Genesis* 9.4-5) Certainly we can see in this verse that no one was meant to live by eating the flesh and blood of others. If one did so, then he would have to pay with his own blood, as it says, "your blood of your lives will I require." This is merely a reference to the law of *karma*: for every animal who suffers because of you, you will also similarly suffer: "at the hand of every beast will I require it."

"To what purpose is the multitude of your sacrifices unto me? Saith the Lord: I am full of the burnt offerings of rams, and the fat of fed beasts; and I delight not in the blood of bullocks, or of lambs, or of goats. When ye spread forth your hands, I will hide Mine eyes from you: yea, when ye make many prayers, I will not hear, for your hands are full of blood." (*Isaiah* 1.11,15)

"It shall be a perpetual statute for your generations throughout all your dwellings, that ye eat neither fat nor blood. (*Leviticus* 3.17). . . And whatsoever man there be of the house of Israel, or of strangers who sojourn among you, that eateth any manner of blood; I will even set My face against that soul that eateth blood." (*Leviticus* 17.10)

From these verses and others not included here, we can certainly see that God's law, as set down in the Bible, was against the eating of flesh and blood and the killing of other entities. However, there are some people who try to legitimize the eating of meat by draining the blood and, thus, make the meat "kosher." Of course, this idea is completely absurd. Blood permeates meat, so how can one be free from eating blood by trying to drain it from the flesh? This is not very realistic, and it certainly does not free one from the violence that must be inflicted on the animal when it is killed in order to eat its flesh. The real point of the matter is not to kill. This is clearly stated in *Exodus* (20.13) in the Hebrew *lo tirtzach*, which, when accurately translated, means "thou shalt not kill."

There are a few verses, however, which I am sure some students of the Bible will reach for that seem to support the eating of flesh. But in every case, this is due to inaccurate translations as we shall see.

For example, in *John* (4.8) it states: "For his disciples were gone away unto the city to buy meat." The word *meat* was taken from the Greek word *trophe*, which actually means *nourishment*. This is exactly the same case in *Acts* (9.19): "And when he had received meat, he was strengthened." When translated accurately it means that by receiving nourishment, he felt stronger.

In *Luke* (8.55) we find, "And her spirit came again and she arose straightaway: and he (Jesus) commanded to give her meat." The word *meat* in this case was translated from the Greek word *phago*, which translated correctly simply means *to eat*.

In *I Corinthians* (8.8) it states: "But meat commendeth us not to God, for neither, if we eat, are we the better; neither if we eat not, are we the worse." The word for *meat* here is *broma*, which actually means *food*. Therefore, this verse signifies that eating or not eating food has little to do with our relationship to God and not, as some people think, that eating meat holds no wrong.

In *Romans* (14.20-21) the verses are: "For meat destroy not the word of God. All things indeed are pure; but it is evil for that man who eateth with offence. It is good neither to eat flesh, nor to drink wine, nor anything whereby thy brother stumbleth, or is offended, or is made weak." The word for *meat* here is *broma*, which actually means *foods*, and the word for *flesh* is *kreas*, which does mean *flesh*. Therefore, this verse makes it clear that flesh eating is unacceptable.

If the Bible explains that eating meat is wrong, then what is the proper thing to eat? *Genesis* (1.29) clearly states: "And God said, Behold, I have given you every herb bearing seed, which is on the face of all the earth, and every tree, in which is the fruit of a tree yielding seed; to you it shall be for meat." This makes it quite obvious that the food for human beings is herbs, seeds, grains, and fruits.

We also find in *Isaiah* (7.14-15): "Therefore the Lord Himself shall give you a sign; Behold, a young woman shall conceive, and bear a son, and shall call his name Immanuel. Butter and honey shall he eat, that he may know to refuse the evil, and choose the good." The first verse is often quoted by Christians for proof that Jesus was the saviour, but the next verse shows that he will be a vegetarian to know the difference between right and wrong.

As mentioned earlier, meat-eating is a sign of spiritual ignorance and tends to keep one from developing compassion and mercy towards our fellow living entities. To be merciful only to man and yet be an enemy to animals by killing and eating them is Satan's philosophy. One will never live in true harmony with God while performing such activities. This is often overlooked by the Christians, Muslims, and others. If these verses were actually understood and the meaning fully realized and practically applied by the Christians and others, I am sure it would bring beneficial reactions the world over in their spiritual development. After all, one of the ten commandments specifically says thou shalt not kill.

In *Bhagavad-gita*, however, we also find similar verses on what is recommended for human consumption. Lord Krishna says, "If one offers Me with love and devotion a leaf, a flower, fruit or water, I will accept it." (*Bg.*9.26) This means that not only should one be a vegetarian and eat only fruits, water, grains, vegetables, etc., but such items should be made as an offering to God with love. The reason is that, "The devotees of the Lord are released from all kinds of sins because they eat food which is offered first for sacrifice. Others, who prepare food for personal sense enjoyment, verily eat only sin." (*Bg.*3.13)

As further elaborated in *Bhagavad-gita* by Lord Sri Krishna: "O son of Kunti, all that you do, all that you eat, all that you offer and give away, as well as all austerities that you may perform, should be done as an offering unto Me. In this way you will be freed from all reactions to good and evil deeds, and by this principle of renunciation you will be liberated and come to Me." (Bg.9.27)

As the *Vedas* explain, what we eat is an important factor in the process of purifying ourselves and remaining free from accumulating bad *karma*. It actually is not so difficult to be vegetarian, and it gives one a much higher taste in eating and in one's spiritual realization. For those of you who would like to learn more about what a vegetarian diet can do for you and how to cook vegetarian meals easily, there are plenty of books available to help you get started. Or write to me for additional information.


## KARMA OF THE NATION

The *Manu-samhita* (8.304-309) describes how a king or ruler of a country receives one sixth of the total *karma* of the subjects he rules. If the majority of people are pious and spiritually oriented, and the ruler protects those citizens to maintain a peaceful society in which such people can flourish, then the king will also share in the good activities and good *karma* of the citizens. Otherwise, if the ruler does not properly protect and maintain the citizens but allows criminals to run loose and create havoc, while still collecting taxes from the people, the overall *karma* will be extremely dark. Such a ruler will take upon himself the foulness of his countrymen and sink into hell.

From this description, we can see that if the ruler is so much affected by the total *karma* of the citizens of the country, then the nation itself fosters its future according to the good or bad activities of the citizens. So whatever reactions this country will endure in its future, whether it be harvests of plenty, good economy, or starvation from famine and drought, or victory over our enemies or destruction from war, depends on the way we live today.

History has noted many countries and civilizations in the past who, although seeming to be so powerful while living a frivolous, decadent, and spoiled lifestyle, finally met their doom. Such a downfall was usually quite unexpected at the time. However, by understanding the law of *karma*, such a collapse can be fairly predictable. We can see this in the analysis of the Roman Empire.

The last great civilization in the West was the Roman Empire, of which historians have noted five characteristics that helped cause that great society to fall apart. First, there was a love of show and luxury. Everyone was eager to acquire material things as a sign of affluence. This also helped cause the second factor, which was a widening gap between the very rich and the very poor.

The third factor was a complete obsession with sex. In the latter days of the Roman Empire, sex became the sole interest, whether in ordinary conversations, or in art, culture--everything. Pompeii was a big resort for this kind of licentious living and sex. (And we all know of the earthquake in A.D. 69 that damaged Pompeii, and then the volcanic eruptian in A.D. 79 that finally buried it.)

A fourth factor in the downfall of the Roman Empire was a freakishness and abandonment in the arts which masqueraded and pretended to be originality. This can easily be found now in modern art, music, sculpture, etc.

The fifth factor was the creation of the welfare state and the increasing desire amongst the people to live off the government. Even today, there are places where anyone can get welfare and not have to work, and with more sex, the more children that are born, which entitles the welfare recipient to more money.

We should carefully regard these points and take note of where our modern American Empire stands because history repeats itself. We find an increase in these same things here in the United States. For example, almost all advertising nowadays evolves around the idea of having or getting sex appeal, no matter whether it is in buying a car, or buying anything that people are told they need, or attaining a successful career. And it does not take much to figure out why everyone wants sex appeal. So the present times merely reflect attitudes and changes that have taken place before, as in the Roman Empire.

For example, modern philosophy, whether in sociology, psychology, art, politics, the sciences, etc., usually presents the idea that there is no absolute law or standard. In other words, whatever turns you on, do it; whatever you believe in, it's O.K. There is no absolute, and anyone who thinks there is becomes regarded as a fanatic. Similarly, in the Roman Empire, there was no emphasis on God or faith in moral standards. There were many denominations, but the attitude was anyone could believe anything he wanted. But those who were serious about their religion were severely persecuted.

In the case of the Christians, they were thrown to the lions in the amphitheaters as a spectator sport. The people would watch in the stands and applaud the utter brutality of it all. One reason for this was that the Christians refused to accept the Roman gods. They believed in only one God as a pure, infinite being who set down the law, which if not followed would cause one to go to hell. Romans accepted gods who drank wine, ate meat, had sex, and so on. Therefore, Romans looked on Christians as if they were fanatics. This is the same way modern philosophers, politicians, and liberals today look at people who seem to be overly dedicated to a law of God, such as the law of *karma*. Rather than understanding the law of *karma*, such people would rather criticize it and simply carry on with their frivolous and whimsical habits, while remaining ignorant of the consequences.

We should point out, however, that *karma* is not a belief system but is a science. One may believe that he can do whatever he wants and that there is no jail house, but if he acts like a criminal and gets caught and thrown into confinement, then he will be forced to adjust his thinking and face the results of his activities. Similarly, people may think they can escape the universal laws and do whatever they like, but when they are forced by the law of *karma* to face their destined punishments after death, it will be too late.

When we see, therefore, that people in certain areas of the country are suffering from drought, that farmers cannot grow their crops, that fires are consuming vast forests and destroying homes, that storms are causing destruction and devastation to cities and towns, or incurable diseases are affecting more and more people all the time, we should not miss the message. It is easy to ask ourselves, "Why has God done this to me?" and try to put the blame on someone else. But why should such reversals in life not happen to us? What have we done to avoid it? Usually nothing. Therefore, we must understand how the law of *karma* affects everyone.

When we stop to consider that as many as 134 million animals and 3 billion birds are slaughtered every year, and hundreds of thousands more are tortured and killed for useless scientific experiments, is it any wonder why there should not be a heavy reaction to the cries of pain from so many innocent living beings as they are butchered in order to satisfy mankind's thoughtless cravings? Everyone wants to be happy and live in peace, but how can this be peace when so many other entities suffer from the most painful experiments in so-called scientific laboratories, or are methodically killed each day at slaughterhouses so that their corpses can be sold in supermarkets? But it is not just commercial enterprises that do this but also the government. In 1986, the Office of Technology Assessment reported that 84% of all painful animal experimentation is carried out by the military. The In Defense of Animals group also stated that of 22 military bases, 83,389 animals were used in 1987, and 142,735 in 1988, of which pain was used in 99% of the experiments on dogs, 81% on cats, and 43% on primates. Therefore, when society in general has such a cruel and callous attitude towards other living entities, or are too wasteful in regards to the planet's natural resources, or live a decadent lifestyle, nature arranges reactions in various ways, one of which is in the form of wars. From time to time we all have to watch as we ship our young men and women off to be killed or maimed in the slaughterhouse of war. As long as there are large numbers of innocent animals being unnecessarily killed and tortured day after day throughout the year, there will never be peace for long, for war will always exist somewhere, in which we will be forced to become involved. But war also means war in the family, such as discontent, arguments, separation, and divorce; war in the community, such as gang wars, crime, robberies, murders, and rape; and industrial and economic wars as well as international wars and terrorism. These reactions affect many millions of people every day and *it is nothing more than the workings of nature as it reflects the consciousness of the people who inhabit this world.*

When the majority of people in a country are influenced by commercialism and addicted to the previously mentioned four most *karmically* implicating activities--meat-eating, intoxication, illicit sex, and gambling--there will definitely be reactions to endure in the future. This is the universal law. There is no amount of economic planning, defense buildup, agricultural arrangement, or even weather forecasting that will help us to avoid unexpected *karmic* reactions. If the ruler of a country receives one-sixth of the aggregate good or bad *karma* of the citizens, then the citizens themselves will also experience the reactions that the country is destined to receive, as arranged by nature.

By understanding the law of *karma* and abiding by the four principles which are especially recommended for this age--namely, truthfulness, cleanliness, austerity, and mercy--the people of this country will surely become strong, develop good moral character, be concerned for the welfare of all others, acquire a sound state of mind, and will attain a great destiny like no other country in the world. We all want to make this country and this world a better place, and there is a method which will enable us to do that, which we are revealing in this book. But we must understand that there is more to it than the obvious plan-making that goes on amongst our politicians, economic advisors, judiciaries, etc. There is the subtle aspect that goes on and is determined by the decisions and activities of each and every individual. Therefore, those who take the time to understand the law of *karma* and try to abide by it can certainly be understood to be people who are working for a better future, not only for themselves, but for a better America and, indeed, for a better world.

# CHAPTER SIX

# *The Modes of Nature: Determining Your Future Existence*

In the last chapter, there were several references to the modes of material nature. So now, I will explain what they are. There are three modes, called *gunas*. One is the mode of goodness, *sattva-guna*; one is the mode of passion, *raja-guna*; and the other is the mode of ignorance or darkness, called *tama-guna*. By understanding the modes of nature, we can realize in which mode we are situated and, thus, determine what our next existence is likely to be. Most books on spiritual topics do not include anything about these modes. That is generally because the authors do not know anything about them. Only by studying the Vedic literature can one understand what the modes of nature are. Therefore, I am including a chapter on the subject because understanding the modes of material nature and how they work is an integral part of comprehending how the laws of *karma* and reincarnation affect us. And since the readers of this book are going to be far superior in their spiritual understanding than the reader of the average occult book, it is necessary to give a full elaboration on the topic. Therefore, in this chapter, you will learn what the modes are, how they influence us, how to recognize them, and how to get free from these forces that compel us to act in particular ways.

## WHAT THE MODES OF NATURE ARE

First of all, let us understand that no one in the material atmosphere is free from the modes of nature, as stated in *Bhagavad-gita*: "There is no being existing, either here or among the demigods in the higher planetary systems, which is freed from the three modes of material nature." (*Bg*.18.40)

These material modes manifest within one's mind and are always in competition with each other. According to a person's activities, we can

115

understand his state of mind as well as by which particular mode he is being influenced. "Material nature consists of the three modes--goodness, passion and ignorance. When the living entity comes in contact with nature, he becomes conditioned by these modes. The mode of goodness, being purer than the others, is illuminating, and it frees one from all sinful reactions. Those situated in that mode develop knowledge, but they become conditioned by the concept of happiness. The mode of passion is born of unlimited desires and longings, and because of this one is bound to material fruitive activities. The mode of ignorance causes the delusion of all living entities. The result of this mode is madness, indolence, and sleep, which bind the conditioned soul. Sometimes the mode of passion becomes prominent, defeating the mode of goodness. And sometimes the mode of goodness defeats passion, and other times the mode of ignorance defeats goodness and passion. In this way there is always competition for supremacy." (Bg.14.5-8,10)

From this description, we can begin to recognize the fact that the mind, which is the center of our senses and an instrument that operates on the material platform, is what creates the illusion of our material happiness and distress due to the influence of the modes of nature. As stated in Srimad-Bhagavatam: "Rather, it is the mind alone that causes happiness and distress and perpetuates the rotation of material life. The powerful mind actuates the functions of the material modes, from which evolve the different kinds of material activities in the modes of goodness, ignorance, and passion. From the activities in each of these modes develop the corresponding statuses [one's position or species] of life." (Bhag.11.23.42-43)

What this means is that by embracing the mind and body as being our real identity, we become subjected to the control of the modes of material nature. From this, we are practically forced to engage in the struggle of trying to attain our likes and avoid our dislikes. This is the materialistic occupation of the living entity which keeps one bound to the cycle of birth and death. Therefore, whatever material activity we decide to engage in is our choice of which mode or combination of modes with which we will associate. It is this choice which determines our status in this life and the next.

How the living entity identifies with the body and then engages in bodily activities which cause one to undergo various reactions is explained in the following verses: "The material senses create material activities, either pious or sinful, and the modes of nature set the material senses into motion. The living entity, being fully engaged by the material senses and modes of nature, experiences the various results of fruitive work. As long as the living entity thinks that the modes of material nature have separate existences, he will be obliged to take birth in many different forms and will experience varieties of material existence. Therefore, the living entity remains completely dependent on fruitive activities under the modes of nature." (Bhag.11.10.31-32)

In this way, the living being experiences the good or bad results of his past activities, which were instigated by the influence of the material modes. In other words, as long as we are absorbed in materialistic activities, we are just like puppets being controlled and motivated by the strings of the modes of material nature that influence us to act in particular ways or take birth in particular species of life. Although one may think he is free to act in any way he chooses to accomplish various goals, in reality these activities are simply the maneuverings of the modes of nature in accordance with one's past *karma*. *Bhagavad-gita* confirms this: "The bewildered spirit soul, under the influence of the three modes of material nature, thinks himself to be the doer of activities which are in actuality carried out by nature." (*Bg*.3.27)

In the material world, we may think we are free to choose what we will do, but our freedom is limited to choosing only which combination of material modes with which we will relate. Therefore, due to the mode of goodness, someone may become a clean and healthy person, searching for higher aspects of life. Due to the mode of passion, a person may become a workaholic, desiring to achieve fame, fortune, and distinction. Due to the mode of ignorance, another person may become a lazy drunkard who simply feels sorry for himself for not attaining the success which he feels life owes him. In this way, we create our destiny and are forced to face the consequences of the choices we make depending on the modes with which we decide to associate.

Real free will means to be free from the binding forces of the modes of material nature which affect the way we see things and how we make our choices through life. We, therefore, must understand how the modes work, how to recognize their influence on us, and the process to get free from them.

## HOW THE MODES OF NATURE WORK

Besides affecting the individual, the modes also have particular influences over the whole universe. The Vedic literature establishes that during the creation of the material world the time element agitates the modes, which thus pro˙ ices past, present, and future, or creation, maintenance, and annihilation c˙ the world. This is explained as follows: "Nature exists originally as the equilibrium of the three material modes, which pertain only to nature, not to the transcendental spirit soul. These modes--goodness, passion, and ignorance--are the effective causes of the creation, maintenance, and destruction of this universe. In this world the mode of goodness is recognized as knowledge, the mode of passion as fruitive work, and the mode of darkness as ignorance. Time is perceived as the agitated interaction of the material modes, and the totality of functional propensity is embodied by the primeval *sutra* or *mahat tattva* (total material energy)." (*Bhag*.11.22.12-13)

The effects that the modes have can also be seen through the unfolding of history. "With the increase of the mode of goodness, the strength of the demigods similarly increases. When passion increases, the demoniac become strong. And with the rise of ignorance, O Uddhava, the strength of the most wicked increases." (Bhag.11.25.19) Therefore, just as a change of wind direction brings a change of weather, time brings changes in the influence of the modes of nature, causing various types of people, civilizations, ideas, or styles of art and music, etc., to become at first dominant in society and to again recede. What was popular and acceptable at one time, may be the reverse later on because of a change in the predominating modes of nature.

Whatever we are inclined to do on a material or bodily basis can be recognized as the effects of interacting with the modes. This is pointed out in Srimad-Bhagavatam (11.25.30-31): "Therefore material substance, place, result of activity, time, knowledge, work, the performer of work, faith, state of consciousness, species of life and destination after death are all based on the three modes of material nature. O best of human beings, all states of material being are related to the interaction of the enjoying soul and material nature. Whether seen, heard of, or only conceived within the mind, they are without exception constituted of the modes of nature."

To recognize the modes and how they influence us, further elaboration is given in Srimad-Bhagavatam (11.25.2-18): "Mind and sense control, tolerance, discrimination, sticking to one's prescribed duty, truthfulness, mercy, careful study of the past and future, satisfaction in any condition, generosity, renunciation of sense gratification, faith in the spiritual master, being embarrassed at improper action, charity, simplicity, humbleness and satisfaction within oneself are qualities of the mode of goodness.

"Material desire, great endeavor, audacity, dissatisfaction even in gain, false pride, praying for material advancement, considering oneself different and better than others, sense gratification, rash eagerness to fight, a fondness for hearing oneself praised, the tendency to ridicule others, advertising one's own prowess and justifying one's actions by one's strength are qualities of the mode of passion.

"Intolerant anger, stinginess, speaking without scriptural authority, violent hatred, living as a parasite, hypocrisy, chronic fatigue, quarrel, lamentation, delusion, unhappiness, depression, sleeping too much, false expectations, fear and laziness constitute the major qualities of the mode of ignorance. Now please hear about the combination of these three modes.

"My dear Uddhava, the combination of all three modes is present in the mentality of 'I' and 'mine.' The ordinary transactions of this world, which are carried out through the agency of the mind, the objects of perception, the senses and the vital airs of the physical body, are also based on the combination of the modes. When a person devotes himself to religiosity, economic development and sense gratification, the faith, wealth and sensual enjoyment obtained by his endeavors display the interaction of the three modes of nature. When a man desires sense gratification, being attached to family life, and when he consequently becomes established in religious and occupational duties, the combination of the modes of nature is manifest. A person exhibiting qualities such as self-control is understood to be predominantly in the mode of goodness. Similarly, a passionate person is recognized by his lust, and one in ignorance is recognized by qualities such as anger.

"Any person, whether man or woman, who worships Me [Sri Krishna] with loving devotion, offering his or her prescribed duties unto Me without material attachment, is understood to be situated in goodness. When a person worships Me by his prescribed duties with the hope of gaining material benefit, his nature should be understood to be in passion, and one who worships Me with the desire to commit violence against others is in ignorance.

"The three modes of material nature--goodness, passion and ignorance--influence the living entity but not Me. Manifesting within his mind, they induce the living entity to become attached to material bodies and other created objects. In this way the living entity is bound up. When the mode of goodness, which is luminous, pure and auspicious, predominates over passion and ignorance, a man becomes endowed with happiness, virtue, knowledge and other good qualities. When the mode of passion, which causes attachment, separation and activity, conquers ignorance and goodness, a man begins to work hard to acquire prestige and fortune. Thus in the mode of passion he experiences anxiety and struggle. When the mode of ignorance conquers passion and goodness, it covers one's consciousness and makes one foolish and dull. Falling into lamentation and illusion, a person in the mode of ignorance sleeps excessively, indulges in false hopes, and displays violence toward others.

"When consciousness becomes clear and the senses are detached from matter, one experiences fearlessness within the material body and detachment from the material mind. You should understand this situation to be the predominance of the mode of goodness, in which one has the opportunity to realize Me.

"You should discern the mode of passion by its symptoms--the distortion of the intelligence because of too much activity, the inability of the perceiving senses to disentangle themselves from mundane objects, an unhealthy condition of the working physical organs, and the unsteady perplexity of the mind.

"When one's higher awareness fails and finally disappears and one is thus unable to concentrate his attention, his mind is ruined and manifests ignorance and depression. You should understand this situation to be the predominance of the mode of ignorance."

By studying these explanations, we can distinguish by which mode we are being influenced. We can also understand that the individual spirit soul is above the modes, but as long as one identifies with the mind, where the modes manifest, and remains on the material platform, one continues being controlled by the various combinations of these modes. This, along with one's past *karma*, is how one continues in the cycle of birth and death and remains attached to material objects and activities. "Due to this external energy, the living entity, although transcendental to the three modes of material nature, thinks of himself as a material product and thus undergoes the reactions of material miseries." (*Bhag*.1.7.5)

How the modes of nature and the law of *karma* work together can be explained through this example. Say that according to one's *karma*, a person is meant to be very successful, with a good career, nice beautiful wife, lovely children, a big house, and fancy cars, etc. Then at one point in life his *karma* dictates that many reversals will take place in his career. When this happens, he may make some bad decisions. Somehow the owners of the business he works with relieve him of his job. Thus, he also loses his money and his career is ruined. It affects his marriage, and the beautiful happy home he once had now becomes a depressing place of misery.

In this situation, he has no control over his *karma* or destiny. He is going to face some reversals in his career and that is all there is to it. At this point, he will suffer due to being affected by the modes of passion and ignorance. But how much he is affected is up to him. He has free choice in how he handles the situation. He may become depressed for a little while and then decide to pull out of it and look for ways he can improve his life. Or he may fall deep into the mode of ignorance and feel he should get revenge for being fired from his job.

In whatever way he handles the situation, it is up to his own free choice. But once he makes his choice, the modes take over either to help him get past the hurdle and carry on, or to get revenge. In this way, he is independent and decides for himself whether to associate with the mode of goodness, passion, or ignorance. But by being enlightened with knowledge of how the modes affect us, and by controlling our mind by our intellect, we can have better command over our lives and remain on a progressive and upward path, no matter what may happen to us. No matter what our *karma* may be, we have to remember that it is not what happens to us but how we react to it that makes the difference.

## ACTION AND CONSCIOUSNESS IN VARIOUS MODES

By now you probably understand that our consciousness, viewpoint, attitude, desires, and the outcome of those all depend on how we interact with the modes of nature. By studying the following descriptions of the kind of work, faith, knowledge, sacrifices, austerities, food, and happiness that are found in the three modes of material nature, we can understand which of the modes affect us the most. Depending on which mode or combination of modes in which we are situated determines our whole outlook on life and the kind of results we can expect to attain. We can also analyse the activities of our friends to understand in which modes they are situated and what results are likely to take place in their lives, along with what affect their association is likely to have on us.

## Action and Work

"As for actions, that action in accordance with duty, which is performed without attachment, without love or hate, by one who has renounced fruitive results, is called action in the mode of goodness. But action performed with great effort by one seeking to gratify his desires, and which is enacted from a sense of false ego, is called action in the mode of passion. And that action performed in ignorance and delusion without consideration of future bondage or consequences, which inflicts injury and is impractical, is said to be action in the mode of ignorance.

"The worker who is free from all material attachments and false ego, who is enthusiastic and resolute and who is indifferent to success or failure, is a worker in the mode of goodness. But that worker who is attached to the fruits of his labor and who passionately wants to enjoy them, who is greedy, envious and impure and moved by happiness and distress, is a worker in the mode of passion. And that worker who is always engaged in work against the injunction of the scripture, who is materialistic, obstinate, cheating and expert in insulting others, who is lazy, always morose and procrastinating, is a worker in the mode of ignorance." (*Bg*.18.23-28)

## Residence

"Residence in the forest is in the mode of goodness, residence in a town is in the mode of passion, residence in a gambling house or [similar places such as bars, racetracks, brothels, etc.] displays the quality of ignorance, and residence in a place where I [the Supreme, or Deity of the Supreme] reside is transcendental." (*Bhag*.11.25.25)

## Faith

"Faith directed toward spiritual life is in the mode of goodness, faith rooted in fruitive work is in the mode of passion, faith residing in irreligious activities is in the mode of ignorance, but faith in My devotional service is purely transcendental." (*Bhag*.11.25.27)

## Understanding

"O son of Pritha, that understanding by which one knows what ought to be done and what ought not to be done, what is feared and what is not to be feared, what is binding and what is liberating, that understanding is established in the mode of goodness. And that understanding which cannot distinguish between the religious way of life and the irreligious, between action that should be done and action that should not be done, that imperfect understanding is in the mode of passion. That understanding which considers irreligion to be religion and religion to be irreligion, under the spell of illusion and darkness, and strives always in the wrong direction is in the mode of ignorance." (*Bg*.18.30-32)

### Knowledge

"That knowledge by which one undivided spiritual nature is seen in all existences, undivided and divided, is knowledge in the mode of goodness. That knowledge by which a different type of living entity is seen to be dwelling in different bodies is knowledge in the mode of passion. And that knowledge by which one is attached to one kind of work as the all in all, without knowledge of the truth, and which is very meager, is said to be in the mode of darkness." (*Bg*.18.20-22)

### Sacrifices

"Of sacrifices, that sacrifice performed according to duty and to scriptural rules, and with no expectation of reward, is of the nature of goodness. But that sacrifice performed for some material end or benefit or performed ostentatiously, out of pride, is of the nature of passion. And that sacrifice performed in defiance of scriptural injunctions, in which no spiritual food is distributed, no hymns are chanted and no remunerations are made to the priests, and which is faithless--that sacrifice is of the nature of ignorance." (*Bg*. 17.11-13)

### Austerities

"The austerity of the body consists in this: worship of the Supreme Lord, the *brahmanas*, the spiritual master, and superiors like the father and mother. Cleanliness, simplicity, celibacy and nonviolence are also austerities of the body. Austerity of speech consists in speaking truthfully and beneficially and in avoiding speech that offends. One should also recite the *Vedas* regularly. And serenity, simplicity, gravity, self-control and purity of thought are the austerities of the mind. This threefold austerity, practiced by men whose aim is not to benefit themselves materially but to please the Supreme, is of the nature of goodness. Those ostentatious penances and austerities which are performed in order to gain respect, honor and reverence are said to be in the mode of passion. They are neither stable nor permanent. And those penances and austerities which are performed foolishly by means of obstinant self-torture, or to destroy or injure others, are said to be in the mode of ignorance." (*Bg*. 17.14-19)

### Charity

"The gift which is given out of duty, at the proper time and place, to a worthy person, and without expectation of return is considered to be charity in the mode of goodness. But charity performed with the expectation of some return, or with a desire for fruitive results, or in a grudging mood, is said to be charity in the mode of passion. And charity performed at an improper place and time and given to unworthy persons without respect and with contempt is charity in the mode of ignorance." (*Bg*.17.20-22)

## Foods

"Food that is wholesome, pure and obtained without difficulty is in the mode of goodness, food that gives immediate pleasure to the senses is in the mode of passion, and food that is unclean and causes distress is in the mode of ignorance." (*Bhag.*11.25.28)

"Foods in the mode of goodness increase the duration of life, purify one's existence and give strength, health, happiness and satisfaction. Such nourishing foods are sweet, juicy, fattening and palatable. Foods that are too bitter, too sour, salty, pungent, dry and hot, are liked by people in the modes of passion. Such foods cause pain, distress and disease. Food cooked more than three hours before being eaten, which is tasteless, stale, putrid, decomposed and unclean, is food liked by people in the mode of ignorance." (*Bg.*17.8-10)

## Happiness

"Now please hear from Me about the three kinds of happiness which the conditioned soul enjoys, and by which he sometimes comes to the end of all distress. That which in the beginning may be just like poison but at the end is just like nectar and which awakens one to self-realization is said to be happiness in the mode of goodness." (*Bg.*18.36-37)

This refers to happiness in connection with spiritual practices which may not always seem like they cater to the pleasure of the senses, for which our mind is always craving. Following rules and regulations for spiritual advancement sometimes appears difficult. But as we become more advanced, our taste for spiritual practices increases and the happiness found therein becomes unlimited. Whereas the happiness found in enjoying our senses seems very pleasurable at first, in the end, after repeating such acts many times, it becomes distasteful, as confirmed in the following verse:

"That happiness which is derived from contact of the senses with their objects and which appears like nectar at first but poison at the end is said to be of the nature of passion. And that happiness which is blind to self-realization, which is delusion from beginning to end and which arises from sleep, laziness and illusion is said to be of the nature of ignorance." (*Bg.*18.38-39)

"Happiness derived from the self is in the mode of goodness, happiness based on sense gratification is in the mode of passion, and happiness based on delusion and degradation is in the mode of ignorance. But that happiness found within Me is transcendental." (*Bhag.*11.25.29)

The following verses from the *Manu-samhita* further elaborate on which activities reflect the qualities of particular modes:

"When a man having done, doing or being about to do any act, feels ashamed, the learned may know that all such acts bear the mark of the quality of Darkness (ignorance)." (*Manu.*12.35)

This kind of act also depends on one's conscience. If a person has no moral training, then he may do anything and never feel any shame or remorse. If such is the case, we can understand that his consciousness is in the mode of ignorance, like that of an animal.

"But when a man desires to gain by an act much fame in this world and feels no sorrow on failing, know that it bears the mark of the quality of Activity (passion). But that bears the mark of the quality of Goodness which with his whole heart he desires to know, which he is not ashamed to perform, and at which his soul rejoices. The craving after sensual pleasures is to be the mark of Darkness, the pursuit of wealth the mark of Activity, and the desire to gain spiritual merit the mark of Goodness; each later named quality is better than the preceeding one." (*Manu.* 12.36-38)

## WHERE THE MODES TAKE US

After reading the descriptions of how the modes of material nature work and affect us, and in which of the modes various activities are situated, it is now time to find out what our destination is by associating with these modes.

The point is that by performing various material activities that are closely linked to the modes of nature, our consciousness and existence will develop accordingly. For example, as the *Bhagavad-gita* explains: "The manifestations of the mode of goodness can be experienced when all the gates of the body are illuminated by knowledge. When there is an increase in the mode of passion, the symptoms of great attachment, uncontrollable desire, hankering, and intense endeavor develop. When there is an increase in the mode of ignorance, madness, illusion, inertia and darkness are manifested." (*Bg.* 14.11-13)

How we can begin to increase or decrease the effects the modes of nature have on us can be understood by studying the previous descriptions of actions in the modes and then adjusting our lifestyle accordingly. For instance, if we live in a hotel with a bar and topless nightclub, and eat food that has been cooked by low-class and unclean people, and drink liquor and spend our time gambling and going through the emotions of anger, attachment, lamentation, moroseness, etc., as we win or lose at the betting games, then this will submerge us deep into the mode of ignorance. Thus, we will be obliged to suffer the necessary consequences of anxiety, disease, and short duration of life that accompany the lifestyle in that mode.

On the other hand, if we live a peaceful life in the country, breathing the fresh air and eating ripe fruits and vegetables, working only as necessary to maintain ourselves while engaged with proper faith and understanding in spiritual pursuits, then we will certainly be in the mode of goodness and experience the uplifting results. This is pointed out in *Bhagavad-gita*: "By acting in the mode of goodness, one becomes purified. Works done in the mode of passion result in distress, and actions performed in the mode of ignorance result in foolishness." (*Bg*.14.16)

As we continue through life, we develop habits that may last for many years. This certainly has a great bearing on our mind and consciousness at the time of death. This is very important to understand, because when we die in a particular mode, as can be discerned by our thoughts and activities, we are thus given the immediate effect. "When one dies in the mode of goodness, he attains to the pure higher planets. When one dies in the mode of passion, he takes birth among those engaged in fruitive activities; and when one dies in the mode of ignorance, he takes birth in the animal kingdom. (*Bg*.14.14-15). . . Those situated in the mode of goodness gradually go upward to the higher planets; those in the mode of passion live on the earthly planets; and those in the mode of ignorance go down to the hellish worlds." (*Bg*.14.18)

"Made to wander as the reaction of his fruitive work, the conditioned soul, by contact with the mode of goodness, takes birth among the sages or demigods. By contact with the mode of passion he becomes a demon or human being, and by association with the mode of ignorance he takes birth as a ghost or in the animal kingdom. Just as one may imitate persons whom one sees dancing and singing, similarly the soul, although never the doer of material activities, becomes captivated by material intelligence and is thus forced to imitate its qualities." (*Bhag*.11.22.52-53)

The *Manu-samhita* gives more specific information on the destination of one who dies in any of the material modes.

"But know this threefold course of transmigration that depends on the three qualities to be again threefold; low, middling, and high, according to the particular nature of the acts and of the knowledge of each person. Immovable beings [such as plants], insects both great and small, fishes, snakes, tortoises, cattle and wild animals, are the lowest conditions to which the quality of Darkness heads. Elephants, horses, *shudras*, and despicable barbarians, lions, tigers and boars are the middling states caused by the quality of Darkness. Caranas, Suparnas [a class of great birds], and hypocrites, Rakshashas [demons who eat human flesh and can assume many forms] and Pishacas [evil demons who are often invisible and can possess people] belong to the highest rank of conditions among those produced by Darkness.

"Ghallas, *mallas* [wrestlers and jesters], *natas* [actors], men who subsist by despicable occupations and those addicted to gambling and drinking form the lowest order of conditions caused by Activity (passion). Kings and *kshatriyas* [warriors], the domestic priests of kings, and those who delight in the warfare of disputations constitute the middling rank of the states caused by the mode of Activity. The Gandharvas [angel-like beings], the Guhyakas [spirits with luminous bodies who exercise their powers from secret places], and the servants of the gods, likewise the Apsaras [heavenly dancing girls], belong to the highest rank of conditions produced by Activity." (*Manu*.12.41-47)

"Hermits, ascetics, *brahmanas*, the crowds of the Vaimanika deities [those who move in the air on their chariots], the lunar mansions, and the Daityas [the giants who were descendants of Diti] form the first and lowest rank of the existences caused by Goodness. Sacrificers, the sages, the gods, the [personified] *Vedas*, the heavenly lights, the years, the *manes* [ancestors], and the Sadhyas [semi-divine celestial beings or intermediate gods], constitute the second order of existences caused by Goodness. The sages declare Brahma, the creators of the universe, the law, the Great One [Supreme Lord], and the Undiscernible One [Paramatma or Supersoul] to constitute the highest order of beings produced by Goodness. Thus the result of the threefold action, the whole system of transmigration which consists of three classes, each with three subdivisions, and which includes all created beings, has been fully pointed out." (*Manu.* 12.48-51)

Of course, this description is not complete in detailing all the various species of life within the universe or the conditions one attains as a result of associating with particular material modes. However, one can definitely see that living entities will raise or lower themselves according to their involvement with the modes of nature. This is made clear in *Srimad-Bhagavatam* (11.25.21-22): "Learned persons dedicated to Vedic culture are elevated by the mode of goodness to higher and higher positions. The mode of ignorance, on the other hand, forces one to fall headfirst into lower and lower births. And by the mode of passion one continues transmigrating through human bodies. Those who leave this world in the mode of goodness go to the heavenly planets, those who pass away in the mode of passion remain in the world of human beings, and those dying in the mode of ignorance must go to hell. But those who are free from the influence of all modes of nature come to Me [the Supreme]."

As long as we are engaged in activities or involved with ideas that are affected by any of the modes of material nature, we will continually transmigrate from one situation to another within this enclosed, cosmic creation. It is similar to a penitentiary or correctional facility. We may be locked up in a big jail cell or a small cell, one with a television or without, or serve as a cook or in making license plates. But whatever the case, we are still in jail. Likewise, as long as we remain influenced by the modes of material nature, we will never experience the freedom outside the material energy. We will always be forced to accept the good or bad results given to us by our *karma* according to the modes with which we associate.

## BECOMING FREE FROM THE MODES

By recognizing which modes are affecting us from the qualities of our acts and thoughts, we can understand what kind of future life we are creating for ourselves. And by understanding the law of *karma*, we can know what sort of reactions we may enjoy or suffer. Therefore, it becomes obvious how important it is to learn the process of becoming free from the modes of material nature.

The advantage of becoming free from the material modes is explained in *Bhagavad-gita*: "When the embodied being is able to transcend these three modes, he can become free from birth, death, old age and their distresses and can enjoy nectar even in this life." (*Bg*.14.20)

Being born, working hard for so many things, only to grow old, diseased, and finally die is certainly not something to which we happily look forward. So, who would not be interested in learning a way to avoid these unwanted miseries? According to *Bhagavad-gita*, there certainly is a way to be free from these distresses, and the process is to transcend the modes. So, how do we do this?

This question was also asked by Arjuna five thousand years ago to Lord Krishna. "Arjuna inquired: 'O my dear Lord, by what symptoms is one known who is transcendental to those modes? What is his behavior? And how does he transcend the modes of nature?' The Blessed Lord said: 'He who does not hate illumination, attachment and delusion when they are present, nor longs for them when they disappear; who is seated like one unconcerned, being situated beyond these material reactions of the modes of nature, who remains firm, knowing that the modes alone are active; who regards alike pleasure and pain, and looks on a clod, a stone and a piece of gold with an equal eye; who is wise and holds praise and blame to be the same; who is unchanged in honor and dishonor, who treats friend and foe alike, who has abandoned all fruitive undertakings--such a man is said to have transcended the modes of nature. One who engages in full devotional service, who does not fall down in any circumstance, at once transcends the modes of material nature and thus comes to the level of Brahman.'" (*Bg*.14.21-26)

Actually, in our present stage of life, it is our duty to become free of the material modes because only in this human form do we have the ability to do so. "Therefore, having achieved this human form of life, which allows one to develop full knowledge, those who are intelligent should free themselves from all contamination of the modes of nature and engage exclusively in loving service to Me." (*Bhag*.11.25.33)

Getting free from the modes is a scientific process that is meant for everyone. The system for arranging society, according to the *Vedas*, is to provide the facility for all people to elevate themselves from whatever their situation is to a higher level of existence. This means raising oneself from the mode of ignorance or passion to at least the mode of goodness. "One must conquer the modes of passion and ignorance by developing the mode of goodness, and then one must become detached from the mode of goodness, by promoting oneself to the platform of *sudha sattva* [the transcendental platform of pure goodness]. All this can be automatically done if one engages in the service of the spiritual master with faith and devotion. In this way one can conquer the influence of the modes of nature." (*Bhag*.7.15.25)

In the mode of goodness, one can begin to understand spiritual knowledge very easily. But in our search for spiritual progress, we must have a teacher or spiritual master to guide us and give us transcendental knowledge. By accepting such guidance from a bonafide and pure spiritual representative, one can swiftly conquer the modes of nature, even the mode of material goodness, and reach pure goodness, the transcendental, spiritual atmosphere.

In this way, by the practice of yoga and following the instruction of the spiritual master, one may remain aloof from material activities by being fixed on the spiritual platform. Thus, one avoids acting within the modes. "A person fixed in transcendental knowledge is freed from conditioned life by giving up his false identification with the products of the material modes of nature. Seeing these products as simply illusion, he avoids entanglement with the modes of nature, although constantly among them. Because the modes of nature and their products are simply not real, he does not accept them." (Bhag.11.26.2)

Being fixed in spiritual consciousness, one no longer transmigrates after death to the destinations acquired by those who are influenced by the modes of nature. "O gentle Uddhava, all these different phases of conditioned life arise from work born of the modes of material nature. The living entity who conquers these modes, manifested from the mind, can dedicate himself to Me by the process of devotional service and thus attain pure love for Me." (Bhag.11.25.32)

"As soon as irrevocable loving service is established in the heart, the effects of nature's modes of passion and ignorance, such as lust, desire and hankering, disappear from the heart. Then the devotee is established in goodness, and he becomes completely happy." (Bhag.1.2.19)

Once we are free from the modes, we will be able to engage in our natural, spiritual activities. This is the kind of freedom for which we are always hankering. We never like to be detained or limited in our pursuits for happiness, but in material life we experience all kinds of problems or responsibilities with which we do not necessarily want to deal. Therefore, Sri Krishna explains that, "A wise sage, free from all material association and unbewildered, should subdue his senses and worship Me. He should conquer the modes of passion and ignorance by engaging himself only with things in the mode of goodness. Then, being fixed in devotional service, the sage should also conquer the material mode of goodness by indifference toward the modes. Thus pacified within his mind, the spirit soul, freed from the modes of nature, gives up the very cause of his conditional life and attains Me." (Bhag.11.25.34-35)

Of course, there may be those who do not agree with this analysis, but their disagreements are simply further proof of their interaction with the modes of nature. For example, there may be philosophers and scientists who try to understand how things go on in this world. But as long as they are controlled by the modes of nature or the universal laws, they will never get a clear understanding of how they work. It is like trying to analyze the cause of a fire while being blinded by the smoke. You must first be free from the smoke to see the fire clearly. That is why Lord Krishna explains, "When philosophers argue, 'I don't choose to analyze this particular case in the same way as you have,' it is simply My own insurmountable energies [the modes] that are motivating their analytic disagreements. By interaction of My energies different opinions arise. But for those who have fixed their intelligence in Me, controlling the senses, differences of perception disappear, and consequently the very cause for argument is removed." (*Bhag.*11.22.5-6)

Once the dualities in material vision, caused by the modes of nature, are removed, the Absolute Truth can be perceived, and by experiencing the Absolute, all reasons for argument are eliminated. Thus, one can understand what reality is and be completely satisfied within himself. The process of devotional service, *bhakti-yoga*, to the Supreme Lord has been described as the process which removes the influence of the modes of nature and which invites the Lord to reveal Himself to the living entity. This state of perfection is described by Lord Krishna in *Srimad-Bhagavatam* (11.25.36): "Freed from the subtle conditioning of the mind and from the modes of nature born of material consciousness, the living entity becomes completely satisfied by experiencing My transcendental form. He no longer searches for enjoyment in the external energy, nor does he contemplate or remember such enjoyment within himself."

This, therefore, is real freedom from the modes of material nature by which one is able to be released from further entrapment in *karma* and the cycle of repeated births and deaths.

# CHAPTER SEVEN

# Heaven And Hell
# And the Basic
# Structure of the Universe

The last few chapters have explained how a person can attain a good or bad future according to the kinds of activities that he or she performs. It was mentioned that people can attain heaven or hell in consequence to their actions. This is due to a combination of *karma* that a person has acquired and from the particular modes of material nature with which one has decided to associate. But what exactly are heaven and hell? Is heaven a place where we can eternally enjoy life with everyone we ever knew and loved? Is hell a place where we suffer eternal damnation for having made the mistake of not living life the way some people believe we should? Or are we given only one chance in this lifetime to attain heaven or be condemned to eternal hell? Or is it all just a state of mind?

A lot of people have many misconceptions about what heaven and hell are. Most fundamentalists agree that living a sound religious life to attain heaven is the highest goal. But to set things straight, we have to have a detailed description of what heaven and hell are, and this kind of knowledge can easily be found in the Vedic literature.

First of all, the Vedic writings agree that this earthly planetary system is the middle planetary system in the universe. From here one can go up to the heavenly planets or down into the hellish planets. The universe is composed of a total of fourteen planetary systems, and just as we have taken birth on this planet earth, we can qualify ourselves by our activities to take birth in any of the lower or higher planetary regions. To get a better idea of how this takes place, we should first understand where heaven and hell are located within this universe.

## THE BASIC UNIVERSAL STRUCTURE

To begin with, it is explained that the material cosmic creation is like a cloud within a corner of the unlimited spiritual sky. Within this cloud there are unlimited universes. Each universe is enclosed by a shell of the material elements, making the interior completely dark except for the light of the sun. The *Srimad-Bhagavatam* (3.11.41) explains: "The layers of elements covering the universes are each ten times thicker than the one before, and all the universes clustered together appear like atoms in a huge combination."

This indicates that if we were to travel to the dark outskirts of the universe, we would run into a shell of earth that encircles the universe. The thickness of this shell would be ten times thicker than the universe is wide. After that would be a layer of water ten times thicker than the layer of earth. Then there are layers of fire, air, ether, mind, intelligence, and false ego. Of course, the form of the elements in these layers is more subtle than what we normally find on this planet. The interior of the universe is very small in comparison to the layers of elements which encircle it. Obviously, therefore, no one can ever get out of this universe by means of any mechanical arrangement or material perfection.

The sun is situated in the central part of the universe, according to Vedic literature. As described in *Srimad-Bhagavatam* (5.20.43-46): "The sun is situated in the middle of the universe, in the area between Bhurloka and Bhuvarloka [planetary systems], which is called *antariksha*, outer space. . . The sun planet divides all the directions of the universe. It is only because of the presence of the sun that we can understand what the sky, the higher planets, this world and the lower planets are. It is also only because of the sun that we can understand which places are for material enjoyment, which are for liberation, which are hellish and subterranean. All living entities, including demigods, human beings, animals, birds, insects, reptiles, creepers and trees, depend upon the heat and light given by the sun-god from the sun planet. Furthermore, it is because of the sun's presence that all living entities can see, and therefore he is called *drig-isvara*, the Personality of Godhead presiding over sight."

The Vedic texts often describe the various planets as *dvipas* or *varshas*, which mean islands or shelters for many living entities within the great ocean of space. Each planet is arranged differently with its own climate, features, wonders, and completely equipped with the necessities for its particular kind of inhabitants. It is described in the *Padma Purana* that there are 8,400,000 species of life and each species has its dwelling in a particular kind of environment found on the various planets. Some species live in water, some in air, some in and on the earth, and others in heat or fire. Therefore, it should be no wonder that other planets are inhabited, as it is described in the *Vedas*, whether we can perceive such life or not with our blunt material senses and instruments.

This earth planet, situated in the middle planetary system, is called Bharata-varsha or Jambudvipa. The *Srimad-Bhagavatam* (5.20.3-42) describes six other major islands above Jambudvipa. These are Plaksadvipa and then Salmalidvipa. Above that is Kusadvipa, or the moon planet. Beyond Kusadvipa is Krauncadvipa which has a width of 12,800,000 miles. The island of Sakadvipa, the planet of the pious, is next whose inhabitants practice *pranayama* and mystic yoga, and in trance worship the Supreme Lord in the form of Vayu.

The next planet is Puskaradvipa or Brahmaloka, which is 51,200,000 miles in diameter and is surrounded by an ocean of very tasteful water. On this planet is a great lotus flower with 100,000,000 pure golden petals, as effulgent as the flames of fire. That lotus is considered the sitting place of Lord Brahma, who is the most powerful living being in the universe and who is therefore sometimes called Bhagavan. The inhabitants of this planet worship the Supreme as represented by Lord Brahma. In the middle of that island is a great mountain named Manasottara, which forms the boundary between the inner side and outer side of the island. Its breadth and height are 80,000 miles.

On that mountain, in the four directions, are the residential quarters of demigods such as Indra. In the chariot of the sun-god, the sun travels on the top of the mountain in an orbit called the Samvatsara, encircling Mount Meru. The sun's path on the northern side is called Uttarayana, and its path on the southern side is called Daksinayana. One side [6 months, our warm season] represents a day for the demigods, and the other [6 months, our winter season] represents their night. In this way, we can understand that one of our years is but a day for the demigods. Therefore, their life is very long, almost like an eternity compared to ours. That is why some religions suggest that life in heaven is eternal.

Needless to say, this is only a partial description of the upper planets and their locations as described by the mystics in the Vedic literature. But, as we can easily begin to see, only the pious and spiritually advanced can enter into the topmost heavenly planets. Therefore, those who are faithless and godless can only enter into the lower planets.

*Srimad-Bhagavatam* (5.24.1-6) explains that below the higher planets, yet still above the earth, are other planets beginning with the planet Rahu which is 80,000 miles below the sun. It moves like one of the stars but is a dark planet and invisible; yet, its existence can be seen occasionally when there is an eclipse. Below Rahu by 80,000 more miles are the planets known as Siddhaloka [where live the Siddhas, or those who are naturally endowed with the mystic perfections, such as flying from one planet to another without machines], Caranaloka [where live Caranas or wandering minstrel-like entities], Gandharvaloka [where the Gandharvas or angels live], and Vidyadhara-loka [where live Vidyadharas, beneficial aerial spirits of great beauty and wisdom]. Beneath these planets are the places of enjoyment for the Yakshas [mysterious spirits that frequent fields and forests], Rakshashas [demon spirits who wander at night and may assume forms such as dogs, vultures, owls, dwarfs, etc.], Pishacas [demoniac spirits who eat flesh, may possess people and congregate at creamation grounds or cemeteries with other ghostly beings], and other creatures like ghosts and so on. Below these dark and invisible planets by several hundred miles is the planet earth.

"Beneath the earth are seven other planets, known as Atala, Vitala, Sutala, Talatala, Mahatala, Rasatala and Patala. . . In these seven planetary systems, which are also known as the subterranean heavens [*bila-svarga*], there are very beautiful houses, gardens and places of sense enjoyment, which are even more opulent than those in the higher planets because the demons have a very high standard of sensual pleasure. Most of the residents of these planets enjoy life without disturbances. Thus they are understood to be very attached to illusory happiness." (*Bhag*.5.24.8-9)

The *Bhagavatam* goes on to explain that the planet below Atala is Vitala, where Lord Shiva lives with his personal associates, the ghosts and similar beings. The next lower planet is Sutala where Bali Maharaja, who is celebrated as the most pious king, resides even now. Beneath the planet of Sutala is Talatala, which is ruled by the Danava demon named Maya. Maya is known as the *acarya* [master] of all the *mayavis* [magicians], who can invoke the powers of sorcery. The planetary system below Talatala is known as Mahatala. It is the abode of many hooded snakes, descendants of Kadru, who are always very angry.

Beneath Mahatala is the planetary system known as Rasatala, which is the abode of the demoniac sons and descendants of Diti and Danu. They are extremely powerful and cruel and are all enemies of the demigods. Beneath Rasatala is another planetary system, known as Patala or Nagaloka, where there are many demoniac serpents. The chief among them is Vasuki. They are all extremely angry, and they have many, many hoods. These hoods are bedecked with valuable gems, and it is the light emanating from these gems that illuminates the entire planetary system of *bila-svarga*.

Approximately 240,000 miles beneath the planet Patala lives another incarnation of the Supreme Lord. He is the expansion of Lord Vishnu known as Lord Ananta or Lord Sankarshana. Lord Sankarshana is the ocean of unlimited spiritual qualities, and thus is known as Anantadeva. He is nondifferent from the Supreme Personality of Godhead. For the welfare of all living entities within this material world, He resides in His abode, restraining His anger and intolerance.

At the time of devastation, when Lord Anantadeva desires to destroy the entire creation, He becomes slightly angry. Then from between His two eyebrows appears three-eyed Rudra, carrying a trident. This Rudra, an expansion of Lord Shiva, appears in order to devastate the entire creation.

The demigods, the demons, the Uragas, the Siddhas, the Gandharvas, the Vidyadharas, and many highly elevated sages constantly offer prayers to Lord Anantadeva. He pleases His personal associates, the foremost demigods, by the sweet vibrations emanating from His mouth. Dressed in bluish garments and wearing a single earring, he holds a plow on His back with His two beautiful and well constructed hands. Appearing as white as the heavenly King Indra, He wears a golden belt around His waist and a *vaijayanti* garland of ever-fresh *tulasi* blossoms around His neck. In this way, the Lord enjoys His very magnanimous pastimes.

The *Srimad-Bhagavatam* describes that there is no end to the great and glorious qualities of that powerful Lord Anantadeva. Indeed, His prowess is unlimited. Though self-sufficient, He Himself is the support of everything. He resides beneath the lower planetary systems on the Garbhodaka Ocean and easily sustains the entire universe.

Above the abode of Lord Anantadeva, in the intermediate space between the three worlds and the vast Garbhodaka Ocean, which fills the lower portion of the universe, is where all the hellish planets are situated. They lie on the southern side of the universe, beneath Bhu-mandala, and slightly above the water of the Garbhodaka Ocean. Pitriloka, the planet of the ancestors, is also located in this region between the Garbhodaka Ocean and the lower planetary systems. All the residents of Pitriloka, headed by Agnisvatta, meditate in great *samadhi* on the Supreme Lord and always wish their families well.

## DESCRIPTION OF HELL

The hellish planets are the destination of those doomed to suffer for all of their wicked and nefarious activities. Of course, if people could decide for themselves if they wanted to go to hell or not, no one would go there. But this is not for us to decide and depends on higher authorities who witness and judge our acts. There is a common misconception amongst many people that as long as whatever we do does not harm anyone or is not seen by anyone, then we are free to do almost anything we want. But the Vedic texts point out that, "The sun, fire, sky, air, demigods, moon, evening, day, night, directions, water, land and Supersoul Himself all witness the activities of the living entity." (*Bhag.*6.1.42) Due to these witnesses, living beings are not able to go any place where there is no one to see what they do.

The King of the hellish planets and the ruler in the after life of those destined for the darker regions of the universe is Yamaraja. The *Srimad-Bhagavatam* describes that he resides in Pitriloka with his personal assistants and, while abiding by the rules and regulations set down by the Supreme Lord, has his agents, the Yamadutas [soldiers of Yamaraja], bring all the sinful men to him immediately upon their death. After bringing them within his jurisdiction, he properly judges them according to their specific sinful activities and sends them to one of the many hellish planets for suitable punishments.

"Some authorities say that there is a total of twenty-one hellish planets, and some say twenty-eight. The names of the different hells are as follows: Tamisra, Andhatamisra, Raurava, Maharaurava, Kumbhipaka, Kalasutra, Asipatravana, Sukaramukha, Andhakupa, Krmibhojana, Sandamsa, Taptasurmi, Vajrakantakasalmali, Vaitrani, Puyoda, Pranarodha, Visasana, Lalabhaksa, Sarameyadana, Avici, Ayahpana, Ksarakardama, Raksogana-bhojana, Sulaprota, Dandasuka, Avatanirodhana, Paryavartana and Sucimukha. All these planets are meant for punishing the living entities." (Bhag.5.26.7)

Throughout Vedic literature, especially the *Puranas*, there are descriptions of the hellish planets. We will only include a small portion of these so as not to make this chapter unnecessarily long, but at least to see what kind of place the hellish planets are and what kind of people are taken there.

"A person who appropriates another's legitimate wife, children or money is arrested at the time of death by the fierce Yamadutas, who bind him with the rope of time and forcibly throw him into the hellish planets known as Tamisra. On this very dark planet, the sinful man is chastised by the Yamadutas, who beat and rebuke him. He is starved, and he is given no water to drink. Thus the wrathful assistants of Yamaraja cause him severe suffering, and sometimes he faints from their chastisements." (Bhag.5.26.8).

"In this life, an envious person commits violent acts against many living entities. Therefore after his death, when he is taken to hell by Yamaraja, those living entities who were hurt by him appear as animals called *rurus* to inflict very severe pain upon him. Learned scholars call this hell Raurava. Not generally seen in this world, the *ruru* is more envious than a snake." (Bhag.5.26.11)

In regard to this, anyone can see that there are people who possess a demoniac mentality and take pleasure in destroying things or hurting others for no justifiable reason. Such people who commit violent acts toward other beings are taken to Raurava, where the living entities they harmed in the past take the form of *rurus* and give them untold misery, as explained in the following verse:

"Punishment in the hell called Maharaurava is compulsory for a person who maintains his own body by hurting others. In this hell, *ruru* animals known as *kravyada* torment him and eat his flesh. For the maintenance of their bodies and the satisfaction of their tongues, cruel persons cook poor animals and birds alive. Such persons are condemned even by man-eaters. In their next lives they are carried by the Yamadutas to the hell known as Kumbhipaka, where they are cooked in boiling oil." (Bhag.5.26.12-13)

"The killer of a *brahmana* is put into the hell known as Kalasutra, which has a circumference of eighty thousand miles and which is made entirely of copper. Heated from below by fire and from above by the scorching sun, the copper surface of this planet is extremely hot. Thus the murderer of a *brahmana* suffers from being burned both internally and externally. Internally he is burning with hunger and thirst, and externally he is burning from the scorching heat of the sun and the fire beneath the copper surface. Therefore he sometimes lies down, sometimes sits, sometimes stands up and sometimes runs here and there. He must suffer in this way for as many thousands of years as there are hairs on the body of an animal." (Bhag.65.26.14)

"In his next life, a sinful king or governmental representative who punishes an innocent person, or who inflicts corporal punishment upon a *brahmana*, is taken by the Yamadutas to the hell named Sukharamukha, where the most powerful assistants of Yamaraja crush him exactly as one crushes sugarcane to squeeze out the juice. The sinful living entity cries very pitiably and faints, just like an innocent man undergoing punishments. This is the result of punishing a faultless person." (*Bhag*.5.26.16)

"A person who in the absence of an emergency robs a *brahmana*--or indeed, anyone else--of his gems [or valuables] and gold is put into a hell known as Sandamsa. There his skin is torn and separated by red-hot iron balls and tongs. In this way, his entire body is cut to pieces." (*Bhag*.5.26.19)

While writing this and residing in Detroit, it is not uncommon to hear of the plight of old people who have no money and are hungry and struggling simply to live from day to day. In many cases, one of the reasons they no longer have the necessary money to take better care of themselves is because they have been robbed, not once or twice, but many times. This makes it extremely difficult for these people to live their final years with any peace or happiness. From the above verse, however, we learn that thieves who burglarize, steal, and also beat innocent citizens for their possessions end up in Sandamsa. Such criminals may escape the laws of the local authorities, but they can never avoid the laws of nature as instituted by the Supreme. At the time of death, such criminals are immediately grabbed by the soldiers of Yamaraja and punished by having their skin torn from their bodies by hot iron tongs. If any thief knew such a fate awaited him after death for the suffering he has caused to others, he would be insane to continue such activities.

"A man or woman who indulges in sexual intercourse with an unworthy member of the opposite sex [or anyone other than one's spouse] is punished after death by the assistants of Yamaraja in the hell known as Taptasurmi. There such men and women are beaten with whips. The man is forced to embrace a red-hot iron form of a woman, and the woman is forced to embrace a similar form of a man. Such is the punishment for illicit sex." (*Bhag*.5.26.20)

These punishments on the hellish planets may sound extremely cruel, but a person becomes sorry and repentent by suffering while remembering one's past sinful activities. Such people may also retain the memory of such suffering deep in their subconsciousness in their next life and, thus, will refrain from performing similar activities in future lives.

"In the province of Yamaraja there are hundreds and thousands of hellish planets. The impious people I have mentioned--and also those I have not mentioned--must all enter these various planets according to the degree of their impiety. Those who are pious, however, enter other planetary systems, namely the planets of the demigods. Nevertheless, both the pious and impious are again brought to earth after the results of their pious or impious acts are exhausted." (*Bhag*.5.26.37)

From this verse, we can understand that hell is not a place where one resides eternally after death. It is simply the reaction for particular nefarious activities. But due to the intensity of the suffering, it may seem like an eternity. After the reactions to one's impious acts are used up, the person generally enters back into the earthly atmosphere to begin again. Then he can continue evolving through the different levels of planetary systems until, gradually, he has experienced every aspect of material existence, from the lower to the upper heavenly planets. However, we should know that to evolve continually through the different planetary systems, or different species of life, is not the way to find real happiness. The happiness which we are always hankering for lies beyond our captivity within this realm of material ups and downs, or temporary heavens and hells in this universe.

## DESCRIPTION OF HEAVEN

We all know that given a choice, everyone would like to go to heaven. And most people have some kind of conception of heaven that makes them convinced that heaven will be a wonderful place. Even if our life on earth is far from ideal, once we get to heaven, everything is going to be alright. But every time someone tells me what kind of place heaven is, I get a different opinion.

In the Vedic writings, we get explicit information about what heaven is. For instance, we can see areas right here on earth that are practically like heaven. If you visit a tropical island with long, sunny beaches of white sand, with cool breezes blowing through the trees carrying the aroma of exotic flowers, and the sound of the waves of crystal clear water reaching the shore, and, let us not forget, beautifully shaped young girls dressed in colorful garments tending to our every need, would you not feel like you were in heaven? No doubt a lot of people would like that kind of experience, because everyone is interested in material sense enjoyment. The only problem is that such places seem to be either difficult to reach, or it costs too much money to live there for long, or we have to leave after a short visit. We can never get enough of it and always want to return or visit similar places again and again.

The *Srimad-Bhagavatam* describes that such heavenly places are where the living entities use up the results of their past pious activities. Heavenly abodes are found in three places: here on earth, the lower heavenly planets, and the upper, celestial, heavenly planets. Only the most elevated of pious people can enter into the celestial planets. Other people can only experience the lesser heavenly atmospheres found on earth or the lower planets.

It is explained in *Srimad-Bhagavatam* (5.17.12) that in the upper heavenly regions, including earth before the advent of the age of Kali several thousand years ago, residents live ten thousand years, and all the inhabitants are almost like demigods. "They have the bodily strength of ten thousand elephants and their bodies are as sturdy as thunderbolts. The youthful duration of their lives is very pleasing, and both men and women enjoy sexual union with great pleasure for a long time. After years of sensual pleasure when a balance of one year of life remains--the wife conceives a child. Thus the standard of pleasure for the residents of these heavenly regions is exactly like that of the human beings who lived during Treta-yuga [when there were no disturbances]."

Even the earth planet used to be a heavenly place during the ages of Satya-yuga and Treta-yuga. Everyone was very pious and practiced yoga. They cared little about material sense enjoyment, though it was available. Thus, the earth supplied the residents with all that they needed in a most pleasant atmosphere. Only later, with the advent of Dvapara-yuga and especially in the present age of Kali-yuga, did the earth begin to withhold her resources and the atmosphere changed and was no longer so heavenly. Now, as Kali-yuga progresses, the atmosphere is becoming more and more polluted and hellish. And it seems that, as time slips away, we are losing the areas that are still considered nice or heavenly, like those found on the upper planets as described as follows:

"There are many gardens filled with flowers and fruits according to the season, and there are beautifully decorated hermitages as well. Between the great mountains demarcating the borders of those lands lie enormous lakes of clear water filled with newly grown lotus flowers. Aquatic birds such as swans, ducks, water chickens, and cranes become greatly excited by the fragrance of lotus flowers, and the charming sound of bumblebees fills the air. The inhabitants of those lands are important leaders among the demigods. Always attended by their respective servants, they enjoy life in gardens alongside the lakes. In this pleasing situation, the wives of the demigods smile playfully at their husbands and look upon them with lusty desires. All the demigods and their wives are constantly supplied with sandalwood pulp and flower garlands by their servants. In this way, all the residents of the eight heavenly varshas enjoy, attracted by the activities of the opposite sex." (Bhag.5.17.13)

From this description, we can see that the heavenly pleasure experienced by the residents of the higher planets is often based on sex and is simply a more refined form of sense enjoyment. This is not much different than what people on earth can experience. One difference is that the residents of the higher planets enjoy like that uninterruptedly for years if they wish; whereas, the residents on earth can enjoy in a similar fashion for only a short time.

Another description of the heavenly regions on the higher planets is about the Trikuta mountain, which is 80,000 miles high and surrounded by an ocean of milk. Just as earth is surrounded by an ocean of salt water, the higher planets also have oceans, but of more pleasing substances.

"The three principal peaks of the Trikuta mountain are made of iron, silver and gold, and beautify all directions and the sky. The mountain also has other peaks, which are full of jewels and minerals and are decorated with nice trees, creepers and shrubs. The sounds of the waterfalls on the mountain create a pleasing vibration. In this way the mountain stands, increasing the beauty in all directions. The ground at the foot of the mountain is always washed by waves of milk that produce emeralds all around in the eight directions. The inhabitants of the higher planets--the Siddhas, Caranas, Gandharvas, Vidyadharas, serpents, Kinnaras and Apsaras--go to that mountain to sport. Thus all the caves of the mountain are full of these denizens of the heavenly planets." (Bhag.8.2.2-5)

"The valleys beneath Trikuta Mountain are beautifully decorated by many varieties of jungle animals, and in the trees, which are maintained in gardens by the demigods, varieties of birds chirp with sweet voices. Trikuta Mountain has many lakes and rivers, with beaches covered by small gems resembling grains of sand. The water is as clear as crystal, and when the demigod damsels bathe in it, their bodies lend fragrance to the water and the breeze, thus enriching the atmosphere." (Bhag.8.2.7-8)

On the heavenly planets, the bodies of the maidens are not only beautiful, but they lend fragrance to the lakes and breezes as well. On this earthly planet, everyone can experience that if our bodies are not bathed daily, they begin to smell bad. To cover this problem, people often use deordorants or artificial fragrances to give their body a nice scent or even to hide the fact that they do not bathe regularly. This, indeed, is far from heavenly when we have to tolerate the unpleasant odor of the bodies of the people around us. This, therefore, is a good comparison to understand how the heavenly planets are thousands of times more opulent than this planet earth.

By studying the Vedic literature, we can learn about such places as heaven. But by trying to attain such knowledge through our limited senses and instruments such as telescopes, which are only extensions of our faulty senses, we will never be able to evaluate properly the conditions of the higher planets. Therefore, we can get an idea of what the higher planets are like by the descriptions found in such books as *Srimad-Bhagavatam*, which describes the grand opulence of Lord Indra, the King of heaven, as follows:

"Hiranyakasipu, who possessed all opulence, began residing in heaven, with its famous Nandana garden which is enjoyed by the demigods. In fact, he resided in the most opulent palace of Indra, the King of heaven. The palace had been directly constructed by the demigod architect Visvakarma and was as beautifully made as if the goddess of fortune of the entire universe resided there. The steps of King Indra's residence were made of coral, the floor was bedecked with invaluable emeralds, the walls were of crystal, and the columns of *vaidurya* stone. The wonderful canopies were beautifully decorated, the seats were bedecked with rubies, and the silk bedding, as white as foam, was decorated with pearls. The ladies of the palace, who were blessed with beautiful teeth and the most wonderfully beautiful faces, walked here and there in the palace, their ankle bells tinkling melodiously, and saw their own beautiful reflections in the gems." (Bhag.7.4.8-11)

Most of us cannot even imagine a house with crystal walls, coral steps, floors bedecked with emeralds, chairs bedecked with rubies, and bedding decorated with pearls. But here is a description of a huge palace of this kind, where many people lived. This is the heavenly region where only those who are qualified can enter. We will not be able to go there by means of rockets or space capsules. The only way we can actually enter into the celestial, heavenly atmosphere is by means of pious works, good *karma*, or mystic perfection. However, for those who are actually wise, attaining heaven is not so important.

## THE OPPORTUNITY IN THIS EARTHLY EXISTENCE

A wise man with knowledge of how this universe works knows that in the heavenly planets, as everywhere else, there is birth and death. Residents of the upper planets live a very long time by earthly calculations, but life ultimately comes to an end there as well. After all, it is still within this material universe, where everything gradually breaks down, deteriorates, and falls apart. Just as one may, after saving his money, go on vacation to Hawaii or someplace and spend the whole time enjoying, relaxing, and doing only the things he likes, when the money runs out he has to return home and go back to work. Similarly, after one has performed many good works and accumulated an abundance of good *karma*, one may enter the heavenly region to live and enjoy for thousands of years. But when the accumulated pious reactions are used up, one's heavenly existence comes to an end and he again enters the middle or earthly planetary system to start over. This is explained in the *Mundaka Upanishad* (1.2.10): "Considering sacrifice and good works as the best, these fools know no higher good, and having enjoyed (their reward) on the height of heaven, gained by good works, they enter again this world or a lower one."

Knowledgeable sages, therefore, consider heaven and all its opulence to be nothing more than phantasmagoria, a spectacular but temporary dream. That, in fact, is all that life is on any level of existence within this cosmic creation. Lord Sri Krishna therefore explains in *Bhagavad-gita*: "From the highest planet in the material world down to the lowest, all are places of misery wherein repeated birth and death take place. But one who attains to My abode, O son of Kunti, never takes birth again." (*Bg*.8.16)

Those who are seriously engaged on the spiritual path have no concern whether they enter heaven or hell. For them, heaven can be hell without worship of the Supreme and hell can be heaven simply by meditating on the spiritual atmosphere. It is not so important where you are, but how you utilize your time that makes the difference, as explained in the following verse:

"O Lord, we pray that You let us be born in any hellish condition of life, just as long as our hearts and minds are always engaged in the service of Your lotus feet, our words are made beautiful [by speaking of Your activities] just as *tulasi* leaves are beautified when offered unto Your lotus feet, and as long as our ears are always filled with the chanting of Your transcendental qualities." (*Bhag.*3.15.49)

By now we can begin to see that the middle planetary system, earth, is the place where one can go to heaven, or to hell, or to the spiritual world which is completely beyond this material creation. In heaven, the atmosphere is so conducive to sense enjoyment that one can hardly concentrate on the need to make spiritual advancement. In the lower planets, life is too painful and distressing, or society too materialistic to engage in spiritual activities. But in the middle planetary system, life is generally neither too heavenly nor too hellish. Therefore, it is a proper environment for one to pursue the spiritual path.

"Since the human form of life is the sublime position for spiritual realization, all the demigods in heaven speak in this way: How wonderful it is for these human beings to have been born in the land of Bharata-varsha [planet earth]. They must have executed pious acts of austerity in the past, or the Supreme Personality of Godhead Himself must have been pleased with them. Otherwise, how could they engage in devotional service in so many ways? We demigods can only aspire to achieve human births in Bharata-varsha to execute devotional service, but these human beings are already engaged there." (*Bhag.*5.19.21)

"After performing the very difficult task of executing Vedic ritualistic sacrifices, undergoing austerities, observing vows and giving charity, we have achieved this position as inhabitants of the heavenly planets. But what is the value of this achievement? Here we are certainly very engaged in material sense gratification, and therefore we can hardly remember the lotus feet of Lord Narayana. Indeed, because of our excessive sense gratification, we have almost forgotten His lotus feet." (*Bhag.*5.19.22)

"A short life in the land of Bharata-varsha is preferable to a life achieved in Brahmaloka for millions and billions of years because even if one is elevated to Brahmaloka, he must return to repeated birth and death. Although life in Bharata-varsha, in a lower planetary system, is very short, one who lives there can elevate himself to full Krishna consciousness and achieve the highest perfection, even in this short life, by fully surrendering unto the lotus feet of the Lord. Thus one attains Vaikunthaloka [the spiritual planets], where there is neither anxiety nor repeated birth in a material body." (*Bhag.*5.19.23)

"Bharata-varsha offers the proper land and circumstances in which to execute devotional service [*bhakti-yoga*], which can free one from the results of *jnana* [speculation] and *karma*. If one obtains a human body in the land of Bharata-varsha, with clear sensory organs with which to execute the *sankirtana-yajna* [chanting or singing the glories of the Supreme], but in spite of this opportunity he does not take to devotional service, he is certainly like liberated forest animals and birds that are careless and are therefore again bound by a hunter." (*Bhag.*5.19.25)

These verses from *Srimad-Bhagavatam* directly point out the rare opportunity we have now that we find ourselves on this planet earth. One who does not utilize such an opportunity to engage in pursuits for spiritual advancement is certainly living only to die without making any tangible progress toward getting free from material existence. Even the demigods pray to take birth on Bharata-varsha. Therefore, we can understand how valuable such a birth is. But another reason why Bharata-varsha is so valuable is because the Supreme Being personally appears here to attract the living entities by performing a portion of His unlimited pastimes on this planet.

"We are now living in the heavenly planets, undoubtedly as a result of our having performed ritualistic ceremonies, pious activities and *yajnas* [sacrifices for spiritual merit] and having studied the *Vedas*. However, our lives here will one day be finished. We pray that at that time, if any merit remains from our pious activities, we may again take birth in Bharata-varsha as human beings able to remember the lotus feet of the Lord. The Lord is so kind that He personally comes to the land of Bharata-varsha and expands the good fortune of its people." (*Bhag.*5.19.28)

Therefore, any activity, either pious or impious, which causes the living entity further entanglement in heaven or hell does not solve the problem of continued birth and death. When one understands the living being's never-ending evolution throughout the upper, middle, and lower planetary systems, as well as through the 8,400,000 species of life, the futility of continued material existence becomes obvious. Only by engaging in spiritual activities in connection with the Supreme are we really able to bring an end to our material existence.

* * *

So far, in these chapters, we have covered the subjects of our real spiritual identity, the law of *karma*, reincarnation, the modes of material nature, heaven and hell, how we are entangled in them, and how we can get free from them. Now, in the next chapter, we will put it all together to describe the process that the living entities undergo in their evolution throughout the various levels of material existence in their search for happiness within this cosmic creation.

# CHAPTER EIGHT

# *The Soul's Evolution Through Life, Death, and Beyond*

As soon as the living beings find themselves in a particular body within this material creation, they immediately begin to identify with the kind of form in which they are situated. They may be male or female, black or white, human or animal, aquatic or whatever. In any case, they begin to chase after those things which they think will give them pleasure. A male chases after a female, or a female looks for a male. A cat looks for a mouse to eat to satisfy its hunger, while a tiger looks for a deer or some other large animal. In this way, all living entities search for different kinds of pleasure according to the kind of body and consciousness they possess. As they search and try to acquire that which they feel will satisfy their body and mind, they will go through a variety of material experiences and psychological changes which take them to various levels of consciousness and different conceptions of happiness. As these changes continue, the living entities evolve and incarnate through many types of bodies and regions of the universe which facilitate the consciousness and desires the living beings have. According to the *Vedas*, this is the process of evolution that we all undergo.

## DARWIN'S THEORY

To most of us, when we hear of evolution, we think of Darwin's theory. However, let us not forget that Darwin's theory is only a theory and nothing more than that, although many people have accepted it as a fact of life. But this version of evolution explains that in the beginning of time there was no life; yet, by chance a very primitive form of life began in some kind of primordial soup. From that life form various other species of life appeared and gradually became more and more developed through random variation and natural selection. From

143

a single-celled organism that was accidently sparked to life by a lightning bolt that struck the puddle of life-producing chemicals in just the right way thousands of years ago, we now have large complicated cities run by man who descended from the monkeys. Even though many people accept such a hypothesis, scientists are still trying to piece together the evidence they need to prove their claims. But to this date, no one has ever observed life or consciousness being spontaneously produced from any combination of inert chemicals.

If someone asks where the planets came from, along with all the chemicals found in the life-producing primordial soup, one is then presented with another hypothesis: the big bang theory. This theory introduces the idea that in the beginning all matter was concentrated into a single point of infinite density and temperature which somehow exploded with colossal force, thus creating subatomic particles at first, then atoms, stars, planets, etc. This may sound very erudite, but there is a problem with this idea. On a mathematical basis such a situation is called a "singularity" or, in other words, an impossibility.

There are many problems with the theory of evolution and the big bang, of which more scientists are becoming aware and who readily admit their reluctance to wholeheartedly accept such theories. For example, in breeding fruits, flowers, or insects, researchers have discovered limits in the degree of change they can make in a species. Once the species is allowed to breed by natural selection, it returns to its standard form. This seems to indicate an antievolutionary characteristic, which means that it may be possible to cause slight changes in the existing form but not for creating entirely new species.

Actually, in *The Origin of Species*, Darwin himself confessed the difficulty in completely accepting his own theory in every case. He says, "To suppose that the eye with all its inimitable contrivances for adjusting the focus to different distances, for admitting different amounts of light, and for the correction of spherical and chromatic aberration, could have been formed by natural selection, seems, I freely confess, absurd in the highest degree."

Mr. Goldsmith, a noted biologist, also arrived at the same conclusion in the case of the eye. By taking away any part of the eye, such as the retina, the eye simply will not function. Thus, the whole eye had to be created simultaneously in order for it to have come into existence. Plus, there had to have been some way for it to be connected with the brain for it to be useful at all. Mr. Goldsmith said that there were seventeen such organs in the body which cannot be explained by the theory of evolution.

Furthermore, Russel Wallace, an English naturalist and friend of Charles Darwin, also arrived at an independent theory of evolution, but he exempted the human spirit from the evolutionary process. He concluded that human consciousness was a special creation that could not be accounted for through biological evolution.

There are other scientists who also regard evolution as very unlikely. The distinguished scientist Professor Simpson estimates that the probability of a mutation taking place in the nucleus of a cell may happen once in 274 billion years. And Mr. Thompson, a noted mathematician, figures that for evolution to take place once would take 64 to the power of 80,000 times the history of this earth. Considering that, according to most scientists, the earth is about 4 to 5 billion years old, this would mean that evolution is completely impossible. This does not include the time required for the many millions of mutations and changes needed for evolution to produce a complex living being like a human.

Herewith, we can see that the theories of evolution and the big bang rest on very shaky foundations and are essentially only attempts to explain the universe in a mechanistic way. Such a viewpoint advocates that there is no God or designer of the creation and that it works simply as a machine. In this way, the world and man are no more than by-products of the machine working according to physical laws. If such is the case, then through science we can eventually learn how to control and manipulate this universe in whatever way we choose.

The Vedic literature, however, does not accept these modern theories of creation and evolution because such ideas are marred by imperfect knowledge. As soon as one says "by chance there was a big bang," or "by chance a species evolved," it simply indicates insufficient knowledge. Whether in materialistic laws or laws set in motion by a Supreme designer, there is no "chance" involved. Everything takes place according to specific principles.

Even if evolution did exist according to Darwin's theory, then who was it that originally made the arrangements for it? Scientists may say it takes place according to nature's laws, but who originated such laws? Since we can only begin to understand how the laws of nature work after much study and observation, we can easily surmise that it is a higher authority who maintains the laws of nature. But even if the universe did work in nothing more than a mechanistic fashion, then where is the mechanic who put the machine together? Or where is the operator who pressed the button that put the machine in motion? Has anyone ever seen a machine that could build itself, start itself, and continue to maintain itself in an organized manner without a designer or operator? If we saw a model of the universe in someone's house, would we think that it suddenly popped into existence? No. We would know that someone made the model. Similarly, to think that this universe has no designer or operator defies logic.

Scientists may say that the universe started from a big bang and slowly became more organized, or that life started from a one-celled organism and gradually developed into a highly evolved and complex life form. But where is the evidence for such a theory? Any person with common sense can see how everything around us gradually breaks down. Buildings get old and begin to crumble. Our bodies deteriorate and die. Even mountains slowly wear away. Has anyone seen a building get stronger as the years go by and need no maintenance? Has anyone seen a car that does not slowly wear and rust away the more it is driven, or need no new replacement parts or oil changes or new tires? Has anyone seen someone who after the age of 30, 40, or 50 years starts getting younger and more healthy with every year that goes by, without getting wrinkles, and continue to improve for several hundred years?

Material nature does not work like that. In fact, the second law of thermodynamics states that if things are left to themselves, rather than becoming more evolved, they go from complex to simple. So how can they expect us to believe that life came from nothing yet somehow gradually evolved until we now have complex organisms such as human beings on the planet? If material elements are always breaking down, deteriorating and falling apart, how can they expect us to believe that this universe formed itself from nothing and gradually became a highly organized creation with planets with specific orbits like the earth, with seasons and days and nights?

Scientists may try to prove their theory of evolution by digging up old bones and piecing them together like jigsaw puzzles, but they do not even understand all the bones they do find. They may have found bones that they have labeled as part of the Neanderthal man or Cro-Magnon man, but they have also found other bones in the same areas in the shape of modern man. They have analyzed and tested these bones and found them to be as old as the Neanderthal man, but the researchers who have found them and announced their findings are often criticised as quacks and ridiculed by other scientists who say such findings are impossible. Then they lose their credibility and position, and that is the last you hear of them. Why does this happen and why not look at all the facts? Obviously, they are not only biased about what they want to believe, but the theory of evolution also has some pretty big cracks in it that some people do not want to discuss. Let us provide some examples of this.

Remember, the modern theory of evolution presents the idea that homo sapiens came into existence only 40,000 years ago. But it was G. Ragazoni, professor of geology, who, in 1860 on the southern flanks of the Alps, discovered human fossils in a hillside excavation at the bottom of a five foot thick layer of blue pliocene clay. (Pliocene is the strata of that which existed 1.8 to 5 million years ago.) In 1880, the bones of a full human man and child were found a few yards away at the same depth. In both cases, it was determined that the overlieing layers of soil were undisturbed, ruling out the possibility of burial from above. A little later, the bones of a fully developed human woman were found at a slightly higher level. This provided excellent evidence for the existence of fully developed homo sapiens in northern Italy as far back as two million years ago.

During the 1850's in Lisbon, stone tools were found in the miocene strata, providing evidence for the existence of homo sapiens from 5 to 23 million years ago. Other tools were found in the Oligocene strata in France, which dates them back from 23 to 37 million years ago.

Although some anthropologists have rejected such finds because they do not fit in with their ideas of evolution, a number of scientists have discovered abundant evidence from all around the world for human presence in the pliocene, miocene, and earlier periods. This indicates that fully evolved homo sapiens were existing on this planet not just 40,000 years ago as the modern theory of evolution presents but even millions of years earlier. Obviously, this kind of evidence contradicts many aspects of the theory of evolution as it is presented today. This is why someone who has studied the Vedic literature will not accept the modern theories of evolution and the big bang. The science of the soul completely negates Darwin's theory. Only by understanding this spiritual knowledge can one get a comprehensive view of what evolution really is.

## OUR IGNORANCE OF LIFE

As explained in previous chapters, the real identity of the living being is spiritual: he is not a material product. He appears in this material world because he has fallen from the spiritual strata.

When the living beings are in the material world, they are born in ignorance and do not know their origin or why they are in this material creation. People tend to think we are all here by accident and that when this life is over, everything is finished. They can see everything is functioning in a systematic manner, but no one knows why or who arranged it. Therefore, they go about making their whimsical goals in search of whatever pleasure they can attain by material endeavor. However, such hard labor produces results which last only a short time. Therefore, the material happiness people hope to find soon deteriorates to lamentation, and the living beings do not understand why. But because they do not know the purpose of this material creation and how it works, they become frustrated, and by thinking that painful circumstances are actually pleasurable, they remain content to continue struggling with the material energy. This is elaborated upon in the following verses:

"The Personality of Godhead said: As a mass of clouds does not know the powerful influence of the wind, a person engaged in material consciousness does not know the powerful strength of the time factor, by which he is being carried. Whatever is produced by the materialist with great pain and labor for so called happiness, the Supreme Personality, as the time factor, destroys, and for this reason the conditioned soul laments. The misguided materialist does not know that his very body is impermanent and that the attractions of home, land and wealth, which are in relationship to that body, are also temporary. Out of ignorance only, he thinks that everything is permanent. The living entity, in whatever species of life he appears, finds a particular type of satisfaction in that species, and he is never averse to being situated in such a condition. The conditioned living entity is satisfied in his own particular species of life; while deluded by the covering influence of the illusory energy, he feels little inclined to cast off his body, even when in hell, for he takes delight in hellish enjoyment." (*Bhag*.3.30.1-5)

Due to not knowing one's real identity, the living entity does not know what real happiness is, nor how to avoid misery. He simply thinks he is the body and thus becomes absorbed in material activity and succumbs to the law of actions and reactions in his life. He does not know how he got into it nor how to get out. Thus, for lack of an alternative, the living being continues to evolve through the various high and low situations material nature gives him due to the results of his activities and *karma*. But if he is able to evolve to a stage of life in which he can understand spiritual knowledge, he can then find the passage that allows his escape from the material entrapment. That is real evolution.

## THE FIVE BASIC STAGES OF HUMAN EVOLUTION

How the consciousness and concerns of an individual in the human form evolve from the beginning to the end of human life can be explained according to the descriptions in the Vedic texts. There are five basic stages. In the first stage, when one is a child, the living entity is food conscious and most concerned about getting enough to eat. When one has gotten nice food to satisfy the tongue and stomach, he is satisfied. This is called *annamaya*. After this stage, one becomes very concerned about continuing to exist by protecting or defending himself from being attacked or destroyed. This is called *pranamaya*, in which one is happy simply by continuing to live. These first two stages are the most primitive levels of consciousness. Generally, living entities in the animal kingdom never evolve beyond this type of awareness. So, if a person remains in these lower stages, he is still considered to be in animalistic consciousness. Above this, the third stage, is *manomaya* in which one becomes involved on the mental platform of figuring out his desires and values of life.

These are the three stages in which most of society is absorbed. But if one continues to evolve through the mental platform and reaches the intellectual platform of philosophical life, or *vijnanamaya*, and begins to progress into spiritual knowledge, understanding that he is not the body but the soul within, then he may also begin to understand the Supreme Soul. By understanding one's relationship with the Supreme, one reaches the *anandamaya* platform of bliss, spiritual knowledge, and eternity. In this final stage, one reaches the goal of life and becomes liberated from further material existence and returns to the spiritual atmosphere.

This, of course, is a short summary of one's successive evolvement through the five different stages of life. However, the Vedic literature offers much more detailed descriptions of a person's evolutionary growth, including the painful experience of living in the womb up to the stage of death and the afterlife.

## LIFE IN THE WOMB AND BIRTH OF THE LIVING ENTITY

According to the results of activities performed in our past life, we are given a particular kind of body suitable for satisfying our materialistic desires as well as suffering or enjoying our good or bad *karma*. For this, we are placed in the womb of a mother and soon thereafter begin the life for which we are destined. "In this way the living entity gets a suitable body with a material mind and senses, according to his fruitive activities. When the reaction of his particular activity comes to an end, that end is called death, and when a particular type of reaction begins, that beginning is called birth." (*Bhag*.3.31.44)

"The Personality of Godhead said: Under the supervision of the Supreme Lord and according to the result of his work, the living entity, the soul, is made to enter into the womb of a woman through the particle of male semen to assume a particular type of body. On the first night, the sperm and ovum mix, and on the fifth night the mixture ferments into a bubble. On the tenth night it develops into a form like a plum, and after that, it gradually turns into a lump of flesh or an egg, as the case may be. In the course of a month, a head is formed, and at the end of two months the hands, feet and other limbs take shape. By the end of three months, the nails, fingers, toes, body hair, bones and skin appear, as do the organs of generation and the other apertures in the body, namely the eyes, nostrils, ears, mouth and anus.

"Within four months from the date of conception, the seven essential ingredients of the body, namely chyle, blood, flesh, fat, bone, marrow and semen, come into existence. At the end of five months, hunger and thirst make themselves felt, and at the end of six months, the fetus, enclosed in the amnion, begins to move on the right side of the abdomen. Deriving its nutrition from the food and drink taken by the mother, the fetus grows and remains in that abominable residence of stools and urine, which is the breeding place of all kinds of worms.

"Bitten again and again all over the body by the hungry worms in the abdomen itself, the child suffers terrible agony because of his tenderness. He thus becomes unconscious moment after moment because of the terrible condition. Owing to the mother's eating bitter, pungent foodstuffs, or food which is too salty or too sour, the body of the child incessantly suffers pains which are almost intolerable.

"Placed within the amnion and covered outside by the intestines, the child remains lying on one side of the abdomen, his head turned towards his belly and his back and neck arched like a bow. The child thus remains just like a bird in a cage, without freedom of movement. At that time, if the child is fortunate, he can remember all the troubles of his past one hundred births, and he grieves wretchedly. What is the possibility of peace of mind in that condition? Thus endowed with the development of consciousness from the seventh month after his conception, the child is tossed downward by the airs that press the embryo

during the weeks preceding delivery. Like the worms born of the same filthy abdominal cavity, he cannot remain in one place. The living entity in this frightful condition of life, bound by seven layers of material ingredients, prays with folded hands, appealing to the Lord, who has put him in that condition."
(*Bhag*.3.31.1-11)

The *Garbha Upanishad* states that while in the womb the living entity has knowledge of all his good and bad deeds and knows he has lived in a mother's abdomen thousands of times before. He knows that with each birth he has also lived and died, and whoever enjoyed the results of his hard work is gone and only he will suffer the consequences. While in the womb he prays that if he can escape the wretched situation, he will surely turn to Lord Narayana and study yoga to be delivered from this repeated cycle of birth and death once and for all.

The above quotations explicitly describe that the embryo, the living being within the womb, is alive and conscious of his situation. He can even remember past lives and is aware of the Supreme Lord and why he is in the womb. He is affected by the worms that bite him and the spicy foods that the mother eats. He can also experience the feelings and emotional changes of the mother. However, once the child has been placed in a womb according to his destiny, if the mother decides to abort the pregnancy, the soul will then be forced to take shelter of a different womb. This is a great hindrance to the evolutionary progress of the living being. It is also a great *karmic* impediment to the mother, who must then suffer the sinful reaction for killing the developing body of the unborn child. Therefore, the *Vedas* recommend that one must atone for child-killing or be prepared to face the dreadful reactions after death.

Even though the child in the womb is aware of many things, he at last begins to experience the process of birth as he is pushed out of the womb, which is such an ordeal that, upon being released, he immediately forgets his previous life within his mother's abdomen.

"Pushed downward all of a sudden by the wind (that helps parturition), the child comes out with great trouble, head downward, breathless and deprived of memory due to severe agony. The child thus falls on the ground, smeared with stool and blood, and plays just like a worm germinated from the stool. He loses his superior knowledge and cries under the spell of *maya*.

"After coming out of the abdomen, the child is given to the care of persons who are unable to understand what he wants, and thus he is nursed by such persons. Unable to refuse whatever is given to him, he falls into undesirable circumstances. Laid down on a foul bed infested with sweat and germs, the poor child is incapable of scratching his body to get relief from his itching sensation, to say nothing of sitting up, standing or even moving. In his helpless condition, gnats, mosquitoes, bugs and other germs bite the baby, whose skin is tender, just as smaller worms bite a big worm.

"The child, deprived of his wisdom, cries bitterly. In this way, the child passes through his childhood, suffering different kinds of distress, and attains boyhood. In boyhood also he suffers pain over desires to get things he can never achieve. And thus, due to ignorance, he becomes angry and sorry. With the growth of the body, the living entity, in order to vanquish his soul, increases his false prestige and anger and thereby creates enmity towards similarly lusty people. By such ignorance the living entity accepts the material body, which is made of five elements, as himself. With this misunderstanding, he accepts nonpermanent things as his own and increases his ignorance in the darkest region.

"For the sake of the body, which is a source of constant trouble to him and which follows him because he is bound by ties of ignorance and fruitive activities, he performs various actions which cause him to be subjected to repeated birth and death. If, therefore, the living entity again associates with the path of unrighteousness, influenced by sensually minded people engaged in the pursuit of sexual enjoyment and the gratification of the palate, he again goes to hell as before. He becomes devoid of truthfulness, cleanliness, mercy, gravity, spiritual intelligence, shyness, austerity, fame, forgiveness, control of the mind, control of the senses, fortune and all such opportunities." (*Bhag*.3.31.23-33)

In this way, one forgets his previous suffering in the womb and by chasing after lusty desires engages in the same activities that create the same useless *karma* to endure as he had before in previous lives. But no one should expect anything else when a person's goal in life is simply to pamper and cater to the whims of the temporary body. The human form of life is a rare opportunity. To waste it by performing nothing but activities for temporary sense pleasure is certainly not the way to solve the real problems of life. Devoting one's life to such materialistic concerns is similar to committing suicide. Since he hardly accomplishes anything that is relative to his real identity as a spiritual being, he lives only to die. As it states in *Srimad-Bhagavatam*: "Any person who engages himself within this material world in performing activities that necessitate great struggle, and who, after obtaining a human form of life--which is a chance to attain liberation from miseries--undertakes the difficult tasks of fruitive activities, must be considered to be cheated and envious of his own self." (*Bhag*.4.23.28)

Being cheated in life means to be absorbed in so many illusory things that one forgets the real importance of spiritual progress. Though continually engaged in many mental and physical activities, the clock of life keeps ticking until finally there is no time left. Then one is forced to give up his life without having made any preparation for his next existence. Thus, he has lost the opportunity that was meant to be found in human existence.

## LIFE IN THE MATERIAL WORLD

As one grows older, there are any number of goals one may give himself in one's attempt to find happiness. But the primary goal is to counteract and solve one's suffering and problems. The way this usually happens is elaborated upon in *Srimad-Bhagavatam*. We should remember as we read the following description that it was written thousands of years ago, but it is just as applicable today as it was then.

"The attached householder remains in his family life, which is full of diplomacy and politics. Always spreading miseries and controlled by acts of sense gratification, he acts just to counteract the reactions of all his miseries, and if he can successfully counteract such miseries, he thinks that he is happy. He secures money by committing violence here and there, and although he employs it in the service of his family, he himself eats only a little portion of the food thus purchased, and he goes to hell for those for whom he earned the money in such an irregular way.

"When he suffers reverses in his occupation, he tries again and again to improve himself, but when he is baffled in all attempts and is ruined, he accepts money from others because of excessive greed. Thus the unfortunate man, unsuccessful in maintaining his family members, is bereft of all beauty. He always thinks of his failure, grieving very deeply.

"Seeing him unable to support them, his wife and others do not treat him with the same respect as before, even as miserly farmers do not accord the same treatment to their old and worn-out oxen." *(Bhag.3.30.9-13)*

"Family members in this material world go under the names of wife and children, but actually they behave like tigers and jackals. A herdsman tries to protect his sheep to the best of his ability, but the tigers and foxes take them away by force. Similarly, although a miserly man wants to guard his money very carefully, his family members take away all his assets forcibly, even though he is very vigilant." *(Bhag.5.14.3)*

"In this material world, when the conditioned soul cannot arrange for his own maintenance, despite exploiting others, he tries to exploit his own father or son, taking away that relative's possessions, although they may be very insignificant. If he cannot acquire things from his father, son or other relatives, he is prepared to give them all kinds of trouble." *(Bhag.5.14.14)*

"The conditioned soul may earn money for the advancement of Krishna consciousness [spiritual progress], but unfortunately the uncontrolled senses plunder his money through sense gratification. The senses are plunderers because they make one spend his money unnecessarily for seeing, smelling, tasting, touching, hearing, desiring and willing. In this way the conditioned soul is obliged to gratify his senses, and thus all his money is spent." *(Bhag.5.14.2)*

"Sometimes the conditioned soul is absorbed in finding residential quarters or apartments and getting a supply of water and riches to maintain his body. Absorbed in acquiring a variety of necessities, he forgets everything and perpetually runs around the forest of material existence [simply trying to satisfy bodily desires]." *(Bhag.5.14.8)*

"The conditioned soul sometimes personally appreciates the futility of sense enjoyment in the material world, and he sometimes considers material enjoyment to be full of miseries. However, due to his strong bodily conception, his memory is destroyed, and again and again he runs after material enjoyment, just as an animal runs after a mirage in the desert." (*Bhag.*5.14.10)

"Sometimes, to mitigate distresses in this forest of the material world, the conditioned soul receives cheap blessings from atheists. He then loses all intelligence in their association. This is exactly like diving in a shallow river. As a result one simply breaks his head. He is not able to mitigate his sufferings from the heat, and in both ways he suffers. The misguided conditioned soul also approaches so-called *sadhus* and *svamis* who preach against the principles of the *Vedas*. He does not receive benefit from them, either in the present or in the future." (*Bhag.*5.14.13)

"Government men are always like carnivorous demons called Rakshashas [man-eaters]. Sometimes these government men turn against the conditioned soul and take away all his accumulated wealth. Being bereft of his life's reserved wealth, the conditioned soul loses all enthusiasm. Indeed, it is as though he loses his life." (*Bhag.*5.14.16)

"Sometimes, due to bodily hunger and thirst, the conditioned soul becomes so disturbed that he loses his patience and becomes angry with his own beloved sons, daughters and wife. Thus, being unkind to them, he suffers all the more." (*Bhag.*5.14.19)

"In the forest of the material world, the conditioned soul is sometimes bitten by envious enemies, which are compared to serpents and other creatures. Through the tricks of the enemy, the conditioned soul falls from his prestigious position. Being anxious, he cannot even sleep properly. He thus becomes more and more unhappy, and he gradually loses his intelligence and consciousness. In that state he becomes almost perpetually like a blind man who has fallen into a dark well of ignorance." (*Bhag.*5.14.21)

"The conditioned soul is sometimes attracted to the little happiness derived from sense gratification. Thus he has illicit sex or steals another's property. At such a time he may be arrested by the government or chastised by the woman's husband or protector. Thus simply for a little material satisfaction, he falls into a hellish condition and is put into jail for rape, kidnapping, theft and so forth." (*Bhag.*5.14.22)

"As far as transactions with money are concerned, if one person cheats another by a farthing or less, they become enemies." (*Bhag.*5.14.26)

"Although people may be enemies, in order to fulfill their desires again and again, they sometimes get married. Unfortunately, these marriages do not last very long, and the people involved are separated again by divorce or other means." (*Bhag.*5.14.37)

"Sometimes the conditioned soul, fearing the approach of death, wants to worship someone who can save him from imminent danger. Yet he does not care for the Supreme Personality of Godhead, whose weapon is the indefatigable time factor. The conditioned soul instead takes shelter of a man-made god described in unauthorized scriptures. Such gods are like buzzards, vultures, herons and crows. Vedic scriptures do not refer to them. Imminent death is like the attack of a lion, and neither vultures, buzzards, crows nor herons can save one from such an attack. One who takes shelter of unauthorized man-made gods cannot be saved from the clutches of death." (*Bhag.*5.14.29)

"The pseudo *svamis*, yogis, and incarnations who do not believe in the Supreme Being are known as *pasandis* [atheistic cheaters]. They themselves are fallen and cheated because they do not know the real path of spiritual advancement, and whoever goes to them is certainly cheated in his turn. When one is thus cheated, he sometimes takes shelter of the real followers of the Vedic principles [*brahmanas* or devotees], who teach everyone how to worship the Supreme Personality of Godhead according to the Vedic rituals. However, being unable to stick to these principles, these rascals again fall down and take shelter among *sudras* who are very expert in making arrangements for sex indulgence. Sex is very prominent among animals like monkeys, and such people who are enlivened by sex may be called descendants of monkeys." (*Bhag.*5.14.30)

The evolutionists are always describing mankind as being the descendants of monkeys, and now we find the Vedic texts agree but in a very different sense. Here it is explained that those people who are always very much eager to engage in animalistic pleasures show signs of descending from lusty animals in their past life, such as monkeys. But by continuing to pursue animalistic propensities in this life, they again develop the consciousness of an animal so that after death they will return to the animal species of life. This is how, instead of progressing higher on the evolutionary path, one can actually go backwards.

As we have now related in this chapter, the living being evolves from the womb and goes through life up to the moment of death, searching all the while for happiness according to the dictates of his mind and senses. This goes on lifetime after lifetime on the material path unless a person can find a true spiritual guide who can teach how to get free.

"In this materialistic life, there are many difficulties, as I have just mentioned, and all of these are insurmountable. In addition, there are difficulties arising from so-called happiness, distress, attachment, hate, fear, false prestige, illusion, madness, lamentation, bewilderment, greed, enmity, insult, hunger, thirst, tribulation, disease, birth, old age, and death. All these combine together to give the materialistic conditioned soul nothing but misery." (*Bhag.*5.14.27)

"Learned scholars and transcendentalists therefore condemn the materialistic path of fruitive activity because it is the original source and breeding ground of material miseries, both in this life and in the next." (*Bhag.*5.14.23)

## OLD AGE AND DEATH

As people become old they begin to experience various diseases. The eyes and ears become weak, making it difficult to see and hear clearly. The teeth become rotten and the mouth is often fitted with false teeth in order for one to chew his food. The muscles and joints do not bend or function as they used to and a cane is often needed to help one walk. The throat and lungs may fill up with mucus, and one may suffer severe coughing. Even passing urine or stool may be very troublesome and painful. In many cases, people can no longer take care of themselves properly, what to speak of taking care of others. Thus, as we have often seen, as people enter old age their existence becomes the responsibility and burden of others.

"The foolish family man does not become averse to family life although he is maintained by those whom he once maintained. Deformed by the influence of old age, he prepares himself to meet ultimate death. Thus he remains at home just like a pet dog and eats whatever is so negligently given to him. Afflicted with many illnesses, such as dyspepsia and loss of appetite, he eats only very small morsels of food, and he becomes an invalid who cannot work anymore." (Bhag.3.30.14-15)

"In this way, he comes under the clutches of death and lies down, surrounded by lamenting friends and relatives, and although he wants to speak with them, he no longer can because he is under the control of time. Thus the man, who engaged with uncontrolled senses in maintaining a family, dies in great grief, seeing his relatives crying. He dies most pathetically, in great pain and without consciousness." (Bhag.3.30.17-18)

At the time of death, the living being does not want to leave his body. He wants to go on associating with friends and relatives in the hope of enjoying life and fulfilling his plans and desires. He thinks of his sons, daughters, grandchildren, servants, pets, wealth, and other accumulated possessions and does not want to leave them. The dying man remembers the past affectionate dealings he had with his wife and children and worries about how they will go on without him. In this way, he is completely absorbed in thoughts of family life while passing from this world. He may want the physician to extend his life in any way possible, but regardless of the expert treatment given by the doctor, the old man is forced to die, for his time has arrived. Death is the door to that journey from which no one returns, and where that journey will take him is rarely known. For one who is unprepared, the thought of death can cause great fear regardless of how he tries to rationalize it in his mind.

Even though he is anxious to continue living, the high fever known as *prajvara* or *vishnujvara* makes him feel as if he is in the middle of a blazing fire and he begins to blackout. His temperature begins to rise up to 107 degrees at which time he dies. His body then starts to become cold and stiff. For an ordinary person who is bereft of advancement in yoga, he may experience a sensation of traveling down a tunnel and then, along with his life air, he is forced out of the body, passing through the rectum or other bodily opening. After leaving the body, the soul, along with the subtle body, is carried over to the next form of existence.

"Those who are interested only in a so-called beautiful life--namely remaining as a householder entangled by sons and a wife and searching after wealth--think that such things are life's ultimate goal. Such people simply wander in different types of bodies throughout this material existence without finding the ultimate goal of life." (Bhag.4.25.6)

If, however, a person is ready to leave the body, either by attaining spiritual enlightenment or through detachment from one's situation (as in the case of someone who has a deseased body and has grown tired of the suffering), death is not necessarily a painful experience but a relief, a transition from one realm to the next. A spiritually enlightened person is not so disturbed at the end of life because, as Sri Krishna explains in Bhagavad-gita (2.12,13,20,22): "Never was there a time when I did not exist, nor you, nor all these kings; nor in the future shall any of us cease to be. As the embodied soul continually passes, in this body, from boyhood to youth to old age, the soul similarly passes into another body at death. The self-realized soul is not bewildered by such a change. . . For the soul there is never birth nor death. Nor, having once been, does he ever cease to be. He is unborn, eternal, ever-existing, undying and primeval. He is not slain when the body is slain. . . As a person puts on new garments, giving up old ones, similarly, the soul accepts new material bodies, giving up the old and useless ones."

Understanding one's spiritual identity, the self-realized soul is not agitated or confused at the time of death. For him it is simply a change of body, and if he is liberated from the material conception of life, his next body will be a spiritual body and he will be completely free from anymore birth and death. For those who are eager to reach this spiritual perfection, the Supreme guides them from within as Supersoul. Thus, a person is able to attain a position, either in this life or the next, where he can make actual spiritual advancement. However, those who are interested only in sense gratification are averse to hearing the Supreme and how to make spiritual progress. Thus, they continue in the cycle of repeated birth and death. This is explained in the following verses from Srimad-Bhagavatam:

"The living entity labors under the bodily conceptions of 'I am this, I am that. My duty is this, and therefore I shall do it.' These are all mental impressions, and all these activities are temporary; nonetheless, by the grace of the Supreme Personality of Godhead, the living entity gets a chance to execute all his mental concoctions. Thus he gets another body." (Bhag.4.29.62)

"Such persons, impelled by the mode of passion, are full of anxieties and always aspire for sense gratification due to uncontrolled senses. They worship the forefathers and are busy day and night improving the economic condition of their family, social or national life. Such persons are called *trai-vargika* because they are interested in the three elevating processes [which includes religion on the fundamental or mundane level, economic development, and sense gratification]. They are averse to the Supreme Personality of Godhead, who can give relief to the conditioned soul. They are not interested in the Supreme Personality's pastimes, which are worth hearing because of His transcendental prowess. . . Such materialistic persons are allowed to go to the planet called Pitriloka by the southern course of the sun, but they again come back to this planet and take birth in their own families, beginning again the same fruitive activities from birth to the end of life." (*Bhag.*3.32.17-18,20)

From this we can understand that those who are extremely attached to the materialistic path will again have a chance to come back and engage in the same materialistic pursuits as they did before. Of course, how successful they will be in their endeavors depends on their *karma*. Still, they will have every opportunity to struggle in the attempt to experience the same joys, accomplishments, victories, etc., along with the same sorrows, disappointments, anxieties, and, last but not least, the pain of death. Life in the material world is considered to be like a dream that is vanishing right in front of us with the passing of time. We may think we are a man or woman, a father or mother, a great politician, a president of a company, or a simple factory worker. But everything we become and all that we accumulate are immpermanent, like in a dream we have at night. And we are forced to wake up to the reality of the good or bad consequences of our activities when we must face the afterlife. Thus, everything we have done is tested at the time of death.

## THE AFTERLIFE--HEAVEN, HELL, OR BEYOND

The *Manu-samhita* (12.20-21) explains that in this life, "If the soul chiefly practises virtue and vice only to a small degree, it obtains bliss in heaven, clothed with those very elements. But if it chiefly cleaves to vice and only to virtue in a small degree, deserted by the elements [of the physical body], it suffers the torments inflicted by Yamaraja."

This is also mentioned in *Srimad-Bhagavatam* (3.30.30-31): "After leaving this body, the man who maintained himself and his family members by sinful activities suffers a hellish life, and his relatives suffer also. He goes alone to the darkest regions of hell after quitting the present body, and the money he acquired by envying other living entities is the passage money with which he leaves this world. Thus, by the arrangement of the Supreme Personality of Godhead, the maintainer of kinsmen is put into a hellish condition to suffer for his sinful activities, like a man who has lost his wealth. Therefore a person who is very eager to maintain his family and kinsmen simply by black methods certainly goes to the darkest region of hell, known as Andha-tamisra."

In this way, it is described that when one lives by unfair means, he only takes the sinful reactions with him. But how do the sinful reactions cling to the living entity? This question was asked and answered thousands of years ago. "[King Pracinabarhi inquired:] 'The expert knowers of the Vedic conclusions say that one enjoys or suffers the results of his past activities. But practically it is seen that the body that performed the work in the last birth is already lost. So how is it possible to enjoy or suffer the reactions of that work in a different body?' The great sage Narada continued: 'The living entity acts in a gross body in this life. This body is forced to act by the subtle body, composed of mind, intelligence, and ego. After the gross body is lost, the subtle body is still there to enjoy or suffer. Thus there is no change.'" (Bhag.4.29.59-60)

Herein, we can understand that sinful reactions affect the subtle body of the person immediately after death. For example, it is related in the Vedic literature that when a particular selfish king died, who had killed numerous living entities in rituals and on hunting excursions, he was instantly attacked by those he had killed. "The most unkind king, Puranjana, had killed many animals in various sacrifices. Now, taking advantage of this opportunity [the death of the king], all these animals began to pierce him with their horns. It was as though he were being cut to pieces by axes." (Bhag.4.28.26) This is how one may suffer after death at the hands of those he unjustly mistreated. But, as previously stated, by practicing evil one also goes to the hellish planets. Descriptions of how this takes place are also found in the Vedic texts.

"At death, the dying person sees the messengers of the lord of death [the Yamadutas, soldiers of Yamaraja] come before him, their eyes full of wrath, and in great fear he passes stool and urine. As a criminal is arrested for punishment by the constables of the state, a person engaged in criminal sense gratification is similarly arrested by the Yamadutas, who bind him by the neck with strong rope and cover his subtle body so that he may undergo severe punishment. While carried by the constables of Yamaraja, he is overwhelmed and trembles in their hands. While passing on the road he is bitten by dogs, and he can remember the sinful activities of his life. He is thus terribly distressed." (Bhag.3.30.19-20)

So, as a dying person sees the horrible and fierce soldiers of Yamaraja, he is so affected by fear that he passes stool and urine. This is not an uncommon incident when a person dies. Furthermore, just as it has been reported in near-death experiences that the person who temporarily leaves his body seemes to enter a pleasant light, there have also been reports by others to have seen frightful looking creatures who were threatening to take them away. Nurses in hospitals and hospices have told of experiences in which dying persons had been afraid of something he or she was seeing and would try to get away or shout in protest or fear just before dying. In fact, I have heard one report in which, as a family was at the bedside of their dying relative, the man who was quietly lying on the bed suddenly rose up, raised his hand as if to keep something away from him, fearfully yelled out, "No, no," and then instantly collapsed dead. No one could understand what he had seen, but it could very likely have been the soldiers of Yamaraja coming to take him away. Where they take such a person is further described.

"Under the scorching sun [on the subtle platform of existence], the criminal has to pass through roads of hot sand with forest fires on both sides. He is whipped on the back by the constables because of his inability to walk, and he is affected by hunger and thirst, but unfortunately there is no drinking water, no shelter and no place for rest on the road. While passing on that road to the abode of Yamaraja, he falls down in fatigue, and sometimes he becomes unconscious, but he is forced to rise again. In this way he is very quickly brought to the presence of Yamaraja. Thus he has to pass ninety-nine thousand *yojanas* [eight miles equal one *yojana*] within two or three moments, and then he is at once engaged in the torturous punishment which he is destined to suffer.

"He is placed in the midst of burning pieces of wood, and his limbs are set on fire. In some cases he is made to eat his own flesh or have it eaten by others. His entrails are pulled out by the hounds and the vultures of hell, even though he is still alive to see it, and he is subjected to torment by serpents, scorpions, gnats, and other creatures that bite him. Next his limbs are lopped off and torn asunder by elephants. He is hurled down from hilltops, and he is also held captive either in water or in a cave. Men and women whose lives were built upon indulgence in illicit sex life are put into many kinds of miserable conditions in the hells known as Tamisra, Andha-tamisra, and Raurava." (*Bhag*.3.30.21-28)

This is the detailed description of the descent into hell of the wicked and the horrible punishment awaiting them. If one has been too wicked and has greatly misused the human form of life by causing pain to others and chasing after immoral forms of enjoyment, he will not see the human form of life again for many years. In fact, his punishment simply prepares him for his future existence in the lower species of life.

However, "Having gone through all the miserable, hellish conditions and having passed in a regular order through the lowest forms of animal life prior to human birth, and having thus been purged of his sins, one is reborn again as a human being on this earth." (*Bhag*.3.30.34)

This is also confirmed in the *Manu-samhita* where it states: "The individual soul, having endured those torments of Yama, again enters, free from taint, those very five elements [earth, air, fire, water, and ether--the physical body], each in due proportion." (*Manu*.12.22)

Herein, it is explained that entrance into hell or taking birth in the lower species of life is not eternal, but lasts only as long as our sinful reactions need to be worked out. Once we have endured such reactions, we are again free to take a human form of birth to start again.

On the other hand, rather than entering hell, if we have performed pious or virtuous activities, we can ascend to the heavenly planets to take birth and live there. "When the conditioned soul accepts the shelter of the creeper of fruitive activity, he may be elevated by his pious activities to higher planetary systems and thus gain liberation from hellish conditions, but unfortunately he cannot remain there. After reaping the results of his pious activities, he has to return to the lower planetary systems. In this way he perpetually goes up and comes down." (*Bhag.*5.14.41)

This is how all living entities evolve within this material cosmic manifestation, through the higher and lower planetary systems, and high and low species of life. According to the consciousness and desires existing in the conditioned soul's subtle body, one acquires a particular type of gross body in order that he may attempt to satisfy those desires. "The mind is the cause of the living entity's attaining a certain type of body in accordance with his association with material nature. According to one's mental composition, one can understand what the living entity was in his past life as well as what kind of body he will have in the future. Thus the mind indicates the past and future bodies." (*Bhag.*4.29.66) Thus, by analyzing the mind and the living entity's desires, as we have discussed in Chapter Six, we can understand where we have come from and where we are going. This is the real science of evolution as found in the *Vedas*.

All the experiences we go through, lifetime after lifetime in this temporary universe, is considered to be nothing more than a dream which is taken as reality by the mind. The dream of material life comes forth and then fades away before our very eyes in the stages of past, present, and future, as it fluctuates within the three modes of material nature. As verified in *Srimad-Bhagavatam* (4.29.2B): "Everything happening within time, which consists of past, present and future, is merely a dream. That is the secret understanding in all Vedic literature."

Through this dream, we experience the various levels of material consciousness as we evolve through our different desires and conceptions of life. Yet, just as our life is temporary and comes to an end, similarly this whole cosmic creation and everything in it and all that takes place inside has a beginning and an end. One day it will be completely annihilated by the will of the Supreme. At such a time this grand illusion exists no more and has no further meaning. But, in the meantime, how long we continue to evolve through the various types of material experiences, searching for lasting pleasure and happiness, depends on us.

Obviously, since this whole cosmic creation is temporary, whatever happiness, misery, or meaning we find within it is also temporary. How could anyone expect otherwise? Therefore, the only real way to reach a stage of full and unfading happiness is to search for that realm which is beyond this temporary material nature. The only actual way to wake up from this temporary material dream is through spiritual enlightenment. Otherwise, the dream continues.

The *Bhagavad-gita* explains that after many lives a wise man finally reaches the highest point of evolutionary development, which is to understand the Supreme Truth. Such a great soul is very rare because most everyone is more concerned about his position and well-being within this world. But the fact of the matter is that only by understanding the Supreme can one finish his wandering through the highs and lows of this cosmic creation. This is also confirmed in *Srimad-Bhagavatam*: "Philosophical research culminates in understanding the Supreme Personality of Godhead. After achieving this understanding, when one becomes free from the material modes of nature, he attains the stage of devotional service. Either by devotional service directly or by philosophical research, one has to find the same destination, which is the Supreme Personality of God." (*Bhag*.3.32.32)

As the Vedic teachings explain, this is the final goal for which everyone should strive, and is, indeed, the ultimate solution for ending one's problems within this material existence. This is specifically stressed in *Bhagavad-gita* by Lord Sri Krishna, where He says: "After attaining Me, the great souls, who are yogis in devotion, never return to this temporary world, which is full of miseries, because they have attained the highest perfection. From the highest planet in the material world down to the lowest, all are places of misery wherein repeated birth and death take place. But one who attains to My abode, O son of Kunti, never takes birth again." (*Bg*.8.15-16)

These verses clearly explain that one can jump over any further entanglement in the material world by engaging in the process of devotional yoga. Such a process ends any fear of death because one can directly regain his or her spiritual position and enter into the kingdom of God immediately after being released from the material body. "That is the way of the spiritual and godly life, after attaining which a man is not bewildered. Being so situated, even at the hour of death, one can enter into the kingdom of God." (*Bg*.2.72)

"[This spiritual nature] is eternal and is transcendental to this manifested and unmanifested matter. It is supreme and is never annihilated. When all this world is annihilated, that part remains as it is. That supreme abode is called unmanifested and infallible, and it is the supreme destination. When one goes there, he never comes back. That is My supreme abode." (*Bg*.8.20-21)

* * *

Here, then, in this chapter is the explanation of the process of evolution according to the *Vedas*. The spiritual living entity can evolve throughout all the different 8,400,000 species of life or the different higher and lower planetary systems, so that one is fully experienced in all aspects of material existence. But only in the human form can one understand this spiritual knowledge. This is the rare opportunity of the human stage of the living being's evolution. By realizing the Supreme Truth, one has reached the highest destination of evolutionary development and can enter into the spiritual dimension.

If, however, one is interested only in the animalistic propensities, such as eating, sleeping, mating, and defending, without consideration for spiritual development, then after death he will regress into the animal species for which he is more suitable. After all, a dog is not expected to act like anything but a dog, but a human being who acts like an animal simply becomes a disturbance to the rest of society. Therefore, in such a case, nature will award him with an appropriate animal body. Only after evolving through the various species of life will he get another opportunity of a human birth. By understanding this, one can recognize the value and responsibility of this human form of life.

But, someone may likely ask, if material existence can be such a struggle, and if after falling into the cosmic creation it is so difficult to get back out or even find the way to get out, then why do we have to go through this? Why is it necessary to evolve through 8,400,000 species of life or go to heaven or hell? Indeed, why is there anything at all? That is the question we will tackle in our next chapter.

# CHAPTER NINE

# *Why Is There Anything?*

"Why is there anything?" is a question not often asked by everyone. Most of us have settled into a routine that curbs our thinking towards the day to day concerns of paying the rent, going to school or work, doing our job, and raising the children. So, we may not often think about it. But there are still many times when we find ourselves indirectly asking this same question: "Why is there anything?" For example, how many times have we heard someone ask, "Why is this happening to me?" or "Why do things have to be like this?" Or people will make comments to each other like, "Things never seem to go as you plan," or "You just can't win for losing, can you?" This is a way of indirectly questioning our existence.

Children, however, in their state of youthful awareness and curiosity, are more direct. They may often ask their parents why there is a sun or a moon, why do people have to die, or other questions about life that their parents often do not know how to answer. Although there may be so many different ways to ask, they all reflect the same essential questions: Why is there a sun? Why is there a moon and stars? Why is there a universe? Why is there life? Why is there death? What am I supposed to do in this life? Why is there anything at all?

## WHY THE MATERIAL WORLD EXISTS

Before we can begin to understand why we exist in this material universe, we must remember that our real identity is spiritual. The living entities are actually from beyond this temporary, inferior, material creation and have a pure spiritual existence in the spiritual atmosphere. When the living being enters this material creation, one's original spiritual body and intelligence become covered over by matter. At that point, one thinks he is a product of the material world and that this temporary creation is his real home. Then, he immediately has so

163

many desires to fulfill and necessities to secure. In this way, the infinitesimal living being attempts to satisfy his desires for material enjoyment by trying to control various aspects of material nature. The material world exists in order to supply a place where the living entity can try to fulfill these illusory materialistic desires.

The material world is, therefore, created for the conditioned souls who want to lord over and control various aspects of material nature, or become a false lord for sense enjoyment. In other words, they have come here to imitate God to one degree or another. But there is only the Supreme who is the Lord of everything and controller of all. In *Bhagavad-gita*, Sri Krishna says: "I am the source of all spiritual and material worlds. Everything emanates from Me. The wise who know this perfectly engage in My devotional service and worship Me with all their hearts." (*Bg.*10.8)

Those who do not wish to acknowledge the authority of God would rather be the Supreme themselves, or at least act like it if only inside their little houses. But as the *Koran* simply states, there is no god but God. Thus, in their ignorance, the conditioned souls compete amongst themselves in their attempt to attain power, strength, position, fame, etc., and in some cases, if it were possible, the position of God. Many people would like to be rich and powerful to do and have whatever they want. This is why it is not unusual in this material world to find those who strive to be recognized, praised, and rewarded for being the best at what they do. And if someone gets in their way, immediately there are ill-feelings, disturbances, or even fights. This is the nature and cause of the endless competition in this world.

We can explain the purpose of this material world in another way. Say, for instance, the mother of a family is preparing an evening meal. She is very busy and along comes her small daughter who wants to help. She starts asking her mother questions and pulling out various pots and pans with the idea that she will help her mother cook something. Actually, she does not know what she is doing and simply gets in the way. To end this unnecessary disturbance, the mother sends her daughter into the playroom. There, the little girl has a toy stove and refrigerator, and toy pots, pans, dishes, etc. She pretends to make all kinds of preparations. Maybe she even imagines herself to be the cook on a television show in which many people are watching to learn and admire her brilliant cooking abilities. Of course, she is not really cooking anything, but she is having fun and is no longer a disturbance to her mother. However, if she continues to desire to be a good cook, then one day she will be allowed to use the real kitchen and may render valuable service to her mother. Until then, she can go on engaging in playful pastimes, out of the way of those who are more responsible.

In this way, the material world is the playground area for those who want to go on pretending to be something other than what they are. Of course, this is one's God-given independence. But a misuse of this independence by performing harmful or sinful activities causes suffering for the conditioned soul. It is not that such suffering is deliberately imposed on them, but the conditioned souls create their own suffering by means of their own acts. Material activities generate further material existence, and as long as one is covered by the material body and materialistic consciousness, suffering cannot be avoided. As long as one has even a slight desire to enjoy lording over material nature for sense gratification, he must continue his existence in these material bodies to try to fulfill such bodily desires. Thus, there is no chance of being freed from the material atmosphere.

Desiring to enjoy the temporary cosmic creation for one's own selfish purposes means to remain ignorant of one's real spiritual identity and one's relationship with the Supreme. It is said that unless one forgets his eternally blissful spiritual nature, it is impossible for him to remain content living within the limited and temporary conditions of the material world. In the spiritual world, there is no forgetfulness; so, there is no desire to enjoy temporary sense gratification. But in order to think one is enjoying the illusory happiness that comes from pampering the senses, it is necessary to forget one's spiritual nature. Therefore, a basic principle of this material world is forgetfulness of one's true identity.

False identification with the material world brings many kinds of problems upon the living entity. When one thinks he is the material body, he also exhibits the fear of death. If one is the body, then everything ends when the body is finished. But we see many people trying to improve the condition of the body to make it healthier, better looking, younger, etc. This is natural because everyone wants to continue living. Everyone generally tries to ignore the morbid subject of our inevitable death. But when we are faced with the problem of death, we become afraid because we do not want to lose everything for which we have been working and we do not know exactly what to expect after death. When all our work is on the material platform, then there is nothing that we have done that can help us at the moment of death. But one who has worked towards spiritual realization and understands that the soul neither takes birth nor dies is not afraid of death.

Another problem that comes from material identification is false proprietorship. We work hard to acquire things which we then think belong to us. Of course, everyone has a particular quota of items that they need to survive in this world. But we can also see that we are born into this life with nothing, and we take nothing with us when we die. So, everything we have in the meantime is not permanently ours. However, when we become entrapped with the sense of false ownership, we feel great anxiety about losing our property and make big arrangements to protect our wealth.

Practically, when someone is on the bodily platform of life, he may take great pride in his accomplishments, even to the point of advertising himself as a self-made man, a servant of no one. But in reality, he will spend his whole life, 24 hours a day if necessary, being the humble and most obedient servant of his mind, senses, and ego. He will gladly cater to their every whim. He eats, sleeps, works, and makes great plans simply for satisfying the mind and body. Such engagement does nothing but secure one a future birth in which he will face the same problems he has now. Being trapped in another material body guarantees that such things as hunger, thirst, disease, old age, and death will surely follow.

Actually, this cosmic creation is manifested only because the living entities want to enjoy it. The material world is not created by the personal will of the Supreme. "My dear Lord, although it is not Your desire, You manifest this creation of gross and subtle elements just for our sensual satisfaction." (*Bhag*.3.21.20) But the point of allowing the living entities to enter it and try to enjoy it is to show the uselessness of it. The spiritual living being trying to enjoy the material atmoshpere is like a fish trying to exist on dry land. The situation is incompatible. After all, who would gladly accept living in a world where one is forced to take birth, old age, disease, and death as the normal course of events? Nobody wants to grow old. Nobody likes being sick. Nobody looks forward to death. Yet, everyone must undergo these problems, not to mention all the other things that can disturb our life. Therefore, we can see that our natural inclination to live forever in a young, healthy, and beautiful body cannot be fulfilled in this material world. It is like looking for water in a desert.

We should understand that there are several reasons for this material manifestation. Naturally, as we have explained, it is a place for the conditioned souls to engage in sense gratification and forget one's real identity. But there are 8,400,000 species of life, which means there are over 8,400,000 levels of forgetfulness. Only in the human form does the living entity have a chance to begin rectifying his misidentification with the material world and realize who he or she really is. Out of compassion, the Lord creates this material world to give a chance to the conditioned souls who are asleep in forgetfulness to awaken to the real life of spiritual consciousness. This is confirmed in *Srimad-Bhagavatam* (9.24.58) where it says: "The Supreme Personality of Godhead acts through His material energy in the creation, maintenance, and annihilation of this cosmic manifestation just to deliver the living entity by His compassion and stop the living entity's birth, death, and duration of materialistic life. Thus He enables the living being to return home, back to Godhead."

This is the Supreme's desire when He decides to create this material manifestation. However, it is not a question of forcing one to spiritual consciousness. As it is said, you can lead a horse to water, but you cannot make him drink. Similarly, the means and methods to spiritualize our consciousness are provided. But if we neglect the opportunity to utilize such methods, there is no hope. One who avoids the means to wake up will remain asleep, drifting aimlessly in the dream of material existence. Therefore, the Lord is not responsible for the entity's living condition.

When the living entity finally reaches the stage of being frustrated with trying to satisfy his bodily desires for so long, he may begin to inquire about his real position. At that time, one may ask such questions as, "Why am I suffering? Why am I going through this? What am I supposed to do? What's life in this world all about?" There may be any number of ways of asking what the purpose of life is, but when one begins sincerely questioning, he becomes eligible for finding the truth.

If, however, there were no difficulties in the material world, no one would ever question the purpose of life or want to change his or her situation and get out of this material world. Who would want to change anything if all we did was wake up to a gorgeous day of sunny weather to do only what we wanted to do? But since such situations are temporary and most people must work hard and experience difficulties in life, it provides an impetus to question what we are doing here. Thus, with such inquiry, one can begin the path of realizing his or her true, spiritual nature.

It is explained that because this world is not our real home and because the Lord is the Supreme Father of all living entities, out of His compassion He brings spiritual knowledge in the form of the Vedic literature, such as *Bhagavad-gita*, so that the conditioned souls can understand things as they are. He also incarnates in this world to teach and perform amazing pastimes to attract us to Him. Or He may also send His representative, the pure devotee, to help guide us on the path back to the spiritual world. If, however, one remains in this material world, he will be annihilated with it when the material manifestation is withdrawn back into the body of the Supreme. At that time, all the conditioned souls will remain in a dormant condition until the Supreme again decides to manifest this cosmic creation. As Lord Krishna states in *Bhagavad-gita*: "O son of Kunti, at the end of the millennium every material manifestation enters into My nature, and at the beginning of another millennium, by My potency I again create." (*Bg*.9.7)

The Supreme is transcendental and exists before the material creation is manifested. When the Supreme decides to create the material worlds, He glances over the material ingredients, which immediately become active and form the cosmic creation. This is confirmed in *Aitareya Upanishad* (1.1): "The Lord glanced at material nature." In this way, the creation of the material world can be taken as one of the pastimes of the Supreme. The Lord is the source of both the superior, unlimited, spiritual energy as well as the inferior, limited material energy. So, naturally, God will occasionally want to exhibit the material creation, especially to give another chance to the conditioned souls within to return to the spiritual world.

No one can say when the living entities first desired to engage in material existence. The cause is untraceable. But since we are all originally spiritual, there was a point when material life began. When the living beings appear in the material world, they identify with material nature and transmigrate from one kind of body to another. They identify with a particular species, or when they are in the human form they think of themselves as belonging to a particular race, nation, sex, or religion, and forget their real identity as eternal, spiritual parts and parcels of the Supreme. As this whole world goes on under this illusion, one out of millions of people will take to understanding spiritual life and leave the material world behind. Such a soul is very rare; yet, everyone, sooner or later, must return to this level of consciousness. This is the real goal of life in the material creation.

## WHY THERE IS LIFE AT ALL

Someone may ask why the infinitesimal spirit souls are created at all. The answer is that the Supreme Being is complete when He is both infinite and infinitesimal. If the Supreme was infinite only, He would not be complete. After all, what meaning would there be in the word *lord* if there were no other beings to overlord?

Furthermore, the infinitesimal living entities are emanations from the original Infinite Spirit. In other words, we have the same spiritual qualities as the Supreme but in extremely small quantities. We do not have the same power as the Lord but share the same transcendental characteristics, just as sparks are limitedly similar to the blazing fire from which they emanate. But just as sparks lose their potency when they leave the blazing fire, the living entities, upon entering the material atmosphere, forget their eternally blissful, spiritual nature and are overcome with the hard struggle for existence.

Since we are all emanations from the Supreme, we are all sons and daughters of the same Supreme Father and share a special relationship between each other and the Father. But the living beings and the Father are all individuals. They are not all the same or all one. Some proclaim that ultimate reality is that in which all living beings merge together with the Supreme Being to become One. But if the son and the father were one person, there would be no relationship between them. Without individuality, there would also be no activity that they could share with each other. Without activity to share, there is no fun, no adventure, nor loving exchange. In that case, without individuality, there would be no infinitesimal living entities, and the Lord would be inactive in a spiritual world that offered no variegatedness. In other words, everything would be void. If such were the case, there would also be no need for a material creation where individual, conditioned souls could chase after their own particular material desires. Thus, there would be no material world, no spiritual world, no anything. But as we can plainly see, such is not the case.

Due to the infinite, spiritual desires of the loving Supreme Personality, there is the spiritual world and the innumerable parts and parcels of the Lord, the living entities. Within the spiritual realm, they all engage in eternal, blissful, loving pastimes. It is these pastimes and this eternal, blissful condition for which we, deep within ourselves, are always hankering, whether we realize it or not. It is natural for the Infinite to have infinitesimal portions which are His inseparable parts and parcels because they compliment His position. There would not be one without the other. However, the relationship between them is variegated and spontaneous, not like the master/servant relationship in the material world where the servant serves only as long as the master pays.

In the spiritual world, there is a natural loving reciprocation between the Supreme and His infinitesimal parts and parcels. The individual living entities help serve and satisfy all the desires of the Supreme and by doing so, in such a personal loving relationship with the Absolute, they also feel unlimited pleasure. They feel many millions of times more pleasure and happiness by satisfying the spiritual senses of the Supreme Soul than the materialists who are trying to satisfy their own dull senses in this material world. Therefore, those who are serving the Supreme directly, or serving the other devotees of the Supreme, feel that there is nothing else that could give them more pleasure. They are perfectly satisfied in what they do. Thus, the Lord and all His parts and parcels in the spiritual world feel very happy in their loving reciprocation. This is the nature of the spiritual world. The energies of the Lord are always expanding, and one's happiness from serving the Supreme in the spiritual world is also ever-increasing. In fact, one of the names of God, *Krishna*, means "the greatest pleasure." So, it is easy to understand that working for Krishna means to work for one's best interest and for the greatest pleasure.

It is no wonder, therefore, that materialists in this world are often frustrated with their endeavors and their search for love. They do not know where to look, neither will anything they find last very long. A marriage that seemed so special loses its spark and ends in divorce. An exciting career later becomes dull and boring. Or a happy and beautiful life ends tragically with death. Nobody wants it like this. So, naturally, when the spiritual living entity, who is by nature eternal, blissful, and full of knowledge, enters into the material elements which are temporary, miserable, and unconscious, he will feel frustrated and inadequately satisfied.

Therefore, the more we understand about the real reason for our existence and the difference between the spiritual and material worlds, the more sense it makes to strive for spiritual advancement and leave this material world behind by going back home, back to the spiritual abode. Working toward this end and helping others to do the same is the goal of human life and the only solution which will solve all our problems. Once the infinitesimal living entity regains his or her spiritual consciousness and begins rendering pure devotional service to the Infinite Supreme Lord, one's spiritual life and loving propensity will fully blossom. In such a state, one is completely satisfied. This is the conclusion as it is presented in the Vedic texts and by those who are spiritually realized.

# CHAPTER TEN

## *Personal God Or Impersonal Force?*

In the last chapter, I mention that the Supreme and the infinitesimal living entities are all individual; otherwise, if they all merged into oneness, there could not be loving relationships between them. Yet, we find that in all religious and theistic philosophies around the world that there are two schools of thought. One holds the idea that God is a personal being to whom we can pray, on whom we can meditate, and from whom we can expect some reciprocal exchange. The impersonalistic school advocates that God is an impersonal force, a void, or a great white light from which everything has emanated and back into which everything merges.

Many people, not having a clear understanding of what God is, are left with nothing more than their imagination to help them figure out what God must be. With such a lack of spiritual realization, one generally comes to the conclusion that either there is no God, or God may be present everywhere but is seen nowhere and must, therefore, be impersonal. In that case, we would accept Him to be nothing more than a great force or all-pervading energy within this universe. If our understanding is more fundamental, we may simply say that God is love. Or we may refer to God as the unfathomable, ever-new joy, the one-ness, the Supreme Eternal, highest bliss, the all-pervading, the Brahman, the Self, and so on. These are all obscure names touching only the outer edges of understanding God and do not reach the depth of God's real form or personality as described in the *Vedas*.

Any scripture or philosophy that has no distinct description of the form of God has the potential for leaving its students or followers with no alternative than to accept the possibility that God is impersonal and has no specific form. This only means that they do not know what God is. This is the danger of incomplete knowledge. Therefore, rather than to speculate, we need to use the Vedic texts to increase our understanding of what God actually is.

# GOD IS PERSONAL AND IMPERSONAL

The Vedic literature points out that God is both personal and impersonal. God's impersonal aspect is called different names by different people. Generally, the impersonal aspect is known as the Brahman effulgence or *brahmajyoti*. A description of the Brahman can be found in various portions of the Vedic literature, including the *Mundaka Upanishad* (2.2.10-12) where it says: "In the spiritual realm, beyond the material covering, is the unlimited Brahman effulgence, which is free from material contamination. That effulgent white light is understood by transcendentalists to be the light of all lights. In that realm there is no need of sunshine, moonshine, fire or electricity for illumination. Indeed, whatever illumination appears in the material world is only a reflection of that supreme illumination. That Brahman is in front and in back, in the north, south, east and west, and also overhead and below. In other words, that supreme Brahman effulgence spreads throughout both the material and spiritual skies."

To realize or attain entrance into the impersonal Brahman, one must practice yoga for many years without falling down from such strict practice. One must be celibate, chant the *om mantra* correctly, raise the life airs within the body to the top of the head, and leave the body while meditating on the Brahman. If one cannot void his mind of all sensual engagement and concentrate on the Brahman for hours at a time without agitation, one will not be successful. If one is successful, one can be liberated from material existence by merging into the Brahman, where there is eternity and knowledge. However, there is no *ananda* or bliss there. The only pleasure in the *brahmajyoti* is the freedom from all material suffering. Some yogis think such pleasure, which may be felt on elementary levels of meditation, is a sign of reaching the final goal. But real *ananda* is found only in spiritual engagement. Without understanding this, one's spiritual knowledge is incomplete.

The goal of the impersonalists is to merge into the Brahman effulgence, where they lose all of their individual characteristics. If they succeed, they remain there as an inactive spiritual spark, floating in the rays of the *brahmajyoti*. They do not develop a spiritual body that would give them the opportunity to engage in various spiritual activities because they do not know about such engagement that can be found on the spiritual Vaikuntha planets that exist within the Brahman effulgence. So, if they again have any yearning for engaging in activities, they cannot go upward to the spiritual planets because they are not qualified to do so. Thus, they are forced to seek shelter in the material world, where they start over again.

The problem is that it is our natural inclination to be active, always doing something. So if the soul is so active while within the material body, how can the impersonalist philosophers suggest that once we are liberated we will be completely inactive? This is not very logical. The *Vedas* state that once one has attained liberation and reaches the *brahmajyoti*, he will not stay there, but he will again desire to return to the material world for engagement. Therefore, the *brahmajyoti* is not considered the highest form of spiritual liberation, although some so-called sages today speak of it as if it is.

Such impersonalist yogis or philosophers either do not know or simply reject the fact that beyond *nirvana* and the outskirts of the Brahman effulgence are the Vaikuntha planets of the spiritual sky. Thus, due to their ignorance or rebelliousness against God, they concentrate only on the impersonal Brahman. One can enter that region by the difficult, mechanical yoga process for controlling the mind, but cannot go any higher. Just as a person cannot escape the material world if he still has material desires, he cannot enter the spiritual planets if he is still absorbed in the void. In this way, such people are unable to enter into the spiritual life of complete eternity, knowledge, and bliss. Therefore, the idea of achieving spiritual liberation by merging into the Brahman effulgence is considered the process of a cheating religion. Why it is considered this is that it destroys the opportunity for people to reestablish their loving relationship with the Supreme. This is confirmed in the *Caitanya-caritamrita* (*Adi*.1.92): "The foremost process of cheating is to desire to achieve liberation by merging in the Supreme, for this causes the permanent disappearance of loving service to Krishna." Therefore, those who have reached mature spiritual realization look upon merging into the Brahman effulgence as a great mistake.

The impersonal realization of the Brahman effulgence is the indirect process of understanding the Absolute Truth and is considered a difficult path according to *Bhagavad-gita*. "But those who fully worship the unmanifested, that which lies beyond the perception of the senses, the all-pervading, inconceivable, fixed and immovable--the impersonal conception of the Absolute Truth--by controlling the various senses and being equally disposed toward everyone, such persons, engaged in the welfare of all, at last achieve Me. For those whose minds are attached to the unmanifested, impersonal feature of the Supreme, advancement is very troublesome. To make progress in that discipline is always difficult for those who are embodied." (*Bg*.12.3-5)

By realizing this impersonal Brahman, one only realizes the bodily effulgence of the Absolute. In other words, the all-pervading spiritual force has a source. This is clearly described in the *Caitanya-caritamrita*, (*Adi*.2, 5 & 15):

"What the *Upanishads* describe as the impersonal Brahman is but the effulgence of His body, and the Lord known as the Supersoul is but His localized plenary portion. He is the Supreme Personality of Godhead, Krishna Himself, full with six opulences. He is the Absolute Truth, and no other truth is greater than or equal to Him. . . The opulences of the impersonal Brahman spread throughout the millions and millions of universes. That Brahman is but the bodily effulgence of Govinda [another name of Krishna]."

The fifteenth and sixteenth *mantras* of the *Isa Upanishad* also acknowledge that from the personal body of God comes the rays of the Brahman effulgence: "O my Lord, sustainer of all that lives, Your real face is covered by Your dazzling effulgence. Please remove that covering and exhibit Yourself to Your pure devotee. O my Lord, O primeval philosopher, maintainer of the universe, O regulating principle, destination of the pure devotees, well-wisher of the progenitors of mankind--please remove the effulgence of Your transcendental rays so that I can see Your form of bliss. You are the eternal Supreme Personality of Godhead, like unto the sun, as am I."

From these verses it is clear that without going beyond the Brahman effulgence, one cannot see the real form of the Supreme. If one reaches the stage of realizing the Brahman and becomes convinced that he has attained the Ultimate, then he does not have complete understanding or full realization. He still must go further until he has reached the source of the Brahman, which, according to the *Isa Upanishad*, is the Supreme Personality.

## THE ABSOLUTE TRUTH IS A PERSON

Many times there are so-called gurus or saints who say that the Absolute Truth, especially in referring to the void or Brahman effulgence, cannot be described with words. Of course, if that were actually the case, why would they expect people to attend their lectures when they spoke about the Absolute? But the *Vedanta-sutras* (1.1.5) point out that, "Brahman is not inexpressible by words, because it is seen that He is so expressly taught in the *Vedas*." The Absolute may not be completely expressable and understood by words alone, but there is a great deal that one can learn by this means. Beyond this, one can learn by practical experience and realization for which the various yoga practices are described. This is what the Vedic texts teach.

If the Brahman had no personality or characteristics, then, obviously, Brahman would be very difficult to describe. But the *Vedanta-sutras* correct this viewpoint in the very second verse: "He, from whom proceeds the creation, preservation and reconstruction of the universe, is Brahman." This is further substantiated in the *Mundaka Upanishad* (1.1.9) where it states that the Brahman comes from Him who knows all: "From Him who perceives all and who knows all, whose penance consists of knowledge, from Him (the highest Brahman) is born that Brahman, name, form and matter." Therefore, Brahman ultimately means a person. The conclusion, according to the Vedic texts, is that the Absolute Truth is that source from which everything emanates, and that source is, ultimately, the Supreme Person.

Since the Brahman effulgence is considered to be but one of the opulences of the Supreme, it should be understood that whenever the Vedic texts speak of Brahman, they are indicating the Supreme Personality of God. In fact, it is stated that in the *Vedas* the word *Brahman* means, "in whom all the attributes reach to the infinity." In this way, it is clear that Brahman primarily means the Supreme Person, of whom the *Vedas* are full of descriptions of various aspects of His infinite qualities and characteristics. The *Caitanya-caritamrita* clearly states: "The word 'Brahman' indicates the complete Supreme Personality of Godhead, who is Sri Krishna. That is the verdict of all Vedic literature." (*Cc.Madhya-lila*, 6.147)

The *Caitanya-caritamrita* (*Adi*.7.112) also explains that, "Everything about the Supreme Personality of Godhead is spiritual, including His body, opulence and paraphernalia. Mayavadi philosophy, however, covering His spiritual opulence, advocates the theory of impersonalism."

The Mayavadi impersonalists say that God is formless and has no attributes other than eternity and knowledge. But the truth of the matter is that God has no *material* form because He is completely spiritual. He is a transcendental person. Just as we are individuals, God is also an individual and has His form. If He were formless only, then He would be less than that which has form. Therefore, God, the complete whole, must have that which is formless as well as that which has form. Otherwise, He would not be complete. In this way, the Supreme has immense potencies, including everything within as well as beyond our experience. Krishna says: "I am the origin of everything. Everything emanates from Me." (*Bg.*10.8) Thus, the Supreme expands Himself into everything but does not lose His original form. This is also confirmed in the first verse of *Isa Upanishad* where it says: "Because He is the complete whole, even though so many complete units emanate from Him, He remains the complete balance."

The impersonalists believe that after God has expanded Himself into matter and into the innumerable living entities, He must no longer exist, just as a large piece of paper no longer exists once it has been torn into many little pieces. If such were the case, then matter and the living beings are equal to or the same as God. In other words, the impersonalists say that we are God but are temporarily undergoing the pains and pleasures in this material world due to forgetfulness of our godlike position. Once we are free from this illusory forgetfulness, or our individuality, we can merge back into the Absolute and again become God. But impersonalists fail to explain how the individual soul became separated from the Brahman effulgence to exist within this material world. Furthermore, if the soul is the same as God, how could it fall into the illusion of identifying itself as a material body? How could we, if we are God, be controlled by the illusory energy? This would mean that material nature is more powerful than God, which would negate God's supremacy.

In the logic of this kind of philosophy, there is no point in praying to God, singing praises to Him, or serving Him since, being formless, God has no ears to hear you or eyes to see you. In fact, such a formless God would have very little to do with us. He could not judge what is right or wrong or reward the righteous or punish the wrongdoers. This impersonal viewpoint actually pervades much of our society today and allows people to reason that anyone can do anything he or she wants to do and face no retribution from God or the universal laws He sets in motion.

Another point is that if God is impersonal, then it puts the process of the creation of the universe in a different light. If God were simply a mass of energy, it would not be possible for God to create the material manifestation and then watch over and control it. Thus, the way the world was created might have happened in any number of different ways. This is the point of view many people have, especially the scientists who try to piece together proof to show that the theory of evolution is truth and the world started from a big bang. The idea that God is simply an impersonal force or does not exist at all is the one factor which gives theories like evolution and the big bang some potential for credibility. But in spite of the popularity of these theories, no one has yet proved them to be true.

These various impersonalist beliefs, as briefly described above, are not supported by the *Vedas*. The *Brihadaranyaka Upanishad* says, *purnam idam purnat purnam udacyate*: "Although He expands in many ways, He keeps His original personality. His original spiritual body remains as it is." Thus, we can understand that God can expand His energies in many ways, but is not affected or diminished in His potency.

The *Svetasvatara Upanishad* (6.6) also states: "The Supreme Personality of Godhead, the original person, has multifarious energies. He is the origin of material creation, and it is due to Him only that everything changes. He is the protector of religion and annihilator of all sinful activities. He is the master of all opulences." This verse specifically points out that only due to God's multipotencies does the world continue to change and be maintained. He also protects religion, which could not be done if He were impersonal. This is only logical since it takes a person to watch over, protect, or maintain anything.

In the *Katha Upanishad* (2.2.13) there is the important verse; *nityo nityanam cetanas cetananam eko bahunam yo vidadhati kaman*: "He is the supreme eternally conscious person who maintains all other living entities." From these descriptions in the Vedic texts, we can clearly understand that God is the Supreme Person who is the source of everything and controller of all. This Supreme Person is the Absolute Truth, as confirmed in the *Caitanya-caritamrita* (*Adi*.7.111): "According to direct understanding, the Absolute Truth is the Supreme Personality of Godhead, who has all spiritual opulences. No one can be equal to or greater than Him."

Since it is established in the Vedic texts that the Absolute is a person, then meditating on the personal form of God rather than the impersonal feature is the highest form of meditation. This is verified in *Bhagavad-gita* (12.2): "The Supreme Personality of Godhead said: 'He whose mind is fixed on My personal form, always engaged in worshiping Me with great and transcendental faith, is considered by Me to be the most perfect.'"

Herein, we can understand that realizing the Absolute Truth in the form of the Supreme Person is much easier and much more attractive than struggling to merge into the great white light of the *brahmajyoti*. By understanding the

Supreme Personality, all other aspects of the Absolute, such as the Brahman effulgence and Paramatma or Supersoul, are also understood. In fact, those who are absorbed in Brahman realization can easily become attracted to understanding the Supreme Personality as did such sages as Sukadeva Gosvami and the Kumaras, as noted in *Srimad-Bhagavatam*:

"Let me offer my respectful obeisances unto my spiritual master, the son of Vyasadeva, Sukadeva Gosvami. It is he who defeats all inauspicious things within this universe. Although in the beginning he was absorbed in the happiness of Brahman realization and was living in a secluded place, giving up all other types of consciousness, he became attracted by the most melodious pastimes of Lord Sri Krishna. He therefore mercifully spoke the supreme *Purana*, known as *Srimad-Bhagavatam*, which is the bright light of the Absolute Truth and which describes the activities of Lord Krishna." (*Bhag.*12.12.68)

"When the breeze carrying the aroma of *tulasi* leaves and saffron from the lotus feet of the lotus-eyed Personality of Godhead entered through the nostrils into the hearts of those sages [the Kumaras], they experienced a change in both body and mind, even though they were attracted to impersonal Brahman understanding." (*Bhag.*3.15.43)

How the *jnani* and other yogis absorbed in the impersonal realization of the Absolute become attracted to the personal form of God is further described in the *Caitanya-caritamrita* (*Madhya-lila*, 17.137,139-140): "The mellows of Lord Krishna's pastimes, which are full of bliss, attract the *jnani* from the pleasure of Brahman realization and conquer him. . . The transcendental qualities of Sri Krishna are completely blissful and relishable. Consequently Lord Krishna's qualities attract even the minds of self-realized persons from the bliss of self-realization. Those who are self-satisfied and unattracted by external material desires are also attracted to the loving service of Sri Krishna, whose qualities are transcendental and whose activities are wonderful. Hari, the Personality of Godhead, is called Krishna because He has such transcendentally attractive features."

Many of the Gosvamis of Vrindavan who had personally realized the attractive features of the Supreme wrote many books about the transcendental personality of God. One of the greatest of these saints was Rupa Gosvami (1489-1564 A.D.) who wrote a list of Krishna's characteristics in his book, *Bhakti rasamrita-sindhu*. This list describes 64 different qualities of God that are mentioned in the Vedic literature. Some of these are; beautiful bodily features, strong, ever-youthful, effulgent, highly learned and intelligent, artistic, grave, gentle, heroic, happy, expert in joking, talks pleasingly, source of all other incarnations, giver of salvation, performs wonderful pastimes, attracts everyone by His flute playing, and so on. All of these qualities are those of someone who has a highly developed form and personality.

Even the Bible verifies that God has a most beautiful form and is not formless, as is shown in the next few verses that are very similar to the Vedic description of God's form: "My beloved is white and ruddy, the chiefest among ten thousand. His head is as the most fine gold, his locks are bushy, and black as a raven. His eyes are as the eyes of doves by the rivers of waters, washed with milk, and fitly set. His cheeks are as a bed of spices, as sweet flowers; his lips like lilies, dropping sweet smelling myrrh. His hands are as gold rings set with the beryl; his belly is as bright ivory overlaid with sapphires. His legs are as pillars of marble, set upon sockets of fine gold; his countenance is as Lebanon, excellent as the cedars. His mouth is most sweet; yea, he is altogether lovely. This is my beloved, and this is my friend." (*Song of Solomon* 5.10-16)

Obviously, there is no more elevated truth or higher bliss than the personal form of the Supreme. As Sri Krishna says: "O conqueror of wealth [Arjuna], there is no truth superior to Me." (*Bg.*7.7) Many great transcendental scholars have accepted this fact, including Lord Brahma, who, after performing many austerities for spiritual purification, became perfectly self-realized and, getting a glimpse of the Lord's spiritual nature, composed the *Brahma-samhita* many thousands of years ago and described what his confidential realizations were.

## DESCRIPTIONS FROM THE BRAHMA-SAMHITA

### Text 1

Krishna, who is known as Govinda, is the Supreme Personality of Godhead. He has an eternal blissful spiritual body. He is the origin and He is the prime cause of all causes.

### Text 29

I worship Govinda, the primeval Lord, the first progenitor who is tending the cows, yielding all desires, in abodes built with spiritual gems, surrounded by millions of purpose trees, always served with great reverence and affection by hundreds of thousands of *lakshmis* [goddesses of fortune] or *gopis*.

### Text 30

I worship Govinda, the primeval Lord, who is adept in playing on His flute, with blooming eyes like lotus petals, with  head bedecked with peacock's feather, with the figure of beauty tinged with the hue of blue clouds, and His unique loveliness charming millions of cupids.

### Text 31

I worship Govinda, the primeval Lord, round whose neck is swinging a garland of flowers beautified with the moon-locket, whose two hands are adorned with the flute and jewelled ornaments, who always revels in pastimes of love, whose graceful three-fold bending form of Syamasundara is eternally manifest.

### Text 32

I worship Govinda, the primeval Lord, whose transcendental form is full of bliss, truth, substantiality and is thus full of the most dazzling splendor. Each of the limbs of that transcendental figure possesses in Himself, the fullfledged functions of all the organs, and eternally sees, maintains and manifests the infinite universes, both spiritual and mundane.

### Text 33

I worship Govinda, the primeval Lord, who is inaccessible to the *Vedas*, but obtainable by pure unalloyed devotion of the soul, who is without a second, who is not subject to decay and is without a beginning, whose form is endless, who is the beginning, and the eternal *purusha*; yet He is a person possessing the beauty of blooming youth.

### Text 34

I worship Govinda, the primeval Lord, only the tip of the toe of whose lotus feet is approached by the yogis who aspire after the transcendental and betake themselves to *pranayama* by drilling the respiration; or by the *jnanins* who try to search out the nondifferentiated Brahman by the process of elimination of the mundane extending over thousands of millions of years.

### Text 38

I worship Govinda, the primeval Lord, who is Syamasundara, Krishna Himself with inconceivable innumerable attributes, whom the pure devotees see in their heart of hearts with the eye of devotion tinged with the salve of love.

### Text 39

I worship Govinda, the primeval Lord, who manifested Himself personally as Krishna and the different *avataras* in the world in the forms of Rama, Nrsimha, Vamana, etc., as His subjective portions.

### Text 40

I worship Govinda, the primeval Lord, whose effulgence is the source of the nondifferentiated Brahman mentioned in the *Upanishads*, being differentiated from the infinity of glories of the mundane universe, appears as the indivisible, infinite and limitless truth.

### Text 51

The three worlds are composed of the nine elements, viz., fire, earth, ether, water, air, direction, time, soul and mind. I adore the primeval Lord Govinda from whom they originate, in whom they exist and into whom they enter at the time of the universal cataclysm.

## Text 55

I adore the primeval Lord Govinda, the meditators of whom, by meditating upon Him under the sway of wrath, amorous passion, natural friendly love, fear, parental affection, delusion, reverence and willing service, attain to bodily forms befitting the nature of their contemplation.

## Text 58

When the pure spiritual experience is excited by means of cognition and service [bhakti], superexcellent unalloyed devotion characterized by love of Godhead is awakened towards Krishna, the beloved of all souls.

# CHAPTER ELEVEN

# *Recognizing*
# *The Existence of God*

Sometimes we hear people ask, "Can you show me God?" as if seeing God face to face will be the proof they expect in order for them to have faith in spiritual philosophy. In other instances, they seem to think that if they follow a yoga system or spiritual path, they will one day become God. This only reveals their utter ignorance of spiritual existence.

In order to see or perceive God, one must be qualified. You cannot order the Supreme to appear any more than you can expect the sun to rise before its proper time. The Lord will reveal Himself when and to whom He chooses. He is not anyone's order carrier. But from the Vedic literature, we get information on how anyone can recognize the Supreme's existence and influence in every aspect of life, as well as what process in which to engage that will enable us to reach the stage of attaining direct perception of God.

First of all, one should understand that God is not material and certainly cannot be seen with material eyes. However, God can be seen from within by spiritual eyes that are opened by spiritual development. As long as one's spiritual eyes are closed due to attachment for material things, one cannot see God. But when one becomes spiritually advanced and attachment to the temporary material world is diminished, one can easily see God. Until then, however, a person has no qualification for such vision and must, therefore, develop the right attributes if one expects to perceive the truth of the Supreme Being's existence. When one's spiritual vision has matured, he will understand that the Lord is beyond anything material, as explained in *Srimad-Bhagavatam* (3.9.36): "Although I am not easily knowable by the conditioned soul, you have known Me today because you know that My personality is not constituted of anything material, and specifically not of the five gross and three subtle elements."

Those who have become spiritually developed can practically see God everywhere by dint of their freedom from material attachments and limitations. "Steady in the Self, being freed from all material contamination, the yogi achieves the highest perfectional stage of happiness in touch with the Supreme Consciousness. A true yogi observes Me in all beings, and also sees every being in Me. Indeed, the self-realized man sees Me everywhere. For one who sees Me everywhere and sees everything in Me, I am never lost, nor is he ever lost to Me." (Bg.6.28-30)

This is similar to what we find in the Yajur-veda (40.5-7): "God is far distant from the irreligious and ignorant, and near the yogis. He is within this entire universe, and surrounds it externally. The man who sees all animate and inanimate creation in God, and God pervading all material objects, falls not a prey to doubt. A man contemplating upon God, feels in Him all beings like unto himself. Such a yogi looking upon God as an unequalled One, becomes free from delusion and grief."

From this description, we can understand that the spiritually self-realized person always sees the influence of God everywhere and constantly feels the presence of God in all his undertakings. Because of this vision, he remains free from the competition of materialistic society and is never without purpose or ever confused about life. In fact, as explained in Bhagavad-gita (5.29): "The sages, knowing Me [Sri Krishna] as the ultimate purpose of all sacrifices and austerities, the Supreme Lord of all planets and demigods and the benefactor and well-wisher of all living entities, attain peace from the pangs of material miseries."

This is the formula for attaining real peace. By understanding that God is the ultimate enjoyer of all activities, that He is the supreme proprietor of all worlds and the supreme friend and well-wisher of all living entities, one becomes peaceful because he understands things as they are. No one else can be the ultimate enjoyer or permanent proprietor of anything. Our existence in these bodies is temporary. And although we may care about the condition of other living beings, our ability to take care of them is very limited. Therefore, we are not the ultimate friend of everyone. But by understanding that the Supreme is the master of material energy, and by working within the framework of the Lord's plan for this creation and helping others to do the same are what can make this world a peaceful place, where all can live in unity. This is the highest service one can do for others in this world.

Unfortunately, there are many who do not recognize the power of God. "Fools deried Me when I descend in the human form. They do not know My transcendental nature and My supreme dominion over all that be. Those who are thus bewildered are attracted by demoniac and atheistic views. In that deluded condition, their hopes for liberation, their fruitive activities, and their culture of knowledge are all defeated." (Bg.9.11-12)

Obviously, those who do not recognize the authority of God and in their foolishness try to figure out the purpose of life or attempt to solve the problems of the world on their own have little hope of being successful. Such fools feel that God has no relevance and, therefore, do not consider God's instructions as found in the Vedic texts. Some even proclaim that God is dead. Thus, they feel that the world goes on in a mechanical way and whatever happens for better or worse completely depends on the decisions of man. Is there any wonder, therefore, why moral standards, the crime rate, or things like murder, terrorism, war, etc., continually get worse?

The tendency is that people are becoming more godless. They feel that they are the ones in control and that God has little to do with them. Thus, they know little about what to do in life and often go through times of confusion and depression in their futile attempts to make sense of it all. Being attracted by demoniac or atheistic viewpoints, there is no doubt that things will only get worse for such people, as well as for those around them. Unless they can be guided by someone who is spiritually realized, their destiny will remain unknown.

Those who are not in a deluded condition and are aware of the constant and active supremacy of God realize that there is actually no truth superior to the Supreme. "Of all that is material and all that is spiritual in this world, know for certain that I [Sri Krishna] am both its origin and dissolution. O conqueror of wealth [Arjuna], there is no Truth superior to Me. Everything rests upon Me, as pearls are strung on a thread." (Bg.7.6-7)

"O son of Pritha, those who are not deluded, the great souls, are under the protection of the divine nature. They are fully engaged in devotional service because they know Me as the Supreme Personality of Godhead, original and inexhaustible. Always chanting My glories, endeavoring with great determination, bowing down before Me, these great souls perpetually worship Me with devotion. Others who are engaged in the cultivation of knowledge, worship the Supreme Lord as the one without a second, diverse in many, and in the universal form. But it is I who am the ritual, I the sacrifice, the offering to the ancestors, the healing herb, the transcendental chant. I am the butter and the fire and the offering." (Bg.9.13-16)

"I am the father of this universe, the mother, the support, and the grandsire. I am the object of knowledge, the purifier and the syllable om. I am also the Rig, Sama, and the Yajur [Vedas]. I am the goal, the sustainer, the master, the witness, the abode, the refuge and the most dear friend. I am the creation and the annihilation, the basis of everything, the resting place and the eternal seed. O Arjuna, I control heat, the rain and the draught. I am immortality, and I am also death personified. Both being and nonbeing are in me. . . I am the only enjoyer and the only object of sacrifice. Those who do not recognize My true transcendental nature fall down." (Bg.9.17-19,24)

In this description from Bhagavad-gita, we not only understand the characteristics of those who are not deluded by the material energy, but we also begin to see how the power of God can be recognized around us. It says that God is the mother and father of the universe, the object of all knowledge, the creation and basis of everything. Those that realize this are under the protection of the divine nature and fully engage in devotional service because they see the evidence of God's supremacy in all aspects of life. The *Atharva-veda* specifically mentions that one can recognize the existence of God simply by seeing all that God has created. "Just as the sun is brought forth from day to day, derives its origins from Him, so the existence of God is perceived by beholding the universe, which in reality is created by Him." (*Atharva*, 13.4.29)

We too can realize and see how everything is an expansion of the energies of the Absolute by studying the descriptions found in the Vedic writings. In fact, by submissively hearing these descriptions, we can look out across this material world with a totally different vision. Everyone is always looking for an enlightening or thrilling experience. We always appreciate something which has a profound affect on us. The Vedic descriptions which follow can actually bring us to the level of perceiving the influence of God very easily. We can begin to see that everything is but a display of the energy of God and all that happens is ultimately caused by the direction of the Supreme.

"As the mighty wind, blowing everywhere, always rests in ethereal space, know that in the same manner all beings rest in Me. . . The whole cosmic order is under Me. By My will it is manifested again and again, and by My will it is annihilated at the end. . . This material nature is working under My direction, O son of Kunti, and it is producing all moving and unmoving beings. By its rule this manifestation is created and annihilated again and again." (*Bg*.9.6,8,10)

"O son of Kunti [Arjuna], I am the taste of water, the light of the sun and the moon, the syllable *om* in the Vedic *mantras*; I am the sound in ether and ability in man. I am the original fragrance of the earth, and I am the heat in fire. I am the life of all that lives, and I am the penances of all ascetics. O son of Pritha, know that I am the original seed of all existences, the intelligence of the intelligent, and the prowess of all powerful men. I am the strength of the strong, devoid of passion and desire. I am sex life which is not contrary to religious principles, O Lord of the Bharatas [Arjuna]. All states of being--be they goodness, passion or ignorance--are manifested by My energy. I am, in one sense, everything--but I am independent. I am not under the modes of this material nature." (*Bg*.7.8-12)

Lord Krishna says here that He is the intelligence of the intelligent and the prowess of the powerful. It is interesting to remember this when we so often see people who are very proud of their accomplishments. Whether they are great athletes, artists, scientists, etc., who have worked hard to achieve or discover something, let us not forget that, as it is pointed out, the ability in them is a fragmental portion of the power of the Supreme. The scientists strive so hard to create life and boast of their accomplishments while giving no credit to God who has already created everything. They may say that life began in some primordial soup and that due to their unique intelligence they will soon discover what the ingredients are, but they do not even know from where they have gotten their intelligence. They did not make their own brain; so, who gave it to them?

Therefore, when they boast about their discoveries in the search to find how life began, they are, in effect, simply advertising their ignorance. They do not even understand how the planets keep their orbits. Yet, we can easily find the explanation for this and more information about the Absolute in the following verses from *Bhagavad-gita*:

"I [Sri Krishna] enter into each planet, and by My energy they stay in orbit. I become the moon and thereby supply the juices of life to all vegetables. I am the fire of digestion in every living body, and I am the air of life, outgoing and incoming, by which I digest the four kinds of foodstuff. I am seated in everyone's heart, and from Me come remembrance, knowledge and forgetfulness. By all the *Vedas* am I to be known; indeed I am the compiler of Vedanta, and I am the knower of the *Vedas*." (*Bg*.15.13-15)

"The splendor of the sun, which dissipates the darkness of this whole world, comes from Me. And the splendor of the moon and the splendor of fire are also from Me." (*Bg*.15.12)

"I am the Self, seated in the hearts of all creatures. I am the beginning, the middle and the end of all beings. Of the Adityas I am Vishnu, of lights I am the radiant sun, I am Marici of the Maruts, and among the stars I am the moon. Of the *Vedas* I am the *Sama-veda*; of the demigods I am Indra; of the senses I am the mind, and in living beings I am the living force [knowledge]." (*Bg*.10.20-22)

". . . of bodies of water I am the ocean. Of the great sages I am Bhrigu; of vibrations I am the transcendental *om*. Of sacrifices I am the chanting of the holy names [*japa*], and of immovable things I am the Himalayas." (*Bg*.10.24-25)

"Among the Daitya demons I am the devoted Prahlada; among subduers I am time; among the beasts I am the lion, and among birds I am Garuda, the feathered carrier of Vishnu. Of purifiers I am the wind; of the wielders of weapons I am Rama; of fishes I am the shark, and of flowing rivers I am the Ganges. Of all creations I am the beginning and the end and also the middle, O Arjuna. Of all sciences I am the spiritual science of the Self, and among logicians I am the conclusive truth. Of letters I am the letter A, and among compounds I am the dual word. I am also inexhaustible time, and of creators I am Brahma, whose manifold faces turn everywhere. I am all-devouring death, and I am the generator of all things yet to be. Among women I am fame, fortune, speech, memory, intelligence, faithfulness and patience. Of hymns I am the *Brihat-sama* sung to the Lord Indra, and of poetry I am the *Gayatri* verse, sung daily by the *brahmanas*. Of months I am November and December, and of seasons I am flower-bearing spring. I am also the gambling of cheats, and of the splendid I am the splendor. I am victory, I am adventure, and I am the strength of the strong." (*Bg*.10.30-36)

"Among punishments I am the rod of chastisement, and of those who seek victory, I am morality. Of secret things I am silence, and of the wise I am wisdom. Furthermore, O Arjuna, I am the generating seed of all existences. There is no being--moving or nonmoving--that can exist without Me. O mighty conqueror of enemies, there is no end to My divine manifestations. What I have spoken to you is but a mere indication of My infinite opulences. Know that all beautiful, glorious, and mighty creations spring from but a spark of My splendor. But what need is there, Arjuna, for all this detailed knowledge? With a single fragment of Myself I pervade and support this entire universe." (*Bg*.10.38-42)

As stated, it is impossible to understand the extent of the opulence of the Absolute. This entire universe is pervaded by the tiniest fragment of the Supreme's energy, not to mention what lies beyond this world. Therefore, the opulences of the Supreme are unlimited.

There is still another aspect of understanding the all-pervading opulences of the Lord in the Vedic philosophy known as the *virat-rupa*, or the universal form of the Lord.

## THE UNIVERSAL FORM

In the conception of the universal form, the entire universe is the body of the Absolute and everything within this universe is described as part of that body. The universal form, however, is not transcendental and is, therefore, temporary. But it is considered easier for the neophyte to concentrate on the material aspects of the Absolute when one is not yet spiritually advanced. The universal form of the Lord is described in *Srimad-Bhagavatam*, Second Canto, Chapter One, so that people can understand how everything is an expansion of the Lord's energies.

The feet and ankles of the universal form are composed of the lower planets such as Patala, Rasatala, and Mahatala planets. The knees are the Sutala planetary system and the thighs are the Vitala and Atala planetary systems. The depression of His navel is the region of outer space. The chest of the gigantic form of the Lord is the luminary planetary system, His neck is the Mahar planets, His forehead is the Tapas planetary system, and Satyaloka is His head. His arms are the demigods, the ten directional sides are His ears, and His mouth is the blazing fire. The eyeball is the sun as the power of seeing. His eyelids are the day and night, and His jaws of teeth are Yama, god of death, who punishes the sinners.

Modesty is the upper portion of His lips, hankering is His chin, religion is the breast of the Lord, and irreligion is His back. The ocean is His waist, and the hills and mountains are the stacks of His bones. The rivers are the veins of the gigantic body, the trees are the hairs of His body, and the omnipotent air is His breath. The passing ages are His movements, and His activities are the reactions of the three modes of material nature.

The clouds which carry water are the hairs on His head, and the supreme cause of material creation is His intelligence. His mind is the moon, the reservoir of all changes. Varieties of birds are indications of His masterful artistic sense. The celestial species of human beings, like the Gandharvas, Vidyadharas, Caranas, and angels all represent His musical rythm, and the demoniac soldiers are representations of His wonderful prowess. His face is the *brahmanas*, His arms are the *kshatriyas*, His thighs are the *vaishyas*, and the *sudras* are under the protection of His feet. It is said that those who desire liberation should concentrate their mind on this form of the Lord, because there is nothing more than this in the world.

Another most amazing description of the universal form is in *Bhagavad-gita* wherein the Lord directly shows this form of His to Arjuna. This is found in Chapter Eleven in which Arjuna, although having heard the teachings of Krishna and attained complete freedom from illusion, still wants to see how the Lord entered into the universe. So he asks Lord Krishna to reveal that all-pervading form of His.

Arjuna petitioned Sri Krishna: "O greatest of personalities, O supreme form, though I see here before me Your actual position [the two armed form of Lord Krishna], I yet wish to see how you have entered into this cosmic manifestation. I want to see that form of Yours. If You think I am able to behold that cosmic form of Yours, O my Lord, O master of all mystic power, then kindly show me that universal self." (*Bg.*11.3-4)

"The Blessed Lord said: My dear Arjuna, O son of Pritha, behold now My opulences, hundreds of thousands of varied divine forms, multicolored like the sea. O best of the Bharatas, see here the different manifestations of Adityas, Rudras, and all the demigods. Behold the many things which no one has ever seen or heard before. Whatever you wish to see can be seen all at once in this body. This universal form can show you all that you now desire, as well as whatever you may desire in the future. Everything is here completely. But you cannot see Me with your present eyes. Therefore I give to you divine eyes by which you can behold My mystic opulence." (*Bg.*11.5-11)

"Sanjaya said: O King, speaking thus, the Supreme, the Lord of all mystic power, the Personality of Godhead, displayed His universal form to Arjuna. Arjuna saw in that universal form unlimited mouths and unlimited eyes. It was all wondrous. The form was decorated with divine, dazzling ornaments and arrayed in many garbs. He was garlanded gloriously, and there were many scents smeared over His body. All was magnificent, all-expanding, unlimited. This was seen by Arjuna. If hundreds of thousands of suns rose up at once into the sky, they might resemble the effulgence of the Supreme Person in that universal form. At that time Arjuna could see in the universal form of the Lord the unlimited expansions of the universe situated in one place although divided into many, many thousands. Then bewildered and astonished, his hair standing on end, Arjuna began to pray with folded hands, offering obeisances to the Supreme Lord." (*Bg.*11.9-14)

"Arjuna said: My dear Lord Krishna, I see assembled together in Your body all the demigods and various other living entities. I see Brahma sitting on the lotus flower as well as Lord Shiva and many sages and divine serpents. O Lord of the universe, I see in Your many, many forms--bellies, mouths, eyes-- expanded without limit. There is no end, there is no beginning, and there is no middle to all this. Your form adorned with various crowns, clubs and discs, is difficult to see because of its glaring effulgence, which is fiery and immeasurable like the sun. You are the supreme final objective; You are the best in all the universe; You are inexhaustible, and You are the oldest; You are the maintainer of religion, the eternal Personality of Godhead. You are the origin without beginning, middle or end. You have numberless arms, and the sun and moon are among Your great unlimited eyes. By Your own radiance You are heating this entire universe. Although You are one, You are spread throughout the sky and the planets and all space between. O great one, as I behold this terrible form, I see that all the planetary systems are perplexed." (Bg.11.15-20)

"All the demigods are surrendering and entering into You. They are very much afraid, and with folded hands they are singing the Vedic hymns. The different manifestations of Lord Shiva, the Adityas, the Vasus, the Sadhyas, the Visvadevas, the two Asvins, the Maruts, the forefathers and the Gandharvas, the Yaksas, Asuras, and all perfected demigods are beholding You in wonder. O mighty-armed one, all the planets with their demigods are disturbed at seeing Your many faces, eyes, bellies and legs and Your terrible teeth, and as they are disturbed, so am I." (Bg.11.21-23)

"O all-pervading Vishnu, I can no longer maintain my equilibrium. Seeing Your radiant colors fill the skies and beholding Your eyes and mouths, I am afraid. O Lord of lords, O refuge of the worlds, please be gracious to me. I cannot keep my balance seeing thus Your blazing deathlike faces and awful teeth. In all directions I am bewildered. O Lord of lords, so fierce of form, please tell me who You are. I offer my obeisances unto You; please be gracious to me. I do not know what Your mission is, and I desire to hear of it." (Bg.11.24-25,31)

"The blessed Lord said: Time I am, destroyer of the worlds, and I have come to engage all people. With the exception of you [the Pandavas], all the soldiers here [at the battle of Kuruksetra] on both sides will be slain. Therefore get up and prepare to fight. After conquering your enemies you will enjoy a flourishing kingdom. They are already put to death by My arrangement, and you, O Savyasacin, can be but an instrument in the fight. All the great warriors--Drona, Bhisma, Jayadratha, Karna--are already destroyed. Simply fight, and you will vanquish your enemies." (Bg.11.32-34)

Arjuna began falteringly to reply as follows: "O Hrishikesa [master of all senses], the world becomes joyful upon hearing Your names and thus everyone becomes attached to You. Although the perfected beings offer You their homage, the demons are afraid, and they flee here and there. All this is rightly done. O great one, who stands above even Brahma, You are the original master. Why should they not offer their homage up to You, O limitless one? O refuge of the universe, You are the invincible source, the cause of all causes, transcendental to this material manifestation. You are the original Personality of Godhead. You are the only sanctuary of this manifested cosmic world. You know everything, and You are all that is knowable. You are above the material modes. O limitless form! This whole cosmic manifestation is pervaded by You! You are air, fire, water, and You are the moon! You are the supreme controller and the grandfather. Thus I offer my respectful obeisances unto You a thousand times, and again and yet again! Obeisances from the front, from behind and from all sides! O unbounded power, You are the master of limitless might! You are all-pervading and thus You are everything!" (Bg.11.36-40)

"You are the father of this complete cosmic manifestation, the worshipable chief, the spiritual master. No one is equal to You, nor can anyone be one with You. Within the three worlds, You are immeasurable. You are the Supreme Lord, to be worshipped by every living being. Thus I fall down to offer You my respects and ask Your mercy. Please tolerate the wrongs that I may have done to You and bear with me as a father with his son, or a friend with his friend, or a lover with his beloved. After seeing this universal form, which I have never seen before, I am gladdened, but at the same time my mind is disturbed with fear. Therefore please bestow Your grace upon me and reveal Your form as the Personality of Godhead, O Lord of lords, O abode of the universe. O universal Lord, I wish to see You in Your four-armed form, with helmeted head and with club, wheel, conch and lotus flower in Your hands. I long to see You in that form." (Bg.11.43-46)

"The Blessed Lord said: My dear Arjuna, happily do I show this universal form within the material world by My internal potency. No one before you has ever seen this unlimited and glaringly effulgent form. O best of the Kuru warriors, no one before you has ever seen this universal form of Mine, for neither by studying the Vedas, nor by performing sacrifices, nor by charities or similar activities can this form be seen. Only you have seen this. Your mind has been perturbed by seeing this horrible feature of Mine. Now let it be finished. My devotee, be free from all disturbance. With a peaceful mind you can now see the form you desire." (Bg.11.47-49)

"Sanjaya said to Dhritarastra: The Supreme Personality of Godhead, Krishna, while speaking thus to Arjuna, displayed His real four-armed form, and at last He showed him His two-armed form, thus encouraging the fearful Arjuna." (Bg.11.50)

Sri Krishna then showed Arjuna His four-armed form, which is called Vishnu or Narayana, holding a lotus flower, chakra, club, and conchshell in each of His four hands. And then He showed His most attractive two-armed form. "When Arjuna thus saw Krishna in His original form, he said: Seeing this humanlike form, so very beautiful, my mind is now pacified, and I am restored to my original nature." (Bg.11.51)

"The Blessed Lord said: My dear Arjuna, the form which you are now seeing is very difficult to behold. Even the demigods are ever seeking the opportunity to see this form which is so dear. The form which you are seeing with your transcendental eyes cannot be understood simply by studying the *Vedas*, nor by undergoing serious penances, nor by charity, nor by worship. It is not by these means that one can see Me as I am. My dear Arjuna, only by undivided devotional service [*bhakti-yoga*] can I be understood as I am, standing before you, and can thus be seen directly. Only in this way can you enter into the mysteries of My understanding." (*Bg*.11.52-54)

In the final verses of this description of the universal form, we find the formula for entering into the mysteries of understanding the Supreme Being. Not only can one understand His all-pervading universal aspects by which one can recognize everything in this world as an expansion of His energy, but one can also learn about the personal form of the Supreme up to and including directly seeing His original form as if He were standing before you. This becomes possible by following the above-mentioned process of *bhakti-yoga* with determination. The proof of our progress is in one's ability to see how everything in this world is an expansion of the Supreme's energy and part of God's universal form, as related in this chapter. This in itself is spiritual vision and a perception of God.

The more we study the information in this chapter and recognize God's influence everywhere, and by increasingly seeing in this way on a day-to-day basis, the more we will get in touch with the Supreme and the divine nature. This is confirmed by Sri Krishna, who says: "My dear Arjuna, one who is engaged in My devotional service, free from the contamination of previous activities and from mental speculation, who is friendly to every living entity, certainly comes to Me." (*Bg*.11.55)

Thus, as we engage in *bhakti-yoga*, our spiritual vision increases, and we thoroughly understand ourselves, this world, how things are taking place, and the nature of God. Because of this increase in spiritual awareness, we do not succumb to the confusion, anxiety, and bewilderment that so often affects the consciousness of common men. Because we know and can recognize the existence of God, we can also more easily know the plan of God and are not surprised by the way things take place within this material world. This is pointed out in *Bhagavad-gita* (15.11) where it states: "The endeavoring transcendentalist, who is situated in self-realization, can see all this clearly. But those who are not situated in self-realization cannot see what is taking place, though they may try to." This, therefore, is just one of the benefits of attaining spiritual vision as described in this chapter.

# CHAPTER TWELVE

# *Description of*
# *The Spiritual World*

The culmination of all spiritual knowledge and practices of all religious or yogic systems is to return to our real home, the spiritual world. That is the ultimate goal. But what exactly is the spiritual world and where is it located? Is it a real place or just a state of mind? The answers to these questions are not to be found, except within the Vedic literature.

To begin with, the Vedic texts explain that the whole cosmic creation is considered to be nothing more than a cloud in a corner of the spiritual sky. Within this cloud are the many variegated forms of material energy, including the innumerable universes, planets, and all species or forms of material existence. What separates the material energy from the spiritual world, according to the *Padmottara-khanda* (225.57), is the Viraja River, the unusual water which surrounds the cosmic creation. Beyond the Viraja River is the spiritual sky, the Brahman effulgence, in which unlimited spiritual planets known as Vaikunthalokas are located. *Vaikuntha* means no anxiety, lamentation, or fear. On each Vaikuntha planet lives an expansion of the Supreme Personality of God. Each planet is also billions of miles in diameter and the residents of those planets are full in the six opulences of strength, knowledge, beauty, fame, wealth, and renunciation.

The spiritual world is said to be three-fourths of all the energies of the Supreme Being, while the material creation is the remaining one-fourth. This material world can hardly be fully understood by even the most intelligent people; so, trying to understand the most basic aspects of the spiritual world is even more difficult. The spiritual kingdom is not a place we easily can reach, but since we are essentially spiritual in nature, it is our real home. Even though it may seem difficult for us to understand what the spiritual world is really like while we are in our state of material conditioning, there are descriptions that allow us to get a glimpse of its natural beauty.

In the *Srimad-Bhagavatam*, Third Canto, Fifteenth Chapter, there is the following description of the kingdom of God: "In the spiritual sky there are spiritual planets known as Vaikunthas, which are the residence of the Supreme Personality of Godhead and His pure devotees and are worshiped by the residents of all the material planets. In the Vaikuntha planets all the residents are similar in form to the Supreme Personality of Godhead. They all engage in devotional service to the Lord without desires for sense gratification.

"In the Vaikuntha planets is the Supreme Personality of Godhead, who is the original person and who can be understood through the Vedic literature. He is full of the uncontaminated mode of goodness, with no place for passion or ignorance. He contributes religious progress for the devotees.

"In those Vaikuntha planets there are many forests which are very auspicious. In those forests the trees are desire trees, and in all seasons they are filled with flowers and fruits because everything in the Vaikuntha planets is spiritual and personal.

"In the Vaikuntha planets the inhabitants fly in their airplanes, accompanied by their wives and consorts, and eternally sing of the character and activities of the Lord, which are always devoid of all inauspicious qualities. While singing the glories of the Lord, they deride even the presence of the blossoming *madhavi* flowers, which are fragrant and laden with honey. When the king of bees hums in a high pitch, singing the glories of the Lord, there is a temporary lull in the noise of the pigeon, the cuckoo, the crane, the *chakravaka*, the swan, the parrot, the partridge and the peacock. Such transcendental birds stop their own singing simply to hear the glories of the Lord. Although the flowering plants like the *mandara*, *kunda*, *kurabaka*, *utpala*, *champaka*, *arna*, *punnaga*, *nagakesara*, *bakula*, lily and *parijata* are full of transcendental fragrance, they are still conscious of the austerities performed by *tulasi*, for *tulasi* is given special preference by the Lord, who garlands Himself with *tulasi* leaves.

"The inhabitants of Vaikuntha travel in their airplanes made of lapis lazuli, emerald and gold. Although crowded by their consorts, who have large hips and beautifully smiling faces, they cannot be stimulated to passion by their mirth and beautiful charms. The ladies in the Vaikuntha planets are as beautiful as the goddess of fortune herself. Such transcendentally beautiful ladies, their hands playing with lotuses and their leg bangles tinkling, are sometimes seen sweeping the marble walls, which are bedecked at intervals with golden borders, in order to receive the grace of the Supreme Personality of Godhead.

"The goddesses of fortune worship the Lord in their own gardens by offering *tulasi* leaves on the coral-paved banks of transcendental reservoirs of water. While offering worship to the Lord, they can see on the water the reflection of their beautiful faces with raised noses, and it appears that they have become more beautiful because of the Lord's kissing their faces.

"It is very much regrettable that unfortunate people do not discuss the description of the Vaikuntha planets but engage in topics which are unworthy to hear and which bewilder one's intelligence. Those who give up the topics of

Vaikuntha and take to talk of the material world are thrown into the darkest region of ignorance.

"Lord Brahma said: My dear demigods, the human form of life is of such importance that we also desire to have such life, for in the human form one can attain perfect religious truth and knowledge. If one in the human form of life does not understand the Supreme Personality of Godhead and His abode, it is understood that he is very much affected by the influence of external nature.

"Persons whose bodily features change in ecstasy and who breathe heavily and perspire due to hearing the glories of the Lord are promoted to the kingdom of God, even though they do not care for meditation and other austerities. The kingdom of God is above the material universe, and it is desired by Brahma and other demigods."

This description provides a little insight into the nature of the spiritual world. Just as there are husbands and wives and planets and airplanes in this universe, you will find a similar arrangement in the spiritual world. But there is a big difference between the two. It is stated that the material world is simply a perverted reflection of the spiritual world. Whatever beautiful things we see here are just reflections of the beauty in the spiritual sky. There, everything is based on attraction to the Supreme, while here everything is based on attraction to these dull, material bodies, especially in the form of sex life. The temporary sex pleasure enjoyed by the residents of this material creation cannot compare to the eternal bliss that is available to those in the spiritual world.

It is unfortunate that many people have no interest in discussing this most valuable information about the spiritual world. As it is stated, even the demigods discuss this knowledge amongst themselves and long for attaining the spiritual strata. But those who are on the regressive path leading to the darker regions of the universe have no interest in such things. Their concern is only for eating, sleeping, having sex, and getting money. Such temporary concerns keep one bound up within the modes of material nature to continue the struggle of trying to smooth out the constant ups and downs of life. When one is in the ocean, being tossed about by the waves, the best thing one can do is simply to get out. If, however, a person is determined to stay in the ocean of material nature with hopes of smoothing out the tossing of the waves, then this does not show much intelligence. If someone will not hang on to the lifeboat of spiritual knowledge in order to be rescued, then there is nothing that can be done. He will go on drowning in the ocean of birth and death for millions of lifetimes.

This, unfortunately, is to be expected because it is said that only a very few in this world will ever hear of the spiritual world as it is. It is not that it is a secret, but those unfortunate people who are so preoccupied with material endeavors never take an interest in finding out about the spiritual realm beyond this temporary material creation. And of those who are fortunate enough to hear about it, some may think that it is so fantastic that it must be a dream or myth from someone's imagination. Of course, we cannot understand all the aspects of the spiritual realm immediately, but if we continue on our spiritual path and study and discuss these topics with other spiritually advanced people, our realizations about the eternal characteristics that are found there will increase.

The Vedic texts describe that in the center of all the spiritual Vaikuntha planets is the planet known as Krishnaloka or Goloka Vrindavana, which is the personal abode of the original Supreme Personality of God, Sri Krishna. Krishna enjoys His transcendental bliss in multiple forms on that planet, and all the opulences of the Vaikuntha planets are found there. This planet is shaped like a lotus flower and many kinds of pastimes are taking place on each leaf of that lotus, as described in *Brahma-samhita*, verses two and four: "The superexcellent station of Krishna, which is known as Gokula, has thousands of petals and a corolla like that of a lotus sprouted from a part of His infinitary aspect, the whorl of the leaves being the actual abode of Krishna. The whorl of that eternal realm, Gokula, is the hexagonal abode of Krishna. Its petals are the abodes of *gopis* [friends] who are part and parcel of Krishna to whom they are most lovingly devoted and are similar in essence. The petals shine beautifully like so many walls. The extended leaves of that lotus are the garden-like *dhama*, or spiritual abode of Sri Radhika, the most beloved of Krishna."

The only business that Sri Krishna has in the spiritual realm is transcendental enjoyment. The only business of Krishna's eternal servants or devotees is to offer enjoyment to Him. The more enjoyment the devotees offer to Krishna, the happier He becomes. The happier Krishna becomes, the more His devotees become enlivened and taste eternal, transcendental ecstasy. In this way, there is an ever-increasing competition of spiritual ecstasy between Krishna and His parts and parcels. This is the only business in the spiritual world, as confirmed in *Brahma-samhita*, verse 6: "The Lord of Gokula is the Transcendental Supreme Godhead, the own Self of eternal ecstacies. He is superior to all superiors and is busily engaged in the enjoyments of the transcendental realm and has no association with His mundane [material] potency."

There are many stories in the Vedic literature which narrate how Krishna engages in loving activities with His friends and relatives and how He performs amazing feats which thrill and astonish everyone. Descriptions of the many activities and pastimes which go on in the spiritual world are found in such texts as *Srimad-Bhagavatam*, *Caitanya-caritamrta*, and Sanatana Goswami's *Brihat Bhagavatamritam*, which explains the many levels and unlimited nature of the spiritual realm. Indeed, the body of the Lord is described as full of eternal bliss, truth, knowledge, the most dazzling splendor, and source of all that exists.

Though it is not possible to experience spiritual pastimes or to see the form of the Supreme with ordinary senses, by spiritualizing our senses by the practice of yoga we can reach the platform of perceiving the Supreme at every moment. At that time we start becoming Krishna conscious and can begin to enter into the pastimes of Krishna, although situated within this material body.

If we become fully spiritualized in this manner, there is no doubt that when we give up this material body, we will return to the spiritual world. Until then, we can continue studying the Vedic texts to remember and be conversant about the beauty and loveliness of the spiritual world, as described as follows:

"Vrindavana-*dhama* is a place of ever-increasing joy. Flowers and fruits of all seasons grow there, and that transcendental land is full of the sweet sound of various birds. All directions resound with the humming of bumblebees, and it is served with cool breezes and the waters of the Yamuna River. Vrindavana is decorated with wish-fulfilling trees wound with creepers and beautiful flowers. Its divine beauty is ornamented with the pollen of red, blue and white lotuses. The ground is made of jewels whose dazzling glory is equal to a myriad of suns rising in the sky at one time. On that ground is a garden of desire trees, which always shower divine love. In that garden is a jeweled temple whose pinnacle is made of rubies. It is decorated with various jewels, so it remains brilliantly effulgent through all seasons of the year. The temple is beautified with bright-colored canopies, glittering with various gems, and endowed with ruby-decorated coverings and jeweled gateways and arches. Its splendor is equal to millions of suns, and it is eternally free from the six waves of material miseries. In that temple there is a great golden throne inlaid with many jewels. In this way one should meditate on the divine realm of the Supreme Lord, Sri Vrindavana-*dhama*." (*Gautamiya Tantra* 4)

"I worship that transcendental seat, known as Svetadvipa where as loving consorts the *Lakshmis*, in their unalloyed spiritual essence, practice the amourous service of the Supreme Lord Krishna as their only lover; where every tree is a transcendental purpose-tree; where the soil is the purpose-gem, water is nectar, every word is a song, every gait is a dance, the flute is the favorite attendant, effulgence is full of transcendental bliss and the supreme spiritual entities are all enjoyable and tasty, where numberless milch-cows always emit transcendental oceans of milk; where there is eternal existence of transcendental time, who is ever present and without past or future and hence is not subject to the quality of passing away even for the duration of half a moment. That realm is known as Goloka only to a very few self-realized souls in this world." (*Brahma-samhita*, 56)

By studying and hearing about the beauty of the spiritual world, we will understand that everything we are looking for in life has its origin in that eternal realm. There, it is described, one finds freedom from all pains and suffering, and the atmosphere is unlimitedly full of ever-expanding beauty, joy, happiness, knowledge, and eternal, loving relationships. It is a world full of recreation only, without the struggle for maintaining our existence. There is never any hunger, and we can feast and never get full. Neither is there any lamentation over the past or fear of the future. It is said that time is conspicuous by its absence. Thus, the needs of the soul for complete freedom and unbounded happiness are found in the spiritual atmosphere. That is our real home.

# Conclusion

Although in the past one hundred years man has made more technological advancement than at any other time in recorded history, and has invented newer forms of comforts and entertainment that can seem very exciting, we still have not found all the necessary answers to our problems through these means. There are still political upheavals, international intrigue, war, racial tension, crime, new diseases, suicides, the threat of economic failures, etc., not to mention other problems, such as the 80 billion pounds of hazardous wastes that are produced every year by our industries that are destroying our lakes, rivers, land, air, forests, and many other resources on which we depend in order to survive. This would seem to make any person question whether we are really advancing or simply bringing about a slow suicide for the human race.

As there are more and more problems that become apparent in society, there are also more and more organizations, clubs, support groups, etc., that are formed to help deal with and try to solve these problems. However, most of these groups use nothing more than the trial and error method in their attempts to solve these issues. This means that they have no guide from which to get additional directions other than their own past experience. This is basically the way it is throughout society, from the top levels of government to the man in the street. This can be seen when organizations such as our government, our educational institutions, and even mainstream religions continually modify the way they do things to suit the ever-changing situation or the constant variations in the likes and dislikes of society. It simply shows that all they have is merely relative truth, or knowledge based on the way things seem to be at the time. As soon as things change, they have to change or update their views. In other words, they have no real knowledge.

This lack of insight and wisdom certainly does not easily help them to attain the goals they set for themselves or avoid the critical problems that perplex them. Actually, it becomes questionable if they ever reach their goals at all or really solve their problems, though they may display some premature optimism by finding some meager relief in merely taking the burden from one shoulder and placing it on the other. This kind of jugglery, which is often found in the diplomacy of politics, does not do anything. The problem is still there and will remain so until they find a more permanent solution. It is like a blind man trying to find his way out of a room by bumping into the walls. If he keeps at it, sooner or later he will find the door. But until he does, how many times will he bang his head? Better to take a little instruction from someone who has knowledge and who can tell you, "Here, go this way and stop wasting time."

Real knowledge is spiritual truth, which does not change. When one approaches the highest truth, all other mysteries and questions are automatically solved and answered. In order to understand things completely, we must use complete knowledge. Our senses can pick up only so much information, but there is more that affects us that is beyond our sense perception. These are the things we must understand if we are to comprehend who we are, where we have come from, where we are going, what the purpose of everything is, and how to utilize it to our best advantage. Once we understand this and actually realize it, then we can easily see the proper course of action. If we neglect this point, then we can go on speculating about life and our problems until we die and never find a real solution. What is the benefit of that? So to avoid this, it would be wise to look at the timeless Vedic wisdom and the universal truths that have been handed down through the ages to see where we have gone off track.

Certainly, anyone can recognize the great need in human society for this spiritual knowledge which can enlighten us about perfecting life. What we do not need is religion or philosophy based on speculation or blind faith. If such is allowed to spread and become predominant, then real spiritual understanding becomes less and less accessable to the general mass of people. Religion or philosophy based on man's questionable speculations or blind sentiments must be given up because spiritual truth and the process that enables one to attain his own spiritual realizations do not exist in one's limited conjectures. We must go much deeper than that. We must find and approach that source of spiritual truth which delivers the knowledge as it is and provides the process by which the Absolute Truth can be directly perceived and experienced. If one comes in contact with such a source of unadulterated spiritual knowledge, he or she should take it very seriously, for such an opportunity may happen only once in one's life. Thus, we have tried to provide this kind of knowledge in a condensed form within the context of this book. For those who have appreciated it and are interested in learning more, Volume Two of *The Eastern Answers to the Mysteries of Life*, called *The Universal Path to Enlightenment*, continues where this volume leaves off.

# SEEING SPIRITUAL INDIA (PART 1)

## *The Historical Holy Sites And Temples of South India*

Reading about Eastern philosophy is one thing, but going to Eastern lands and actually experiencing it is quite another. Seeing the local people who understand and practice this knowledge in their customary surroundings can be very enlightening, but it can also be perplexing if you don't know what is happening or the reasons behind what people do.

India, like other places in the world that have unusual mystical traditions, is a land that can be both physically and mentally demanding. India is an exotic, beautiful, and wondrous country, depending on what aspects of it you see. Living and traveling there can be pleasant and exciting, but it is also likely to provide you with many trying situations. It can be terribly hot, dry, and dusty. Good food and water may not always be readily available, and living conditions and transportation can often leave much to be desired. But it is a total experience on every level; a testing ground that is not for everyone. It can separate the serious from the frivolous; the real truth-seekers from the superficial and worldly sight-seeing tourists. But if you want the real treasure of India, the spiritual heritage of the East, it can be found if you are determined. But you have to know where to look and how to find it.

Entering India, you'll most likely go through one of three places: Calcutta, Bombay, or New Delhi. Like any big city, they can be somewhat overwhelming if you don't know where to go or how to handle the various situations that one is likely to encounter, especially in such a different culture. Some people may handle it quite easily, while others will find that the difference in lifestyle will make them ask, "Why did I ever think I wanted to come to this place?" For those, India may be a country where they stop long enough merely to see the Taj Mahal, the Jaipur Palace, and a few other places before going on to some other part of the world. Then they can say that they've been to India. But whether they actually see the real life of the people is another thing.

When visiting India, you have to be willing to readjust the way you see the world. It is a country that moves slowly: trains and buses are often late. You must have patience and plenty of tolerance, otherwise you may experience much to complain about and little of the beauty and wonder that exists there. You have to look beyond the poverty, the dirt, dust, smells, and overcrowded living conditions in the cities if you expect to enter into the mysteries of India's spiritual culture.

If you are attached to your Western ways or particular standards of comfort and are not willing to adjust, then, quite honestly, you have no business going to India, not at least if you are looking for its spiritual aspects. To do that requires you to get out amongst the people, especially the *sadhus* or holy men, and see them as they are, doing their regular business, visiting their temples and attending their religious festivals. Whether you understand it all or not, it is bound to awaken a part of you that you never knew existed or have rarely experienced. You may either be confused by it, or you may find that you are quite at home with it, feeling a spiritual tranquility, the likes of which you've hardly attained before.

Attaining this spiritual serenity is a matter of evolving in your consciousness. And how can your consciousness evolve if you don't decondition yourself from the habitual materialistic thought patterns in which you have grown accustomed? You must set aside your normal (or is it unnormal?) everyday ways of thinking in order to look at things from an entirely new perspective, a different state of mind. This is what consciousness expansion and becoming aware of higher realms of existence is all about. And this is the real spiritual heritage of India. It offers an individualistic process of personal transformation and development for understanding yourself, your position in the universe, and your relationship with the Supreme. However, let us remember that the goal of Eastern philosophy or yoga is not to escape or cut yourself off from the outside world, but it is to BRING IN the awareness of self, the understanding of your real identity. Upon attaining this perception, one is never shaken in any situation. Of course, this doesn't mean that if you go to India you will see everyone intensely absorbed in this aspect of life. Like any place else, most people will simply be engaged in the struggle to survive. Nonetheless, the people of India, generally speaking, are the most spiritually oriented people in the world.

In one's attempt to see the spiritual side of India, it's very important to know where to go and what to see in order to maximize whatever spiritual experiences you're looking for. Naturally some places have more to offer than others, and certain towns are more sacred to specific religions or spiritual paths.

There are places in India like Vrindavan, Mathura, Mayapur, Dwarka, Varanasi, Puri, and others, as well as rivers like the Ganges or Yamuna, which exist and can be experienced in the normal three dimensional way. But these places are said to also exist in the spiritual realm, the higher dimension. This means that these places are where the material and spiritual energies overlap. Although the spiritual energy may pervade the universe, at such holy places or *tirthas* the experiences of higher dimensions are easier to attain. This is what gives these places special meaning amongst those who can perceive or know of this multidimensional aspect. This depends, however, on how receptive and elevated the person is in spiritual knowledge and awareness.

For those who are not spiritually aware, these cities and rivers will appear as no different from any other. Such people will say that the Ganges is not a holy river, that the Deities in the temples are merely stone idols, and that the sages are ordinary men. But the Vedic texts say that people with such a vision have a hellish mentality. They are forced by their own limitations of consciousness to be aware of nothing more than the most base level of existence and cannot perceive the higher realms of life that are all around us. For them this three dimensional material universe holds more mysteries than they can imagine, what to speak of the spiritual dimension which they cannot see at all.

From the gross sensory perspective, many of the values the people of India have, as well as activities they perform in the name of spirituality, will be completely bewildering for an uncultured tourist who lacks the spiritual knowledge that we've presented in this book. They may see a variety of activities, customs, and traditions that people enthusiastically perform in their abandonment for unity between the soul and God. Yet the average tourist will have no idea of why or what is the meaning of such customs. Then, as to be expected, they will view everything as being very strange. Therefore, only for those who are spiritually elevated does the higher dimensional realm of India exist, not simply as something to observe or study, but as a reality to be experienced. For others who lack such spiritual awareness, this aspect of India will forever remain a peculiar mystery. However, with the proper knowledge they can understand what is going on and the purpose of the numerous traditions that have existed for many hundreds and thousands of years.

South India is especially the home of real Indian culture. The South was not as influenced by the Muslim invaders or the British Raj as was Northern or Central India, so you will find that it still holds the traditional customs and religious views that it's had for hundreds of years. For example, it is the South that still remains primarily vegetarian. And if you are interested in this kind of diet, there is no reason to eat any meat while you visit South India. Though the food is very different and spicier than that found in the North, there are still preparations that will be very tasty and easy to digest. It is a part of the experience of South India not to be missed. And the architecture is like no where else. The temples, which are generally in the center of town, have towering gates, called *gopurams*, that are amazingly ornate.

Fortunately, when we visit these temples we are not seeing relics of an ancient but extinct society, such as we find when visiting the Egyptian pyramids or ancient temples of the Mayan and Incas in Central and South America. But the temples of India present a living culture. In other words, the religious practice of the people, the festivals, and the rituals in the temples are the same as they were thousands of years ago. They still offer fruits and nicely cooked preparations, beautiful dresses, sandalwood paste, flowers and garlands, ghee and camphor lamps, incense and perfumes to the temple Deities just as they have done throughout the ages.

Spiritually, the temples are like launching pads where one performs those activities that assist in reaching higher dimensions. They are the doorways to more advanced realms and where pilgrims and devotees go to make an outward display of their devotion to their Deities. Though God is within us all, and religion or yoga is very often an inward process, God can manifest externally as the Deity, the *arca-vigraha* incarnation, through which He accepts the devotee's service while he or she is in the material realm. These devotional activities, such as simple *darshan* (seeing the Deity and being seen by the Deity), are considered purifying for one's life and consciousness. The goal is to continue on this path until one's thoughts are purified to the point where one sheds his or her materialistic consciousness and can enter the spiritual realm, at least by the time of death if not before. Thus, everyone tries to visit the nearest temple a few times a day, or tries to make pilgrimages to the famous holy places.

The temples usually have a main shrine with smaller temples or shrines surrounding it. These shrines may have *murtis* or carved images of important spiritual masters, or deities of various demigods, such as Parvati (Lord Shiva's wife), Durga (the warrior aspect of Parvati, sometimes called Kali, Tara, etc.), Sarasvati (goddess of knowledge and intelligence), Lakshmi (goddess of fortune, Lord Vishnu's wife), Ganesh (a son of Shiva, said to destroy obstacles and offer good luck), Murugan (meaning divine child, the Tamil name for Subramaniya, another son of Shiva, especially worshipped in the South), Brahma (born from Lord Vishnu and who engineered the creation of the living beings within the universe), and Shiva (the benevolent one, part of the triad of Brahma, Vishnu, and Shiva who continually create, maintain, and destroy the universe), and Deities of the Supreme, such as Vishnu (incarnation of the Supreme appearing as the All-pervading One, the preserver or maintainer of the universe), or Krishna (the Supreme Being, source of all other incarnations, such as Rama, Vishnu, Narasimha, etc.). The temple is usually dedicated to a particular form of God or demigod which you will find on the main altar.

It is explained that the Deity is not a product of someone's imagination, but is made in accordance with the ancient Vedic texts, called the *Shilpasutras*, which deal with the science of iconography. Everything about the Deity, such as its proportions, the postures, hand gestures, weapons (if any), the emblems, etc., all mean something. Therefore, it is very important that every part of the

Deity is formed properly. The Deity may also have different features which represent different aspects, abilities, powers, or pastimes. After the Deity is formed, there is the elaborate installation ceremony during which the Deity is installed in the temple. At this time the devotees and priests petition the personality of the demigod or Supreme Being to take up residence in the form of the Deity. Only then does the Deity become the *arca-vigraha*, or worshipable incarnation of the Supreme Being or particular demigod.

It is considered that since God is the controller of both material and spiritual energies, He can turn something material into spiritual energy or vice versa. Thus, the Deity, which may appear to be made of common material elements, becomes spiritual and allows us to see spiritual form with our material senses. Out of the causeless mercy of the Supreme, He agrees to reside within the form of the Deity to accept the worship of His devotees. Of course, we should not think He is forced to remain there. If He is neglected or if harm is allowed to come to the Deity, He may leave the form of the Deity at any time.

There are many stories in both traditional Vedic writings and local legends that relate how various Deities have reciprocated with devotees. Such relations have taken place in dreams as well as in the awakened state in which the Deity has come to life to show Himself as He is or partake in pastimes with His devotees. There are also some instances when Krishna or Shiva spontaneously manifested themselves as stone Deities. Such Deities are called self-manifested because they were not formed by any artist or priest. Lord Venkateshvara at Tirupati, Vishvanatha Shiva at Varanasi, and several Krishna Deities at Vrindavan are a few examples of this. Of course, most Westerners of little faith cannot explain such occurrences, and can hardly accept that the Supreme would exhibit Himself in this way. They would rather look for some "logical" or non-mystical explanation for such things. But for the devoted and the sages who have glimpsed and understand the spiritual dimensions of existence, the Deities are a reality. Even if one cannot accept the concept of Deities, then even in the most abstract sense the images, such as in Buddhism, represent cosmic principles which affect us all. Therefore, they remain a part of the reality we experience at every moment. In this way, the temples are the places where one can see and even experience the Divine.

Furthermore, many of the temples are built at locations where ancient historical or holy events involving the incarnations of God or the demigods have occurred. Such temples give evidence for the legends that are described in the *Puranas* which explain how the Supreme Being appeared there. Therefore, these sites become very sacred, even spiritualized for having been the site of the pastimes of the Supreme. It is for this reason that people can acquire great spiritual merit by visiting these places. Thus, these sites become important centers on the pilgrimage routes for many of the devout. In this way, the temples are the most significant of the surviving monuments where religious, social, cultural, and, in many cases, political aspects of history have been preserved.

Historically, the temples were also major centers for education. The larger ones would maintain priests and students for the recitation of the Puranic texts to the people at large. Thus, both literate or illiterate people could be provided with a cultural education. The villages, however, had schools for basic study and learning, but beyond that the temples often had libraries full of books from all branches of learning and teachers who taught all these subjects.

The temples also served as centers for the arts since they would employ many artists to paint scenes from the Puranic legends or carve beautiful sculptures. There were also jewelers and goldsmiths who would make articles for the Deities. Musicians and singers were also employed, and dancing girls would perform exotic dances in times of worship, especially during festivals.

The larger temples had hospitals and doctors and areas for feeding and caring for the poor and destitute. In order to do all this, the temples consumed large amounts of fruits and grains. Thus, the temples were given plots of land that were used mostly by the farmers for growing food for the offerings in the temples. These offerings, however, would then be redistributed amongst the temple employees and the poor. The temples also had systems of banking. Thus, with such a variety of activity centered around them, the temples played a very important part in Indian culture.

In many cases, the temples are still the center of cultural and spiritual activity in the towns. One of the most unique temples to witness how important they can be is the temple near the town of Tirupati, which is a three and a half hour bus ride northwest of Madras. Above Tirupati are the Tirumalla Hills, the home of Lord Venkatesha (Vishnu), also known as Sri Balaji. Many people from all over India come to visit. No other temple in the world draws so many pilgrims, not even Mecca or Rome, which can number up to five thousand on an average day, and many thousands more on a festival day. It is here where we will begin our tour of South India.

The temple of Lord Balaji is perhaps the richest temple in the world. Money comes in from many different sources, but there is much that the administration of this temple does with it. They own and maintain their own bus system as well as the roads that take the pilgrims up and down the hills to see this temple. They also have several large universities that they manage, as well as banks, hospitals, and many programs for the poor and sick. They also give grants to writers of books on Eastern philosophy, and also freely send beautifully carved Deities for installation in new temples in various parts of the world. In fact, to discuss in detail the many projects that this temple is involved in would take several pages.

There are two ways to go to Tirumalla from Tirupati, either by foot or by bus. The bus ride is like taking a roller coaster that climbs steep and winding roads that overlook sheer cliffs that drop hundreds and thousands of feet down the hillside. You occasionally pass other vehicles on the narrow road, or even pilgrims who are walking up. Sometimes the bus comes precariously close to the edge of the road, and will make sharp turns that force you to hang onto your seat. While I was making the trip, one old lady could not hang on tight enough and was thrown to the other side of the bus. And while I was hanging on for dear life, hoping the bus would not crash, a fat man who was sitting next to me was snoring away, oblivious to the whole thing. Sometimes the way the buses are driven during the hour long ride up the hill will make you feel like you are risking your life. But thousands of people do it everyday.

Walking up is a very hefty climb, but it used to be the only way you could go. Some of the more determined pilgrims still prefer to walk up as a spiritual austerity and sign of their sincerity. The footpath starts at the Alipiri tower and continues to the Kali Gopuram at the half-way point, and then on up to the top. There are two temples along the path. The temple of Lord Narasimha, about four miles up, is a required visit. Otherwise, it is considered that your vows may not be fulfilled and the pilgrimage will not be complete. Of course, taking the bus means you by-pass this temple. The other temple is for Ramanuja and marks the place where he would stop to sleep on his way up the hill.

Once we reach the top, we find many buildings and cottages that fill the area between the seven sacred hills. Many people stay here for days or weeks. It is indeed a complete city in itself and has all kinds of shops and stores offering whatever you might need, including free meals for pilgrims at certain halls.

As we get further into the city, we see many people with shaved heads. Some men, women, and children perform the sacrifice of voluntary loss of hair as a way of signifying their surrender of vanity and ego for unity with God. By lessening one's concern for bodily beauty and distinction, it automatically becomes easier to focus the mind on higher goals. This is why pilgrims often shave their heads when they visit Tirumalla. At Kalyana *ghat* many barbers are kept busy assisting people for this purpose. As you tour South India, you will often see individuals or complete families with shaved heads, evidence of their recent visit to Tirumalla.

In the center of the town is the main temple where long lines of people are continually entering through the main gate for *darshan* of the Lord. *Darshan* is the devotional exchange of seeing and being seen by the Deity. It is one of the most important devotional activities for a pilgrim to perform. To enter the temple you have to go to a special gate some distance away from the temple entrance. (Anyone can tell you where it is.) There you can ask for a twenty-five rupee ticket for "special *darshan*." This greatly reduces the waiting time of standing in line. Regular *darshan* may take three to four hours of standing in the queue, while "special *darshan*" takes only about an hour. Of course, on festival days the waiting time may take two to three hours for "special *darshan*" and up to twelve or more hours for regular *darshan*.

There are waiting rooms that can hold large numbers of people where you sit until your room is called. Then, along with everyone else, you stand in the queue that goes around the temple building. The lines are fenced off from the rest of the street and there is a roof to shade you from the sun.

When we finally enter the temple, we can see very opulent halls and pillars. The first hall has bright bronze statues of King Venkatapathi Raya and King Achyuta Raya and his wife and others, all of whom were great devotees of Lord Venkatesha. We make our way through other large halls and pass smaller shrines before arriving at the sanctum sanctorium. The nice thing about this temple is that they allow Westerners and non-Hindus inside to see the Deity, whereas in some temples in the South you are not allowed to enter.

Finally, we pass through the golden gate of the sanctum, walking past the huge figures of the sentinels on either side. You are automatically pushed along in the queue to see the Lord. As the Deity comes into view, many people, with hands folded before them, exclaim, "Jaya Govinda, Jaya Sri Krishna," since Lord Venkatesha (Vishnu) is an expansion or incarnation of Lord Krishna. Some pilgrims have been dreaming of this moment for many years. The devotion they display as they come before the Deity cannot go unnoticed. The feelings these people have for God leave the religious sentiments most Westerners have far behind.

The Deity is very beautiful and from the time you first see Him, it takes maybe two or three short minutes to approach, walk to the Deity, bow slightly or say a short prayer if so inclined, and then turn away. Lord Venkatesha, or Balaji, stands on a pedastal at a height of nine feet. He is richly decorated with jewels, crown, and colorful flower garlands. The *Purana* states that He stands here to forgive everyone of their sins and blesses them by granting whatever devotional requests they have. There are other Deities in the temple room, such as Krishna with Bhumi and Rukmini, and Lord Rama with Lakshmana and Sita, but for lack of time They mostly go unnoticed.

As we exit the sanctum, priests offer you a spoonful of *caranamritam*, the water that has been used to bathe the Deity earlier that morning. This is considered especially powerful for one's spiritual merit. You hold out your right hand and take a few drops in your palm, sip it, and away you go toward the exit as hundreds of other pilgrims are waiting in the line behind you. Sometimes temple attendants have to push people in order for them to move on.

As we make our way out of the temple hallways and back out to the streets, we feel especially lucky for having gotten *darshan* of the Lord at this most popular and opulent temple. We also feel a little exhalted for having been blessed by the Divinity, and maybe a little wiser after witnessing an ancient tradition of this culture in which thousands of people participate everyday.

We can relax for a moment at the edge of Swamipushkarini lake at the north side of the temple. This water tank is the most sacred water on the hill. The *Brahmananda Purana* explains that the goddess Sarasvati Devi herself has taken the form of this water tank to wash away the sins of all who bathe in it. If we've brought the right clothes, we can take a dip in it. If not, we can at least splash some water over our heads. It is suggested that we bathe in this lake to purify ourselves before seeing Lord Balaji. But for now we can see other Deities in the various shrines on the hill, which will be easier since there won't be such long lines of people. Or we can explore and wander around the area a little further. When we are finished we can catch a bus for the winding and sometimes frightening ride back down to Tirupati.

Back in Tirupati, there is the big Govindaraja Swami temple established by the great spiritual leader Ramanujacarya. It is worth visiting and many people stop to see it. The temple is in the centre of three enclosures, each entered through ornately carved gates. The first gate or *gopuram* is the most impressive and is seven storeys tall. Inside are two halls that are used for various festivals. The smaller second *gopuram* has many carved panels inside with scenes of Krishna from the stories in the *Puranas*, as well as scenes from the *Ramayana*. In the second enclosure we find the minor shrines to Garuda, Hanuman, and incarnations of Vishnu. Through the third and smallest *gopuram* we reach the two main shrines. One has a Deity of Krishna holding a bow, and the other has a Deity of reclining Vishnu. The Deity here is a sleeping Vishnu lying on Seshanaga, Vishnu's serpentine bed, with Lakshmi and Bhudevi nearby. Vishnu's bird carrier, Garuda, and the devotee Narada Muni are in attendance as well. Brahma is also there on the lotus flower coming from Vishnu's navel. There is another temple room for Kothalakshmi and Mahalakshmi.

Two miles from Tirupati, a ricksha ride away, is the temple of Goddess Padmavathi at Tiruchanur. Padmavathi is considered to be the wife of Lord Venkatesha, thus many pilgrims also visit this temple. This is also the place where Lord Srinivasa did penance seeking reunion with Mahalakshmi, and also where the sage Sukhadeva did penance many years ago.

A distance west of Tirupati, 85 miles north of Bangalore, is the town of Lepakshi. Though this is not a historical holy site, some people may want to visit the Virabhadra temple that is located on a little hill in this town. It was Virupanna, a Vijayanagara governor, who used state funds to build it in 1530. Though externally it is rather plain, this temple complex is in a walled enclosure and contains many well preserved sculptures and beautiful frescoed ceilings. The paintings, for which this temple is especially known, depict the popular stories from the *Mahabharata, Ramayana*, and *Puranas*. The detail and vibrant colors of the dress and facial characteristics are outstanding. The stone carvings display deities, sages, animals, guardians, musicians, dancers, etc. On the sides of the temple entrance are carved figures of the goddesses Ganga and Yamuna. A boulder on the east side is carved into a coiled serpent with multi-hoods sheltering a granite *linga*.

The principal deity is a life-size Virabhadra carrying weapons and bedecked with skulls, and is housed in the main sanctuary. Another shrine for Maheshvara and Uma is partly cut out of a boulder on the east side of the main temple. A shrine to Lord Vishnu is also found here. A distance from the temple is an image of Nandi, Shiva's bull carrier, which has been carved out of a granite boulder and is said to be the biggest in India.

On the bus route between Tirupati and Madras, 22 kilometres away, is the Kalahasthi temple, a famous Shiva temple. Kalahasthi is an important place of pilgrimage in this region. It is here that the hunter devotee Kannappa attained salvation by offering his eyes to Lord Shiva. A small sanctuary with his image is on the summit of the hill above the temple, which is reached by following the path from the temple's south *gopuram*.

The temple is surrounded by high walls and is entered from the south. The temple's main *gopuram* is six storeys tall and faces the Svarnamukhi River. Inside the enclosure you will find the usual assortment of columned pavilions and smaller structures and shrines. It has four main shrines, the principal one to the west houses the main object of worship: the Vayu (air) Linga which appears as an anthill. Proof that it is the Vayu Linga is that the nearby lamp keeps flickering in spite of the fact that there is no air circulating in the temple. The other shrines are for Jnanaprasumbha to the east, Dakshinamurti to the south, and Ganesh to the north.

Our next stop is in Madras, a pleasant city that is important for business, politics, and culture. Madras was founded only 350 years ago in 1640 when Francis Day and Andrew Gogan built a fortified structure on a piece of land that was given by the local Vijayanagara governor. They called the place Fort St. George. From that British bastion evolved the city of Madras. Inside the Fort are a variety of buildings that are used by the Tamil Nadu Government. There is also St. Mary's Church, built in 1680, which is the oldest Protestant church in Asia, and one of the oldest British buildings in India.

There are a few temples worth visiting in Madras. The most important is the Parathasarathy temple, which is popular with many Hindus. It is dedicated to Lord Krishna as Parathasarathy, the chariot driver of Arjuna, as described in the *Mahabharata*. The Deity of Parathasarathy is made of black metal and has a very powerful appearance. The temple has some very nice Deities of Krishna, His consort Rukmini, His brother Balarama and others. No other temple worships Krishna's entire family as they do here. There is also a separate shrine for Sri Ranganatha, the reclining form of Vishnu resting on Adisesha. The incarnations of Vishnu as Narasimha and Varaha are also seen here. Unfortunately, they do not allow Westerners into the temple. So, if you're a Western tourist or pilgrim, going to this temple may not be very fruitful. But you can try to go in if you are dressed in a *dhoti* or devotional clothes.

Another temple is the Kapaleeshvara temple complex, devoted to Shiva. The principal shrine houses a large Shiva Linga and an image of Subramanya, Shiva's son. A smaller shrine to goddess Parvati is nearby. Legend has it that Parvati, Shiva's wife, once incarnated as a peacock and worshiped Lord Shiva here to obtain deliverance. There are many sculptures depicting a number of the local legends. However, they do not allow Westerners into the sanctum sanctorium. Nonetheless, it is an interesting temple, and when I was there a wedding ceremony was going on with nearly a hundred people in attendance.

The ceremony included a simple ritual as the bride and groom sat in the middle of the crowd. The groom was dressed in a silk *dhoti* and shirt, while the bride had a beautiful red sari and gold bangles and hair pieces. After the short ritual, there was an exchange of flower garlands between the bride and groom, and the groom marked the bride's forehead with the red dot that means she is a chaste and married lady. The senior ladies, all dressed in their most opulent and colorful saris, came forward to bestow their blessings on the bride by placing their hands on her head and saying some prayers or offering her some advice. Soon the ceremony was over. Then everyone very happily gathered around to congratulate each other. The people at the wedding received me very nicely and were glad I was interested in watching it. They gave me some fruits that had been offered in the ceremony, as well as some other *prasada* that was being passed around to everyone. They also wanted me to meet the bride and groom. It was as if I had become a part of the celebration. Afterwards, I made my way through the courtyard and out the temple gate feeling quite satisfied by this chance encounter.

One word of caution: if you leave your shoes at the shoe minder's stall near the temple entrance, pay only 10 to 25 paise at the most when you pick up your shoes. This is the standard price at any temple. Don't allow yourself to be cheated by paying up to 10 rupees if they ask for that. Many times shoe minders, guides, *ricksha* drivers, or even shop keepers will automatically charge Westerners considerably more than local people. For a *richsha* it is best to find out what the going rate is from someone who is impartial and then stick with that. However, *ricksha* and taxi rates do change a little according to the region. So be aware of what it is.

A few minutes drive from the Kapaleeshvara temple is an important church for local Christians. This is the San Thome Basilica which was originally built in 1504 and rebuilt in 1898 on the ruins of the original Portuguese church which housed the remains of the Apostle "Doubting" Thomas Didymus who used to preach every day in this area after he had arrived in India. He was originally buried on the nearby beach, but then was moved to a crypt where the Basilica was built. Near the airport is St. Thomas' Mount where he died. A small Portuguese church is there with relics of the saint. It has a tranquil atmosphere and a great view of Madras.

South of the San Thome Basilica is the Adyar River estuary where the Theosophical Society has its world headquarters, founded in 1882 by Madame H. P. Blavatsky. This place has hundreds of acres of gardens with magnificent buildings, shrines, and a world-class library. In the gardens is a 200 year old banyan tree, one of the biggest in India. On the way to Elliot's Beach is the Ashtalakshmi temple, dedicated to goddess Mahalakshmi, one of the few shore temples in the country.

Madras also has the very interesting Government Museum and Art Gallery on Pantheon Road. It has excellent displays of a variety of Deities and artwork from different regions and historical periods. This will give you some insight into the spiritual heritage and culture of India if nothing else in Madras will.

I must say one thing regarding temples that are restrictive about who they let inside. First of all, I can understand why those who are disrespectful should not be allowed entrance. And there is certainly a history of the white Christian missionaries who came to India to preach and blaspheme against the "pagan gods." But for those who are sincerely trying to understand Eastern philosophy and have respect and veneration while in the temple, I see no reason why they should not be allowed inside. Otherwise, the local priests are simply keeping the temples to themselves without any concern for the spiritual well-being of others. This is due to their callous blindness. They do not see the soul that exists within everyone. All they can see is that this person is Indian or Hindu, and that person is a Westerner. This person can come in, and that person must stay out. This is not proper. Spiritual understanding will not spread like that. They should be happy that people other than Indians are interested in their culture and philosophy, but if they don't want to assist in this exchange, then their selfishness and lack of concern will be all that is recognized.

Maybe Westerners in general have engaged in what to the *brahmana* priests are very low activities, such as eating meat, or taking intoxicants, not bathing daily, etc. But God is God of everyone, the Supreme Pure, and, obviously, must be able to purify anyone who comes before Him. So any old *brahmana* who feels that Westerners will only disturb or spoil the atmosphere of the temple lacks real spiritual understanding. And who can say who is really worthy of entering a temple? While riding the trains I have seen Indian *brahmanas* eating eggs and smoking cigarettes. This kind of activity certainly does not give them the qualities that differentiates them from anyone else. It merely shows their own hypocrisy. In fact, according to the orthodox view, once a *brahmana* eats such food, like eggs or meat, he immediately is considered to have lost his caste. He can no longer be a *brahmana*. So how can they enter a temple to see the Deities when other Westerners who may be following a more pure or virtuous lifestyle cannot go in? This is ludicrous. I have seen many Westerners adopt a spiritual path that includes no meat-eating, no intoxication, no illicit sex, etc.: habits that many Indians as well as some *brahmanas* cannot give up. Yet they hold sway over their temples to exclude these sincere souls from entering.

From Madras we take a 72 kilometre bus ride to Kanchipuram, another small but interesting temple town. It is one of the seven most sacred cities of India, which include Varanasi, Hardwar, Ujjain, Mathura, Ayodhya, and Dwarka. As you approach Kanchipuram by bus, you will see the tall temple *gopurams* from miles away. There are many temples in this town, but there are five main ones that pilgrims and tourists visit. The best way to see them is to hire a *ricksha* for several hours or rent a bicycle. But if you don't know the town and your time is limited, a *ricksha* driver will know where to take you with a lot less hassle, though it may cost a little more.

Starting on the west side of town we first visit the Kailasanatha temple, dedicated to Shiva. It's no longer a functioning temple and the only person there is the guard who will show you around and explain some of the more interesting aspects of the temple, if you can understand his English. It was built around 700 A.D. by Rayasimha, a Pallava king. It is enclosed by a wall that has numerous carved figures and small shrines in it. The outside of the temple has many sculptures of various aspects of Shiva, and there is a fine sculpture of Ardhanaresvara, the half-male and half-female form of Shiva/Parvati. The top of the temple is a pyramidal structure that rises a few storeys high, and inside the sanctum is a Shiva *lingam*. It's a quiet place, although the local children will follow you while asking for a pen. But you'll get that almost anywhere you go.

The Ekambareshvara temple is our next stop. This is still a functioning temple dedicated to Shiva and many visitors are continuously coming and going. It's also one of Kanchipuram's newest and largest temples that was built in 1509 by the Vijayanagar king Krishna Devaraja. It covers nine hectares and has a *gopuram* that stands 192 feet tall. There is a large water tank on the north side of the temple next to the long columned *mandapa* hall in front of the main entrance to the temple. You can walk around and get a feel for the place, but you'll not be able to go directly into the temple if you're a Westerner. In the main sanctuary is the Prithvi Lingam, a Shiva *lingam* representing the element of earth. The principal shrine is surrounded by a corridor that has many stone carvings of animals and lotus flowers.

From here we go to the Kamakshiamman temple, dedicated to the goddess Parvati, Shiva's wife. This temple is also enclosed by a wall with a gateway in each direction. Within the enclosure is an ornate columned hall and a water tank with stepped sides. In one corner of the enclosure is a shelter where they keep a couple of elephants for temple functions. All of the visitors briefly stop here to see them. This is another temple complex you can walk around in, but if you're a Westerner you won't be allowed into the main temple, which has a golden sculpted dome above it. When I wanted to take a photo of the golden dome, I was immediately stopped by an old toothless temple assistant who made a big commotion when I got my camera out. I thought to myself, "Boy, I'm in trouble now." Though he spoke no English, he conveyed to me that as soon as no one was looking I could take the photo I wanted if I paid him ten rupees. Though I realized it was just a scam that he played to get a foreigner's money, I played along with it anyway and got the picture I wanted. Inside the temple, the goddess is worshiped as a *chakra*, which is placed before the deity. There is also an image of Sankaracarya, the spiritual teacher who advocated monism.

Now we go to the Vaikunthaperumal temple, which was built around 700 A.D. Inside the surrounding wall you'll see many pillars with sculpted lions on them, a forerunner of the later 1000 pillared halls that we find in temples further south. There are also sculptures depicting some of the Pallava history, such as coronation scenes, as well as images of Vishnu and His incarnations in scenes from the *Puranas*. This temple is dedicated to Lord Vishnu and is worth visiting if you're in Kanchipuram. It is still a functioning temple and when the priest is there he'll show you the Deity. The Deity is a beautiful black stone Vishnu, standing with four hands and nicely decorated with shiny brass ornaments. I was quite impressed and upon leaving a 30 rupee donation, the priest gave me *caranamrita*, *tulasi* leaves (an important plant whose leaves are used in the worship of Vishnu or Krishna), and *prasada* (food that has been offered to the Deity and is considered to be spiritually very powerful) in the form of little sweets. The temple consists of three sanctuaries, one above the other, although only the lower one is used.

The guide also took me to a few parts of the temple that were kept locked. This allowed me a look at other stairways that have carved images on the walls as well as a much closer look at the carvings on the central dome over the temple. After my tour I felt quite satisfied. Other Western tourists were there, too, but, not understanding Eastern culture, they soon left and unknowingly did not get the opportunity to see the beautiful Deity of Vishnu, the real reason for the temple's existence.

Another important Vishnu temple in Kanchipuram is for Varadaraja. This temple is said to be on the site where Lord Brahma performed a fire (*yajna*) ritual to invoke Lord Vishnu. The central enclosure of the temple is supposed to conform to the raised altar that Brahma had used for the ritual.

The temple is built on a hill and has two high *gopurams* on the east and west sides of the temple compound that lead into the first enclosure, and a smaller gate leads into the inner enclosures. There are 96 elaborately carved columns in the *mandapa* hall that show many figures and scenes of the Vaishnava iconography. Nearby is a water tank with a small central pavilion, and another tank at the east side of the enclosure. Other shrines and pavilions are also found, such as the shrines for Perundevi, the consort of Varadaraja. The main temple is entered by climbing a flight of steps. The raised structure contains bronze images of Vishnu with His consorts. Other shrines and paintings of Vaishnava divinities are located in the corridor that surrounds the central sanctuary. The temple has beautiful examples of workmanship. One such example is a huge chain carved from one piece of stone.

Although Kanchipuram has as many as 125 recognized shrines, other noteworthy temples include the Kachapeswara Shiva temple, the Chitragupta temple, the Kumarakottam temple dedicated to Subramaniya, the Iravataneshvara, Matangeshvara, Mukteshvara, and Jvarahareshvara Shiva temples. Another point of interest in Kanchipuram is the highly regarded and valued silk saris that are made here. The weavers use vibrant colors and rich designs, and sometimes use gold thread in the borders. These saris are often sold by the weight of the material. There are numerous shops that sell silk and cotton saris and your *ricksha* driver will want to take you to see a shop or factory where they make them. This is because if you buy any, he is likely to get a commission for bringing you there. Nonetheless, if you need any saris, this is a good place to purchase a few.

From Kanchipuram we take a bus to Mahabalipuram (officially renamed Mamallapuram) which is situated on the coast 59 kilometres south of Madras. This small town is known for its rock-cut cave temples, stone carvings, and shore temple on the beach. The shore temple, one of Mahabalipuram's most noted landmarks, is dedicated to Shiva and has a 16 sided *lingam* and a relief of Somaskanda. The steep pyramidal tower above the temple is capped by an octagonal dome.

From here we go up the road toward the hill that dominates the town. On our right as we walk along we can see the main temple of the town which we can visit if it's open. (One thing to remember is that most temples are closed from noon until 4 PM.) The temple, dedicated to Sri Vishnu, is still active and receives many visitors. The sanctum sanctorium is rather dark, so the priest will take a ghee lamp to provide a little light so you can make out the features of the reclining Vishnu. This form of Vishnu is popular in the South, so take a good look since there may be other temples with a similar Deity that may not allow Westerners to enter.

As we leave the temple and reach the hill, we see a huge boulder 90 feet long by 30 feet high with 153 different figures of deities, humans, and various animals carved on it. This is a most fascinating composition of Indian art. It has a large assortment of animals and beings, gods and goddesses that are included in it. It depicts the story of Arjuna doing penance in order to attain a boon from Lord Shiva. It also shows the story of the Ganges descent from the Himalayas.

From here you can continue up the hill to follow the path and read the signs and see the rock-cut temples and halls that are scattered around the hill. These include the Krishna Mandapa with its stone carving depicting Krishna protecting the residents of Vrindavan from the heavy rains by lifting Govardhana Hill to use as a huge umbrella. Heading south and going clockwise around the hill, there is the Dharmaraja Cave Temple, and then the Adivaraha Cave Temple, with an image of Varaha and panels depicting Lakshmi and Durga. Next is the Mahishamardini Cave Temple, which has a carving of Vishnu reclining on Seshanaga surrounded by the demigods. Further along the path is the Trimurti Cave Temple that has three shrines in a row with stone carvings of Brahma (left), Vishnu (middle), and Shiva (right), and a niche for Durga. The Varaha Cave Temple has a large carving on the wall showing Varaha lifting Bhudevi (left) and Trivikrama (right), and Lakshmi and Durga are on the rear wall. The Ganesha Ratha is after that. Most of the carvings and halls were completed by the 7th and 8th century A.D. Just south of the hill are the Five Rathas, which are small temples used as prototypes for Dravidian architecture. Each is dedicated to one of the Pandavas, namely Draupadi, Arjuna, Bhima, Dharmaraja, and one for Nakula and Sahadeva.

Mahabalipuram has always been known for its stone work, which you can still find plenty of today. There are many shops around to sell you little Deities or souvenirs, or even take custom orders for works of carved stone.

Fourteen kilometres from Mahabalipuram is Tirukkalikundram. This place is known for its hilltop temple on Vedagiri Hill, which is a climb up 565 steps. The temple is dedicated to Shiva as Sri Vedagiriswara. It is built on three huge blocks of stone, which form its inner walls. On the walls are sculptures of Shiva and Parvati and Subramanya, and the main Deity in the central room is a Shiva *lingam*. The priests are friendly and gladly show you around, so be sure to leave a little donation, which is customary at any temple. But I have a rule that if I don't get *darshan* of the Deity, I give no donation. At this temple the priests will also give you some Deity remnants.

This temple is also called Pakshi Tirtha, holy place of the birds, and is famous for the two eagles that arrive every day at noon and are fed by the temple priests. After being fed, the eagles fly to the other side of the hill to clean their beaks where there are large indentations in the hillside from this being done for so many years. Legend has it that they were once two sages who had sinned and were cursed by Lord Shiva to repeatedly take birth as eagles. They come to the temple to offer respects to Shiva for their salvation. This daily event has been going on for hundreds of years. It is even mentioned in the *Puranas*. No one is sure where the eagles come from, but some say that they fly from Varanasi. Five hundred years ago Sri Caitanya Mahaprabhu also visited this hilltop temple to offer respects to Lord Shiva and saw the eagles being fed.

From the hilltop are excellent views of the area, especially of the temple below. The temple at the base of the hill is also very interesting with tall *gopurams*, through which you enter the complex. It has many carved pillars and hallways, and when I visited there were a number of students sitting about studying textbooks. This temple is also dedicated to Shiva and the priests allow you to see the Deities here, one of a Shiva *linga*, the other of Subramanya.

To visit this temple it's good to take a short day trip by bus from Mahabalipuram. But go in the morning because if you arrive after the temples open in the afternoon, you'll miss the feeding of the eagles and it may start getting dark before you're ready to return. After dark is not a good time to be trying to get a bus. Buses can be full and will drive past without stopping. And some of the local people who live along this road are not the kind with whom you will want to be alone after dark. Especially if they are poor and intoxicated peasants who look at you as a person who has money.

Leaving Mahabalipuram, we board a bus for Tindivanam and from there head west some 66 kilometres to Tiruvannamalai. This is another temple town, said to have over 100 temples. But the town is dominated by the central Shiva-Parvati temple, one of the largest in India. The main *gopuram* reaches 66 metres (217 feet) in height, and there are massive walls all the way around the complex. There are several smaller shrines and temples within, but the main temple is dedicated to Shiva in the form of the Jyothir Lingam, representing fire.

Next to that temple is the one for Parvathi. The management here is quite organized and for a yearly donation they will send you Deity *prasada* and remnants every month to wherever you live. During the month of Keshava, November-December, there is a big festival during which a huge bonfire is lit on top of Arunachalla Hill. The fire can be seen for miles and devotees offer obeisances to it, considering it to be the manifestation of Shiva's fiery form.

One thing you may be questioning is why Lord Shiva is almost always represented as a *lingam*. According to the *Puranas*, there was a great sacrificial ceremony that was going to take place many hundreds of years ago. The great sage Narada Muni was invited to it and asked who would receive the effects of the sacrifice. No one could answer, so the sages who were present asked him who should receive it. Narada said that Sri Vishnu, Brahma, and Shiva were all eligible, but they would have to find out which one had the most patience and purity to be the receiver of the sacrifice. So he chose the great sage Brighu to learn the answer.

Brighu had many mystic powers and was able to travel to the domain of the demigods. So first he went to see Lord Brahma, but Brahma was preoccupied and did not notice Brighu'spresence. Feeling insulted, Brighu cursed Brahma, "You are so proud of your power of creation, you did not notice my arrival. For this you shall have no temples on earth." Thus, there are very few temples of Brahma on earth. Next, Brighu went to see Shiva in Kailash, but Shiva also did not notice Brighu's arrival. Brighu, again feeling offended, cursed Shiva to be worshiped only as a *lingam* on earth. This is the reason why Lord Shiva is primarily worshiped as a *lingam*.

Then, to continue the story, Brighu went to see Lord Vishnu, who also did not recognize Brighu's presence. Brighu was so angered that he went forward and kicked Vishnu's chest. Lord Vishnu apologized if He had hurt Brighu's foot and began praising Brighu. Brighu immediately felt pleased and could understand that Vishnu was actually the most qualified to receive the offerings from the sacrifice. However, Lakshmidevi, the goddess of fortune and Lord Vishnu's wife, was very displeased by Brighu's action and, therefore, does not bestow much mercy on the *brahmanas* who, as a result, are often without much money.

Behind the Shiva-Parvati temple complex is Arunachala Hill where several Hindu seers and saints have perfected their lives. One can climb the hill by taking the stone path behind the Ramana Maharshi Ashrama. Everyone climbs the hill barefoot and it's a hefty walk up. I had to stop and rest several times. At the end of the path, half-way up the hill, is Skandashrama, the place where Ramana Maharshi lived and attained enlightenment. This place is like a little heaven on earth. Amidst the barren rock of the hill, there are trees for shade, refreshing breezes, a pleasant house, and a well with very nice water that tastes exceptionally good after the hard climb up. It's a great place for solitary meditation. You can look out over the city and get great views of the temple below as you sit and relax until you're ready for the walk back down. But don't wait too long. I went up in the morning and by the time I came back down at 11 AM, the rocks on the path had already soaked up so much heat from the sun that I felt like they were burning my feet. And this was in March. So you must plan accordingly. The best time to visit South India is between the months of October and March. After that it starts getting very hot and is not a good time to visit if you're not used to the kind of heat that you'll experience here.

By the time I got back down the hill at 11.30, they were serving lunch at the Ramana Maharshi Ashrama, and for a small donation it was well worth it. Tiruvannamalai is not a town that seems to cater to Westerners. There's not a lot of English signs or English speaking people. But when lunch was served at the *ashrama*, I was surprised to see all kinds of Westerners show up. Obviously, many people come here to study yoga and the Shaivite form of Hinduism at the Ramana Maharshi Ashrama. The *ashrama* also has a temple dedicated to Shiva in the form of a *lingam*, and the rooms where Ramana Maharshi lived are kept as a memorial. They also have living quarters for guests and students.

Another *ashrama* that's popular with Westerners is in Pondicherry, the Sri Aurobindo Ashram. This was founded in 1926 and has many programs in the evening that are open to all visitors. There is, however, some controversy surrounding the *ashrama* and it tends to be somewhat unpopular with local people due to the way it has managed the society. It's spiritual philosophy is based on a combination of yoga and modern science. Whether this is effective or not for you is something you'd have to find out for yourself, but opinions tend to sway either way.

Auroville, 10 kilometres north of Pondicherry, a project of the Aurobindo Ashram, was to be an example of how all people could live in peace and harmony above the distinctions of race and creed. It was started in 1968 and at first attracted many people, particularly Europeans, and many organizations donated lots of money for its growth. But a power struggle followed for control of Auroville when "The Mother" died in 1973. She was Mirra Alfassa who joined Aurobindo's household in 1920. It was actually under her management that the original small group of students became a community of over 1200 participants, later to be called the Sri Aurobindo Society. And it was also Mirra who envisioned the Auroville project. But at one point after her death, things got so bad that construction on many buildings was stopped and help was needed to prevent many of the residents from going hungry. Later, the Indian government had to step in to make some managerial decisions for its continued operation. Nonetheless, some construction has gone on and there are now new forests where there was once only dry land, and there are over 700 residents. There are still a number of projects going on at Auroville, but if you're looking for the traditional Eastern or spiritual culture, you may be disappointed. Of course, if you're in the area you can always drop by to check it out.

From the largest temple of India at Tiruvannamalai, we now go to one of the oldest. We take a bus from Tiruvannamalai to Villupuram, where we can continue by bus or take a train to Chidambaram. In our case, we'll take a train. The roads between cities are often very narrow with only one lane most of the time. And when oncoming buses meet, they drive straight toward each other until the last minute when they turn just enough to miss each other by inches. Occasionally, they don't quite clear each other, and you can see the damaged vehicles for days afterwards before the reckage is moved. This kind of driving can get rather nerve racking after a while, so we take a train when it's convenient since it's a little less hazardous.

The Chidambaram temple is dedicated to Nataraja, dancing Shiva. To the right of the image of Nataraja in the sanctum is a circular arch from which hangs a string of golden *vilva* leaves which represents Shiva as *akasha*, or the element of air. Also used in worship on special ocassions is a small crystal or ruby which represents a Shiva *lingam*.

Close to the main Shiva temple is also a Vishnu temple with a reclining Vishnu and Parathasarthi Deities. In fact, a unique thing about this place is that from one position in the sanctum you can have *darshan* of both Shiva (by looking straight ahead) and Lord Vishnu (by looking to your left). So Shaivites can worship Lord Vishnu and Vaishnavas can offer respects to Lord Shiva. No other temple complex is like this. Plus, there is another Vishnu temple in the complex with Lakshmi-Narayana Deities. And in the Nritta Sabha court, which is carved to resemble a large chariot with horses and wheels, there is a temple of Shiva in his angry form. Throughout the complex are smaller temples and shrines for personalities such as Shivakumasundari (Shiva's consort whose name means the beautiful girl who invoked Shiva's love), Durga, Ganesh, Nandi, Subramanya, and many other aspects of Shiva. So regardless of what portion of Hinduism or Vedic study you're interested in, it can be accomodated here.

The temple complex is large and located in the center of town. It covers 13 hectares of land and its *gopurams* reach up to 49 metres high on the north and south sides. It also has a hall of 1000 pillars, which is open only at certain times of the year. The temple employs 300 families to help with its operation. In this temple, the *puja* (worship) is performed strictly according to the Vedic rites and the *brahmanas* receive no salary for doing the worship. There are three *pujas* in the morning and three in the evening. There are also several festivals held each year, but one of the most important is, of course, Shiva Ratri, which is a big 10 day celebration.

According to the *Puranas*, this temple is where Lord Shiva exhibited his cosmic (Paramanantha, very joyful) dance to many demigods and sages thousands of years ago. After the dance, the sages Patanjali and Vyagrapada requested him to accept worship and exhibit his dance forever in this place for the good of his devotees. Thus, Shiva granted their request for the benefit of the world. Though the present temple was built in the 10th century A.D., the history of this place dates back much further.

The history of the temple is said to go back to the Chola king,

Simhavarman, who, before being crowned king, was suffering a prolonged disease. While wandering around the country, he was told by a hunter about the self-manifesting Shiva *linga* in the Tillai forest, Chidambaram. Simhavarman reached the forest and met Vyagrapada and Patanjali and requested that they cure his disease. They instructed him to bathe in the water of the sacred tank Shivagangai (presently the large pool on the north side of the temple) and to worship the Shiva *linga*. Having done so, he was at once cured of his disease and his body turned golden in color, for which he was named Himayavarman. After being crowned king, he returned to the Tillai forest with great wealth and built a big temple for Lord Shiva and the many Gods and demigods who had witnessed Lord Shiva's dance many hundreds of years earlier. In the days of later Chola kings, they also served this temple and through the years added many structural additions.

Chidambaram is a great temple. If you are in South India, be sure to stop in to see this place. Visitors come from all over India. Group tours of Westerners regularly come through, but being able to visit on your own or with a few friends and take some time to absorb the atmosphere is the best way to see it. The nice thing about it is that you are allowed to see as much as anyone else. You can watch all the ceremonies and Deity worship along with the Indian visitors. You can also take photographs of almost anything except the Deities. Thus, the temple is a great place to study and learn Eastern philosophy and watch how real Vedic *brahmanas* live and perform their rituals.

When I was there they had a special bathing ceremony in which the priests bathed the crystal *lingam* of Shiva in a variety of elements. Many people came to see it. I stood near the right side of the temple platform, just outside the silver doors. Directly in front of me was a spout where the water and milk used in the bathing drained down from the platform. Many people came to collect the *caranamritam* water in their hands and sip it or pour some over their heads. Others had containers to collect larger quantities. But everyone treated it with special regard. After the bathing, they set the Shiva deity up on the altar again and then performed the *arati*, the ceremony in which they offer the deity of Nataraja (dancing Shiva) sweet incense and large flames in the ghee lamps. It was a most interesting experience.

The reason Lord Shiva is often worshipped by pouring Ganges water over the *lingam* is that it represents the Ganges descending from heaven on to Shiva's head. The legend is that when the Ganges first began to flow to the earthly planet from the heavenly region, the force of it would've destroyed the earth. To prevent this, Lord Shiva agreed to let the river first fall on his head before forming into a river.

You can spend plenty of time wandering around the grounds and hallways of this complex, finding the different temples and getting *darshan* of the Deities. If you're not sure where to look, just ask. Temple assistants can guide you. Although some tour books say not to bother with taking on a guide, it really depends on the temple, how big it is, and how much time you have. If your time is limited and you want to see a lot of the temple quickly, then it may be best to have a guide give you a quick tour and then continue on your own. In many cases, however, a guide may be nothing more than a useless waste of time and money.

At Chidambaram my guide was N. Anandhan who has been at this temple for 20 years and spoke fairly good English. He had also helped work on Mike Wood's video on Chidambaram for the B.B.C. He helped show me where the many temples were and after he saw that I was also an initiated *brahmana*, he arranged for me to get *darshans* of the Deities of Vishnu and Shiva, and get closer than some of the regular Indian visitors were allowed. He also arranged for me to receive Deity remnants like flower garlands and sweets that had been offered to the Deities. He also told me what times the special ceremonies took place so I could be sure to attend, and he was also there to meet me and explain what was taking place. This can be important since some temples may do things differently than others. And you'll want to know exactly what is happening if you've never seen it before so you can understand it, even if you are already familiar with most of the customs. Anyway, I highly recommend him as a guide if you go to Chidambaram.

This temple has played a great part in the lives of many saints and poets of the past, as well as people today. Sri Caitanya also visited this temple nearly 500 years ago. Chidambaram is where you can see how the people of India find harmony and peace in a world full of changes. The people are friendly and enthusiastic for sharing what they get in their abandonment for the soul. Here, or in any holy city of India, the people know why they're in this world, how they fit into it, and who they are, which is more than many people of the West can say for themselves. They may have much less than most Westerners have, materially speaking, but they have much less to worry about as well and are often happier. I actually felt quite at home here. So it was with some regret when I said farewell to my new friend Anandhan and took a *ricksha* to the train station for my next stop at Kumbakonam.

Taking the train in India can be quite an adventure. You can definitely see some great landscapes as you go through hills, valleys, travel past the lakes, cities, villages, farmlands, rice fields, and groves of fruit trees. At the train stations there are often vendors who will come through the train cars or call through your window selling anything from bananas, biscuits (cookies), cool drinks, magazines, nuts, salad, etc. And, of course, there are the tea sellers with their loud and often annoying shouts of, "Chai, chai." There may also be children (or old men and women) who seem to live at the train stations by begging. Or a blind beggar will use his cane to find the door to the train car, board and carefully walk down the aisles asking for donations while playing an instrument and singing songs as the train goes on to its next stop, where he will get off.

There may also be village children who sing songs or play with monkeys as a form of entertainment outside your train window in the hope of getting a few rupees. And while traveling, the people you meet on the train are often very friendly and willing to share conversation, ask you questions, or even share their food. On the average, Indian people are much friendlier than Westerners. But if you are a Westerner you may have to get used to people staring at you, especially when in smaller towns. There were many times when I was the only white person on the train or the bus, and the people couldn't help but be curious and watch every move I made. One time in a small town in Central India I got off the bus to buy a few apples. When I had made my purchase and turned around, I was facing a large crowd of local people who had gathered behind me simply to watch what I was doing. Who knows when the last white man went through their village.

When using the trains, if it's available always travel in the first-class section where it's a little cleaner (most of the time) and more organized and roomier. In second-class, anything can happen and people sometimes squeeze in until there's standing room only. One time I was sitting in the crowded second-class section and with each stop more and more people left the train. So I got on an upper bunk to take some rest. Just as I was getting to sleep the train stopped at a place where the whole village must've tried to get on. There were eight people sitting on benches that were meant for four. I didn't get much sleep that night. Another time I was at a train station waiting for a train when one train pulled out that was completely full. There were no more seats available, the aisle was full, and there were people hanging onto the doors and windows on the outside of the train. How long they could hold on like that I don't know.

Anyway, Kumbakonam is an interesting town with many shops, bazaars, people wandering through the streets, and, of course, many temples. The temples are of all sizes, from quite large to no bigger than a closet. But there are several significant temples to see in this town. The Sarangapani Vishnu temple ranks third with the Srirangam and Tirupati temples in importance and is the largest Vaishnava temple in town. It covers 3 acres of land and the main *gopuram* is 147 feet tall with 12 storeys and is covered with sculptures. The sanctum and front *mandapam* (hallway) enclosed in the building are built to resemble a huge chariot with large wheels and horses. Legend is that the sage Himarishi invoked the aid of Lord Vishnu from this place, who then descended to earth in a chariot.

The Adi Kumbhesvara is the temple after which the town is named. It is in the heart of the city and has a *gopuram* that is 128 feet tall and beautifully carved and painted. It is dedicated to Shiva and the *linga* in the main shrine is in the shape of a *kumbha* (pot), beneath which stands Nataraja, dancing Shiva. The legendary basis of this temple is that Shiva once gave a pot that held the seed of creation to Lord Brahma. During the great deluge the pot was carried to this place where the contents drained out and spread over an area of 10 miles.

This nectar settled in two places: one was the Mahamaham tank on the other side of town, and the other place was the Portamarai tank of the Sarangapani temple. Out of the broken pieces of the pot, Shiva made a *lingam* which he installed here at the Kumbhesvara temple. Although the temple has many painted pillars and fine sculptures, Westerners are not allowed inside.

The next temple is the Chakrapani temple, which is dedicated to Lakshmi, the goddess of fortune and wife of Lord Vishnu. One has to climb a flight of stairs to see the colorful eight-armed image. Many women attend this temple.

From here we go to the Sri Ramaswami temple, which is dedicated to Lord Ramacandra, another incarnation of Lord Vishnu or Krishna. This temple has Deities of Ramacandra, Sita (His wife), Hanuman (His great monkey servant) and Lakshman and Satrughna (Lord Rama's two brothers). They are made out of black stone and decorated with silver jewelry and paraphernalia. All the way around the inside of the walls that enclose the courtyard are many paintings depicting scenes of the Ramayana.

Another important temple is the Nageshvara with shrines to Shiva and different expansions of Parvati. It is said that Adisesha and Surya, the sun god, worshiped Sri Nageshvara in this place. The temple is built in such a way that on the 11th, 12th, and 13th of the month of Chitra (March-April) the sun lights the *lingam* in the sanctum. This temple is known for the fine sculptures of the Chola period.

From here we go to a temple that I really liked. It's a good place to sit and relax away from the heat outside and talk with the temple priests. This temple is dedicated to Lord Brahma, which is rare to find. It's a somewhat poor temple, no fancy *gopurams* to show the way. You just have to know where it is or ask your *ricksha* driver to take you there. But once you enter and go through the hall of carved pillars, you reach the sanctum where there are three altars with beautiful Deities. One altar has a big image of Brahma with four heads and four hands, made of black stone and holding silver items in his hands. At his sides are goddesses Sarasvati and Bhumi. The central altar has Lord Vishnu, Lakshmi, and Bhumi. And the third altar has a big Lord Narasimha and Lakshmi. I wish I could've taken photos, but they tend to be quite fussy about that.

If one wishes, you can go to the big Mahamaham water tank, which covers 20 acres. There are 16 different shrines in the shape of small pavilions along the banks which are dedicated to a variety of Vedic divinities. Once every 12 years on the full moon day of Magha (January-February) there is a festival attended by thousands of pilgrims who bathe here. At that time it is considered that all the holy rivers of India enter this tank. Taking a dip in this tank on that day is believed to give the person the merit of bathing in all the holy rivers. The last festival was in 1992. Other temples in Kumbakonam include the Banapurishvara, the Gautameshvara, and Vishvanatha temples.

Four kilometres west of Kumbakonam is Dharasuram, a small town with two old but well preserved temples. They are built side by side, separated by their huge outer walls. The first temple, the Daivanayaki Ammoan goddess temple, is interesting and built much like the second temple next to it. The second temple, the Airateshvara, is in much better shape and is a good example of Chola architecture. It was built in the 12th century and is little used but is still a functioning temple. The temple is in a rectangular court surrounded by a colonnade, which is entered through two gateways. The exterior of the temple building has rows of stone sculptures and images of demigods, goddesses, saints, folk art, etc. Inside the temple, which has a large *mandapa* hall in front of the sanctum, there are many more stone images, especially different aspects of Shiva. Lotus designs and musicians are carved on the ceilings. The entrance hall is built to resemble a chariot. You can go into the sanctum, which is topped by a structure that reaches 85 feet high, and see the Shiva *linga*, and the old priest will show you around and tell you all about this place. He is remembered with fondness by all who visit. This temple is definitely worth visiting.

Another four kilometres farther west is the town of Swamimilai with its Swaminathaswamy temple. This temple is dedicated to Murugan, who appears in the form of teaching his father, Lord Shiva, the Pranava (*om*) *mantra* which Shiva had forgotten. The temple is reached by climbing 60 steps up a hill. Thirty steps up you'll see the life-like image of Murugan teaching Shiva the *mantra*. The presiding deity in the sanctum, Sri Swaminathaswamy, is a six foot tall granite image of Murugan in a standing position. On the ground floor are other shrines for Sri Sundareshwarar, goddess Meenakshi, and Vinayaga. This town also features artists who still make bronzes by hand in the traditional way of their Chola ancestors.

If you are going to be staying in Kumbakonam for a while and want to see more of the spiritual culture of India in the area, there are more temples short distances away. Ten kilometres from Kumbakonam near Swamimilai is Tiruvalamjuli with its temple of Sri Vinayaka. It is noted for its architectural grandeur, intricate stone windows, and fine sculptures. The sanctum that houses a white deity of Sri Vinayaka is full of architectural splendor. Smaller shrines are also found in the complex. The legendary basis of this temple is that when the demigods churned the ocean of milk for the special nectar for immortality, they had ignored the worship of Sri Vinayaka and, thus, first produced poison from the ocean, which was swallowed by Shiva. When they realized their mistake, the demigods took the white foam from the ocean and fashioned an image of Vinayaka; hence, the white color of the deity in the temple.

Suryanarcoil, 15 kilometres east of Kumbakonam, is said to be the only temple in the south dedicated to Surya, the sun god. The *navagrahas* (nine planets) are believed to influence the destinies of people. Thus, they are worshiped to acquire peace, prosperity, longevity, and other good results. The central shrine of this temple complex faces west and is dedicated to the sun. The other eight planets, namely Brihspati, Rahu, Sukra, Ketu, Chandra, Angaraka, Budha, and Sani, also have shrines in the courtyard.

Eight kilometres from Kumbakonam is the village of Tribhuvanam with its temple dedicated to Shiva as Sri Kampaharesvara. It is an impressive and colorful temple, built in the 13th century similar to the temple in Tanjore. The tower and sides of the temple are full of sculpted figures depicting scenes from the *Puranas*. There is also a shrine to Sarabha, the form Shiva took to subdue the divine fury of Vishnu when He appeared as Lord Narasimha.

Gangakondacholapuram, 35 kilometres north of Kumbakonam, has an enormous temple, also built smaller but similar to the temple in Tanjore in the 11th century by King Rajendra Chola. Dedicated to Shiva, it has many beautiful sculptures and a large water tank said to have received many large pots of Ganges water. In the interior of the temple is a huge representation of the nine planets (*Navagrahas*) installed on the shape of a chariot. Surya (the sun) occupies the prominent position in the chariot and Saturn is the driver, while the other planets are on the sides. Not many people come here to visit and it is no longer a functioning temple, so it is now only a grand reflection of the past.

When you're ready to leave Kumbakonam, we hop on the train for a couple hours to our next stop, Tanjore. This town is said to have over 40 temples, but the main attraction here is the Brihadeshvara Temple fort. If you didn't see the other temples outside of Kumbakonam, this is the temple after which many of them were styled. It was built a thousand years ago by Raja Raja I, the Chola king who was also a pious devotee. Entering the courtyard through *gopurams* that are 90 feet high and that have sculpted figures with clubs that guard the doorway, we see a large pavilion under which is a monolithic Nandi deity (12 feet tall by 19 feet high), considered the second largest in India. The main temple has a huge tower (217 feet high) over the sanctum covered with carved figures which is topped by a dome cut from a single piece of granite (81 tons). The dome was put into position by using an inclined plane starting at the village Sarapallam four miles away. Westerners are allowed inside the temple to see the large cave-like hall and the biggest Shiva *linga* I saw anywhere in India. It must be about seven or eight feet in diameter and 10 to 12 feet high, and is noted as being the largest in India. There are tall platforms around it so that priests can climb up to pour liquid offerings (usually Ganges water) over it in worship, which then drain through a spout and into a small tank outside the temple.

There is a continual flow of Indians and Westerners alike who visit this temple. It is worth taking some time to walk around and see everything this place has to offer. In the northwest corner is a small shrine to Subramanya, built in the 17th century, which is a real gem of decorative stone work. There are other small shrines in the complex, including one for Chandeshvara near the temple entrance, and a small museum is on the south side. The huge walls surrounding the courtyard have open rooms filled with Shiva *lingas* and small shrines. On the other side of town there is also the museum and art gallery that has displays of many deities that one can see and photograph, including many figures in granite and bronze of Shiva, as well as Brahma, Buddha, Vishnu,

Krishna, etc. There is also a 190 feet tall lookout, built like a *gopuram*, that provides a good view over the city if you climb through the narrow stairways to reach the top. But the Shiva temple is the main reason people come to this city. On His South Indian tour Sri Caitanya also visited this temple 500 years ago.

If you want, you can also take a day trip to Tiruvarur, a town 40 km east of Tanjore that is easily reached by bus and is famous for its temple of Shiva as Sri Thyagaraja. The original structure of this temple, built in the 10th century, was the shrine to Vanmikanatha (Shiva), and the adjacent Thyagaraja shrine has divinities of Shiva with Uma (Parvati) and Skanda (son of Shiva and Parvati, also known as Karttikeya, Kumara, and Subrahmanya), and was built in the 13th century. In a different part of the complex is a temple to Achaleshvara, another aspect of Shiva, also built in the 10th century. Additions to this complex continued up to the 17th century, which include several columned halls, *gopuras*, and ceilings that are adorned with many fine sculptures and paintings.

East of Tiruvarur along the coast is the town of Vedaranyam, also called Dakshina Kailasam. This is a sacred place for Hindus because Lord Rama was supposed to have stopped here when He was returning from Lanka. Nearby is a mound where one can find the preserved footprints of Lord Rama.

After spending a day or two wandering around Tanjore and the area, we get our things together and take the 7 PM train to Tiruchirappali, otherwise called Trichy. When we arrive, it is dark but the streets and shops are busy with people shopping, socializing, or whatever. After making our way out of the noisy train station, we get a *ricksha* ride to a nearby hotel to get a room and settle in for the night, knowing full well that tomorrow will be a busy day.

Trichy has three major attractions. One is the Rock Fort temple in the heart of the old city. To get there we board the number 1 bus near our hotel and ride to a place several blocks away from the hilltop temple. We walk past the Teppakulam water tank and find the entrance to the Rock Fort temple in the Chinna Bazaar. We leave our shoes at the shoe minder's stall and proceed up more than 400 steps that are cut through the rock of the hill. It is a steep and laborious climb to the summit 273 feet up where the views are great. If it's not too hazy, you can see the Srirangam temple to the north.

Westerners are, unfortunately, not allowed inside the hilltop temple to see the image of Vinayaka, known here as Uchi Pillayar. The legend is that Vibhishan, the brother of the demon king Ravana of the *Ramayana* epic, was returning to Sri Lanka from Ayodhya with a Vishnu Deity that had been presented to him by Lord Rama. He stopped at Srirangam to perform his worship on the banks of the Kaveri river. He gave the Deity to a *brahmana* boy with instructions not to place it on the ground. But the boy placed it on the earth anyway and then the Deity could not be moved. Vibhishan became angry and struck the boy who ran to the summit of the rock and stood transformed as Vinayaka. Even now the image of Vinayaka has a depression on his face where he had been struck.

The shrine to Thayumanavar, Shiva, is located half-way up the hill, also closed to non-Hindus. Legend explains that when a pious mother could not cross the Kaveri river to tend to her daughter who was in labor with child, Shiva appeared to help the daughter as a midwife to avoid her being disappointed. When the real mother arrived, Shiva disappeared. Thus, Shiva is called Thayumanavar, the one who became the mother. This temple was excavated in the 8th century and belongs to the Pandya era. It is, basically, a columned *mandapa* hall with two side shrines with wall carvings of Vishnu and Shiva. In niches in the rear wall are images of Ganesh, Subrahmanya, Brahma, Surya, and Durga.

From the Rock Fort temple we walk back to the bus stop to catch a bus to the Sri Ranganathaswamy temple on the north side of town. This is another very large temple complex, a town in itself, and one of the most important Vishnu temples in the South. It has 21 *gopurams* marking the gateways through seven walls that surround the main temple. The largest *gopuram* is the south entrance which was completed in 1987 and reaches a height of 236 feet, one of the tallest in India. The outer walls contains an area of 3000 feet by 2400 feet. It is situated on the island of Srirangam which is between two branches of the Kaveri river. Thousands of pilgrims, especially Vaishnavas, visit this temple all year long. The legend is that the Deity of Sri Ranganatha was once worshiped by Lord Rama thousands of years ago. He gave the Deity to Vibhishan who unwittingly allowed it to be placed on the ground. When the Deity could not be moved, a temple was built at the spot.

The main Deity is an 18 foot long reclining black Vishnu lying on His serpentine couch of Seshanaga. Near His feet are His consorts Bhu Devi and Nila Devi. Just in front is the beautiful standing Vishnu Deity, adorned with flowers and jewelry. Images of Nathamuni, Yamunacarya, and Ramanujacarya are also found in the sanctum. The great saint Sri Ramanujacarya was also buried here at Srirangam. Unfortunately, once again, they do not let most Westerners into the main temple nor a few of the many smaller shrines, some of which are for Sri Krishna, Narasimhadeva, Ganesh, Garuda, etc. But there are plenty of other things to see, including a variety of shops and commercial enterprises. Tour companies also bring in groups of foreigners to see and photograph this temple. But there is a camera fee of ten rupees. Nonetheless, you can see many colorful sculptures and pillared halls, watch the people and learn about the different aspects of the life that goes on in this place. This is an important temple and still plays a significant role in the spiritual traditions that are found in the East. This is another temple visited by Sri Caitanya Mahaprabhu where He danced in ecstasy many years ago.

Some Westerners who have accepted the path of *sanatana-dharma* (*bhakti-yoga*) and dress accordingly are allowed into the sanctum to have *darshan* of the Deity and see the worship. In fact, Iskcon devotees are welcomed by the head *pandita*, Sri Rangaraja Bhatta, who is a descendant of Sri Gopala Bhatta

Gosvami's father, Vyenkata Bhatta. His house is located in the temple complex and is called "Mahaprabhu Sadan" for being the place where Sri Caitanya Mahaprabhu had stayed for four months with Vyenkata Bhatta while He visited Sri Rangam. In this way, our visit to Sri Rangam to have *darshan* of the Deities and get association with other spiritually oriented people can be very uplifting. This is the reason for our pilgrimage to such temples.

Outside the main gates of the temple complex we catch the bus to the other side of the main road and walk down the lane to the Sri Jambukesvara temple, dedicated to Shiva. It's not as big as the Sri Ranganatha temple, but is nearby and quite interesting. It has massive carved pillars in its huge hallways, along with outside courtyards, water pool, etc. And for ten rupees you can photograph most any part of it. Here, as at the previous temple, you may be approached by a guide or temple assistant who will want to show you around.

There are two main temples in this complex, one to Parvati (Akilandesvari), and one to Lord Shiva. The main deity is a Shiva *linga*, Sri Jambhukeshvara or Appulingam, which is half submerged under the water of a natural spring next to it. They do not allow non-Hindus into the main temple, but upon seeing that I was an initiated *brahmana*, I was allowed in to see the sanctum. Of course, that also means that the priests will do a special *puja* ceremony for you, offering lamps and *mantras* to the deity, and then expecting some nice donations for it. But this is an aspect of worship that many pilgrims perform and is spiritually beneficial and fascinating to observe and partake in. Thus, for our own spiritual merit, we also participate.

After returning to our hotel, getting something to eat and relaxing a while, we can now prepare to catch the evening train for the short ride to our next stop, which is Madurai, one of the most interesting temples in the South and a big attraction for tourists and pilgrims alike. However, if you're a devotee of Murugan, you might want to stop at Dindugal to get a connecting train to Palni (or Palani).

Lord Murugan, one of the sons of Shiva, is very popular in Tamil Nadu and Kerala. The main temple at Palni is the most renown of the six temples of Murugan. It is located on the hilltop and reached by climbing 659 steps, or by taking an electric winch. The Murugan deity is in the form of an ascetic who has renounced the world, standing with a staff in his right hand and *rudraksha* beads around his neck. The deity is said to be made from nine different kinds of poison which, mixed together, resembles wax. The exact proportions, calculated by a sage named Bhoga, is unknown. But substances that touch the deity are believed to acquire healing powers. The deity is bathed daily with different liquids, such as milk, rose water, sandal paste, etc., all of which becomes *prasadam* with strong healing potencies. There are a series of festivals through the year at this hilltop temple that draw thousands of pilgrims from Tamil Nadu. At the foot of the hill in Palni is another temple dedicated to Subramanya (Murugan) with his consorts Valli and Devayanai.

The legend behind the deity of the main temple is that Lord Shiva once showed his sons, Ganesh and Murugan, a rare fruit and said it would be the prize for the one who first returned from circumambulating the world. Murugan immediately started out, riding on his peacock carrier. Ganesh, however, simply walked around his parents and said that since the universe rests in them this was equal to traveling around the world. So Shiva gave the fruit to him. When Murugan returned and found out what had happened, he became angry and renounced all worldly connections.

When we reach Madurai, you'll find it is a very interesting city. If you travel through the south, this is a place you should not miss. It leaves an indelible impression on all visitors and enriches their knowledge of South Indian art, architecture, and spiritual culture. Madurai has a population of 817,000, but it's not as big as you'd expect. If you get a hotel that's centrally located, you can walk to most of the places you'd be interested to see. Of course, if you stay at a larger hotel across the river, you may have to take a taxi or *ricksha* to get around. It's not far from the train station to the central hotels, or from the hotels to decent restaurants. The fruit vendors and shops that sell most anything you might need are also nearby. There are lots of little stores and small industries. The city stays busy all day and into the evening. Lots of people wander the streets, shopping or selling, all adding to the variety this place has to offer. You'll see people from all over India as well as from any part of the world. Tour companies bring large groups of tourists here, especially to visit the Meenakshi temple. And it's been said that the temple attracts as many as 10,000 visitors a day.

The Meenakshi temple is located in the center of the old town. It's a huge complex (covering 847 feet by 729 feet) with four towering *gopurams* (the south tower is the tallest at 169 feet) that dominate the landscape and mark the entrances through the outer walls. The *gopurams* are some of the most famous in India since they are tall and covered from top to bottom with colorful and intricate images of gods, goddesses, scenes from the *Puranas* and Vedic epics, guardians, animals, and so on.

The main entrance to the temple complex is on the east side. Over the entrance you'll see the sculpted representation of the wedding of Meenakshi. As you go in you'll soon be greeted by the temple elephant and its attendant. A little crowd of people, especially children, is usually gathered around it and are fascinated by the way it takes an offering of money from their hands and then gently blesses them with a tap on their head with its trunk.

Further into the temple you'll find a long hallway with many little shops selling everything from bangles, spices, and miniature deities and pictures, to toys for children. It is quite interesting to stand back for a bit and watch the incredible variety of people who walk through. There are the expected Indian tourists, pilgrims, and holy men dressed in saffron, as well as Westerners from America or different parts of Europe, some not knowing what to make of it all, or others who are living and studying the ways of the East and familiar with what it's all about. A most fascinating mixture.

It is also in this area that you buy your ticket to the Temple Art Gallery. Then you enter the impressive Hall of 1000 Pillars, at the end of which is a large deity of Nataraja, dancing Shiva. From this hallway you can wander through the museum, which has a good selection of wood, stone, and metal deities of all sizes from different eras. Some of the displays need maintenance, but it is worthwhile nonetheless.

After seeing the museum, you can continue into the temple and explore its many shrines, sculptures, the long cave-like hallways, and almost get lost in it for hours. The halls are filled with columns and sculptures of many incarnations of Vishnu, demigods, goddesses, and forms of their varied personalities. There are also many images of animals and statues of kings and rulers who either helped build the temple or were devoted to the deities. To understand them all would take much time and you'd have to have a very knowledgeable guide to explain them. The walls around the Golden Lotus tank have murals which depict the 64 miracles that were performed by Lord Sundaresvara in and around Madurai. Across from the tank is the sanctuary for Meenakshi, the Divine Mother, where she stands with a parrot and a bouquet in her right hand.

In a separate temple, Sundaresvara is the Shiva *linga*. In front of the Sundaresvara shrine is the Kambathadi *mandapa* which has many fine sculpted pillars, among which is one that depicts the wedding of Meenakshi to Shiva, and shows Lord Vishnu giving away His sister, Meenakshi, to Shiva. After wandering through the temple complex, you can even have your future foretold by the palmists and astrologers who are sitting in the shade in the courtyard on the northside of the building.

The legends concerning this temple go back thousands of years. It begins with Indra, the king of heaven, who was wandering through the universe looking for a means to purify himself from the sin of killing a *brahmana*. While near the Kadamba forest of Madurai, he discovered that he had become purified. He realized the cause of it was due to the presence of a Shiva *lingam* under a tree. So he bathed in what is now the temple's Golden Lotus tank, and using golden lotus flowers he worshiped the *lingam*. Afterwards, he built a little shrine for it and then returned to his heavenly abode.

Much later, King Kulashekara Pandyan learned of this incident and went to the forest to see and worship the *lingam*. It was he who started building the temple and city of Madurai into greater prominence. Malayadwaja Pandyan succeeded the throne and, since he and his wife were childless, performed a sacrifice to beget a child. From the sacrificial fire appeared a three year old girl who had three breasts. They were told that the third breast would disappear when she met the person she would marry.

The child, Thadathagati, an incarnation of Shiva's wife Parvati, was raised and trained like a prince and mastered all the arts of war. She succeeded the king and in her warrior spirit conquered all the nearby countries up to the Himalayas, even reaching the abode of Lord Shiva, Mount Kailash. But when she met the gaze of Lord Shiva on the battlefield, her third breast disappeared and she knew he was her husband.

On the order of Lord Shiva, she returned to Madurai and eight days later Shiva came to marry her. They ruled Madurai together for some time and after making their son, Ugra Pandyan (an incarnation of Muruga), the King, they assumed the divine forms as Sundaresvara and Meenakshi.

The temple of Sundaresvara was still a shrine in the 7th century A.D. and the temple of Meenakshi was built in the 12th century. Most of the complex as we see it today was designed by Vishwanatha Nayak in 1560 and built during the 200 year reign of the Nayaka rulers, especially Tirumalai Nayak (1623-55). And it was almost 500 years ago that Sri Caitanya Mahaprabhu also visited this temple to see Sundaresvara and Meenakshi.

Another temple in Madurai is the Kudalalagar Devasthanam Vishnu temple on South Masi Street. It has a nice temple building with a beautiful black Vishnu Deity with gold colored hands and ornaments. He is sitting with Sri Lakshmi on His right and Sri Andal or Bhumi on His left. If the stairway is unlocked you can go to the second floor where there is a standing Vishnu Deity, and up to the third floor where the small temple room has a Deity of a reclining Vishnu. On the south side is a separate temple for Sri Lakshmi and on the north side there is one for Sri Andal or Bhumi.

There will be guides at this temple who will want to show you around and then ask for large tips. They may also take you "for free" to the temple sari shop to show you how they make and dye saris to sell and help support the temple. It's interesting to watch, but they really want you to buy something. There's another smaller temple a few blocks away.

If you are staying for a while in Madurai and want a change from seeing temples, you can visit the Tirumalai Nayak Palace about a kilometre from the Meenakshi temple, or the Gandhi Museum across the river. Several kilometres east of the city is the large (1000 feet by 950 feet) and tranquil pool called Mariamman Theppakulam with a temple structure on the island in the middle of it. Not much happens here except when, in late January or early February on Thai Poosam day, they bring the deities of Meenakshi and Sundaresvara here for the Teppam (float) festival. They place the deities on boats to give them rides across the water. People from all over India attend, so the city can be rather crowded at this time. Another festival in late August or early September takes place when they bring the deities out on big carts that are drawn through the streets of Madurai. Another important festival is the Chitra festival in late April or early May when the wedding of Meenakshi and Shiva is celebrated. For this festival, the Deity of Lord Vishnu from the Alagarcoil temple also attends in a procession that goes to the Vaigai river. This festival draws up to 100,000 devotees from all over India.

Alagarcoil is 12 miles (19 kilometres) east of Madurai where a beautiful Vishnu temple is found on the side of a hill. The bronze Vishnu Deity is Sri Sundararajan. There are many beautiful sculptures here depicting various incarnations of Vishnu as well as paintings of the *Ramayana*. The important event for this temple is the Chitra festival. On the fourth day, the Deity is brought in a procession to Madurai to attend His sister's (Meenakshi's) marriage to Shiva. They also celebrate the marriage of Alagar (Vishnu) to Sri Andal with great pomp. At the top of the Alagar hill is a temple dedicated to Murugan.

In Thirupparankuntram, 7 miles (10 kilometres) south of Madurai, is one of the six famous temples to Lord Murugan. This is a cave temple on the northern side of a hill that marks the place where Murugan married Devayani, daughter of Lord Indra, after he defeated Surapadma. The sanctum is carved out of the rock and Murugan's wedding with Devayani is depicted here. The front of the temple has 48 large pillars carved very artistically. The temple also has separate shrines to Lord Vishnu, Shiva, Ganesh, Durga, etc.

After seeing Madurai, we catch the early morning train for Ramesvaram. If we're traveling first-class, we may have a compartment all to ourselves since this is not a crowded train. It's a relaxing ride (about six hours) as we head toward the coast. Ramesvaram is a tropical island surrounded by coral reefs and sandy beaches with coconut palms and tamarind trees. It is a major center of pilgrimage for both Vaishnavas and Shaivites. The Sri Ramanathaswamy temple is one of the most important in India. It is a massive complex with a number of shrines, holy wells, *gopurams*, and several long hallways, one reaching 4000 feet in length, the longest in the country. The halls are adorned with many large pillars, some of which are covered with scrollwork, lotus designs, animals, and other figures, and colorful painted medallions are on the ceilings.

According to legends, this temple was originally started by Lord Rama. Lord Rama had gone to Sri Lanka to rescue His wife, Sita, and engaged in a great battle during which He killed the demon Ravana. Afterward, He wanted to absolve Himself of the sin by installing a *lingam* at Ramesvaram. He sent His most trustworthy servant Hanuman to get a Shiva *lingam* from Mount Kailash, but Hanuman was delayed in his return. Since Shiva had to be worshiped by a certain time, Sita made a *lingam* (Sri Ramanatha) out of sand. When Hanuman returned with a *linga*, he was disappointed and angry to find another *linga* already installed. To pacify Hanuman, Rama had the Hanumath *lingam* (Visvalingam) installed next to the Ramanatha *lingam* and ordered that all worship should first go to the Visvalingam. So in this complex the main shrines are for Visvalingam and the Sri Ramanatha *lingam*.

Next to Ramanatha is a shrine to Parvathavardhani (Parvati), the consort of Ramanatha. There's also a separate shrine to Lord Vishnu with a Deity made of white marble, known as Sethu Madhava. The original shrine that housed the *lingas* many years ago was but a simple thatched shed. But the temple as we see it today was begun in the 12th century A.D. and expanded over the centuries by the rulers of the area. Only Hindus are allowed into the sanctum, but fortunately while I was there they brought some of the Deities out for a little parade through the streets of the city, enabling me to see them quite clearly.

Ramesvaram is also the temple where Sri Caitanya Mahaprabhu found the *Kurma Purana*. Within it He found a verse stating that Ravana kidnapped an illusory Sita, and the real Sita was safely hidden by Agni. This information has greatly relieved many devotees of Sri Sri Sita-Rama.

About a mile and a half north of the temple is Gandhamadana Parvatham, a temple that houses the footprints of Lord Rama. It is from this place that Hanuman is believed to have lept across the sea to Lanka. From the top of the temple one can get a beautiful view of the town. Seven miles from the Ramanathaswamy temple is a Vishnu temple known as Thiruppullani or Darbhasayanam. This marks the place where Lord Rama lay on a bed of Darbha grass before proceeding to Lanka. Inside are Deities of Sri Rama lying on His grass bed. Ten miles northeast of Ramesvaram is the coastal village of Devipatnam or Navapashanam. Here is a temple to the nine planets, said to have been originally installed by Lord Rama for worship. The nine stone columns in the sea are said to be all that's left of the original temple.

Jata Thirtam, two and a quarter miles east from Ramesvaram, is a place glorified in Chapter 20 of the *Sanat Kumara Samhita* of the *Skanda Purana*. This place is said to be where Lord Rama first took His bath after killing Ravana and before worshiping the Ramanatha *lingam*.

Five miles east of Ramesvaram is the Kothandaraman temple. It is said that Vibhishana, Ravana's brother, surrendered to Lord Rama at this place. Further out we arrive at Dhanuskodi, which is the long peninsula that extends into the sea. There's not much to see here but the small fishing village where the curious children follow you asking for rupees. But it's here at the confluence of the Bay of Bengal and the Indian Ocean that's considered to be Sethu Bhandan. This is where Lord Rama and His devotees built the stone bridge that reached Lanka in order to rescue Sita, as fully described in the *Ramayana*. At the request of Vibhishan, after having used the bridge, Rama broke it with the end of his bow, causing it to sink. Hence the name Dhanuskodi, which means "bow end." Some people say that the many rocks below the surface of the sea that leads out to Sri Lanka is evidence that such a bridge actually existed. It is at the tip of Dhanuskodi where sincere pilgrims bathe before their pilgrimage to Ramesvaram. And a pilgrimage to Ramesvaram is recommended before one makes a pilgrimage to Varanasi in the eastern part of India. It is said that by taking a holy bath at Dhanuskodi one gets all the fruitive results of performing the *agnistoma* ritual, and simply by visiting Dhanuskodi one is liberated from the cycle of repeated birth and death. As we can see, this area has many important historical connections dating back to the time of Lord Ramacandra as related in the *Ramayana*.

After our visit to Ramesvaram, we board a morning bus for the eight hour ride to Kanyakumari. On the way, 100 kilometers north of Kanyakumari, there is a temple that is over 1000 years old in the coastal town of Tiruchendur that many people stop to see. It's a popular place and one of the six principal temples of Muruga. The legend is that from this location Muruga (Subramanya) launched his attack in the last part of the war against Surapadma. After his victory, he returned in the form of a young child and worshiped Shiva. In the sanctum of the temple is a deity of Balasubramanya, Subramanya as a child. There is also a shrine to Lord Vishnu as Sri Venkatesha. The *gopuram* is 137 feet in height and can be seen from the main road. The beach is only about 200 yards east of the temple.

About 200 yards south of the temple is a well which is 14 feet across and at the bottom of a flight of 14 steps. It is called the Nazhi Kinaru. The water smells sulphurous and is brakish. But inside this well is a smaller well, which covers an area of only one foot and is seven feet deep with sweet and crystal clear water. Bathing in the sea as well as the Nazhi Kinaru is considered spiritually auspicious.

On the bus ride to Kanyakumari, you'll see many agricultural areas, lots of rice fields, groves of coconut and banana trees, and places where they produce salt from sea water. You often pass through little villages with small and simple shops. Huts with thatched roofs nestled in the shade of lots of palm trees are often found on the outskirts of town. It can be very exotic. You'll see the local people going about their business, stopping long enough to watch the bus go by.

At Kanyakumari, the southernmost tip of India (Land's End), we find a small but busy tourist town hosting people from all over the world. It has a resort feel to it with several hotels and guest houses in various price ranges. There are many souvenir shops and lots of vendors selling all kinds of sea shells. This town takes pride in the fact that it is the only place where, during a full moon, you can simultaneously watch the sun set into the sea in the west and the moonrise from the sea in the east. The Bay of Bengal is to the east, the Indian Ocean to the south, and the Arabian Sea to the west. Many people gather at the open monument near the confluence to watch the sunrise and sunset. There is also a bathing *ghat* here and to bathe in the confluence of these three seas is considered sacred. Only after bathing here and worshiping goddess Kanyakumari is one's pilgrimage to Varanasi in the north considered to be complete.

This town is also a holy place of pilgrimage. The temple here is dedicated to Devi Parashakthi's (Parvati's) incarnation as goddess Kanyakumari. The legend is that goddess Kanyakumari did penance here in order to secure Shiva's hand in marriage. But since this attempt was spoiled and she could not get Lord Shiva as her husband in this lifetime, she vowed to remain a virgin (Kanya). It was on the rock island (where Vivekananda's memorial is now located and which may have been part of the mainland at one time) that the goddess Kanya did her penance. There is a small shrine, the Shripada Mandapam, that houses a stone with the goddess Kanya's footprint on it.

The deity in the Kanyakumari temple is in the form of a young girl holding a rosary in her right hand. It is said that the deity, made of blue stone, was installed by Sri Parashurama many hundreds of years ago. The temple also has shrines to Indra Vinayak and Thyagasundari. Westerners can go in to see the beautiful deity, but the shoe minder's stall can be quite crowded and disorderly with people leaving or getting their shoes. When I went to the temple, a priest at the gate objected to my carrying a camera bag into the temple, but my guide, an old man who spoke no English, argued with the priest and got me in. He also took me through the east door, by-passing the queue of people. The deity was very nice to see, though poorly lit with only several ghee lamps hanging from the ceiling, as it is with many temples.

There is also a memorial to Gandhi on the beach where his ashes were displayed before being immersed into the sea. The memorial to Swami Vivekananda is on the rock island 200 metres off the shore. Vivekananda came to this place to meditate in 1892 before traveling around the world as one of India's most renowned spiritual crusaders. A ferry service takes you out to it, if you're willing to wait in the lines for a while. The place offers a good view of Kanyakumari, but you have to check in your camera upon arrival at the island. No photography is allowed, something I could never understand about certain places in India.

At Suchindram, 13 kilometres to the northwest of town, a pleasant taxi ride away, there is the Stanumalayam (Trimurti) temple, an interesting place to visit. The original construction of the temple was in the ninth century, but it was greatly expanded in the 17th century. Once again we find a temple filled with large hallways, temple art, painted ceilings, and beautifully sculpted pillars, some of which are musical and produce different tones when you knock on them. The outside of the temple is covered with carved designs and friezes that depict legends from the *Ramayana* and *Puranas*. Westerners can enter this temple and see all the divinities as well as the *arati* ceremonies, the offering of lamps. However, photography is not allowed. When going in, you'll have to wrap a special *dhoti* over your clothes, and it's best to take a guide (Rs. 10) if you want to quickly find your way around. The temple has several shrines but is dedicated to Trimurti, the three main personalities of Vishnu, Shiva, and Brahma, all on a single *lingam*. The tradition is that Indra, the King of Heaven, worships the *lingam* here every night, as he has done for many years. In one of the halls, there is an impressive image of Hanuman that stands 18 feet tall.

When our visit to Kanyakumari is finished, we board the early morning train to start traveling north along the coast. From Kanyakumari through Kerala and Karnataka, there are a number of interesting and spectacular temples that you should not miss if you are in the area. To go to these various temples, many of which are in small towns, you will have to take a bus or combination of train and bus. Buses in this area give horrendous rides, either driving full speed through the countryside and villages, or braking hard to avoid hitting something, or slowing just enough to let passengers get on or off. This tends to bounce you up and down and throw you back and forth continuously until you feel like you're getting blisters from your seat. Sitting in the back of the bus gives a rougher ride but allows for some relief from the constant shrill noise of the horn which is used every few seconds. It's adventure at its finest.

Starting in the town of Thiruattur, about 50 kilometres south of Trivandrum, is the Adi Keshava temple located near the banks of the Payasvini River. This is the Krishna temple which Sri Caitanya Mahaprabhu visited on His South Indian tour and found a copy of the ancient *Brahma-samhita*. This has become an important text for all Vaishnavas.

In the city of Trivandrum, there is the Sri Padmanabhaswamy temple, a large ornate structure built about 400 years ago, that is popular and busy. It is dedicated to Sri Vishnu as He reclines on His servant, Ananta or Adisesha. In fact, the name Trivandrum is short for Tiruvanandapuram, which means the abode of the serpent Anantha (Sesha). The Deity of reclining Vishnu in the sanctum is flanked on all sides by Sri Devi, Bhudevi, Niladevi, and different sages. From His navel sprouts a lotus on which is Lord Brahma. The Deity, made from 12,000 *salagramas*, is 20 feet long and in a compartment that has three doors in the front. One for His upper body, one showing His midsection, and another for His legs and feet. To get a full view, one has to do obeisances at all three doors. There are other shrines for Krishna, Narasimha, Subramanya, Ganesh, etc. It is open only to Hindus who must wear or rent a *dhoti* to go in.

For a change of pace you may also want to visit the Napier Museum to see its collection of bronzes, costumes, etc., or the Sri Chitra Art Gallery which has works of art from many Asian countries. There is also a zoo, Botanical Gardens, and an aquarium. There is also the Kerala Kalaripaytta demonstration, which is a form of martial arts that is famous all over the world and said to pre-date other forms of Far Eastern martial arts. The Kathakali form of dancing in Kerala, using colorful masks and costumes, is also world famous.

In the coastal town of Varkala, 35 kilometres north of Trivandrum, is a very ancient temple (said to be over 2000 years old) dedicated to Lord Vishnu as Janardhana. This temple is in a beautiful location near the sea and is a fine example of Kerala architecture. The Deity is a standing Vishnu, believed to have been found in the sea by fishermen who installed Him in a temple. This temple has a circular sanctum topped with a conical dome made with sheets of copper.

As we continue to head north, there are drastic changes in the architecture of the temples. No more do we find large pyramid-like stone *gopurams* at the gates of huge complexes with many buildings. Instead, we find carved woodwork and much smaller temples.

At Ettumanoor, 13 kilometres from Vaikam, there is one of the richest temples in Kerala, the Sri Mahadevar temple, dedicated to Shiva in the form of a *linga*. It has some amazing murals inside depicting scenes from the great Vedic texts. It is a large circular building inside a rectangular enclosure. Though non-

Hindus are prohibited, inside the temple is a circular columned hall where a square sanctuary enshrines the Shiva *linga*. It is said that anyone suffering from witchcraft or mental diseases can be relieved by praying for a few days in this temple.

Cranganore, 35 kilometres north of Cochin, has a temple to Kodungallur Bhagavathi Devi. It is one of the most important Devi temples in Kerala. It has beautiful carvings on the granite pillars and wooden ceiling, though the exterior of the building is rather simple.

In the hills east of Ettumanoor, 47 miles southeast of Kottayam and 185 km from Trivandrum, is Sabarimala, otherwise known as Dharma Sastha and Harihara Puthran. This is the abode of Lord Ayyappa, set amidst the Sabari Hills. Reaching this place is not easy. You have to take the road going south from Kottayam and then up to the Pamba River. From the river is an additional three miles of walking through thick forest to this wilderness hill temple. During the main festival season in the month of Narayana (December-January), many pilgrims come to this place while observing strict vows. During this time, many men wearing black can be seen in the nearby cities converging on Sabarimala and singing the chants of Lord Ayyappa. The Sri Ayyappa deity is enshrined in a little sanctuary on a raised area that is reached by climbing 18 steps.

According to the *Puranas*, Lord Vishnu once appeared in His incarnation as the most beautiful woman, Mohini. Shiva became so attracted to Her that he fell in love and passed semen while chasing after Her, although he could not catch Her. The devotees of Ayyappa declare that it was from that semen that Lord Ayyappa was formed. Others, however, claim that there is no Ayyappa and that this idea is based merely on mental speculation and is not substantiated in the *Puranas*, such as *Srimad-Bhagavatam*, which gives no possibility for any son of Shiva to have been born from the incident. So whether there really is a son of Shiva named Ayyappa remains a controversial topic.

The Shiva temple at Vaikom, about 15 miles northwest of Ettumanoor, is a large temple with bright murals between the doorways and windows that depict scenes of dancing Shiva, Parvati, Vishnu, etc. There is a simple square sanctuary that houses a huge *linga*, called Sri Vaikkathappam. The temple feeds many people here every day, but only Hindus are allowed inside, and this usually means that you have to be born in an Indian family to be considered a real Hindu.

North of Vaikom, along the banks of the Alwaye River, is the small town of Kaladi, 48 kilometres northeast of Cochin and 42 km from Trichur. This is a major pilgrimage center where Sri Shankaracarya, the great proponent of impersonalism, was born in the eighth century. He helped defeat Buddhism by his arguments and was considered to be an incarnation of Lord Shiva. One temple at Kaladi has an image of Sri Adi Shankaracarya as Dakshinamurti, and another temple has an image of Saradamba. Near the Sarada temple is the *samadhi* tomb of Sri Shankara's mother. Nearby is a temple that has a Deity of

Krishna installed by Shankaracarya himself, proving that in spite of his impersonalistic preaching, he was actually a devotee of Krishna. There is also the Sri Adi Sankara Keerthi Sthamba Mandapam, which is a nine-storey octogonal tower, 150 feet tall in height. Each floor is commemorated to a period of Shankaracarya's life.

The city of Trichur has the Vadakkunnatham temple, which is one of Kerala's largest temples. The temple is in the center of a rectangular court surrounded by a colonade. There are three main shrines facing west: one for Vadakkunnatha (Paramashiva), one for Shankara Narayana, and another for Lord Rama. Each has an open pavilion in front of it. There are smaller shrines for Ganesh, Krishna, and Parvati. The walls of the shrines, especially in the passageways, are beautifully painted with scenes of Nataraja, Vishnu, and depictions from the *Mahabharata*, etc. The temple also has exquisitely carved wood in its architectural designs. The legend is that the temple was originally established by Lord Parashurama. The temple is known for its Pooram festival in April. They have a parade of some 30 to 40 grandly ornamented elephants accompanied by the fanfare of traditional Keralite musical instruments. Afterwards, there is one of the best fireworks displays you'll find in India that goes on until dawn.

Northwest of Trichur at Guruvayoor is the famous temple dedicated to Lord Krishna. The Deity is a four-armed standing Vishnu with a *chakra* in the right hand, conchshell in the left, and mace and lotus flower in the other two. Sri Krishna showed this form of His only twice during His appearance on earth: once to Arjuna just before the battle of Kurukshetra while speaking the *Bhagavad-gita*, and once to His parents, Vasudeva and Devaki, at the time of His birth. The Deity is said to have been worshiped by Lord Krishna Himself at Dwaraka thousands of years ago. The legend is that when Krishna left this world, He ordered Brihaspati, the guru or spiritual teacher of the demigods, and Vayu, demigod of the wind, to take care of this Vishnu Deity. When they arrived at Dwaraka to get the Deity, the city of Dwaraka had already sunk into the sea. After searching in the water, they found the Deity and went south. Not knowing where to go, they sat down by the side of a lake and began to meditate. Soon, Shiva appeared and after some discussion they decided to start a new temple for the Deity of Vishnu near the Rudratirtha Lake. Since that time 5,000 years ago, the place has been known as Guruvayoor.

As in most temples, the Deity is served from three or four in the morning until nine at night. The service includes bathing, dressing, offering food, and receiving the many hundreds of devotees in the temple for *darshan*. Only Hindus are allowed into the temple, but if you're a Westerner and can show that you are a follower of the Vaishnava path by dressing accordingly, they may let you in. The temple is somewhat dark, however, and the Deity is poorly lit.

The temple manages a large elephant yard and the elephants play a major role during the annual 10-day Ulsavom festival in February-March. There is an elephant race at the start of the festival. Then every evening is the main event, which is a grand procession with the temple elephants bedecked with gold and jewels, one of which carries a miniature of the temple Deity. Then, with instruments playing and people joining, the procession circumambulates the temple complex three times. Afterwards, there are performances of Krishnattom style dancing and other festivities, all based on ecstatic love for Lord Vishnu.

From Guruvayoor, we go north of Mangalore to the coastal town of Udupi (sometimes spelled Udipi), the place where the great spiritual teacher Madhvacaraya was born and lived. Udupi is a small but pleasant town where the famous 13th century Krishna temple is located. Inside, there are several altars, but the main ones are for Madhvacarya's Deity of Lord Krishna and another for a four-armed standing Vishnu Deity. When Sri Caitanya visited this temple, He became completely ecstatic when He saw Madhvacarya's Krishna Deity. Westerners are also allowed in to see the Deities and watch the *puja* rituals that are performed each day as they have been for centuries.

This temple has a unique festival twice a month on *Ekadashi*. On these days, they bring the Deities out to ride the tall ornate carts that are pulled through the streets. The temple elephants are also in the procession and on their backs stand temple priests who wave big whisk fans, one in each hand, to fan the Deities in the nearby carts. It's a fascinating festival to see and many people join the parade. This is the best time to come to Udupi for a visit.

From Udupi, we take a one hour bus ride back to Mangalore and catch another bus to Mysore. It is a journey that takes several hours, but you go through some beautiful and hilly country. You'll see small communities and houses on the hillsides that have been terraced for rice farming, some of which are many miles away from anywhere. You will also pass through the town of Hunsur where you'll see Buddhist monks walking about. The reason is that near this place is a Tibetan refugee settlement and two monasteries. They also have factories that produce Tibetan carpets that you can buy, or they will gladly take your custom orders if you care to stop here to do some business. But it's a small town with little facility for travelers and most people continue on their way.

When you get to Mysore, you will notice that it's a clean, friendly city with many local attractions, and it's easy to get around. It's a great place, so if you're in South India, don't miss it. And if you're looking for a place to buy souvenirs, this town has many shops offering much from which to choose. Mysore is particularly known for its sandalwood. There's sandalwood oil, sandalwood incense, sandalwood soap, and so many sandalwood, rosewood, and teak carvings and furniture that you're bound to find something you'll like. There's also plenty of brassware and paintings. Street vendors also try to get your attention. If you buy something rather large and don't want to carry it while you travel, you can go to the post office and send it home. Don't depend on the store to send it for you unless it's the Cauvery Arts & Crafts Emporium. Many times tourists rely on a store to ship their merchandise back to the West, only to never receive it. There are also decent restaurants that offer something for whatever taste you have. But for fresh produce, go to the local Devaraja Fruit and Vegetable Market. This is an interesting place to watch people do business whether you buy anything or not.

The most interesting time to be in Mysore is for the Dussera celebration in October. The city and the palace are resplendent with lights and festivities that last for ten days. This is when the town celebrates the slaying of the Mahishasura demon by the goddess Chamundeswari, a form of Parvati. The tenth day is the peak of the festivities with a parade a mile long. People come from all over to watch the procession of soldiers, dancers, brass bands, floats, the Camels Corps, and decorated horses and elephants. Near the end of the parade, one gold bedecked elephant carries an image of the city's patron goddess, Chamundeswari. Then there is a grand fireworks display.

The legend is that goddess Chamundeswari protected the people of this area from the demon Mahishasura by killing him, and then made her residence on the hill just south of the city. The city was named after the demon, and is even mentioned in the *Mahabharata* as Mahishmati. The demon's statue is at the top of Chamundi Hill with a sword in one hand and cobra in the other. Nearby is the main temple of the city. The Chamundi temple, 3489 feet above sea level, is entered through a tall outer *gopuram* gateway and a smaller inner *gopuram*. The doors are of embossed silver that depict scenes of the goddess. The temple itself is not so elaborate, and the sanctuary is entered through a small *mandapa* hall. The small deity of Sri Chamundesvari is adorned with rich attire, but you are not allowed to get very close and must view the deity from a short distance. She has eight arms holding various weapons and is in the act of killing the demon Mahisha. To reach this temple, you can either take a bus or walk up the over 1000 steps on the hillside. Three-quarters of the way up is a huge Nandi (Shiva's bull carrier) carved out of solid rock. It's one of the biggest in India and is always visited by pilgrims. Once you reach the hilltop, there are plenty of little shops for refreshments.

Mysore has a lot of history, too. It has some very beautiful palaces and museums, especially the Mysore Palace, completed in 1912, which I found to be incredibly ornate and elegant. It has huge halls, stained glass windows, carved wooden and ivory inlaid doors, mosaic marble floors, some solid silver doors, paintings of the life in Mysore years ago, and displays of silver chairs, a golden throne, musical instruments, fabulous ceiling murals, and much more.

The palace also has several temples on or near the grounds that you can visit. Just outside the fort is the Kodi Bhairavasvami temple dedicated to Shiva in the form of Bhairava. This is historically a significant temple since this is where Yaduraya and Krishnaraya met the royal priest which caused the founding of the Mysore Kingdom in 1399.

There is also the Sri Lakshmiramana Svami temple in the western part of the fort, the Sri Shveta Varahasvami temple dedicated to Varaha, an incarnation of Lord Vishnu, and the Sri Prasanna Krishnasvami temple dedicated to Lord Krishna. This was built because the Mysore dynasty claims its descent is from the Yadu race, which was founded by Lord Krishna.

On the northern side of the fort is the Sri Bhuvanesvari temple. The Sri Gayatri temple, dedicated to Gayatri and Lakshmi, is in the southeast corner, corresponding to the Trinayaneshvara Svami temple, dedicated to Shiva. Nearby is the Venkataramana Svami temple. This was established by Queen Lakshanammanni, wife of Krishnaraja Wadiyar II, after the Deity, Lord Venkataramana, who was in Balamuri at the time, appeared to her in a dream and instructed that He should be installed in a temple in Mysore. So she proceeded to Balamuri and brought the Deity to Mysore where she consecrated and worshiped Him. For this pious act, the kingdom was restored to the Wadiyar dynasty after the death of Tipu Sultan in 1799.

Aside from the fort temples, Mysore is also known for many other unusually attractive temples in the area. The easiest way to see the other temples around Mysore is to simply take a tour. Check with your hotel or local tourist office and book a tour for the temples or places you'd like to see. They usually stop long enough at each place for you to get a good look around and it saves you the trouble of trying to arrange all the transportation yourself.

Sixteen kilometres from Mysore is Srirangapatnam. This was Tipu Sultan's capital in the 18th century when he ruled this part of India. Many people come here to see the historical remnants, such as Tipu's summer palace at Daria Daulet Bagh. There's not much left of the fort at Srirangapatnam, but there is the Sri Ranganathasvamy Temple, the largest in Karnataka. It is a rather plain temple from the outside with a medium size *gopuram* in front, but very popular amongst Hindu pilgrims. It is dedicated to Sri Ranganatha, Vishnu reclining on Adisesha. In its cave-like interior, you'll find several shrines to other aspects of Vishnu, such as Lord Venkatesvara, Narasimha, and Lakshmi, the goddess of fortune, and so on. As you go to each altar, the priest will give you *caranamrita* and Deity remnants, like *tulasi* leaves, etc. All the Deities are very nice looking and They are worshipped and well cared for. On the way out, there are stalls with *prasada* sweets you can purchase. Personally, I felt quite enlivened after visiting this temple.

A little further out from Mysore (82 km) is Sravanabelagola. The name means "the white pond of the ascetic," which no doubt refers to a pond that used to be where the large water tank is presently located at the base of the hill. It's a small town but is the single most important Jain holy site in Southern India, if not all of India, and attracts thousands of them from all over the country. At the top of Vindhyagiri Hill, over 500 steps up, is the Jain temple with an image of Lord Bahubali, Gomateshvara, that stands 58 feet tall. He is considered the son of the first Jain *Thirthankara*, Vrishaba Deva or Adinatha, who was a ruler of a kingdom in northern India until he renounced his throne to become a saint. The image is from the Digambara or "sky-clad" sect. It was built in the 10th century by Chamundaraya, minister to Rachamalla of the Ganga dynasty. Once every 12 years the Maha Masthaka Abhishesha ceremony takes place in which they pour milk, honey, water, coconut milk, turmeric, vermilion, flower petals, and other items over the head of the image. Hundreds of thousands of people attended the last festival in 1981, the 1000th year anniversary of the image. The hill also has the Odegal Basti, which is a plain temple that houses images of Adinatha (south), Neminatha (east), and Shantinatha (west). You'll also pass the Brahmadeva Mandapa, a small pavilion that contains an intricately carved column.

There's a few more temples in town that are worth seeing. The Bhandari Basti enshrines 24 images of *Thirthankaras* arranged in a row in the sanctuary. You'll need someone to explain which one is which if you're interested. And the Jain Matha has several altars with bronze images around a courtyard, some of which date back to the 10th century, along with fascinating wall murals. The paintings depict some scenes of the life of Parsvanatha and Nagakumara. Even if no one is at this Matha, you can still see the images through the large glass windows that protect them. Smaller shrines are scattered around the town.

On Chandragiri Hill, there are a few other Jain temples, including the Parsvanatha Basti from the 12th century that has an image of Parsvanatha that reaches over 16 feet high. The Chamundaraya Basti has images of Neminatha and Parsvanatha, and the Chandragupta Basti, which is the tomb of Chandragupta Maurya, has interesting carved stone work that depicts scenes from the lives of Bhadrabahu and King Chandragupta.

The town has a long history going back to the 3rd century B.C. At that time Chandragupta Maurya, having given up his kingdom, came here with Bhagwan Bhadrabahu, his guru. As Bhadrabahu's disciples spread the Jain teachings throughout the region, Jainism became established in the South. The Ganga dynasty took to Jainism, and between the 4th and 10th centuries it was an important part of the culture of this area.

Other temples in this area are the Hoysala temples at Belur, Halebid, and Somnathpur, which are some of the most amazingly ornate temples you can see near Mysore. They are not as large as many of the other South Indian temples, but they are certainly some of the most beautiful, having the most intricate carvings and designs that you can imagine. You'll find sculptures of a variety of deities, dancing girls, scenes from the *Mahabharata* and Vedic texts, images of the Hoysala rulers, animals, daily life activities, and so on.

The Hoysalas did not really become prominent in their rule of this area until the 11th through 13th centuries when Tinayaditya (1047-78 A.D.) began utilizing the fact that the Gangas and Rashtrakutas were losing power. It was Ramanuja who converted Vishnuvardhana, formerly known as Bittiga, from Jainism to Vaishnavism, the worship of Vishnu. Ramanuja also defeated the Jain texts in public, which took away much of its credibility. Jainism began a rapid decline after this. After Vishnuvardhana's conversion, he began erecting temples devoted to Vishnu and Shiva. The temples at Belur and Halebid were built during the reign of Vishnuvardhana (1110-52 A.D.).

The only one that is still a functioning temple is the Channekeshvara Temple at Belur (155 km from Mysore). This temple is over 800 years old and was built entirely of green chlorite by Vishnuvardhana after his victory over the Chola armies. The temple enshrines the beautiful Deity of Keshava and has remarkably intricate carvings around the doors and over the walls. These consist of guardian figures, many images of Vishnu, dancing girls, musicians, elephants and other animals, geometric designs, etc. This collection easily represents some of the finest of Hoysala art. The central hall in the temple is a pavilion with perforated walls that allows outside air to come through. The ceiling has an octogonal base with an intricately carved dome. There is a search light that can be used to light the detailed craftsmanship, otherwise the temple interior is rather dark. But use of the light costs two rupees. The temple also has a *gopuram* several stories tall at the entrance to the courtyard that surrounds the temple. There are a few other temples in the complex you can also see.

The temple at Halebid (16 km from Belur), which was built in the mid-12th century, is dedicated to Shiva and has two Shiva *lingas* in two separate rooms, Sri Hoysalesvara and Kedaresvara. It is actually two identical temples linked together. In front of each hallway is a detached pavilion with a large Nandi image. This temple has extensive carvings inside and out that show the expertise of the chisel work. The outside walls are decorated with friezes with rows of elephants, lions, scrollwork, and scenes from the *Ramayana* and *Mahabharata*. There are exceptional carvings of Vishnu and Lakshmi, Vishnu's incarnations, Rama and Sita, one of Bishma dying on a bed of arrows, and others. The nearby Archeological Museum has additional stone deities and panels depicting a variety of scenes and divinities of the Vedic pantheon.

The temple at Somnathpur (40 km from Mysore), which is dedicated to Lord Vishnu, is one of the best preserved of the Hoysala temples. It was erected by a Hoysala general, Somnatha, in 1268, and was created by the artist Janakachari, who had a part in the construction of other Hoysala temples. It was said that this temple was so perfect that even the demigods thought of stealing it. This temple is shaped like a star in the center of the courtyard. In the temple are three shrines: the stone Deity of Keshava is in the center, Janardhana is to the north, and Gopala is to the south. All around the temple exterior are carvings of the various incarnations of Vishnu, such as Narasimha, Varaha, Venu Gopala, etc., as well as demigods like Brahma, Shiva, Ganesh, Surya, Lakshmi, and so on. This is another small but beautiful temple that clearly exemplifies how much regard the Vaishnava Hindus gave to the worship of Sri Vishnu and to the construction of the temples they built for Him. Even though it's no longer a functioning temple, many people still visit it as a sign of their devotion.

The Mysore area is a fascinating place. Coming here for a visit can satisfy you regardless of your motive. You may have a tourist's point of view or a pilgrim's vision. It won't matter. But before leaving for new horizons, we can spend an evening at Brindaban Gardens, 19 kilometres from Mysore, below the Krishnarajasagar dam on the Cauvery River. It is known for its beautiful flowers, many water fountains, and evening illumination from its many lights. Numerous Indians and tourists come here to relax with families and friends.

Here, we can casually walk around the fountains or simply sit back and reflect on our tour of South India. After all, we've just completed a pilgrimage that many people can only dream of doing. Now we've actually seen and been a part of some of the most important aspects of Eastern spiritual culture. We've seen the temples that were built many hundreds of years ago, as well as the devotional activity that still goes on in them today. We've heard many legends of antiquity that are associated with some of these famous holy places. And, depending on our consciousness, maybe we were able to enter into the spiritual atmosphere for which these holy places are known. Maybe in our meditations we attained a glimpse of the spiritual vision that the great sages have, and then returned to our external awareness with a new view and deeper understanding of ourselves and the world. Maybe we realized the importance of the path taken by the spiritual masters who have left their teachings for us to ponder. Maybe, if we were fortunate, we realized the essence of the spiritual truths that are explained in the Vedic texts, and will leave South India with memories of a most unforgetable experience.

Certainly, this is a culture which dates back further than most others and is still very much alive. The customs and traditions we see today are quite the same as they were when they were performed thousands of years ago. And the philosophical reasonings and spiritual insights found in the ancient Vedic texts often challenge today's most mature Western theologians. Certainly, the West has yet to produce any literature as deep or as lofty as the *Bhagavad-gita*. Of course, we may recognize that a percentage of Indians have accepted and follow Western religion, like Christianity. But we also see many Westerners studying and accepting yoga and the Vedic philosophy in their search for experiences and answers not attainable in conventional Western philosophy and religion. Surely, the East and West have many things to learn from each other, and a beneficial balance can be reached. It all depends on how open-minded we are in the way we view and explore our cultures.

For now, however, as we sit in the park, the sun has gone down, the air has become cool, the many lights have been turned on, and it will not be long before we board our bus for the ride back to our hotel in Mysore. At the hotel, we'll pack our bags so we can be ready to catch the early morning train for our journey back toward Madras. From Madras, we will head north where we will continue our spiritual adventure in the eastern section of India. There, we will visit various temples, holy places, and cities, some of which are considered by Vaishnavas, Shaivites, Jains, as well as Buddhists and others, to be the most holy in all of India, if not the world.

# PHOTOGRAPHS

PAGE 246: Top, the original path up the Tirumalla Hills.

Bottom, view over the town and the Tirumalla hilltops. The Balaji temple is in the center with the gold-topped dome.

PAGE 247: Top, the Swamipushkarini lake on the north side of the temple, said to be goddess Sarasvati Devi who has taken the form of the lake to wash away the sins of all who bathe in it.

Bottom, main street in front of the Balaji temple.

PAGE 248: Sculpture of Lord Venkatesha (Balaji) on top of a building.

PAGE 249: The front *gopuram* and lines of people going into the Balaji temple.

PAGE 250: Top, the temple on the sea shore at Mahabalipuram.

Bottom, the carved rock displaying Arjuna's penance and descent of the river Ganges, Mahabalipuram.

PAGE 251: Top, a reclining Vishnu carved in the wall at Mahashamardini Mandapam, Mahabalipuram.

Bottom, the Five Rathas, Mahabalipuram.

PAGE 252: The Pakshi Tirtha Shiva temple on the hilltop at Tirukkalikundram.

PAGE 253: The south *gopuram* of the Shiva temple in Tiruvannamalai, the largest in India.

PAGE 254: A smaller *gopuram* entrance into the main shrine of the Shiva temple, Tiruvannamalai. Arunachalla Hill is in the background.

PAGE 255: Top, bathing *ghat* and other *gopurams* inside the temple complex.

Bottom, Shiva temple complex viewed from Arunachalla Hill, easily showing how it is situated in the center of town.

PAGE 256: Top, the ancient and ornate Airateshvara temple at Dharasuram.

Bottom Left, Nataraja, dancing Shiva, 12th century bronze, National Museum, New Delhi.

Bottom Right, top of *gopuram* depicting Shiva's son Murugan (Subramanya) above a small temple at Chidambaram.

PAGE 257: Top, one of the many paintings in the halls of the temple complex at Chidambaram. This one depicts King Simhavarman worshiping the Shiva *linga* and meeting the sages Vyagrapada and Patanjali. Shortly after this he began constructing the ancient temple at Chidambaram.

PAGE 257: Bottom, present day Sivagangai bathing tank where King Simhavarman was cured of his disease.

PAGE 258: Top, people watching the evening *arati* ceremony at the main shrine of the Shiva temple, Chidambaram.

Bottom, after the *arati* everyone circumambulates the temple.

PAGE 259: Top, deep in the halls of the Chidambaram temple complex.

Bottom, people near the sanctum of the Shiva temple, Chidambaram. It's one of those shots you're not supposed to take, but it shows the uniqueness of this temple. The people are watching the *arati* in the temple of Lord Vishnu to their left, while straight ahead is the main altar of the Shiva temple. No other temple combines these two sects so closely as we see here.

PAGE 260: People coming into the large Vishnu temple complex at Sri Rangam, the most important Vishnu temple in South India.

PAGE 261: Top, sculpture of reclining Vishnu above the door of the main temple at Sri Rangam.

Bottom, the many *gopurams* and temple top at Sri Rangam.

PAGE 262: The ornately carved horse pillars at Sri Rangam.

PAGE 263: Rock Fort Shiva Temple above Teppakulam tank, Trichy.

PAGE 264: One of the huge columns inside the halls of the Jambukesvara temple, Trichy.

PAGE 265: Top, Brihadesvara temple, Tanjore.

Bottom, some of the Shiva *lingams* in one of the many rooms in the colonnade that surrounds the Brihadesvara temple complex.

PAGE 266: Top, the Meenakshi temple at night, Madurai.

Bottom, the east entrance to the Meenakshi temple. On the left side of the entrance is Ganesh and on the right is Murugan, Shiva's sons. Above the entrance is a scene depicting the wedding of Shiva and Meenakshi. Goddess Meenakshi is in the center with her brother, Lord Vishnu, who is to the left of her. He is giving her away in marriage to Lord Shiva who is on her right. Other demigods are also in attendance.

PAGE 267: North *gopuram* of the Meenakshi temple showing the many buses parked in front that bring tourists and pilgrims from all over India and the world who visit this temple every day.

PAGE 268: Top, hall of 1000 pillars with an image of dancing Shiva at far end.

Bottom, the bazaar area of the temple. At the far right is the stall for tickets to the museum and hall of 1000 pillars.

PAGE 269: The west *gopuram* of the Meenakshi temple. These towers are some of the most famous in the world for their ornate stone carvings.

PAGE 270: Top Left, sculpture of Lord Vishnu's Universal Form.

Top Right, Shiva & Parvati riding Shiva's bull carrier, Nandi.

Bottom Left, dancing Shiva.

Bottom Right, Ganesh, son of Shiva and demigod who removes obstacles and gives good luck in undertakings when petitioned.

PAGE 271: Painting of Meenakshi Devi, one of the incarnations of Shiva's wife, Parvati or Durga. Durga assumes or incarnates in as many as 64 different forms according to her activities. She is also the personification of material nature and is thus worshiped as the Mother goddess, or Mother Nature.

PAGE 272: One of the longest temple halls in India, Ramesvaram.

PAGE 273: Top Left, Shiva & Parvati in parade at Ramesvaram. This image shows them being carried by the ten-headed demon Ravana. After Ravana had been blessed by Shiva he became so proud that he thought he could lift Shiva's mountain abode, Mount Kailash.

Top Right, Durga on her lion carrier.

Bottom Left, Ganesh on his mouse carrier.

Bottom Right, Murugan (Subramaniya) on his peacock carrier.

PAGE 274: Top, fishing village at Dhanuskodi where Lord Ramacandra had built His stone bridge over the sea to Ravana's kingdom in Sri Lanka to rescue His wife Sita.

Bottom, Kanya Kumari, "Land's End," the southernmost tip of India just behind the Kanya Kumari temple. On the island is the Vivikenanda Memorial, which marks the place where he meditated in 1892 before traveling to the West, and also where goddess Kanya Kumari did penance in an attempt to gain Lord Shiva as her husband.

PAGE 275: Top, watching the sunrise, people are gathered at Kanya Kumari around the bathing *ghat* which is the confluence of the Bay of Bengal, Indian Ocean, and the Arabian Sea.

Bottom, the unique sailboats used by the people of this region.

PAGE 276: The small Krishna Deity of Madhvacarya in Udupi.

PAGE 277: Top, festival carts in front of the 13th century temple of Madhvacarya's Krishna Deity, Udupi.

Bottom, the long path up the hill to the Jain temple, Shravanabelagola.

PAGE 278: The tall image of Bahubali (Gomateshvara) at Shravanabelagola.

PAGE 279: Top, wall painting inside a Jain temple.

Bottom, the intricately carved interior of the Hoysala Shiva temple, at Halebid.

PAGE 280: Top, the extremely ornate Hoysala Narayana (Vishnu) temple at
Belur.
Bottom, the Hoysala Shiva temple at Halebid.

PAGE 281: Top Left, Lakshmi & Vishnu, an example of the fine chisel work
which covers the ornate Hoysala temples, Halebid.
Top Right, another ornate carving at the Belur temple. This depicts
a mischievous but smiling monkey trying to grab the cloth from
a dancing girl who is about to swat the monkey to make it stop.
Bottom Left, a huge Nandi bull carved from a single stone on
Chamundi Hill, Mysore.
Bottom Right, the figure of demon Mahishasura on Chamundi Hill.

PAGE 282: The Deity of Janardhana (Vishnu) at the Hoysala temple in
Somnathpur. On two other separate altars are Deities of Keshava
and Venu Gopala.

PAGE 283: Top, the Hoysala temple at Somnathpur.
Bottom, Mysore Palace.

PAGE 284: Top, Brindaban Gardens just below the Krishnarajasagar dam on the
Cauvery River, 19 kilometres from Mysore.
Bottom, the author at the Five Rathas, Mahabalipuram.

PAGE 285: Top, a group of *brahmana* Vaishnavas engaging in study and
worship at a temple in Jagannatha Puri.
Bottom, group of *sadhus* going on pilgrimage in Vrindavan, which
is one of the holiest towns of India that all pilgrims like to visit.

PAGE 286: Top, little shops like this one are nearby most temples that sell many
things for one's spiritual practice, such as *japa* beads, pictures of
Deities, dresses for one's personal Deities, incense, etc.
Bottom, sweet shop, some are privately operated, others which are
run by a temple offer sweets that are first offered to the temple
Deity, making it *prasadam*. Pilgrims sometimes buy boxes of
these sweets to bring home and distribute to friends and relatives
as sacred *prasadam* from that particular Deity.

PAGE 287: Top, just one of the many vegetable stands at the busy Devaraja
Fruit & Vegetable Market in Mysore.
Bottom, a palmist on the street of Tanjore.

PAGE 288: Top, a family taking sacred bath at the holy Yamuna river. This is
a custom for pilgrims at any holy river, especially at a *tirhta* or
sacred place such as seen here at Vrindavan.
Bottom, college girls from Patiala, Punjab, touring Rishikesh,
which shows that pilgrims are from all kinds of backgrounds.

PAGE 289: Top Left, elephant decorated for a festival. Many temples have their own elephants that they especially use during holy festivals.

Top Right, lady selling garlands near a temple entrance. Devotees buy them to offer to the Deities in the temple.

Bottom Left, bride and groom at the Kapeeleshvara temple, Madras.

Bottom Right, snake charmer in Jaipur, something you might find near tourist attractions or some popular temples. Fortunately cobras a fairly docile except when frightened or attacked.

PAGE 290: Top Left, a *brahmana* priest at Vishrama Ghat in Mathura. He will assist pilgrims in performing various rituals in their worship or in paying their respects to the sacred Yamuna River at this holy place where many spiritual pastimes have taken place many years ago that involved Lord Krishna, Sri Caitanya Mahaprabhu, and others.

Top Right, a wandering Shaivite mendicant temporarily residing at Chidambaram.

Bottom Left, an old Vaishnava sage chanting *japa* at Vrindavan.

Bottom Right, a *sadhu* walking through the streets of Rishikesh.

PAGE 291: Map of South India.

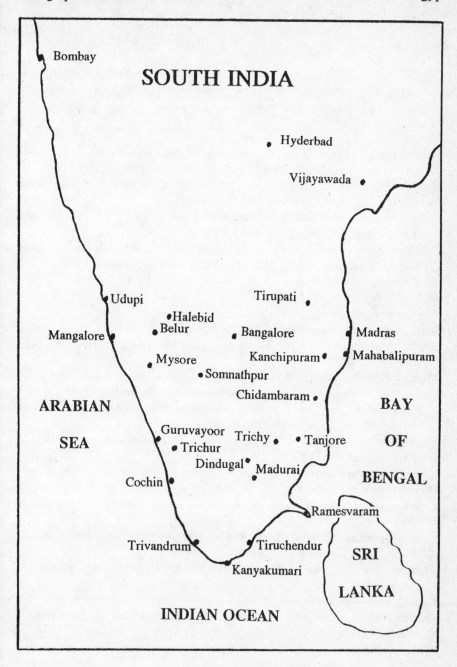

# REFERENCES

The following is a list of all the authentic Vedic and religious texts that were referred to or directly quoted to explain or verify all the knowledge and information presented in this book.

---

*Agni Purana*, translated by N. Gangadharan, Motilal Banarsidass, Delhi, 1984

*Atharva-veda*, translated by Devi Chand, Munshiram Manoharlal, Delhi, 1980

*Bhagavad-gita As It Is*, translated by A. C. Bhaktivedanta Swami, Bhaktivedanta Book Trust, New York/Los Angeles, 1972

*Bhagavad-gita*, translated by Swami Chidbhavananda, Sri Ramakrishna Tapovanam, Tiruchirappalli, India, 1991

*Bhakti-rasamrita-sindhu, (Nectar of Devotion)*, translated by A. C. Bhaktivedanta Swami, Bhaktivedanta Book Trust, New York/Los Angeles, 1970

*Bhakti-sandarbha sankhya*

*Bhavisya Purana*

*Bhavartha-dipika*

Bible, New York International Bible Society, 1981

*Book of Morman*, The Church of Jesus Christ of Latter-day Saints, Salt Lake City, Utah, 1976

*Brahma Purana*, edited by J.L.Shastri, Motilal Banarsidass, Delhi 1985

*Brahmanda Purana*, edited by J.L.Shastri, Motilal Banarsidass, 1983

*Brahma-samhita*, translated by Bhaktisiddhanta Sarasvati Gosvami Thakur, Bhaktivedanta Book Trust, New York/Los Angeles,

*Brahma-Sutras*, translated by Swami Vireswarananda and Adidevananda, Advaita Ashram, Calcutta, 1978

*Brahma-vaivarta Purana*

*Brihad-vishnu Purana*

*Brihan-naradiya Purana*

*Brihadaranyaka Upanishad*

*Caitanya-caritamrta*, translated by A. C. Bhaktivedanta Swami, Bhaktivedanta Book Trust, Los Angeles, 1974

*Caitanya Upanisad*, translated by Kusakratha dasa, Bala Books, New York, 1970

*Chandogya Upanishad*

*Garbha Upanishad*

*Garuda Purana*, edited by J. L. Shastri, Motilal Barnasidass, Delhi, 1985

*Gautamiya Tantra*

*Gheranda Samhita*, translated by Rai Bahadur Srisa Chandra Vasu, Munshiram Manoharlal, New Delhi, 1980

*Gitabhasya of Ramanuja*, translated by M. R. Sampatkumaran, M.A., Ananthacharya Indological Research Institute, Bombay, 1985

*Hari-bhakti-vilasa*

*How to Know God, The Yoga Aphorisms of Patanjali*, translated by Swami Prabhavananda and C. Isherwood, New American Library, 1969

*Jiva Gosvami's Tattvasandarbha*, Stuart Mark Elkman, Motilal Banarsidass, Delhi, 1986

*Kali-santarana Upanishad*

*Katha Upanishad*

*Kaushitaki Upanishad*

*Koran*, translated by N. J. Dawood, Penguin Books, Middlesex, England, 1956

*The Holy Quran*, 'Abdullah Yusaf 'Ali, Amana Corporation, Brentwood, Maryland, 1989

*Kurma Purana*, edited by J. L. Shastri, Motilal Banarsidass, Delhi, 1981

*Linga Purana*, edited by J. L. Shastri, Motilal Banarsidass, Delhi, 1973

*Mahabharata*, translated by C. Rajagopalachari, Bharatiya Vidya Bhavan, New Delhi, 1972

*Mahabharata*, Kamala Subramaniam, Bharatiya Vidya Bhavan, Bombay, 1982

*Matsya Purana*

*The Law of Manu*, [*Manu-samhita*], translated by Georg Buhlerg, Motilal Banarsidass, Delhi, 1970

*Minor Upanishads*, translated by Swami Madhavananda, Advaita Ashram, Calcutta, 1980; contains Paramahamsopanishad, Atmopanishad, Amritabindupanishad, Tejabindupanishad, Sarvopanishad, Brahmopanisad, Aruneyi Upanishad, Kaivalyopanishad.

*Mukunda-mala-stotra*

*Mundaka Upanishad*

*Narada-pancaratra*

*Narada Purana*, tr. by Ganesh Vasudeo Tagare, Banarsidass, Delhi, 1980

*Narada Sutras*, translated by Hari Prasad Shastri, Shanti Sadan, London, 1963

*Narada-Bhakti-Sutra*, A. C. Bhaktivedanta Swami, Bhaktivedanta Book Trust, Los Angeles, 1991

*Narottam-Vilas*, by Sri Narahari Cakravarti Thakur, translator unknown.

*Padma Purana*, tr. by S. Venkitasubramonia Iyer, Banarsidass, Delhi, 1988

*Padmottara-khanda*

*Padyavali*

*Prema-Vilas*, by Nityananda Das

*Purana-vakya*

*Ramayana of Valmiki*, tr. by Makhan Lal Sen, Oriental Publishing Co., Calcutta

*Hymns of the Rig-veda*, tr. by Griffith, Motilal Banarsidass, Delhi, 1973

*Rig-veda Brahmanas: The Aitareya and Kausitaki Brahmanas of the Rigveda*, translated by Arthur Keith, Motilal Banarsidass, Delhi, 1971

*Samnyasa Upanisads*, translated by Prof. A. A. Ramanathan, Adyar Library, Madras, India, 1978; contains Avadhutopanisad, Arunyupanisad, Katharudropanisad, Kundikopanisad, Jabalopanisad, Turiyatitopanisad, Narada-parivrajakopanisad, Nirvanopanisad, Parabrahmopanisad, Paramahamsa-parivrajakopanisad, Paramahamsopanisad, Brahmopanisad, Bhiksukopanisad, Maitreyopanisad, Yajnavalkyopanisad, Satyayaniyopanisad, and Samnyasopanisad.

*Shiva Purana*, edited by Professor J. L. Shastri, Banarsidass, Delhi, 1970

*Siksastaka*, of Sri Caitanya Mahaprabhu.

*Sixty Upanisads of the Vedas*, by Paul Deussen, translated from German by V. M. Bedekar and G. B. Palsule, Motilal Banarsidass, Delhi, 1980; contains Upanisads of the Rigveda: Aitareya and Kausitaki. Upanisads of the Samaveda: Chandogya and Kena. Upanisads of the Black Yajurveda: Taittiriya, Mahanarayan, Kathaka, Svetasvatara, and Maitrayana. Upanisads of the White Yajurveda: Brihadaranyaka and Isa. Upanisads of the Atharvaveda: Mundaka, Prasna, Mandukya, Garbha, Pranagnihotra, Pinda, Atma, Sarva, Garuda; (Yoga Upanisads): Brahmavidya, Ksurika, Culik, Nadabindu, Brahma-bindu, Amrtabindu, Dhyanabindu, Tejobindu, Yoga-sikha, Yogatattva, Hamsa; (Samnyasa Upanisads): Brahma, Samnyasa, Aruneya, Kantha-sruti, Paramahamsa, Jabala, Asrama; (Shiva Upanisads): Atharvasira, Atharva-sikha, Nilarudra, Kalagnirudra, Kaivalya; (Vishnu Upanisads): Maha, Narayana, Atmabodha, Nrisimhapurvatapaniya, Nrisimhottara-tapaniya, Ramapurvatapaniya, Ramottaratapaniya. (Supplemental Upanisads): Purusasuktam, Tadeva, Shiva-samkalpa, Baskala, Chagaleya, Paingala, Mrtyu-langala, Arseya, Pranava, and Saunaka Upanisad.

*Skanda Purana*

*Sri Bhakti-ratnakara*, by Sri Narahari Cakravarti Thakura

*Sri Brihat Bhagavatamritam*, by Sri Srila Sanatana Gosvami, Sree Gaudiya Math, Madras, India, 1987

*Sri Caitanya Bhagavat*, by Sri Vrindavan dasa Thakura

*Sri Caitanya Shikshamritam*, Thakura Bhakti Vinode, Sree Gaudiya Math, Madras, 1983

*Sri Isopanisad*, translated by A. C. Bhaktivedanta Swami, Bhaktivedanta Book Trust, New York/Los Angeles, 1969

*Srimad-Bhagavatam*, translated by A. C. Bhaktivedanta Swami, Bhaktivedanta Book trust, New York/Los Angeles, 1972

*Srimad-Bhagavatam*, translated by N. Raghunathan, Vighneswar Publishing House, Madras, 1976

*Srimad-Bhagavatam MahaPurana*, translated by C. L. Goswami, M. A., Sastri, Motilal Jalan at Gita Press, Gorkhapur, India, 1982

*Sri Sri Krishna Bhavanamrta Mahakavya*, Srila Visvanatha Chakravarti Thakura, completed in 1686

*Sri Srimad Bhagavata-Arka Marichimala*, Thakura Bhakti Vinode, Sree Gaudiya Math, Madras, 1978

*Svetasvatara Upanishad*

*Taittiriya Upanishad*

*Tantra of the Great Liberation (Mahanirvana Tantra)*, translated by Woodroffe, Dover Publications, New York, 1972

*Tattva-Viveka, Tattva-Sutra, Amnaya Sutra*, Srila Bhaktivinode Thakur, Sree Gaudiya Math, Madras, 1979

*Twelve Essential Upanishads*, Tridandi Sri Bhakti Prajnan Yati, Sree Gaudiya Math, Madras, 1982. Includes the *Isha, Kena, Katha, Prashna, Mundaka, Mandukya, Taittiriya, Aitareya, Chandogya, Brihadaranyaka, Svetasvatara,* and *Gopalatapani Upanishad* of the Pippalada section of the *Atharva-veda.*

*Upadesamrta (Nectar of Instruction)*, translated by A. C. Bhaktivedanta Swami, Bhaktivedanta Book Trust, New York/Los Angeles, 1975

*The Upanishads*, translated by Swami Prabhavananda and Frederick Manchester, New American Library, New York, 1957; contains Katha, Isha, Kena, Prasna, Mundaka, Mandukya, Taittiriya, Aitareya, Chandogya, Brihadaranyaka, Kaivalya, and Svetasvatara Upanishads.

*The Upanisads*, translated by F. Max Muller, Dover Publications; contains Chandogya, Kena, Aitareya, Kausitaki, Vajasaneyi (Isa), Katha, Mundaka, Taittiriya, Brihadaranyaka, Svetasvatara, Prasna, and Maitrayani Upanisads.

*Varaha Purana*, tr. by S. Venkitasubramonia Iyer, Banarsidass, Delhi, 1985

*Vayu Purana*, translated by G. V. Tagare, Banarsidass, Delhi, India, 1987

*Veda of the Black Yajus School: Taitiriya Sanhita*, translated by Arthur Keith, Motilal Banarsidass, Delhi, 1914

*Vishnu Purana*, translated by H. H. Wilson, Nag Publishers, Delhi

*Vishnu-smriti*

*Vedanta-Sutras of Badarayana with Commentary of Baladeva Vidyabhusana*, translated by Rai Bahadur Srisa Chandra Vasu, Munshiram Manoharlal, New Delhi, 1979

*White Yajurveda*, translated by Griffith, The Chowkhamba Sanskrit Series Office, Varanasi, 1976

*Yajurveda*, translated by Devi Chand, Munshiram Manoharlal, Delhi, 1980

*Yoga Sutras of Patanjali*


Other references that were helpful are listed as follows:

*Bible Myths and Their Parallels in Other Religions*, T. W. Doane, Health Research, Mokelumne Hill, California, 1910

*The Cult of Jagannatha and the Regional Tradition of Orissa*, edited by A. Eschmann, H. Kulke, and G. C. Tripathi, Manohar Publications, Delhi, 1978

*The Daily Practice of the Hindus*, Rai Bahadur Srira Chandra Vidyarnava, Oriental Books Reprint Corporation, Allahabad, 1979

*Dictionary of Philosophy and Religion*, Reese, Humanities Press, Atlantic Highlands, New Jersey, 1980

*Diet for a Small Planet*, by Francis Moore Lappe, Ballantine, New York, 1971

*Elements of Hindu Iconography*, by T. A. Gopinatha Rao, Motilal Banarsidass, Delhi, 1985

*The Gods of India*, by Alain Danielou, Inner Traditions, New York, 1985

*Harper's Dictionary of Hinduism*, by Margaret and James Stutley, Harper & Row, San Francisco, 1917

*Hindu Samskaras*, by Dr. Raj Bali Pandey, Motilal Banarsidass, Delhi, 1969

*Mathura, The Cultural Heritage*, edited by Doris Meth Srinivasan, American Insitute of Indian Studies, New Delhi, 1989

*Peter Burwash's Vegetarian Primer*, by Peter Burwash & John Tullius, Atheneum, New York, 1983

*Puranic Encyclopaedia*, Vettam Mani, Motilal Banarsidass, Delhi, 1964

*Seven Systems of Indian Philosophy*, by Rajmani Tigunait, Ph.D., Himalayan Publishers, Honesdale, Pennsylvasnia, 1953

*The Surya Siddhanta, A Textbook of Hindu Astronomy*, edited by Phanindralal Gangooly, Motilal Banarsidass, Delhi, 1860

*Vedic Mathematics*, by Sri Bharati Krishna Tirthaji Maharaja, Motilal Banarsidass, Delhi, 1965

*Vedic Tantrism*, [*Rigvidhana of Saunaka*], by M. S. Bhat, Motilal Banarsidass, Delhi, 1987

*Vedic Cosmography and Astronomy*, by Richard L. Thompson, Bhaktivedanta Book Trust, Los Angeles, 1989

*Vijnanabhairava or Divine Consciousness, A Treasury of 112 Types of Yoga*, by Jaideva Singh, Motilal Banarsidass, Delhi, 1979

*Yantra: The Tantric Symbol of Cosmic Unity*, Madhu Khanna, Thames and Hudson, London, 1979

## ABBREVIATIONS

*Bhagavad-gita* is abbreviated in this book as *Bg*.
*Caitanya-caritamrita* is *Cc*.
*Manu-samhita* is *Manu*.
*Srimad-Bhagavatam* or *Bhagavat Purana* is *Bhag*.
*Vishnu Purana* is *VP*.

# GLOSSARY

## A

*Acarya*--the spiritual master who sets the proper standard by his own example.

Achaleshvara--Shiva as Lord of the Hill.

*Acintya-bhedabheda-tattva*--simultaneously one and different. The doctrine Lord Sri Caitanya taught referring to the Absolute as being both personal and impersonal.

Adi Keshava--name of Vishnu.

Adinatha--the first of the 24 Jain *Tirthankaras*.

Adi Varaha--name of Vishnu as the Primeval Boar.

*Advaita*--nondual, meaning that the Absolute Truth is one, and that there is no individuality between the Supreme Being and the individual souls which merge into oneness, the Brahman, when released from material existence. The philosophy taught by Sankaracharya.

Agastya Muni--a sage who was the knower of the *Vedas*.

*Agni*--fire, or Agni the demigod of fire.

*Agnihotra*--the Vedic sacrifice in which offerings were made to the fire, such as ghee, milk, sesame seeds, grains, etc. The demigod Agni would deliver the offerings to the demigods that are referred to in the ritual.

*Ahankara*--false ego, identification with matter.

*Ahimsa*--nonviolence.

Airavateshvara--Shiva as Lord of the heavenly elephant.

*Akarma*--actions which cause no *karmic* reactions.

*Akasha*--the ether, or etheric plane; a subtle material element in which sound travels.

Amba, Ambika--name of Mother Durga.

*Amrita*--the nectar of immortality derived from churning the ocean of milk.

Amriteshvara--Shiva as Lord of Ambrosia.

*Ananda*--spiritual bliss.

*Ananta*--unlimited.

Annapurna--Parvati, a name meaning Filled with Food.

*Apara-prakrti*--the material energy of the Lord.

*Aranyaka*--sacred writings that are supposed to frame the essence of the *Upanishads*.

*Arati*--the ceremony of worship when incense and ghee lamps are offered to the Deities.

*Arca-vigraha*--the worshipable Deity form of the Lord made of stone, wood, etc.

Ardhanarishvara--Shiva as half Shiva and half Parvati.

Aryan--a noble person, one who is on the Vedic path of spiritual advancement.

297

*Asana*--postures for meditation, or exercises for developing the body into a fit
    instrument for spiritual advancement.
*Asat*--that which is temporary.
*Ashrama*--one of the four orders of spiritual life, such as *brahmacari* (celibate
    student), *grihastha* (married householder), *vanaprastha* (retired stage),
    and *sannyasa* (renunciate); or the abode of a spiritual teacher or *sadhu*.
*Astanga-yoga*--the eightfold path of mystic yoga.
*Asura*--one who is ungodly or a demon.
*Atma*--the self or soul. Sometimes means the body, mind, and senses.
*Atman*--usually referred to as the Supreme Self.
*Avatara*--an incarnation of the Lord who descends from the spiritual world.
*Avidya*--ignorance or nescience.
*Aum*--*om* or *pranava*
Ayodhya--the birthplace of Lord Rama in East India.
*Ayurveda*--the original wholistic form of medicine as described in the Vedic
    literature.

## B

*Babaji*--wandering mendicant holy man.
Badrinatha--one of the holy places of pilgrimage in the Himalayas, and home of
    the Deity Sri Badrinatha along with many sages and hermits.
Betel--a mildly intoxicating nut.
Bhagavan--one who possesses all opulences, God.
Bhagiratha--a king who brought the Ganges down from heaven by the austerities
    he performed.
Bhairava--Shiva as the terrifying destroyer.
*Bhajan*--song of worship.
*Bhajan kutir*--a small dwelling used for one's worship and meditation.
*Bhakta*--a devotee of the Lord who is engaged in *bhakti-yoga*.
*Bhakti*--love and devotion for God.
*Bhakti-yoga*--the path of offering pure devotional service to the Supreme.
*Bhang*--pronounced bong, a sweet mixed with hashish.
*Bhava*--preliminary stage of love of God.
Bhavani--name of Parvati.
Bhikshatanamurti--Shiva as a wandering beggar.
Bhu, Bhumidevi--Earth, a goddess associated with Vishnu.
Bhutanatha--Shiva as Lord of the *bhutas*, ghosts.
Bhuvaneshvari--Parvati as Ruler of the World.
*Bidi*--an Indian cigarette.
Binda Madhava--Shiva.
Bodhi--the tree under which Buddha became enlightened.

Brahma--the demigod of creation who was born from Lord Vishnu, the first created living being and the engineer of the secondary stage of creation of the universe when all the living entities were manifested.

*Brahmacari*--a celebate student, usually five to twenty-five years of age, who is trained by the spiritual master. One of the four divisions or *ashramas* of spiritual life.

Brahmani--consort of Brahma.

*Brahmajyoti*--the great white light or effulgence which emanates from the body of the Lord.

Brahmaloka--the highest planet or plane of existence in the universe; the planet where Lord Brahma lives.

Brahman--the spiritual energy; the all-pervading impersonal aspect of the Lord; or the Supreme Lord Himself.

*Brahmana* or brahmin--one of the four orders of society; the intellectual class of men who have been trained in the knowledge of the *Vedas* and initiated by a spiritual master.

*Brahmana*--the supplemental books of the four primary *Vedas*. They usually contained instructions for performing Vedic *agnihotras*, chanting the *mantras*, the purpose of the rituals, etc. The *Aitareya* and *Kaushitaki Brahmanas* belong to the *Rig-veda*, the *Satapatha Brahmana* belongs to the *White Yajur-veda*, and the *Taittiriya Brahmana* belongs to the *Black Yajur-veda*. The *Praudha* and *Shadvinsa Brahmanas* are two of the eight *Brahmanas* belonging to the *Atharva-veda*.

*Brahmastra*--a nuclear weapon that is produced and controlled by *mantra*.

Brahmeshvara--a name of Shiva.

*Brahminical*--to be clean and upstanding, both outwardly and inwardly, like a *brahmana* should be.

*Brijbasi*--a resident of Vraja, Vrindavan.

Buddha--Lord Buddha or a learned man.

# C

*Caitanya-caritamrta*--the scripture by Krishnadasa Kaviraja which explains the teachings and pastimes of Lord Caitanya Mahaprabhu.

Caitanya Mahaprabhu--the most recent incarnation of the Lord who appeared in the 15th century in Bengal and who originally started the *sankirtana* movement, based on congregational chanting of the holy names.

*Candala*--a person in the lowest class, or dog-eater.

*Caranamrita*--the water that has been used to bathe the Deity and is offered in small spoonfuls to visitors in the temple.

Causal Ocean or Karana Ocean--is the corner of the spiritual sky where Maha-Vishnu lies down to create the material manifestation.

*Chakra*--a wheel, disk, or psychic energy center situated along the spinal column in the subtle body of the physical shell.

Chandra--the moon.

Chandrashekara--Shiva as Moon Crested.

*Chhandas*--sacred hymns of the *Atharva-veda*.

Chaturbhuja--Shiva as Four-armed.

Chitragupta--name of Surya, the demigod of the sun.

*Cit*--eternal knowledge.


# D

*Darshan*--the devotional act of seeing and being seen by the Deity in the temple.

Daivanayaki--Parvati.

Dakshinamurti--Shiva as teacher of yoga and universal knowledge.

Dasara--the ten-day festival in September-October when Durga is worshiped and the victory of Lord Rama over the demon Ravana is celebrated.

Dashavatara--the ten incarnations of Lord Vishnu: Matsya, Kurma, Varaha, Narasimha, Vamana, Parashurama, Rama, Krishna, Buddha, and Kalki.

Deity--the *arca-vigraha*, or worshipful form of the Supreme in the temple, or deity as the worshipful image of the demigod. A capital D is used in refering to Krishna or one of His expansions, while a small d is used when refering to a demigod or lesser personality.

*Devaloka*--the higher planets or planes of existence of the devas.

Devaki--the devotee who acted as Lord Krishna's mother.

*Devas*--demigods or heavenly beings from higher levels of material existence, or a godly person.

*Dham*--a holy place.

*Dharma*--the essential nature or duty of the living being.

*Dharmachakra*--Buddhist wheel of law, the first sermon given by Buddha at Sarnath.

*Dharmashala*--a shelter or guesthouse for pilgrims at temples or holy towns.

Digambara--one of the two main Jain sects, sky-clad.

*Diksha*--spiritual initiation.

Diwali--festival of lights, marks the end of the rainy season.

Dualism--as related in this book, it refers to the Supreme as both an impersonal force (Brahman) as well as the Supreme Person.

Durga--the form of Parvati, Shiva's wife, as a warrior goddess known by many names according to her deeds, such as Simhavahini when riding her lion, Mahishasuramardini for killing the demon Mahishasura, Jagaddhatri as the mother of the universe, Kali when she killed the demon Raktavija, Tara when killing Shumba, etc. She assumes or incarnates in as many as 64 different forms, depending on her activities.

*Dvapara-yuga*--the third age which lasts 864,000 years.
Dvarakadisha--Krishna as Lord of Dvaraka.
*Dwaita*--dualism, the principle that the Absolute Truth consists of the infinite Supreme Being along with the infinitesimal, individual souls.

# E

*Ekadasi*--a fast day on the eleventh day of the waxing and waning moon.

# G

*Gana*--Shiva's dwarf attendants.
Ganapati--Ganesh as Lord of the *ganas*.
*Gandharvas*--the celestial angel-like beings who have beautiful forms and voices, and are expert in dance and music, capable of becoming invisible and can help souls on the earthly plane.
Ganesh--a son of Shiva, said to destroy obstacles (as Vinayaka) and offer good luck to those who petition him. It is generally accepted that the way Ganesh got the head of an elephant is that one time Parvati asked him to guard her residence. When Shiva wanted to enter, Ganesh stopped him, which made Shiva very angry. Not recognizing Ganesh, Shiva chopped off his head, which was then destroyed by one of Shiva's goblin associates. Parvati was so upset when she learned what had happened, Shiva, not being able to find Ganesh's original head, took the head of the first creature he saw, which was an elephant, and put it on the body of Ganesh and brought him back to life. The large mouse carrier of Ganesh symbolizes Ganesh's ability to destroy all obstacles, as rodents can gradually gnaw their way through most anything.
Gangadhara--Shiva's name when bearing the weight of the Ganges descent to earth.
*Gangapuja*--the *arati* ceremony for worshiping the Ganges.
Ganges--the sacred and spiritual river which, according to the *Vedas*, runs throughout the universe, a portion of which is seen in India. The reason the river is considered holy is that it is said to be a drop of the Karana Ocean outside of the universe that leaked in when Lord Vishnu, in His incarnation as Vamanadeva, kicked a small hole in the universal shell with His toe. Thus, the water is spiritual as well as being purified by the touch of Lord Vishnu.
Gangeshvara--Shiva as Lord of Ganga.
Gangotri--the source of the Ganges River in the Himalayas.
Garbhodakasayi Vishnu--the expansion of Lord Vishnu who enters into each universe.

Garuda--Lord Vishnu's bird carrier.

Gaudiya--a part of India sometimes called Aryavarta or land of the Aryans, located south of the Himalayas and north of the Vindhya Hills.

Gaudiya *sampradaya*--the school of Vaishnavism founded by Sri Caitanya.

Gauri--name of Parvati meaning Fair One.

Gaurishankara--Shiva and Parvati together.

*Gayatri*--the spiritual vibration or *mantra* from which the other *Vedas* were expanded and which is chanted by those who are initiated as *brahmanas* and given the spiritual understanding of Vedic philosophy.

*Ghat*--a bathing place along a river or lake with steps leading down to the water.

*Godasa*--one who serves the senses.

Goloka Vrindavana--the name of Lord Krishna's spiritual planet.

*Gompa*--Buddhist monastery.

*Gopuram*--the tall ornate towers that mark the gates to the temples, often found in south India.

*Gosvami*--one who is master of the senses.

Govinda--a name of Krishna which means one who gives pleasure to the cows and senses.

Govindaraja--Krishna as Lord of the Cowherds.

*Grihastha*--the householder order of life. One of the four *ashramas* in spiritual life.

*Gunas*--the modes of material nature of which there is *sattva* (goodness), *rajas* (passion), and *tamas* (ignorance).

*Guru*--a spiritual master.


# H


Hanuman--the popular monkey servant of Lord Rama.

Hare--the Lord's pleasure potency, Radharani, who is approached for accessibility to the Lord.

Hari--a name of Krishna as the one who takes away one's obstacles on the spiritual path.

*Haribol*--a word that means to chant the name of the Lord, Hari.

*Harinam*--refers to the name of the Lord, Hari.

Har Ki Pauri--the holy bathing *ghats* in Hardwar where the Ganges leaves the mountains and enters the plains. It is at this spot where the Kumbha Mela is held every twelve years.

*Hatha-yoga*--a part of the yoga system which stresses various sitting postures and exercises.

Hayagriva--Lord Vishnu as the giver of knowledge.

Hinayana--Lesser Vehicle, the Buddhist school that stresses achieving one's own enlightenment.

Hiranyagarbha--another name of Brahma who was born of Vishnu in the primordial waters within the egg of the universe.

Hiranyakashipu--the demon king who was killed by Lord Vishnu in His incarnation as Narasimha.

Hrishikesa--a name for Krishna which means the master of the senses.


# I


Impersonalism--the view that God has no personality or form, but is only an impersonal force (Brahman) which the individual souls merge back into when released from material existence.

Impersonalist--those who believe God has no personality or form.

Incarnation--the taking on of a body or form.

Indra--the King of heaven and controller of rain, who by his great power conquers the forces of darkness.

ISKCON--International Society for Krishna Consciousness.


# J


Jagadambi--Parvati as Mother of the World.

Jagannatha----Krishna as Lord of the Universe, especially as worshipped in Jagannatha Puri.

Jagat Kishora--name of Krishna.

*Jai* or *Jaya*--a term meaning victory, all glories.

Janardhana--name of Vishnu.

*Japa*--the chanting one performs, usually softly, for one's own meditation.

*Japa-mala*--the string of beads one uses for chanting.

*Jiva*--the individual soul or living being.

*Jivanmukta*--a liberated soul, though still in the material body and universe.

*Jiva-shakti*--the living force.

*Jnana*--knowledge which may be material or spiritual.

*Jnana-kanda*--the portion of the *Vedas* which stresses empirical speculation for understanding truth.

*Jnana-yoga*--the process of linking with the Supreme through empirical knowledge and mental speculation.

*Jnani*--one engaged in *jnana-yoga*, or the process of cultivating knowledge to understand the Absolute.

Jyestha--goddess Shakti.

Jyotirlinga--the luminous energy of Shiva manifested at 12 places, such as Kedarnatha, Patan, Ujjain, and Varanasi.

# K

Kailash--Shiva's mountain home.

*Kala*--eternal time, Yama.

Kali--the demigoddess who is the fierce form of the wife of Lord Shiva. The word *kali* comes from *kala*, the Sanskrit word for time: the power that dissolves or destroys everything.

Kali-yuga--the fourth and present age, the age of quarrel and confusion, which lasts 432,000 years and began 5,000 years ago.

Kalki--future incarnation of Lord Vishnu who appears at the end of Kali-yuga.

*Kalpa*--a day in the life of Lord Brahma which lasts a thousand cycles of the four *yugas*.

*Kama*--lust or inordinate desire.

*Kama sutra*--a treatise on sex enjoyment.

Kanyakumari--Parvati as a virgin.

Kapila--an incarnation of Lord Krishna who propagated the Sankhya philosophy.

Karanodakasayi Vishnu (Maha-Vishnu)--the expansion of Lord Krishna who created all the material universes.

*Karma*--material actions performed in regard to developing one's position or for future results which produce *karmic* reactions. It is also the reactions one endures from such fruitive activities.

*Karma-kanda*--the portion of the *Vedas* which primarily deals with recommended fruitive activities for various results.

*Karma-yoga*--system of yoga for using one's activities for spiritual advancement.

*Karmi*--the fruitive worker, one who accumulates more *karma*.

Karttikeya--son of Shiva and Parvati, also known as Skanda, Subramanya, Kumara, or son of the Pleiades (Krittika constellation).

Keshava--Krishna with long hair.

*Kirtana*--chanting or singing the glories of the Lord.

Krishna--the name of the original Supreme Personality of Godhead which means the most attractive and greatest pleasure. He is the source of all other incarnations, such as Vishnu, Rama, Narasimha, Narayana, Buddha, Parashurama, Vamanadeva, Kalki at the end of Kali-yuga, etc.

Krishnaloka--the spiritual planet where Lord Krishna resides.

*Kshatriya*--the second class of *varna* of society, or occupation of administrative or protective service, such as warrior or military personel.

Ksirodakasayi Vishnu--the Supersoul expansion of the Lord who enters into each atom and the heart of each individual.

Kumbha Mela--the holy festival in which millions of pilgrims and sages gather to bathe in the holy and purifying rivers for liberation at particular auspicious times that are calculated astrologically. The Kumbha Mela festivals take place every three years alternating between Allahabad, Nasik, Ujjain, and Hardwar.

Kuruksetra--the place of battle 5,000 years ago between the Pandavas and the
    Kauravas ninety miles north of New Delhi, where Krishna spoke the
    *Bhagavad-gita*.
Kuvera--the pot bellied chief of the *yakshas*, and keeper of earth's treasures.
Kurma--incarnation of Vishnu as a tortoise.


# L

Lakshmi--the goddess of fortune and wife of Lord Vishnu.
*Lila*--pastimes.
*Lilavataras*--the many incarnations of God who appear to display various
    spiritual pastimes to attract the conditioned souls in the material world.
*Linga*--the phallic symbol of Lord Shiva, often represents universal space.


# M

Madana-mohana--name of Krishna as one who fills the mind with love.
Madhava--Krishna.
*Mahabhagavata*--a great devotee of the Lord.
*Mahabharata*--the great epic of the Pandavas, which includes the *Bhagavad-
    gita*, by Vyasadeva.
*Maha-mantra*--the best *mantra* for self-realization in this age, called the Hare
    Krishna *mantra*.
*Mahatma*--a great soul or devotee.
*Mahat-tattva*--the total material energy.
Mahavira--Great Hero, referring to the last of the great Jain teachers, or
    *tirthankaras*.
Maha-Vishnu or Karanodakasayi Vishnu--the Vishnu expansion of Lord Krishna
    from whom all the material universes emanate.
Mahayana--Great Vehicle, the Buddhist school that stresses giving aid to all
    living beings toward enlightenment.
Mahishamardini--Durga as the slayer of the buffalo demon.
Mandakini--another name of River Ganga.
*Mandir*--a temple.
*Mantra*--a sound vibration which prepares the mind for spiritual realization and
    delivers the mind from material inclinations. In some cases a *mantra* is
    chanted for specific material benefits.
Martya-loka--the earth planet, the place of death.
Matsya--Lord Vishnu as the fish incarnation.
*Maya*--illusion, or anything that appears to not be connected with the eternal
    Absolute Truth.

*Mayavadi*--the impersonalist or voidist who believes that the Supreme has no
    form.

Meenakshi--Parvati as Fish-Eyed.

Mitra--the deity controlling the sun, and who gives life to earth.

*Mleccha*--a derogatory name for an untouchable person, a meat-eater.

Mohini--Lord Vishnu's incarnation as the most beautiful woman.

*Moksha*--liberation from material existence.

Mukteshvara--Shiva as the giver of liberation.

Mukunda--Krishna as the giver of spiritual liberation.

*Murti*--a Deity of the Lord or an image of a demigod or spiritual master that is
    worshiped.

Murugan--means the divine child, the Tamil name for Subramaniya, one of the
    sons of Shiva and Parvati, especially worshiped in South India. It is said
    that he was born to destroy the demon Tarakasura. He was born in a
    forest of arrow-like grass and raised by the six divine mothers of the
    Krittika constellation (Pleiades). Thus, he is also called Kartikeya and
    Sanmatura, and he assumed six faces (and twelve arms) to suckle the
    milk of the six mothers. Being young and virile, he is also called
    Kumara or Sanatkumara. He is also called Skanda for being very
    forceful in war. His two consorts are Velli, the daughter of a humble
    chieftan of an agricultural tribe, and Devasena, the daughter of the
    demigod Indra.


# N


Nanda--the foster father of Krishna.

Nandi--Shiva's bull carrier.

Narasimha--Lord Vishnu's incarnation as the half-man half-lion who killed the
    demon Hiranyakashipu.

Narayana--the four-handed form of the Supreme Lord.

Nataraja--King of Dance, usually referring to Shiva, but also Krishna.

Nilakantha--Blue Throated Shiva after swallowing the poison first produced when
    the ocean of milk was churned by the demons and demigods.

*Nirguna*--without material qualities.

*Nirvana*--the state of no material miseries, usually the goal of the Buddhists or
    voidists.


# O


*Om* or *Omkara*--*pranava*, the transcendental *om mantra*, generally referring to
    the attributeless or impersonal aspects of the Absolute.

# P

Padmanabha--Vishnu.

Pan--a concoction of ground betel nut and spices that acts as a mild stimulant or intoxicant. It is very popular and often leaves the teeth stained red.

*Pandal*--a large tent where religious gatherings are held.

Papanasana--Shiva as destroyer of sin.

*Paramahamsa*--the highest level of self-realized devotees of the Lord.

Paramatma--the Supersoul, or localized expansion of the Lord.

*Parampara*--the system of disciplic succession through which transcendental knowledge descends.

Parashurama--incarnation of Vishnu with an axe who cleansed the world of the deviant *kshatriya* warriors.

Parsvanatha--one of the prominent Jain *thirthankaras*.

Parthasarathi--Krishna as Arjuna's chariot driver.

Parvati--Lord Shiva's spouse, daughter of Parvata. Parvata is the personification of the Himalayas. She is also called Gauri for her golden complexion, Candi, Bhairavi (as the wife of Bhairava, Shiva), Durga, Ambika, and Shakti.

Pashupati--Shiva as Lord of the animals.

Patanjali--the authority on the *astanga-yoga* system.

*Pradhana*--the total material energy in its unmanifest state.

Prajapati--deity presiding over procreation.

*Prakriti*--matter in its primordial state, the material nature.

*Prana*--the life air or cosmic energy.

*Pranayama*--control of the breathing process as in *astanga* or *raja-yoga*.

*Pranava*--same as *omkara*.

*Prasada*--food or other articles that have been offered to the Deity in the temple and then distributed amongst people as the blessings or mercy of the Deity.

*Prema*--matured love for Krishna.

*Puja*--the worship offered to the Deity.

*Pujari*--the priest who performs worship, *puja*, to the Deity.

*Purusha* or *Purusham*--the supreme enjoyer.

# R

Radha--Krishna's favorite devotee and the personification of His bliss potency.

Rahu--deity representation of the planetary node that causes solar eclipses.

*Raja-yoga*--the eightfold yoga system.

*Rajo-guna*--the material mode of passion.

Ramachandra--an incarnation of Krishna as He appeared as the greatest of kings.

Ramanuja--Vaishnava philosopher.

*Ramayana*--the great epic of the incarnation of Lord Ramachandra.

*Rasa*--an enjoyable taste or feeling, a relationship with God.

Ravana--demon king of the *Ramayana*.

*Rishi*--saintly person who knows the Vedic knowledge.

# S

Sacrifice--in this book it in no way pertains to human sacrifice, as many people tend to think when this word is used. But it means to engage in an austerity of some kind for a higher, spiritual purpose.

Sati--Shiva's wife who killed herself by immolation in fire.

*Shabda-brahma*--the original spiritual vibration or energy of which the *Vedas* are composed.

*Sac-cid-ananda-vigraha*--the transcendental form of the Lord or of the living entity which is eternal, full of knowledge and bliss.

*Sadhana*--a specific practice or discipline for attaining God realization.

*Sadhu*--Indian holy man or devotee.

*Saguna* Brahman--the aspect of the Absolute with form and qualities.

*Samadhi*--trance, the perfection of being absorbed in the Absolute.

*Samsara*--rounds of life; cycles of birth and death; reincarnation.

*Sanatana-dharma*--the eternal nature of the living being, to love and render service to the supreme lovable object, the Lord.

*Sangam*--the confluence of two or more rivers.

Sankhya--analytical understanding of material nature, the body, and the soul.

*Sankirtana-yajna*--the prescribed sacrifice for this age: congregational chanting of the holy names of God.

*Sannyasa*--the renounced order of life, the highest of the four *ashramas* on the spiritual path.

Sarasvati--the goddess of knowledge and intelligence.

*Sattva-guna*--the material mode of goodness.

Satya-yuga--the first of the four ages which lasts 1,728,000 years.

Shaivites--worshipers of Lord Shiva.

Shakti--energy, potency or power, the active principle in creation. Also the active power or wife of a deity, such as Shiva/Shakti.

*Shastra*--the authentic revealed scripture.

Shiva--the benevolent one, the demigod who is in charge of the material mode of ignorance and the destruction of the universe. Part of the triad of Brahma, Vishnu, and Shiva who continually create, maintain, and destroy the universe. He is known as Rudra when displaying his destructive aspect.

*Sikha*--a tuft of hair on the back of the head signifying that one is a Vaishnava.

Skanda--son of Shiva and Parvati, leader of the army of the gods; also known as Karttikeya and Subramanya or Murugan.

*Smaranam*--remembering the Lord.

*Smriti*--the traditional Vedic knowledge "that is remembered" from what was directly heard by or revealed to the *rishis*.

*Sravanam*--hearing about the Lord.

Sri, Sridevi--Lakshmi, the goddess who embodies beauty and prosperity, wife of Lord Vishnu.

Sridhara--Lord Vishnu.

*Srimad-Bhagavatam*--the most ripened fruit of the tree of Vedic knowledge compiled by Vyasadeva.

*Sruti*--scriptures that were received directly from God and transmitted orally by *brahmanas* or *rishis* down through succeeding generations. Traditionally, it is considered the four primary *Vedas*.

Svetambara--one of the two main Jain sects, white robed.

*Sudra*--the working class of society, the fourth of the *varnas*.

Surya--Sun or solar deity.

*Svami*--one who can control his mind and senses.


# T

*Tamo-guna*--the material mode of ignorance.

*Tapasya*--voluntary austerity for spiritual advancement.

*Thanka*--Tibetan cloth painting, usually based on Buddhist philosophy.

*Tilok*--the clay markings that signify a person's body as a temple, and the sect or school of thought of the person.

*Tirtha*--a holy place of pilgrimage.

*Tirthankara*--the person who is the spiritual guide or teacher in Jainism.

Treta-yuga--the second of the four ages which lasts 1,296,000 years.

Trilochana--Three-eyed Shiva.

Trilokanatha--Shiva as Lord of the Three Worlds.

*Trimurti*--triad of Vishnu, Brahma, and Shiva.

Trivikrama--Lord Vishnu as Vamadeva, the *brahmana* dwarf who covered the entire universe in three steps.

*Tulasi*--the small tree that grows where worship to Krishna is found. It is called the embodiment of devotion, and the incarnation of Vrinda-devi.

# U

Uma--Parvati

*Upanishads*--the portions of the *Vedas* which primarily explain philosophically
   the Absolute Truth. It is knowledge of Brahman which releases one
   from the world and allows one to attain self-realization when received
   from a qualified teacher. Except for the *Isa Upanishad*, which is the
   40th chapter of the *Vajasaneyi Samhita* of the *Sukla* (*White*) *Yajur-veda*,
   the *Upanishads* are connected to the four primary *Vedas*, generally
   found in the *Brahmanas*.

# V

*Vaikunthas*--the planets located in the spiritual sky.

Vaishnava--a worshiper of the Supreme Lord Vishnu or Krishna and His
   expansions or incarnations.

*Vaishnava-aparadha*--an offense against a Vaisnava or devotee, which can negate
   all of one's spiritual progress.

*Vaisya*--the third class of society engaged in business or farming.

*Vajra*--thunderbolt.

Vamana--dwarf incarnation of Vishnu who covered the universe in three steps.

*Vanaprastha*--the third of the four *ashramas* of spiritual life in which one retires
   from family life in preparation for the renounced order.

Varaha--Lord Vishnu's boar incarnation.

*Varna*--sometimes referred to as caste, a division of society, such as *brahmana*
   (a priestly intellectual), a *kshatriya* (ruler or manager), *vaisya* (a
   merchant, banker, or farmer), and *sudra* (common laborer).

*Varnashrama*--the system of four divisions of society and four orders of spiritual
   life.

Varuna--demigod of the oceans, guardian of the west.

Vasudeva--Krishna.

Vayu--demigod of the air.

*Vedanta-sutras*--the philosophical conclusion of the four *Vedas*.

*Vedas*--generally means the four primary *samhitas;* Rig, Yajur, Sama, Atharva.

Venktateshvara--Vishnu as Lord of the Venkata Hills, worshiped in Tirumala.

*Vidya*--knowledge.

*Vikarma*--sinful activities performed without scriptural authority and which
   produce sinful reactions.

Virabhadra--vengeful form of Shiva.

Virajanadi or Viraja River--the space that separates the material creation from
   the spiritual sky.

Vishalakshi--Parvati, consort of Vishvanatha or Vishalaksha, Shiva.

Vishnu--the expansion of Lord Krishna who enters into the material energy to create and maintain the cosmic world.

Vishvakarma--demigod architect of the heavens.

Vishvanatha--Shiva as Lord of the universe, worshiped in Varanasi as a *linga*.

Vishvarupa--universal form of Lord Vishnu.

Vrindavana--the place where Lord Krishna displayed His village pastimes 5,000 years ago, and is considered to be part of the spiritual abode.

Vyasadeva--the incarnation of God who appeared as the greatest philosopher who compiled the main portions of the vedic literature into written form.

# Y

*Yajna*--a ritual or austerity that is done as a sacrifice for spiritual merit, or ritual worship of a demigod for good *karmic* reactions.

Yamaraja--the demigod and lord of death who directs the living entities to various punishments according to their activities.

Yamuna--goddess personification of the Yamuna River.

*Yantra*--a machine, instrument, or mystical diagram used in ritual worship.

Yashoda--foster mother of Krishna.

Yoga--linking up with the Absolute.

Yoga-*siddhi*--mystic perfection.

*Yoni*--sexual emblem of Devi or Durga or Shakti, the universal female energy, often represented as a pedestal for the *Linga*.

*Yuga-avataras*--the incarnations of God who appear in each of the four *yugas* to explain the authorized system of self-realization in that age.

# INDEX

## DISCLAIMER
= = = = = = = = = = = = = = = = = = = = = = = = = = = = = =

# ABOUT THE AUTHOR

Stephen Knapp (photograph on page 284) grew up in a Christian family, during which time he seriously studied the Bible to understand its teachings. In his late teenage years, however, he sought answers to questions not easily explained in Christian theology. So he began to search through other religions and philosophies from around the world and started to find the answers for which he was looking. He also studied a variety of occult sciences, ancient mythology, mysticism, yoga, and the spiritual teachings of the East. After his first reading of the *Bhagavad-gita*, he felt he had found the last piece of the puzzle he had been putting together through all of his research. Therefore, he continued to study all of the major Vedic texts of India to gain a better understanding of the Vedic science.

It is known amongst all Eastern mystics that anyone, regardless of qualifications, academic or otherwise, who does not engage in the spiritual practices described in the Vedic texts cannot actually enter into understanding the depths of the Vedic spiritual science, nor acquire the realizations that should accompany it. So, rather than pursuing his research in an academic atmosphere at a university, Stephen directly engaged in the spiritual disciplines that have been recommended for hundreds of years. He continued his study of Vedic knowledge and spiritual practice under the guidance of a spiritual master. Through this process, and with the sanction of His Divine Grace A. C. Bhaktivedanta Swami Prabhupada, he became initiated into the genuine and authorized spiritual line of the Brahma-Madhava-Gaudiya *sampradaya*, which is a disciplic succession that descends back through Sri Caitanya Mahaprabhu and Sri Vyasadeva, the compiler of Vedic literature, and further back to Sri Krishna. Besides being *brahminically* initiated, Stephen has also been to India several times and traveled extensively throughout the country, visiting most of the major holy places and gaining a wide variety of spiritual experiences that only such places can give.

Stephen has been writing *The Eastern Answers to the Mysteries of Life* series, which so far includes *The Secret Teachings of the Vedas* and *The Universal Path to Enlightenment*. He has also written a novel, *Destined for Infinity*, for those who prefer lighter reading, or learning spiritual knowledge in the context of a fictional, spiritual adventure. Stephen has put the culmination of over twenty years of continuous research and travel experience into his books in an effort to share it with those who are also looking for spiritual understanding.

If you have enjoyed this book, you will also want to get Volume Two in this series:

# he Universal Path to Enlightenment

Although all religions and spiritual processes are meant to lead you toward ghtenment, they are not all the same in regard to the methods they teach, nor in the level hilosophical understanding they offer. So an intelligent person will make comparisons veen them to understand the aims and distinctions of each religion, and which is the most ating.

This book logically analyzes all the major religions and spiritual paths of the world and ribes their histories, philosophical basis, and goals, and shows what level of development is likely to attain from them. It will help you decide which path may be the best for you.

## You Will Learn

w Christianity and Judaism were greatly influenced by the pre-Christian or "pagan" igions and adopted many of their legends, holidays, and rituals that are still accepted and cticed today.

out evidence that shows Jesus may have traveled to the East to learn its spiritual owledge, and then made *bhakti-yoga* the essence of his teachings.

o were the real Vedic Aryans, the founders of the earliest of religions and organized tures, and how early Vedic society was a world power and influenced many other early ilizations, such as Egyptian, Greek, Oriental, etc., and how their Vedic teachings are ll found in Christianity and other traditions today, which makes the Vedic knowledge the rce of the world's spiritual heritage and the most developed of all spiritual processes.

philosophical basis and origin of Christianity, Judaism, Islam, Hinduism, Buddhism, roastrianism, Jainism, Sikhism, and many others.

out the *chakras*, mystic powers, and the yoga systems, such as *raja-yoga, hatha-yoga, akti-yoga, mantra-yoga*, etc., what their goals are, and how practical they are in this age.

at are the many branches of Vedic literature and the different levels of knowledge that y contain, and the ultimate spiritual path they recommend for realizing the Supreme.

at the qualifications are of a genuine spiritual teacher or guru.

w spiritual enlightenment is the cure for the many problems in society.

essential similarities of all religions that all people of any culture can practice, which uld bring about a united world religion, or "THE UNIVERSAL PATH TO LIGHTENMENT."

d, most importantly, what is the real purpose of a spiritual path that you should strive for, d how to practice the path that is especially recommended as the easiest and most effective the people of this age to attain real spiritual enlightenment.

d much more information not easily found elsewhere.

In its 420 pages, there is also a special section on seeing spiritual India. You will tour famous temples and holy places of Eastern India, from Madras in the South to New Delhi e North. You will learn about and see some of the most important and sacred temples and ns in the world where several of the major religions originated. Almost 100 photographs included of a variety of temples, holy sites, art, sculptures, and people engaged in all cts of life in India and Nepal. A must for anyone who would like to travel in this area.

To get your copy, see your local book store to order it (ISBN 0-9617410-2-3), or ly send $14.95, plus $2.50 for postage and handling ($6.50 for overseas orders) to: World Relief Network, P. O. Box 15082, Detroit, Michigan, 48215-0082, U. S. A.